First World War
and Army of Occupation
War Diary
France, Belgium and Germany

23 DIVISION
70 Infantry Brigade
Duke of Cambridge's Own (Middlesex Regiment)
1/8th (T.F.) Battalion,
King's Own (Yorkshire Light Infantry)
8th Battalion
and Sherwood Foresters (Nottinghamshire and Derbyshire Regiment)
11th Battalion.
2 August 1915 - 1 October 1917

WO95/2187

The Naval & Military Press Ltd
www.nmarchive.com
Published in association with The National Archives

Published by

The Naval & Military Press Ltd

Unit 10 Ridgewood Industrial Park,

Uckfield, East Sussex,

TN22 5QE England

Tel: +44 (0) 1825 749494

www.naval-military-press.com

www.nmarchive.com

This diary has been reprinted in facsimile from the original. Any imperfections are inevitably reproduced and the quality may fall short of modern type and cartographic standards.

© **Crown Copyright**
Images reproduced by permission of The National Archives, London, England, 2015.

Contents

Document type	Place/Title	Date From	Date To
Heading	8th Division 70th Infy Bde 23 Div 1-8th Middlesex Regt Aug 1915-Jan 1916 From 28 Div 85 Bde To 56 Div 167 Bde.		
Heading	8th Division 121/0561 1/8th Middlesex Vol III 2.8.15. From 9th March To 28 Aug 15		
War Diary	Doulieu	02/08/1915	31/08/1915
Heading	8th, Division 25th, Brigade. 1/8th, Middlesex Regt. September, 1915		
Heading	8th Division 25th Bde 1/8th Middlesex Vol IV Sept. 15		
War Diary	Doulieu	01/09/1915	01/09/1915
War Diary	Fleurbaix (Rue Biache)	02/09/1915	03/09/1915
War Diary	Saillys Sur La Lys	05/09/1915	07/09/1915
War Diary	Fleurbaix	08/09/1915	14/09/1915
War Diary	Sailly Sur La Lys	15/09/1915	29/09/1915
Miscellaneous	B.M.C.234. Officer Commanding 1/8 Middx. R.	23/09/1915	23/09/1915
Heading	8th Division 1/8th Middlesex Vol V Oct. 15		
War Diary	Sailly-Sur-La-Lys	01/10/1915	06/10/1915
War Diary	Fleurbaix	06/10/1915	31/10/1915
Heading	8th, Division. 70th, Brigade. 1/8th, Middlesex. November, 1915		
Heading	8th Division 1/8 M'sex Nov. 1915 Vol VI		
War Diary	Fleurbaix	01/11/1915	30/11/1915
Miscellaneous	8th Division Special Order 26th November 1915	26/11/1915	26/11/1915
Heading	8th, Division. 70th, Brigade. 1/8th, Middlesex. December, 1915		
Heading	8th Div. 1/8th Middlesex Rgt Dec Vol VII		
War Diary	Steenbecque	01/12/1915	19/12/1915
War Diary	M in Fontaine	20/12/1915	20/12/1915
War Diary	Ham	21/12/1915	21/12/1915
War Diary	La Pierre	22/12/1915	22/12/1915
War Diary	Steenbecque	23/12/1915	31/12/1915
Miscellaneous	Special Order Of The Day.	18/12/1915	18/12/1915
Miscellaneous	First Army Special Order of the Day. by General Sir Douglas Haig, G.C.B. K.C.Y.O., A.D.C. GEN., Commanding 1st Army.	19/12/1915	19/12/1915
Miscellaneous	Programme Of Concert Christmas 1915 The Rest Camp M.I.H.		
Miscellaneous	Programme Of Concert.		
Miscellaneous	A Form. Messages And Signals.	25/12/1915	25/12/1915
Miscellaneous	A Form. Messages And Signals.		
Miscellaneous	A Form. Messages And Signals.	25/12/1915	25/12/1915
Miscellaneous	A Form. Messages And Signals.		
Miscellaneous			
Miscellaneous	A Form. Messages And Signals.	25/12/1915	25/12/1915
Miscellaneous	23rd Inf. Bde.	25/12/1915	25/12/1915
Heading	8th, Division 70th, Brigade. 1/8th, Middlesex. October, 1915		
Heading	8th, Division. 70th, Brigade. 1/8th, Middlesex. January, 1916		

Heading	8th Div 20th Bde 1/8 Middlesex Regt Jan Vol VIII. Transferred to 167th Bde. 56th. Division 5.2.16		
War Diary	Steenbecque	01/01/1916	09/01/1916
War Diary	Vieux Berquin	10/01/1916	10/01/1916
War Diary	Sailly-Sur-La-Lys	11/01/1916	26/01/1916
War Diary	Bac. St.Maur	27/01/1916	31/01/1916
Miscellaneous	A Form. Messages And Signals.	01/01/1916	01/01/1916
Heading	23rd Division 70th Infy Bde 8th Bn K.O.Y.L.I. 191 Aug-1915 Oct To Italy.		
Heading	8th Div. KOYLI June 1916		
Miscellaneous	Egypt & Palestine Vol. II Map Q. The Defence of Jerusalem		
War Diary	Bordon Camp Hants	26/08/1915	26/08/1915
War Diary	Havre	27/08/1915	28/08/1915
War Diary	Zutkerque	29/08/1915	05/09/1915
War Diary	Campagne	06/09/1915	06/09/1915
War Diary	Oultersteen	07/09/1915	11/09/1915
War Diary	Armentieres	12/09/1915	14/09/1915
War Diary	Fme De Biez.	15/09/1915	17/09/1915
War Diary	Ref Map 36 H.18.B.6.8	18/09/1915	21/09/1915
War Diary	Fme De Biez	22/09/1915	25/09/1915
War Diary	H.18.Q.6.8	26/09/1915	29/09/1915
War Diary	Fme De Biez	30/09/1915	04/10/1915
War Diary	Orchard	05/10/1915	08/10/1915
Miscellaneous	Appendix "A" Disposition Of Bombing Parties		
Operation(al) Order(s)	8th K.O.Y.L.I. Operation Order No. 37		
Miscellaneous	Appendix "B" Disposition Of Lewis Guns.		
Miscellaneous	O.C. Companies, 8th Bn. K.O.Y.L.I		
Miscellaneous	Appendix "C" Communication		
War Diary	Albert	01/06/1916	03/06/1916
War Diary	Henencourt Wood	04/06/1916	15/06/1916
War Diary	Long Valley	16/06/1916	18/06/1916
War Diary	Henencourt Wood	19/06/1916	22/06/1916
War Diary	Tylers Redoubt Authville Wood	23/06/1916	25/06/1916
War Diary	Boulincourt Defences	26/06/1916	28/06/1916
War Diary	Authville Wood	29/06/1916	30/06/1916
Miscellaneous	Q/5 Hd. Qr. 70th Inf Bde	22/06/1916	22/06/1916
Heading	70th Inf.Bde. 23rd Div. Battn. With Bde. Rejoined From 8th Div. 17.7.16. 8th Battn. The King's Own (Yorkshire Light Infantry) July 1916		
War Diary	Trenches Near Ovillers	01/07/1916	01/07/1916
War Diary	Long Valley	02/07/1916	31/07/1916
Miscellaneous	Casualties During The Month Of July 1916		
Heading	23rd Division 70th Brigade 1/8th Battalion King's Own Yorkshire Light Infantry August 1916		
War Diary	Somme Sector	01/08/1916	07/08/1916
War Diary	Franvillers	08/08/1916	15/08/1916
War Diary	Rue De Sac	16/08/1916	17/08/1916
War Diary	St Yves Tr	18/08/1916	25/08/1916
War Diary	Rue De Sac	26/08/1916	04/09/1916
War Diary	Zudausques	05/09/1916	11/09/1916
War Diary	Bresle	12/09/1916	15/09/1916
War Diary	Black Wood	16/09/1916	18/09/1916
War Diary	Peake Wood	19/09/1916	19/09/1916
War Diary	Lozenge Wood	20/09/1916	21/09/1916
War Diary	Gourlay Tr	22/09/1916	30/09/1916

War Diary	N-Martinpuich	01/10/1916	02/10/1916
War Diary	Dingle	03/10/1916	04/10/1916
War Diary	Cutting	05/10/1916	08/10/1916
War Diary	Bresle	09/10/1916	12/10/1916
War Diary	In The Train	13/10/1916	13/10/1916
War Diary	Francieres	14/10/1916	14/10/1916
War Diary	Argenvillers	15/10/1916	15/10/1916
War Diary	Poperinghe	16/10/1916	16/10/1916
War Diary	Ouderdom	17/10/1916	17/10/1916
War Diary	Ypres	18/10/1916	18/10/1916
War Diary	Zillebeke	19/10/1916	21/10/1916
War Diary	Ypres	22/10/1916	26/10/1916
War Diary	Zillebeke	27/10/1916	29/10/1916
War Diary	Poperinghe	30/10/1916	04/11/1916
War Diary	Ypres	05/11/1916	09/11/1916
War Diary	Trenches	10/11/1916	15/11/1916
War Diary	W/N Trenches	16/11/1916	16/11/1916
War Diary	Montreal Camp	17/11/1916	22/11/1916
War Diary	Trenches	23/11/1916	29/11/1916
War Diary	Ypres	30/11/1916	30/11/1916
Operation(al) Order(s)	? K.O.Y.L.I. Operation Order No. 71	15/11/1916	15/11/1916
War Diary		01/12/1916	05/12/1916
War Diary	Trenches	06/12/1916	07/12/1916
War Diary	Camp	08/12/1916	15/12/1916
War Diary	Ypres	16/12/1916	19/12/1916
War Diary	Trenches	20/12/1916	23/12/1916
War Diary	Ypres	24/12/1916	27/12/1916
War Diary	Trenches	28/12/1916	31/12/1916
War Diary	Montreal Camp	01/01/1917	08/01/1917
War Diary	Ypres	09/01/1917	12/01/1917
War Diary	Trenches	13/01/1917	16/01/1917
War Diary	Ypres	17/01/1917	20/01/1917
War Diary	Trenches	21/01/1917	24/01/1917
War Diary	Montreal Camp	25/01/1917	31/01/1917
War Diary	Ypres	01/02/1917	17/02/1917
War Diary	Ouderdom (Montreal Camp)	18/02/1917	24/02/1917
War Diary	Bollezeele	25/02/1917	25/02/1917
War Diary	Watten	26/02/1917	26/02/1917
War Diary	Mentque	27/02/1917	18/03/1917
War Diary	Moulle	19/03/1917	19/03/1917
War Diary	Bollezeele	20/03/1917	20/03/1917
War Diary	Houtkerque	21/03/1917	04/04/1917
War Diary	Winnipeg Camp	05/04/1917	07/04/1917
War Diary	Zillebeke Bund & Railway Dugouts.	08/04/1917	10/04/1917
War Diary	Frontline Trenches	11/04/1917	14/04/1917
War Diary	Scottish Lines	14/04/1917	21/04/1917
War Diary	Frontline Trenches.	22/04/1917	26/04/1917
War Diary	Railway Dugouts	27/04/1917	30/04/1917
War Diary	Front Line Trenches	01/05/1917	01/05/1917
War Diary	Billets (Watou)	02/05/1917	10/05/1917
War Diary	Scottish Lines	11/05/1917	12/05/1917
War Diary	Front Line	13/05/1917	14/05/1917
War Diary	Billets (Watou)	15/05/1917	24/05/1917
War Diary	Railway Dugouts	25/05/1917	26/05/1917
War Diary	Front Line Trenches	27/05/1917	31/05/1917
War Diary	Camp Near Ouderdom	01/06/1917	03/06/1917

Type	Description	Date From	Date To
War Diary	Trenches	04/06/1917	10/06/1917
War Diary	Near Ouderdom	11/06/1917	12/06/1917
War Diary	Meteren	13/06/1917	13/06/1917
War Diary	Near Meteren	14/06/1917	26/06/1917
War Diary	Camp Near Reninghelst	27/06/1917	27/06/1917
War Diary	Trenches	28/06/1917	30/06/1917
Miscellaneous	Preliminary Instructions And Plan-Of Attack 8th. K.O.Y.L.I.		
Miscellaneous	Plan Of Attack 8th. K. O. Y. L.I.		
Map	Map 14 Scale 1:10.000		
Miscellaneous	8th. K.O.Y.L.I. Administrative Instructions For 2nd Army Offensive.		
Miscellaneous	Reference-8th. E.O.Y.L.I. Administrative Orders.	02/06/1917	02/06/1917
Miscellaneous	To Be Read In Conjunction With Administrative Instructions For The Attack-8th K.O.Y.L.I.	03/06/1917	03/06/1917
Miscellaneous	Headquarters, 8th Bn. K.O. Yorkshire L.I. 3rd June 1917	03/06/1917	03/06/1917
Operation(al) Order(s)	8th K.O.Y.L.I. Administrative Orders. (In of Operation Order No. 115)	04/06/1917	04/06/1917
Miscellaneous	Plan Of Attack. 8th. K. O. Y. L.I.		
War Diary	Trenches	01/07/1917	05/07/1917
War Diary	Micmac Camp.	06/07/1917	11/07/1917
War Diary	Near Steenvoorde	12/07/1917	18/07/1917
War Diary	Near Meteren.	19/07/1917	31/07/1917
War Diary	Meteren	01/08/1917	06/08/1917
War Diary	Arques	07/08/1917	07/08/1917
War Diary	Bouvelinghem	08/08/1917	09/08/1917
War Diary	Bayenghem	10/08/1917	10/08/1917
War Diary	Tunnellers Camp	11/08/1917	23/08/1917
War Diary	Dominion Cp	24/08/1917	25/08/1917
War Diary	Trenches	26/08/1917	31/08/1917
War Diary	Patricia Lines	01/09/1917	02/09/1917
War Diary	En Route	03/09/1917	03/09/1917
War Diary	Buysscheure	04/09/1917	12/09/1917
War Diary	Weamers Cappel	13/09/1917	13/09/1917
War Diary	Steenvoorde	14/09/1917	14/09/1917
War Diary	Dickebush	15/09/1917	15/09/1917
War Diary	Railway Dugouts.	16/09/1917	16/09/1917
War Diary	Trenches	17/09/1917	18/09/1917
War Diary	Mic Mac Camp	19/09/1917	19/09/1917
War Diary	Trenches	20/09/1917	24/09/1917
War Diary	Chippewa Camp	25/09/1917	26/09/1917
War Diary	Trenches	27/09/1917	29/09/1917
Miscellaneous	23rd Division S.G. 62/16/2. X Corps.	30/09/1917	30/09/1917
Miscellaneous	Patrol Report	01/09/1917	01/09/1917
Map	Map. Shewing. Observatory-Ridge. Hill-60. & Canal. Sections.		
Map	Message Map		
Miscellaneous	Message Form		
Map	Message Map		
Miscellaneous	Message Form.		
Miscellaneous	O.C. Cave. Patrol Report. Strength. 1 Officer And 10 Other Ranks.	29/09/1917	29/09/1917
War Diary	Bedford House.	01/10/1917	01/10/1917
War Diary	Ridgewood	02/10/1917	02/10/1917
War Diary	Meteren	03/10/1917	04/10/1917

War Diary	Ypres	05/10/1917	11/10/1917
War Diary	Scottish Wood	12/10/1917	13/10/1917
War Diary	Trenches	14/10/1917	18/10/1917
War Diary	Railway Dugouts	19/10/1917	19/10/1917
War Diary	Scottish Wood	20/10/1917	20/10/1917
War Diary	Esquerdes	24/10/1917	30/10/1917
War Diary	Bedford House	30/10/1917	30/10/1917
War Diary	Esquerdes	31/10/1917	31/10/1917
Heading	Attached 8th Division 70th Infy Bde 23 Div. 8th Bn K.O.Y.L.I. Oct 1915-May 1916		
Heading	8th, Division. 70th, Brigade. 8th, K.O.Y.L.I. 9/10/15-30/11/15. May 1916		
Heading	8th Division 8th K.O.Y.L.I Vol. 3		
War Diary	Fme De Biez.	09/10/1915	11/10/1915
War Diary	Jesus Fme	12/10/1915	16/10/1915
War Diary	La Croix Les Corneux	18/10/1915	18/10/1915
War Diary	La Croix Les Corneux	17/10/1915	21/10/1915
War Diary	Foray Fme	22/10/1915	23/10/1915
War Diary	Weathercock House	24/10/1915	24/10/1915
War Diary	Crucifix Fms	25/10/1915	27/10/1915
War Diary	Cul-De-Sac	28/10/1915	31/10/1915
Miscellaneous	Headquarters 8th Lt. Co. Yorkshire Light Infantry Nov. 30 1915	30/11/1915	30/11/1915
War Diary	Cul-De-Sac Farm	01/11/1915	03/11/1915
War Diary	Wye. Farm	04/11/1915	07/11/1915
War Diary	Crucifix Farms	08/11/1915	08/11/1915
War Diary	Weathercock Hall	09/11/1915	10/11/1915
War Diary	Cul De Sac	11/11/1915	17/11/1915
War Diary	Wye Farm	18/11/1915	22/11/1915
War Diary	Cul De Sac	23/11/1915	24/11/1915
War Diary	Steen Becque	25/11/1915	30/11/1915
Heading	8th, Division 70th, Brigade 8th, K.O.Y.L.I. December, 1915		
Heading	8th Division 8th K.O.Y.L.I. Vol 4 Dec. 15		
War Diary	Steenbecque	01/12/1915	19/12/1915
War Diary	Lynde	20/12/1915	20/12/1915
War Diary	Enguinegatte	21/12/1915	21/12/1915
War Diary	Cauchie D'Ecques	22/12/1915	22/12/1915
War Diary	Steenbecque	23/12/1915	31/12/1915
Heading	8th, Division. 70th, Brigade. 8th, K.O.Y.L.I. January, 1916		
Heading	8th K.O.Y.L.I. Vol. 5		
War Diary	Steenbecque	01/01/1916	10/01/1916
War Diary	Estaires	11/01/1916	11/01/1916
War Diary	Spy. Farm	12/01/1916	15/01/1916
War Diary	Weathercock House	16/01/1916	19/01/1916
War Diary	Spy Farm	20/01/1916	23/01/1916
War Diary	Weathercock House	24/01/1916	26/01/1916
War Diary	Sailly	27/01/1916	31/01/1916
Miscellaneous	G.574/4K.	07/01/1916	07/01/1916
Miscellaneous	Demonstration of Coloured Signal Flares, 8th Jan. 1916	08/01/1916	08/01/1916
Map	Map Square 1 Demonstration 8.1.1916 Use Of Flares In Attack.		
Miscellaneous	8th Battalion K.O. Yorkshire Light Infantry	08/01/1916	08/01/1916
Heading	8th, Division. 70th, Brigade. 8th, K.O.Y.L.I. February, 1916		

War Diary	Sailly	01/02/1916	03/02/1916
War Diary	Pergola. House	04/02/1916	07/02/1916
War Diary	Nye Farm	08/02/1916	11/02/1916
War Diary	Pergola House	12/02/1916	15/02/1916
War Diary	Wye Farm	16/02/1916	19/02/1916
War Diary	Pergola House	20/02/1916	23/02/1916
War Diary	Wye Farm	24/02/1916	27/02/1916
War Diary	Fleurbaix	28/02/1916	29/02/1916
Heading	8th, Division. 70th, Brigade. 8th, K.O.Y.L.I. March, 1916		
Miscellaneous	Headquarters, 8th Bn. K. O. Y. L. I. 4th April 1916	04/04/1916	04/04/1916
War Diary	Fleurbaix	01/03/1916	01/03/1916
War Diary	Wye Farm (Nr Fleurbaix)	02/03/1916	05/03/1916
War Diary	Fleurbaix	06/03/1916	09/03/1916
War Diary	Wye Farm (Nr Fleurbaix)	10/03/1916	13/03/1916
War Diary	Fleurbaix	14/03/1916	17/03/1916
War Diary	Wye Farm (Fleurbaix)	18/03/1916	20/03/1916
War Diary	Sailly	21/03/1916	25/03/1916
War Diary	Calonne	26/03/1916	26/03/1916
War Diary	Vignacourt	27/03/1916	30/03/1916
War Diary	St Gratien.	31/03/1916	31/03/1916
Heading	8th, Division 70th, Brigade 8th, K.O.Y.L.I. April, 1916		
War Diary	Albert	02/04/1916	06/04/1916
War Diary	Trenches Near Albert	07/04/1916	14/04/1916
War Diary	Albert	15/04/1916	17/04/1916
War Diary	Millencourt	18/04/1916	24/04/1916
War Diary	Trenches Near La Boisselle	25/04/1916	30/04/1916
Heading	8th, Division. 70th, Brigade. 8th, K.O.Y.L.I. May, 1916		
War Diary	N.E. Of Albert	01/05/1916	02/05/1916
War Diary	Dernancourt	03/05/1916	08/05/1916
War Diary	Henencourt	09/05/1916	18/05/1916
War Diary	Albert	19/05/1916	26/05/1916
War Diary	Albert (Trenches)	27/05/1916	31/05/1916
Miscellaneous			
Heading	23rd Division 70th Infy Bde 11th Bn Sherwood Foresters 1915 Aug-1917 Oct. To Italy.		
Heading	XXIII Division 11th Sherwood Foresters Vol I		
War Diary	Bordon	20/08/1915	27/08/1915
War Diary	Ostrohove	28/08/1915	29/08/1915
War Diary	Zutkerque	30/08/1915	30/08/1915
War Diary	Campagne	06/09/1915	06/09/1915
War Diary	Outtersteen	07/09/1915	11/09/1915
War Diary	La Chaple d'Armentieres.	11/09/1915	20/09/1915
War Diary	Armentieres.	25/09/1915	03/10/1915
Heading	8th, Division. 70th, Brigade. 11th, Notts & Derby. Oct & Nov, 1915		
Heading	VIII Division Vol. 2 5. Oct-Nov. 15		
War Diary	Armentieres.	05/10/1915	11/10/1915
War Diary	Fleurbaix	18/10/1915	18/10/1915
War Diary	Bac St Maur	22/10/1915	22/10/1915
War Diary	La Coix Les Colneux	23/10/1915	23/10/1915
War Diary	Fleurbaix	24/10/1915	24/10/1915
War Diary	Sailly	27/10/1915	27/10/1915
War Diary	Armentieres	03/10/1915	14/10/1915
War Diary	Bois Grenier	18/10/1915	22/10/1915
War Diary	Sailly	01/11/1915	04/11/1915

War Diary	Trenches	05/11/1915	08/11/1915
War Diary	Fleurbaix	08/11/1915	09/11/1915
War Diary	La Croix Lescornex	10/11/1915	10/11/1915
War Diary	Sailly	13/11/1915	18/11/1915
War Diary	Trenches	19/11/1915	22/11/1915
War Diary	Sailly	23/11/1915	23/11/1915
War Diary	La Couronne	24/11/1915	24/11/1915
War Diary	Steinbecque	25/11/1915	30/11/1915
Heading	8th, Division 70th, Brigade. 11th, Volts & Derby. December, 1915		
Heading	VIII Div. 11th Notts & Derby Vol. 3		
War Diary	Steenbecque	01/12/1915	31/12/1915
Map	8th Division Line		
Miscellaneous			
Heading	8th, Division. 70th, Brigade. 11th, Notts & Derby. January, 1916		
Heading	11th Notts & Derby Vol: 4		
War Diary	Steenbecque	01/01/1916	10/01/1916
War Diary	Neuf Berquin	11/01/1916	11/01/1916
War Diary	Rue De Quesne	13/01/1916	22/01/1916
War Diary	In Trenches	23/01/1916	26/01/1916
Heading	8th, Division 70th, Brigade. 11th, Notts & Derby. February, 1916		
War Diary	Rue Du Quesnoy Sailly	01/02/1916	02/02/1916
War Diary	Trenches	03/02/1916	07/02/1916
War Diary	Fleurbaix	08/02/1916	09/02/1916
War Diary	Trenches	11/02/1916	16/02/1916
War Diary	Fleurbaix	17/02/1916	18/02/1916
War Diary	Trenches	19/02/1916	22/02/1916
War Diary	Fleurbaix	26/02/1916	27/02/1916
War Diary	In Trenches.	27/02/1916	29/02/1916
Heading	8th, Division. 70th, Brigade. 11th, Notts & Derby. March, 1916		
War Diary	In Trenches	01/03/1916	02/03/1916
War Diary	Fleurbaix	04/03/1916	05/03/1916
War Diary	In Trenches	06/03/1916	10/03/1916
War Diary	Fleurbaix	11/03/1916	14/03/1916
War Diary	In Trenches	16/03/1916	17/03/1916
War Diary	Fleurbaix	20/03/1916	20/03/1916
War Diary	Cul De Sac Farm	22/03/1916	26/03/1916
War Diary	Calonne	27/03/1916	27/03/1916
War Diary	Vignacourt	28/03/1916	30/03/1916
War Diary	St Gratien	31/03/1916	31/03/1916
Heading	8th, Division. 70th, Brigade. 11th, Notts & Derby. April, 1916		
War Diary	Albert	01/04/1916	01/04/1916
War Diary	In Trenches	03/04/1916	07/04/1916
War Diary	Albert	08/04/1916	08/04/1916
War Diary	In Trenches	13/04/1916	17/04/1916
War Diary	Henencourt	18/04/1916	24/04/1916
War Diary	Dernancourt	25/04/1916	27/04/1916
War Diary	Becourt Wood	28/04/1916	28/04/1916
War Diary	De Henencourt	29/04/1916	29/04/1916
Heading	8th, Division. 70th, Brigade. 11th, Notts & Derby. May, 1916		
War Diary	In The Trenches	02/05/1916	06/05/1916

War Diary	Hennencourt	09/05/1916	09/05/1916
War Diary	Millencourt	19/05/1916	19/05/1916
War Diary	Albert	27/05/1916	27/05/1916
War Diary	In The Trenches	31/05/1916	31/05/1916
Heading	11th Bn Sherwoods June 1916		
Heading	Egypt & Palestine Vol. II. Map A.		
War Diary	The Trenches	01/06/1916	04/06/1916
War Diary	Henencourt	08/06/1916	12/06/1916
War Diary	Bouzincourt (Defences)	13/06/1916	20/06/1916
War Diary	In The Trenches	26/06/1916	30/06/1916
Operation(al) Order(s)	11th (Service) Battalion The Sherwood Foresters Operation Order No. 6	17/06/1916	17/06/1916
Miscellaneous	Appendix "A"	18/06/1916	18/06/1916
Miscellaneous	To The Quartermaster & Transport Officer	18/06/1916	18/06/1916
Miscellaneous	To The Signalling Officer.	18/06/1916	18/06/1916
Miscellaneous	Reference Operation Order No. 6 Para 12 (A)		
Heading	11th Bn. Notts & Derby Regt July 1916		
Miscellaneous	Subject		
War Diary	In The Field	01/07/1916	31/07/1916
Miscellaneous	Account Of The Part Taken By 11th (Service) Battalion The Sherwood Foresters In The Operations Of 1st July, 1916	01/07/1916	01/07/1916
Miscellaneous	Casualties In Action July 1st, 1916	01/07/1916	01/07/1916
Heading	Appendices To War Diary 11th Notts & Derby Regt. July 1916		
Miscellaneous	Subject		
Map	Scale 1:5000 Trenches Corrected To May 11th 1916		
Map	Scale		
Map	St Yves.		
Miscellaneous			
Map	St. Yves.		
Miscellaneous	For Attachment to August War Diary.		
Map	German Line		
Map	Shows Wire (Efficient Obstacle) May 18 1916		
Map	Sketch Map		
Map			
Map	Ovillers Trenches 10.5.16.s		
Miscellaneous			
Heading	23rd Division 70th Brigade 1/11th Battalion Notts & Derby Regiment August 1916		
War Diary		02/08/1916	30/08/1916
War Diary	Papot	01/09/1916	12/09/1916
War Diary	Bresle	15/09/1916	15/09/1916
War Diary	Black Wood	18/09/1916	18/09/1916
War Diary	Contalmaison	19/09/1916	20/09/1916
War Diary	Lozenge Wood	21/09/1916	22/09/1916
War Diary	Contalmaison	25/09/1916	25/09/1916
War Diary	Front Line	26/09/1916	27/09/1916
War Diary	Trenches	27/09/1916	28/09/1916
War Diary	Support Line	29/09/1916	30/09/1916
Operation(al) Order(s)	Operation Order No. 42 By Major C.E. Hudson, D.S.O., M.C. 11th. (S) Battalion The Sherwood Foresters.	19/09/1917	19/09/1917
Miscellaneous	Administrative Details		

Miscellaneous	Report On Operation From Sept. 20th. 917 Until 1st. Oct. 1917 In Which 11th. (S) Battn. Sherwood Foresters Took Part.		04/10/1917	04/10/1917
War Diary	Front Line		01/10/1917	01/10/1917
War Diary	Dickebush		02/10/1917	02/10/1917
War Diary	Meteren		04/10/1917	07/10/1917
War Diary	Ypres		10/10/1917	11/10/1917
War Diary	Dickebush		12/10/1917	14/10/1917
War Diary	Zillebeke Bund		16/10/1917	17/10/1917
War Diary	Front Line		18/10/1917	19/10/1917
War Diary	Zillebeke Bund		20/10/1917	20/10/1917
War Diary	Hallebast Camp		20/10/1917	23/10/1917
War Diary	Setques		24/10/1917	31/10/1917
Map				
Map	Position after the Attack			
War Diary	Martinpuich		01/10/1916	01/10/1916
War Diary	Le Sarsline		02/10/1916	02/10/1916
War Diary	Lozenge Wood		04/10/1916	08/10/1916
War Diary	Breslewood		10/10/1916	12/10/1916
War Diary	Pont Remy		14/10/1916	14/10/1916
War Diary	Grapennes		15/10/1916	15/10/1916
War Diary	Ouderdom		16/10/1916	18/10/1916
War Diary	Zillebeke Bund.		21/10/1916	29/10/1916
War Diary	Poperinghe		01/11/1916	04/11/1916
War Diary	The Trenches		06/11/1916	09/11/1916
War Diary	Ypres		14/11/1916	16/11/1916
War Diary	Toronto Camp		17/11/1916	22/11/1916
War Diary	Zillebeke Bund		22/11/1916	29/11/1916
War Diary	Trenches		01/12/1916	05/12/1916
War Diary	Zillebeke		06/12/1916	07/12/1916
War Diary	Toronto Camp		10/12/1916	15/12/1916
War Diary	Trenches		19/12/1916	19/12/1916
War Diary	Ypres		20/12/1916	27/12/1916
War Diary	Barracks		28/12/1916	31/12/1916
War Diary	Toronto Camp		01/01/1917	08/01/1917
War Diary	Rudkin House HQ.		09/01/1917	12/01/1917
War Diary	The Bund		13/01/1917	16/01/1917
War Diary	Rudkin House		17/01/1917	20/01/1917
War Diary	The Bund		21/01/1917	24/01/1917
War Diary	Toronto Camp		25/01/1917	31/01/1917
War Diary	Half Way House		01/02/1917	05/02/1917
War Diary	Ypres Barracks		06/02/1917	18/02/1917
War Diary	Toronto Camp		18/02/1917	26/02/1917
War Diary	Nordausques		27/02/1917	28/02/1917
War Diary	Nordausques		01/03/1917	09/03/1917
War Diary	Nordausques.		10/03/1917	24/03/1917
War Diary	Houtkerque		26/03/1917	05/04/1917
War Diary	Toronto Camp		06/04/1917	06/04/1917
War Diary	Bund.		08/04/1917	10/04/1917
War Diary	Hill 60		10/04/1917	14/04/1917
War Diary	Toronto Camp		15/04/1917	22/04/1917
War Diary	Trenches Hill 60		23/04/1917	25/04/1917
War Diary	Hill 60		25/04/1917	30/04/1917
Miscellaneous	Report on Enemy Attack on Centre Battalion of the Hill 60 Sub-Sector on The Night of April 9th,11th		15/04/1917	15/04/1917
Map	Map Showing Right Brigade Area. Scale 1/10.000			

War Diary	Railway Dugouts Ypres	01/05/1917	02/05/1917
War Diary	Near Abeele	03/05/1917	05/05/1917
War Diary	Abeele	06/05/1917	11/05/1917
War Diary	Toronto Camp	12/05/1917	12/05/1917
War Diary	Half Way House	13/05/1917	14/05/1917
War Diary	Abeele	15/05/1917	24/05/1917
War Diary	Trenches Hill 60	25/05/1917	26/05/1917
War Diary	The Bund	27/05/1917	28/05/1917
War Diary	Rudkin House	29/05/1917	31/05/1917
Operation(al) Order(s)	The 11th (S) Battalion The Sherwood Foresters Operation Order No. 15 By Lieut. Colonel H.F. Watson, C.M.G., D.S.O., Comdg.	20/05/1917	20/05/1917
Miscellaneous	Stokes Mortars		
Operation(al) Order(s)	The 11th (S) Battalion, The Sherwood Foresters Operation Order No. 15 By Lieut. Colonel H.F. Watson, C.M.G., D.S.O., Commdg.	20/05/1917	20/05/1917
Miscellaneous	2nd Army Offensive. Administrative Details To Be Read In Conjunction With O.O.	29/05/1917	29/05/1917
Operation(al) Order(s)	2nd Army Offensive Addition To Operation Order No. 15		
War Diary	Trenches	01/06/1917	01/06/1917
War Diary	Halifax Camp	02/06/1917	02/06/1917
War Diary	St Lawrence Camp	04/06/1917	05/06/1917
War Diary	Trenches	06/06/1917	10/06/1917
War Diary	Scottish Lines	11/06/1917	12/06/1917
War Diary	Meteren	14/06/1917	15/06/1917
War Diary	Dickebusch	16/06/1917	28/07/1917
Miscellaneous	2nd Army Offensive Moppers - Up	03/06/1917	03/06/1917
Miscellaneous	2nd Army Offensive Additions And Amendments.	04/06/1917	04/06/1917
Miscellaneous	List of Awards in connection with Offensive of June 7th.		
War Diary	Windmill Camp Near Dicke Busch	01/07/1917	01/07/1917
War Diary	In The Trenches	02/07/1917	05/07/1917
War Diary	Micmac Camp	06/07/1917	12/07/1917
War Diary	Steenvoorde	13/07/1917	13/07/1917
War Diary	Pinchboom	18/07/1917	31/07/1917
War Diary	Meteren	01/08/1917	01/08/1917
War Diary	Arques	06/08/1917	06/08/1917
War Diary	West Becourt	07/08/1917	10/08/1917
War Diary	St Janter Beizen	11/08/1917	23/08/1917
War Diary	Devonshire Camp	24/08/1917	25/08/1917
War Diary	Chateau Segard	26/08/1917	27/08/1917
War Diary	Half Way House	28/08/1917	30/08/1917
War Diary	Wippenhoek	31/08/1917	03/09/1917
War Diary	Oosthoek	09/09/1917	12/09/1917
War Diary	Oosthoek	13/09/1917	13/09/1917
War Diary	Steenvoorde	14/09/1917	14/09/1917
War Diary	Dickebusch	15/09/1917	15/09/1917
War Diary	In The Line	16/09/1917	19/09/1917
War Diary	Mic Mac Camp	19/09/1917	20/09/1917
War Diary	Stirling Castle	22/09/1917	22/09/1917
War Diary	In The Line	23/09/1917	24/09/1917
War Diary	In Line.	24/09/1917	24/09/1917
War Diary	Murrumbridge	25/09/1917	27/09/1917
War Diary	In The Line	29/09/1917	01/10/1917

Miscellaneous	Second Army G.353. X Corps G. 101/17/32. 23rd Divn. S.G. 181/1/11	09/10/1917	09/10/1917
Operation(al) Order(s)	11th. (S) Battalion The Sherwood Foresters Order No. 50	15/10/1917	15/10/1917
Operation(al) Order(s)	11th. (S) Battalion The Sherwood Foresters Order No. 51	15/10/1917	15/10/1917
Operation(al) Order(s)	11th. (S) Battalion The Sherwood Foresters, Order No. 52	19/10/1917	19/10/1917
Miscellaneous	Routine Orders By Brigadier General H. Gordon, C.M.G., D.S.O. Commanding 70th Infantry Brigade.	31/10/1917	31/10/1917
Map	Message Map.		
Miscellaneous	Message From		
Heading	8th Division 70th Infy Bde 23 Div. 11th Bn Notts & Derby Oct 1915-May 1916		

ATTACHED 8TH DIVISION
70TH INFY BDE

23 DIV

1-8TH MIDDLESEX REGT
AUG ~~OCT~~ 1915 - JAN 1916

MAPS/PLANS RECORDED

From 28 DIV   85 BDE

To   56 DIV   167 BDE

Box 2187

8th Division

121/0561

18th Middlesex
Vol III
From March 2.8.15. to 25 Aug 15
reorganised on "operational
formation" 2 Aug 1915
to 25th Bn
27 Aug.

WAR DIARY or INTELLIGENCE SUMMARY

Army Form C. 2118.

8th BATT. (O.C.O) ESSEX REGT

Hour, Date, Place		Summary of Events and Information	Remarks and references to Appendices
Doiran 2nd August	10 am	The remainder of 1/8 Middlesex who had been absorbed into the 1/7 Bn. on 23rd June paraded and were inspected by Lt Col King, C.O. 1/7 Bn prior to departure & wishing them a farewell the Col attached them to the 1st Coy that they had worked and trusted the amalgamation and wished them all good luck in them new start in life. Capt Clapp replied & behalf of the 1/8 Men and the Bn. gave them hearty cheers for Col King, the Battn then marched off. No 2 of the new Cys they were out to Major Grigg who was received with hearty demonstration and on arrival of their billets were welcomed by a large draft which had arrived on 31st July from Gibraltar. In the afternoon the Battn was arranged into its original companies and the draft allotted fourteen junior officers recently joined remainded with 1/7 Bn to complete their course of instruction at the officers class. The Battalion state showed 25 officers and other ranks the officers were :—	

Army Form C. 2118.

WAR DIARY
or
INTELLIGENCE SUMMARY.
(Erase heading not required.)

1st BATT. (C.O.) MIDDX. REGT

Hour, Date, Place	Summary of Events and Information	Remarks and references to Appendices

Major S.O.W. Buggery Commanding
Capt. ? + Chapp — Adj. Adjutant
Capt. Q.M. + Lon Ebart Lomal
Capt. Woodbridge } A Coy
2/Lt. de Behn   }
Lt. Wilett   }
Lt. Pool   } B coy
Lt. Hughson }
Lt. Lacey   } C coy
Capt. Butcherd } D Coy
Lt. Dash   }

The undermentioned Officers were
not at once allotted to their
respective companies, they being with

1/Bn. 2/Lt. Tonkinson *
          Trenlit   *
          Bailey
          Ryan
          Reynolds
          Waldram
          Roult
          Lacey
          Emmer
          Isaacs
          Charlie
                        *
          Howell   *
          Marks

* Reverted to subaltern on
joining Imperial Service
unit.

WAR DIARY
or
INTELLIGENCE SUMMARY.
(Erase heading not required.)

Army Form C. 2118.

9th BATT. 10(?) X. REGT

Hour, Date, Place	Summary of Events and Information	Remarks and references to Appendices
5th August	The battalion arrived in the 23rd Inf Bde of the 8th Division in Divisional Reserve. On its best and transport it was meanwhile. Lieut Burder reported from the ranks of 1/25 London Reg. reported for duty. The strength of the Battalion on organisation and after absorbing drafts was found to be Officers 26 Other ranks 728.	
7 August	The subalterns who arrived with the 1/7 Bn returned and were posted to coys as follows:— A Coy: 2Lt BYHAM, CHALICE, ISAACS, TOMLINSON B Coy: "L" EASMAN, TRUMLETT, MARTIN C Coy: "L" BAILEY, REYNOLDS, WADDAMS D Coy: "L" HOWELL, RYAN, ROUTH, BURDER 2Lt LAREY was appointed to the Machine Guns and attached to C Coy Lieut PONTIFEX gazetted from the ranks of this Battalion left to join the depot of the 10th Middlesex in England	Extract from London Gazette Major S.D.W Gregory to be temporary Lieut Colonel 12/6/15 P.S.C

Army Form C. 2118.

WAR DIARY
or
INTELLIGENCE SUMMARY.
(Erase heading not required.)

5TH BATT. (D.C.O.) 17TH REGT.

Hour, Date, Place	Summary of Events and Information	Remarks and references to Appendices
9th August	The Battalion still being without transport was taken over temporarily by the 24th Inf. Brigade who relieved the 23rd Inf. Bde. It occupied its former billets.	9th August 2/Lts TREMLETT and CHALICE and 63 men of 'A' and 'B' Coys who had not before been in battle went into trenches at 5pm with 1/7 Middx for 48 hrs instruction.
10th August	Two travelling cookers arrived and were taken in charge. The battalion was inspected in the afternoon by General Pulteney, Cmdg 3rd Army Corps, accompanied by Brig-Gen Oxley and staff. The men were paraded outside their billets in clean fatigue dress. The General visited each billet in turn inspecting the men and the billet. The inspection lasting from 6.15pm till 7pm. Remarks generally were passed on the physical fitness and healthy appearance of the men. 396 N.C.Os and men W. 5 Coy. gone on leave 10". 6.15 "inst 2/Lt BURDER goes on leave 11". L.18". inclusive.	
11th August	The Battalion exercised daily in physical drill, handling of arms and route marching.	

Army Form C. 2118.

WAR DIARY
or
INTELLIGENCE SUMMARY.
(Erase heading not required.)

8TH BATT. (D.C.O.) MIDDX. REGT.

Hour, Date, Place	Summary of Events and Information	Remarks and references to Appendices
12" August	The Battalion bathed, the first time for five weeks. 2/Lt MARTIN and REYNOLDS with 64 other ranks went into the trenches on night 11/12 for 48 hours of instruction with 1/r Middx. 11/8/15 The following officers reported for duty, and were posted to Companies as follows:- "L" HUDSON, G.M. to A Coy "L" CAREY, G. to C Coy - SANDERSON to B Coy "L" CAREY, A.S. to D Coy J.C. A party of 4 officers and 64 other ranks went to the trenches to undergo 48 hour instruction with 1/7 Bn. They consisted of 2/Lt WADDAMS, HUDSON, CAREY J., LACEY and men from 5th & 6th draft. The party that went in on the 11" returned without casualties.	
13" August	Brig Gen Oxley C.M.G. 24" I.J. Bde paid an unofficial visit in the evening.	
14" August	No 25781 Cpl Best left for Gt Britain to be transferred to a Home Service unit as a Transfer Tailor. The weather has been fine and cool for the last week and the men around here all so cul entertained in YOC cinemas.	7.P.C.

(9 29 6) W 4141—463 100,000 9/14 H W V Forms/C. 2118/10

Army Form C. 2118.

8th BATT. (D.C.O.) [illegible] REGT.

WAR DIARY
or
INTELLIGENCE SUMMARY.
(Erase heading not required.)

Instructions regarding War Diaries and Intelligence Summaries are contained in F.S. Regs., Part II. and the Staff Manual respectively. Title pages will be prepared in manuscript.

Hour, Date, Place	Summary of Events and Information	Remarks and references to Appendices
15 August	Lt PEAT and LEWY gone on 6 days leave.	
	Capt BUCKLAND with 2nd Lt HOWELL and CHALICE and 48 other ranks go to trenches for 48 hrs instruction. The party that went on 13th returned without casualties.	? J.C.
16 August	Lt TRESAWNA W. R.O.2.C. joined for duty.	? J.C.
17 August	The Battalion was taken over by 23rd Inf Bde on the 24th Inf Bde moving from this district. The last party from the trenches still rest in.e.v. is returned without casualties, the whole Battalion, with the exception of a few infected cases, have now experienced trench life again.	? J.C.
18 August	10 N.C.O. men left to undergo a course of instruction at the 23rd Inf Brigade Grenadier School. Our Col and 3 other ranks R.O.2.C. have joined the Bn as attached for watch duties.	? J.C.

Forms/C. 2118/10

WAR DIARY
or
INTELLIGENCE SUMMARY
(Erase heading not required.)

Army Form C. 2118.

8th BATT. (D.C.O.) MIDDX. REGT.

Hour, Date, Place	Summary of Events and Information	Remarks and references to Appendices
19th August.	Lieut Buxton returns from leave. 5 Officers and 45 other ranks to attend a gas demonstration. Wearing their masks which they enter a building filled with gas and remain there for a few minutes. A working party of 100 is supplied to 15 F Coy R.E. for work on new trench lines. This and other parties as to become daily such. They are conveyed daily in motor lorries and are away from 7am till about 5pm.	
20th August.	A second working party is supplied to 96 F Coy R.E. beginning today. They leave at 7am return about 5pm, being conveyed in motor lorries. This party is also working on a communication trench. A third party of 100 men with Officers & N.C.Os. moved into billets at FLEURBAIX and is working under 24 Inf. Bde. Then work in contact - tramways to the trenches.	7 7 C
21st August.	Lieut ROUTH, C. F. R. leaves for BOULOGNE to undergo an investigation examination in Turkish and another Speck. Scouts which was supplied with duplicate of M.C. only 30 were sent in. He there apparently is repairing it.	See also entry under Aug 26th 7 7 C

Army Form C. 2118.

WAR DIARY
or
INTELLIGENCE SUMMARY.
(Erase heading not required.)

8ᵗʰ BATT, ... ESSEX. REGT

Instructions regarding War Diaries and Intelligence Summaries are contained in F.S. Regs., Part II. and the Staff Manual respectively. Title pages will be prepared in manuscript.

Hour, Date, Place	Summary of Events and Information	Remarks and references to Appendices
22ⁿᵈ August 1915	From *London Gazette*. KING (B.C.O.) 9ᵗʰ Battⁿ. Lieut Q-M Sgt. B H B King from 8ᵗʰ Bn. 8ᵗʰ Co Lancs Regt.— " to be Lieut and seconded for duty with 63ʳᵈ Res. Batt — Aug 20 1915. See Lt King was taken from A Coy when he was to C.Q.M.S. and attached to "C" Coy until he leaves the Battⁿ. Telegram from 25ᵗʰ Inf Bde. BM 817 dated 22.8.15 — 6.30am "There will be no leave boat until further notice will be partial steamer run to and from Boulogne until further intimation is received." There are going on leave are consequently retained. Weather during past week has been cold & hazy, but lowering. The corn has gone on rapidly. Soldiers are often seen assisting the villagers with the harvest. A draft of 31 rank and file arrived from the base at 2.30 pm. The majority of these men have been in 1/8 Bn. before but have left — through wounds, sickness or were left behind in England owing to their youth or wounds. There were from Gibraltar and had been left at Marseille and Rouen as sick when the Bn. left — from Gibraltar arrived at the end of July. 7.30	

Army Form C. 2118.

WAR DIARY
or
INTELLIGENCE SUMMARY.
(Erase heading not required.)

1st BATT. (C.C.) [BLACK] REGT.

Instructions regarding War Diaries and Intelligence Summaries are contained in F. S. Regs., Part II. and the Staff Manual respectively. Title pages will be prepared in manuscript.

Hour, Date, Place	Summary of Events and Information	Remarks and references to Appendices
22nd August 1915	Amongst the transport which arrives daily was four new Vickers machine guns straight from England. The M.G. section are greatly delighted. The health of the troops continues remarkably good. The daily sick report showing for the most part trivial ailments. Hospital cases are confined to influenza and dental trouble. The Battalion was able to obtain the use of a 30yds range this afternoon at which several officers and men practised.	7 C
23rd August	The Brigade inform us that the leave boat from Boulogne will probably resume its services on Tuesday 24 inst and men who were unable to go on Sunday may go in addition to the usual Tuesday men. 300 men with usual proportion of N.C.O. officers resume their daily task behind the firing line under direction of the R.E.	7 C
24th August	2/Lt LEVY returns from leave, return had been delayed owing to stoppage of boat service. Horses arrived today – 1 Riding 2nd L[t] Surgat 11 H Draught	7 C

Forms/C. 2118/10

WAR DIARY
or
INTELLIGENCE SUMMARY
(Erase heading not required.)

Army Form. 2118

4th BATT. (W.L.I.) MIDDX. REGT.

Place	Date	Hour	Summary of Events and Information	Remarks and references to Appendices
JULLUNDUR	12/8/15	11 am	The first men left this Battalion for the Base on discharge on termination of engagement. One man of B Coy was wounded by a stray shot on yesterday's morning parade.	
DO	26 Aug	10.45 am	Wire from Fort Army wrote: "A/Maj. 25th 15 - 2/Lt ROUTH 1/Middlesex Regt accepted by Examiner and orders have been issued for him to proceed to England". 2/Lt ROUTH should now be struck off the strength of that regiment. The four new Machine Guns were tested by a 2 minute range and gave satisfaction but heavy draught horses used sick during the night. The nights effort took her away for the test. Wire from "A" 25 2/Lt Bell aug. BM 835 - 268 15 - 7 Morning from 8th Division began as 3rd Corps approves "Lieutenant" of front un pro INGPEN 2/W Yorks R to temporary command 1/4 R. Middx. Regt. 2/Lt HUDSON with 22 other ranks left to undergo course at 25 2/Bn Bde Grenadier School. Last evening Brig. Gen. STEVENS came and inspected the 310 n. draft that arrived on Sunday. This morning the Bde General with Gen. STEVENS had a private interview with the CO. Today we were to supply for working parties of 100 cal. but we are expected. The 100 of C Coy with machine gun & staff went into billets at A 21 I so Sheet 36. This morning the parties from A & B Coys companies continue to go down daily.	See also notes on 21 Aug.

WAR DIARY
or
INTELLIGENCE SUMMARY
(Erase heading not required.)

Army Form C. 2118

1/8th BATT. (CITY OF LONDON) REGT.

Place	Date 1915	Hour	Summary of Events and Information	Remarks and references to Appendices
Devizes	29 Aug	10.30am	Our first official intimation that we are attached to 25th Inf Bde was conveyed in C'din Staff memo G309/19 K/a dated 27th Aug. The 8th Middlesex Reg having been allotted to 25th Inf Bde will be included in the ordinary roster of working parties furnished by that Brigade. In connection with this a telegram was received from O.C 96 Field Coy. R.E. with whom "D" Coy of 1/8th have been working, in which he begs "to further demand will therefore be made from other units as you Coy working parties to any regd". With reference to an application from "D" Bn for a letter to a Home Service Bath crossing to be in suspense, a reply was received saying he was to be attached to 2nd Bn Suffolk line Reg. "D" Coy left Devizes for Aldershot Hd Hq Battalion and in our Brigade. 2D Bnvok upstit.	Telegram JMP no/2834
	30 Aug	11 am	Div. Routine Order 163 dated 29.8.15 says 2/c 1/8 Bn Middlesex Reg will in future belong to the 25th Inf. by Brigade.	7.T.C
			A 1st Lt. J Laguey attached in Brigade Order 154 of 29th not enrolled at 10am to reguard with the 1st of the been allotted to C Coy Commander. The Re inf. was Captain H.L. RILEY. 5 So 7/Rifle Brigade, a new Servt - Captain J.H.G. RIFFIN 2/Lincolnshire Reg. "D" Townsend 8/2 Middlesex 3rd Lieut. joined us opening at 11am. After a week of fine dry weather the last two days have been colder and stormy. Third of the snow has now been turned out. Its tom blitch plunged. Nothing fir lit no still provided. B.+C Coy cut down 100 acres in still meadow on the front line. And "D" sent another 100 to pg. ente trans. Today the remainder of the Battle works complete.	

Army Form. 2118

WAR DIARY
or
INTELLIGENCE SUMMARY
(Erase heading not required.)

1/8th BATT. (D.O.O.) MIDDX. REGT

Instructions regarding War Diaries and Intelligence Summaries are contained in F.S. Regs., Part II. and the Staff Manual respectively. Title Pages will be prepared in manuscript.

Place	Date	Hour	Summary of Events and Information	Remarks and references to Appendices
DOULIEU	30 Aug	(cont)	The following officers attached & Lieut transfd for instruction, Capt WOODBRIDGE and Lieut WHITE	7 TC
-do-	31 Aug	10.30am	Orders have been received for the Bngde to advance 2th 2/ Bde who are in the Frontline Forward these Battalion are to be in the Front line and these in immediate reserve. We are to be in reserve behind the right section of the Bn. But transport as to move south of the River. The men in tin hangs and likely to be orderly and have again been given orders to the M.G. section. We also are to use the divisional trollies this afternoon We as expect to battle west of the battalion	7 TC

ESWGregory Lieut Colonel
Commanding 8th Batt. (D.O.O.) Middx. Regt

8th, Division.

25th, Brigade.

1/8th, Middlesex Regt.

September, 1915.

$\frac{121}{6930}$

8th Division

26th Bde

1/8th Middlesex

Vol IV

Sept. 15

Camp from 23rd Sept to 23/10/15
to 70th Bde

Army Form. C. 2118

1/8TH BATT. (D.C.O.) MIDDX. REGt

WAR DIARY
or
INTELLIGENCE SUMMARY
(Erase heading not required.)

Instructions regarding War Diaries and Intelligence Summaries are contained in F. S. Regs., Part II. and the Staff Manual respectively. Title Pages will be prepared in manuscript.

Place	Date	Hour	Summary of Events and Information	Remarks and references to Appendices
DOULIEU	1st Sept	9.45am	We are moving today to billets near the front line. Three battalions of the Brigade are going into the trenches to relieve 24th Bde ourselves and two others are going into immediate reserve	
		11 am	Permission just arrived for Capt. BUCKLAND to go on leave from 1st to 8th September. He has gone Left for La Gorgue	7 PC
FLORBAIX (R.N. BIACHE)	2nd Sept	11.20 am	Relief was completed by 9.40 pm. Two Companies with Hd Qrs. at CROIX MARECHAL and an M.O. were lent to 1st London Regt. and two Companies with an M.O. at CROIX MARECHAL, an M.G. were lent to 1st London Regt. Lt Col INGPEN 2/West Yorks arrives and takes over command of the Battalion	
		9 pm	25th Inf Bde Order 690 dated 2nd Sept is as follows. Major (Temporary Lt Colonel) P L INGPEN 2/West Yorkshire Regiment is appointed to Command 1/8 Middlesex Regiment. He assumed command this day.	7 PC
	3rd Sept	4 pm	The C.O., 2nd in command, Coy Commanders and M.O. go to visit the trenches held by 1st London Regiment. They are at present a very wet day	

Army Form. C. 2118

WAR DIARY
or
INTELLIGENCE SUMMARY

(Erase heading not required.)

8th BATT. (D.D.O.) MIDDX. REGT

1915

Place	Date	Hour	Summary of Events and Information	Remarks and references to Appendices
SAILLY SUR LA LYS	5 Sept		Battalion in Trenches - Fine. All quiet on Bn Front. Bn took over [N.5.1, N.5.2, N.5.3] from 1st London Regt on relieving of 2nd Heavy rain. Trenches very wet. [3R,3S,3Q,P,4R]	7d.
	6th Sept		Bn in Trenches - Visited by Brigadier. Trenches much down. Fine. Lt Col Gregory went on leave	7d.
	7 Sept		Total casualties for this period of trenches O.R. killed 1 wounded 1	7.D.C.
Flambaix	8 Sept		Relieved by 1st London Regt & returned to reserve billets at Rue Bacot, Fleurbaix and Cam Morceau last evening.	7.D.C.
	9 Sept	5pm	Draft of 38 other ranks arrived. All had been before with this Battalion in France.	
		3.15pm	Capt Burkland returned from leave. 2/Lt Burdee returns from 2nd Lincolnshire Regt to which he had been attached. Fine.	7.D.C.
	11 Sept		The G.O.C. Brigade inspected the draft that arrived 8th inst.	7.D.C.
	12 Sept	7pm	Bn took over 3R, 3S, 4P, 4Q from 1st London Regt (R.F.) Trenches dry	7.C.
	14 Sept	7.30am	Bn visited by G.O.C. 8th Div. Bgr Hudson, who made a tour of the trenches. 2/Lt g.g. de Sauls was shot through the head whilst looking over the parapet. He was carried away when/Khow away	
SAILLY SUR LA LYS	15 Sept		Bn was relieved on the trenches by 1st Sherwood Foresters (Notts and Derby) Regt and went into billets at man Cross roads Sailly	7.C.
	17 Sept		Bn provide a working party of 200 daily for work on communication trenches	7.D.C.

Army Form. C. 2118

8TH BATT. (D.C.O.) MIDDX. REGT

WAR DIARY
or
INTELLIGENCE SUMMARY
(Erase heading not required.)

Place	Date	Hour	Summary of Events and Information	Remarks and references to Appendices
SAILLY-SUR-LA-LYS	24th Sept 1915	11 am	The Bn. was visited by Brig General Stephens, in fighting order - Brig.r addressed Bn. on the coming advance	
		6.15pm	The Bn. left billets and arrived at bivouac near CROIX BLANCHE at 7.45pm.	
	25th	2 am	The Bn. left their bivouac near CROIX BLANCHE and proceeded to their positions of assembly, 2 Coys in the Rue DE LAYES and 2 Coys at Battn. HQrs in the 250 yards trench from JAY POST, TIN BARN AVENUE. 4 machine guns & 25 Grenadiers under Brigade Machine Gun Officer in 250 yard trench from JAY POST - CITY ROAD. Battn was in Brigade Reserve.	
		7.10 am	Received orders to send forwards 1 machine gun and detachment to report to Headquarters Rifle Brigade in front line trench.	
		7.45 am	Received orders to send two companies to report to OC 2nd Rifle Brigade in front line trench - these two Coys were employed as carrying parties and took up bombs and trench ammunition into the captured German trench.	
		8.15am	Brought up the two companies from the River DE LAYES into the 250 yards trench.	
		10.30 am	Received orders to take up remainder of Battn and take over the front line trench from East end of WELL FARM strand line to Brigade advanced Headquarters. Several carrying parties were supplied from these two companies carrying ammunition to the Battn from captured German trench where they had been sent to assist the Rifle Brigade.	
		12 noon		
		3 pm	Two machine guns and detachments were ordered to report to OC 2nd Lincoln Regt in the BRIDOUX SALIENT.	

WAR DIARY
or
INTELLIGENCE SUMMARY.
(Erase heading not required.)

Army Form C. 2118.

Instructions regarding War Diaries and Intelligence Summaries are contained in F.S. Regs., Part II. and the Staff Manual respectively. Title pages will be prepared in manuscript.

Place	Date	Hour	Summary of Events and Information	Remarks and references to Appendices
SAILLY-SUR-LA-LYS	Sept. 1915 25th	4 p.m.	Received orders to hold the original front line trench from E. of WELL FARM SALIENT CHORD LINE to advanced Bivouac Headquarters until further orders. Rain and mud was very bad.	
		11.30 pm	Battn. relieved in trenches by the Worcesters and went into reserve at ELBOW FARM & POST.	7°C
	26"	2.30 pm	Battn. went back into reserve billets at cross roads SAILLY. Total casualties during past two days. Officers wounded Captain S. BUCKLAND, 2nd Lt. KOENIG-RYAN. Other Ranks killed 6, wounded 15", missing 23 (believed to be in hospital), hospital 5.	7°C 7°C
	27"	9.30 am	Battn. was inspected by Major General HUDSON, Cmdg. 8th Division accompanied by Brig. Gen. STEPHENS. After the inspection the G.O.C. complimented the Battalion on the manner in which they had carried out their duties during the past action.	
		12.30 pm	The 8th and Brigade became Divisional Reserve.	
	29"	10.30 pm	The Brigade was inspected by Lt. General Cmdg. III Army Corps who complimented them on their behaviour during the recent action. The parade was marred by heavy rain.	7°C 7°C 7°C

B/

B.M.C.234.

Officer Commanding,

1/8 Middx. R.

    Under orders from the 1st Army not more than 20 officers per Infantry Battalion are to go into action in the first place. The remainder are to be kept back at the transport lines, and may be taken to replace casualties.

    The Brigadier General Commanding leaves it to Commanding Officers to decide which officers are to remain behind, but where possible an officer of some experience should be included.

23rd September, 1915.

Captain,
Brigade Major,
25th Inf. Bde.

8th Hussars

23rd Oct transferred to Rda for issue to

121/729

18th Lancers.
Vol V
Oct 15

Army Form. C. 2118

WAR DIARY
or
INTELLIGENCE SUMMARY
(Erase heading not required.)

1/8TH BATT. (D.C.O.) MIDDX. REGT

Place	Date 1915	Hour	Summary of Events and Information	Remarks and references to Appendices
BAILLEUL-SUR-LA-LYS	Oct 1st	6 pm	A Regtl. Concert was held at the BAILLY EMPIRE and proved a great success.	
	2"		The Bn. took over trenches I 311 and part of N 5b from 1st Bn. SHERWOOD FORESTERS, CITY POST from 2" EAST LANCS and COMMAND POST from NORTHAMPTONSHIRE REGT. Weather was very wet and the trenches in a very muddy state. Beyond the usual sniping and shelling with field guns the enemy fired occasionally trench mortars and rifle grenades at the front trench.	
	6"		The Battalion was relieved in the trenches by 1st LONDON REGT (Roy Fusiliers) and at CITY POST. Of COMMAND post a Company was left in support to the 1st London. Three days were spent at FLEURBAIX, Leave this division. Other three days were O.R. 2 died of wounds.	
FLEURBAIX			The Battalion was billetted near FLEURBAIX.	
	9"	10 p.m	Lieut DARK went on leave.	
	10" 12" 13/14		The Bn took over trenches T 311 and part of N 5b from 1st London Regt (Roy. Fusiliers) and at City Post. At COMMAND Post a Company was left as support to the 1st line another. The enemy were quiet except on the night 13/14 when they opened rapid fire, at the same time sending our trench mortar, firing a large number of very light, one exploding also that of the enemy, the above lasted at about 10 o'clock. From 11 pm all was quiet, it is thought that the enemy had the idea that we were attacking.	
	14"		The Battn was relieved in the trenches by 1st London Regt (R.F.) and at CITY POST, at COMMAND POST a company was left as support to the 1st London. Casualties during these four days O.R. 3 wounded. The Battn were billetted near FLEURBAIX.	
	15" 16" 17"		The Battn Capt CHIPP went on leave. Lieut DARK returned from leave. 2nd LIEUT HUDSON struck off the strength of the Battalion, on transfer to ENGLAND.	

Army Form. C. 2118

WAR DIARY
or
INTELLIGENCE SUMMARY
(Erase heading not required.)

1/8th BATT. (P.O.O.) MIDDX. REGT

Place	Date	Hour	Summary of Events and Information	Remarks and references to Appendices
FLEURBAIX	Oct 16 18		The Bn took over trenches I 311 from 1st London Regt, and at CITY POST, at COMMAND POST a Company was left in support. The enemy were very quiet during the four days we occupied the trenches.	
	22nd		The Bn was relieved in the trenches by 1st London Regt and 1st Royal Irish Rifles, and at CITY POST by 1st Londons, a company was left at COMMAND POST. Casualties during these four days OR 2 killed	
	23rd		The Bn went billets near FLEURBAIX. CAPT CHIDP returned from leave. The Bn was transferred from the 25th Brigade to the 70th Brigade.	

Army Form C. 2118.

WAR DIARY
or
INTELLIGENCE SUMMARY.

1/8th BATT. (D.C.O.) MIDDX. REGT

(Erase heading not required.)

Instructions regarding War Diaries and Intelligence Summaries are contained in F.S. Regs., Part II. and the Staff Manual respectively. Title pages will be prepared in manuscript.

Place	Hour, Date, 1915	Summary of Events and Information	Remarks and references to Appendices
FLEURBAIX	23rd October 6 p.m.	Took over trenches from 1/7 Bn. D.C.O. (Middx Regt) N51, N41, Mill Road Post, Croix Blanche Post, and Croix Blanche billet. Bn. Hqrs at BASSETT HOME	7.C.
	25th Oct.	Lieut. HUGHMAN from on leave. — Raining continuously	7.C.
	27th Oct.	The following reliefs were effected between Companys. "B" Coy 155A over took N41, "D" Coy took N51 and Mill Road Post, "C" Coy CROIX BLANCHE POST "A" Coy were billeted at CROIX BLANCHE in immediate support.	7.C.
	31st Oct.	"A" Coy relieved "D", and "C" relieved "B". ordinarily for the Battalion have now been in the trenches twelve days except for the change of trenches from I 311 to N4 and N5. Casualties for the month :- (excluding sick) Other ranks 5 killed 4 wounded.	7.C.

P. L. Ingpen .... Lieut. Colonel,
Comdg. 8th "L.S." Batt. D.C.O. (Middx. Regt.) T.F.

8th, Division.

70th, Brigade.

1/8th, Middlesex.

November, 1915.

121/7636

8th Baroun

WAR DIARY
or
INTELLIGENCE SUMMARY

Army Form. C. 2118

1/8th BATT. (D.C.O.) MIDDX. REGT.

Place	Date 1915	Hour	Summary of Events and Information	Remarks and references to Appendices
FLEURBAIX	Nov 1		In the trenches N51 and N41 "A" Coy and "C" Coy "A" Coy one platoon at "MILL ROAD Post." Bn Hqrs "BASSETT HOUSE" "B" & "D" Coys in CROIX BLANCHE post and billet. It rained incessantly. There were frequent collapses of parapet and dugouts.	
	2.		Lieut. SANDERSON went on leave. Rain continued. (All the Battalion on working parties except actual guards in the trenches.)	
	3.		Lieut. HUGHMAN returned from leave. Rain continued.	
	4.		Draft of seventeen O.R. arrived. Two of them had been in France with 1/8 Bn before remainder all new men to the Battalion. Major General commanding 8th Division made a tour of the trenches. "B" & "D" Coys changed with "A" and "C".	
	5.		Stopped raining.	
	6.		A very little rain. All available men engaged on working on Avenues and breastwork.	
	7.		A fine day. Working parties continued.	
	8.		C. of E. service in the morning for the two Coys not in the trenches. Weather fine. "A" and "C" Coys relieved "B" and "D" Coys in the trenches. The latter go to CROIX BLANCHE post and billet.	
	9.		"B" and "D" supply working parties to "A" & "C" in the afternoon. Fine	
	10.		"B" & "D" working parties to "A" & "C" in the trenches. Lieut. SANDERSON returned from leave.	

Army Form. C. 2118

WAR DIARY
or
INTELLIGENCE SUMMARY

8TH BATT. (D.C.O.) MIDDX. REGT

(Erase heading not required.)

Instructions regarding War Diaries and Intelligence Summaries are contained in F. S. Regs., Part II. and the Staff Manual respectively. Title Pages will be prepared in manuscript.

1915

Place	Date	Hour	Summary of Events and Information	Remarks and references to Appendices
FLEURBAIX	Nov. 11		Trenches inspected by Major General Cuthbert. Division. Much rain again. The Battn. relieved by 1/7 Bn. Middlesex Reg and went into Divisional Reserve north of SAILLY-SUR-LA-LYS.	
			The Battalion had been in the trenches and immediate support for 40 days of the last 20 days had been spent continuously in the trenches, one half of the Battalion relieving the other half every few days. The last two weeks it rained nearly every day and night and the trenches were very wet. Despite this the health of the Battn. had been good and there were only some five cases of "trench feet." (slight)	
	12		The Battalion all batted. Rain.	
	13		Rain. Company parades inside Coy Cours. An R.E. working party of 25 was found.	From London Gazette No.534 C.S.M. SAVAGE to be Lieut. 8 Bn. Middx. Rgt. "D" SAVAGE who was serving with the Bn. was posted to B Coy.
	14		A fine day. An R.E. working party of 75 was found.	
	15		An R.E. working party of 175 was found.	
	16		3 officers & 50 O.R. attended a gas demonstration. An R.E. working party of 100 found.	
	17		Rain and hail. 2/Lt. MARTIN and REYNOLDS returned from leave. An R.E. working party of 75 found.	
	18		Working party of 85 found. The Battn. took over trenches I 311, part I 312 and CITY ROAD Post from 1/7 Bn. LONDON ROT. (Roy. Fusiliers) The following officers went on leave:— Major WOODBRIDGE, Majors LEVY, BYHAM, BAILEY, LACEY, SAVAGE. Rain and frost.	

WAR DIARY
or
INTELLIGENCE SUMMARY

1/8 Bn. Middlesex Regt.

Army Form. C. 2118

Place	Date	Hour	Summary of Events and Information	Remarks and references to Appendices
FLEURBAIX	Nov. 19		In the trenches. Cold and fine. Quiet.	
	20		Trenches. Artillery duels otherwise quiet. From London Gazette. "To be temp. Capts. Aug 2nd 1915, Lieut. C.M. HUGHMAN, Lieut A. TOMLINSON."	
	21		In the trenches. Cold and frost.	
	22		The Bn. was relieved in trenches I.311 and part I.312 by 2nd Bn. EAST LANCS. Regt. and in CITY ROAD POST by 2nd Bn. WEST YORKS REGT. Hand frost and roads very slippery. The Bn. went into billets just north of SAILLY-SUR-LA-LYS. Lieut CHALLIS went on leave.	
	23		The Division went into Corps reserve. The Bn. marched from Sailly-Sur-La-Lys to BLEU map 1/40,000 Sheet 36a. and were billeted for the night. All Regt. transport accompanied the Bn.	F. 19. B.
	24		The Bn. marched in Brigade from BLEU to camp No 4 just N.E. of STEENBECQUE, and went under canvas & huts.	C. 30. B.
	25		Settling down and building camp.	
	26		Hail and snow. A Brigade parade was ordered as the Com'd'r in Chief wished to address all ranks of the Division. Owing to the weather the parade was cancelled. The circular memo attached gives the C-in-C's remarks (under training command)	
	27	1st day	Individual and Platoon training. M.Gunners, signallers etc in special brigade and regtl classes. Football competitions. Fine. Offr. from leave... Maj WOODBRIDGE, 2/Lts MADDAMS, BYHAM, LACEY and SAVAGE.	
	28	Sunday	Cold and frosty. Voluntary Divine Service.	
	29	2nd day	Rain. Individual and Platoon training. Football competitions. Camp was visited by G.O.C. II Corps.	
	30	3rd day	Fine. Platoon training. Football. Pioneers and fatigue parties on construction of camp.	

P.L. Ingpen .... Lieut. Colonel,
Comdg. 8th "I.S." Batt. D.G.O. (Middx. Regt.) T.F.

8th DIVISION.

...SPECIAL ORDER...   26th November 1915.

To be read out on Parade to all units.

Owing to the inclemency of the weather, the Field Marshal Commanding in Chief cancelled the parades he had ordered for November 26th. When doing so, he directed me to inform all ranks of the 8th Division, how disappointed he was not to see them, as he particularly wished to speak a few words to them regarding the share taken by the Division in the fighting of the 25th September and following days. The Field Marshal expressed his complete satisfaction with the manner in which the operations had been carried out and spoke in terms of high praise of the gallantry and thoroughness with which the attack had been delivered. The results achieved precisely fulfilled his wishes and expectations, for the attack distracted the enemy's attention from the main point threatened, compelled him to withold and expend his reserves, prevented his moving his artillery, and finally, inflicted considerable loss. Such results could not have been attained had the attack not been pressed home with vigour and determination.

H. Hudson.

Major General,
Commanding 8th Division.

8th, Division.

70th, Brigade.

1/8th, Middlesex.

December, 1915.

Hári Misra Rai

Sac
vol. VII

12/
7930

Army Form. C. 2118

WAR DIARY
or
INTELLIGENCE SUMMARY
(Erase heading not required.)

1/8th BATT. (D.C.O.) MIDDX. REGT

Place	Date 1915 DEC	Hour	Summary of Events and Information	Remarks and references to Appendices
STEENBECQUE	1st		Winter training continued.	
	4th day		Platoon training. Interplatoon football. Pioneers and fatigues on construction of camp. Specialist courses – Grenadier, Machine Guns, Trench Mortar, Signalling. 2/Lt. BAILEY and CHALLIS returned from leave – Fine but turned to wet at night. 7.D.C.	
"	2" 5th day		Training as on 4th – Fine. 7.D.C.	
"	3" 6th day		Training continued. Mild & wet. 7.D.C.	
"	4" 7th day		Training, including CO's kit inspection. Showery, mild. 7.D.C.	
"	5" Sunday		Voluntary Divine Services. Fine. 2/Lt. C.V. BURDER went on leave. 7.D.C.	
"	6" 8th day		Coy training. 2 Coys close order drill. 2 Coys route march. Specialist classes. Showery.	
"	7" 9th day		Training with much wind. 7.D.C.	
"	8" 10th day		Coy training as on 6th. 2/Lt. A.S. CAREY and J. CAREY went on leave. 7.D.C.	
"	9" 11th day		Fine. Training continued. Lecture by Major HEWETT on "Aircraft Photography" attended by C.O., 2i/c, Adjt, O/C Coys. 7.D.C.	
"	10" 12th day		Wet. 2 Coys route march. 2 Coys open order drill.	
"	11 13th day		Wet. Camp waterlogged. 2 Coys route march. 2 Coys open order drill. Lecture on Gas by Capt. BUNKER R.E. to C.O.'s, 2i/c, Coy Comdrs. 2/Lt. Lieut. W.R. HOLLAND joined for duty. 7.D.C.	
"	12" Sunday		Much wind and rain. Continued with Coy training, Camp drainage. 7.D.C.	
"	13 14th day		Voluntary Divine Service. A fine morning, hail in afternoon. 7.D.C.	
			Company training continued. A fine day.	

Army Form. C. 2118

WAR DIARY
or
INTELLIGENCE SUMMARY
(Erase heading not required.)

1/8th BATT. (D.C.O.) MIDDX. REGT

Place	Date	Hour	Summary of Events and Information	Remarks and references to Appendices
STEENBECQUE	1915 Dec 14	15th day	Route training continued	
			Advanced Company Training & Protection when on the move and at rest — The assault. A fine day.	7.o.c.
	15	16th day	Lieut. BURKE returned from leave. 7.o.c.	7.o.c.
			Battalion Training commenced. Route march & advt. gards, with 1st line Transport. Weather fine and cold. 7.o.c.	
	16	17th day	Battalion Training. Two hours close order drill. Instruction in the attack of trenches represented as a flagged field. Lieut. W. TRESAWNA R.A.M.C. went on leave and was relieved by Captain MASKEW R.A.M.C. Lieut. COL and CLIFF 7.o.c.	7.o.c.
	17	18th day	Battalion Route March accompanied by 1st line transport and pack mules. Fell and wet. 7.o.c.	7.o.c.
	18	19th day	Battalion Training. Practice attack of flagged trenches. Revd KEMPSON C.F reported for duty and was attached to the BH4.	7.o.c.
	19	Sunday	A fine day. Capt. T.M. PEAKE and 2/Lt G. TREMLETT went on leave.	7.o.c.
NORRENT FONTES	20	20th day Monday	Divisional Manoeuvres. The Battalion found part of the main body in an advance on THEROUANNE. Map Sheet. At night they were billeted around map square C.21.a.2.5	Map Sheet 36 a /40,000
HAM	21	21st day	Divisional manoeuvres. The advance was continued. The Battalion again being in the main body. The Battalion paraded and marched off at 9am. They reached the village of HAM M.5.B.c at 1.30pm & went into billets. It was followed by 70th Inf Bde practice fighting a rearguard action and acting as part of a rearguard to the Division and retiring on THEROUANNE. Their original parade at 8am was postponed.	
LA PIERRE	22	22nd day	Divisional manoeuvres. The 70th Inf Bde practice fighting a rearguard action and acting as part of a rearguard to the Division and retiring on THEROUANNE. The original parade at 8am was postponed.	LA PIERRE B.9.G.
			At 9.30am at night the Battalion was billeted around LA PIERRE B.9.G.	
MEULETTE	23	23rd day	Divisional manoeuvres. The Division returned to rest camps on completion of the manoeuvres. Camp No.4 was reached at 1.30pm.	
			During the 21st and 22nd at night continued.	

WAR DIARY or INTELLIGENCE SUMMARY

Army Form. C. 2118

1/8th BATT (D.C.O.) MIDDX REGT

(Erase heading not required.)

Place	Date 1915	Hour	Summary of Events and Information	Remarks and references to Appendices
STEENBECQUE	24th	—	A rest day. A general cleaning up after the manoeuvres. 2/Lt A R WINDER joined the Battn. and reported for duty on 23rd inst. Lieut TRESAWNA R.A.M.C. returned from leave and Captn MASKEW R.A.M.C. who had been acting for him returned to the 24th Field Ambulance	7 P.C.
	25th	—	Christmas Day. Divine Service for C of E, R.C., and Nonconformists was held during the morning. The C.O. visited each Coy during the Christmas Dinner, the Officers had a dinner and supper. Coues [Carols] in the evening during which the G.O.C. and officers visited them. Cold in the morning and dull generally, mild	7 P.C.
	26th Sunday	—	At 1 pm the Bath Storm very much in STEENBECQUES square. Divine Services for C of E, R.C., and Nonconfs. The G.O.C. 70th Bde attended the Battn Coy's Service at 9.15 am. A fine morning. Mild	7 P.C.
	27th 24th day	—	Battalion Route March - Steaming with march wind Mild. Capt. T.M. PEAKE and 2/Lt G. TRENLETT returned from leave.	7 P.C.
	28th 25th day	—	Battalion training. Concentration march of Coys to a given point. At the evening a Regt Concert was held in the Boys School STEENBECQUE at which G.O.C. 70th Inf Bde was present. A programme is attached	7 P.C.
	29th 26th day	—	Battn. practised the attack on the Bols Flagged Course - Fine	7 P.C.
	30th 27th day	—	Battalion training. Concentration march of Coys. Practice of artillery formation. A fine day.	7 P.C.
	31st 28th day	—	Battalion training. Practice "putting out" expeditions on Flagged Course. Working party felling on practice tracks under R.E. - Dull	7 P.C.

P.L. Ingpen .... Lieut. Colonel,
Comdg. 8th "I.S." Batt. D.C.O. (Middx. Regt.) T.F.

Special Order of the Day.

By Field-Marshal SIR J. D. P. FRENCH, G.C.B., O.M., G.C.V.O., K.C.M.G., Commander-in-Chief, British Army in the Field.

In relinquishing the command of the British Army in France I wish to express to the officers, non-commissioned officers and men, with whom I have been so closely associated during the last sixteen months, my heartfelt sorrow in parting with them before the campaign, in which we have been so long engaged together, has been brought to a victorious conclusion.

I have however, the firmest conviction that such a glorious ending to their splendid and heroic efforts is not far distant, and I shall watch their progress towards this final goal with intense interest, but in the most confident hope.

The success so far attained has been due to the indomitable spirit, dogged tenacity which knows no defeat, and the heroic courage so abundantly displayed by the rank and file of the splendid Army which it will ever remain the pride and glory of my life to have commanded during over sixteen months of incessant fighting.

Regulars and Territorials, Old Army and New Army have ever shown these magnificent qualities in equal degree.

From my heart I thank them all.

At this sad moment of parting my heart goes out to those who have received life-long injury from wounds, and I think with sorrow of that great and glorious host of my beloved comrades who have made the greatest sacrifice of all by laying down their lives for their country.

In saying good-bye to the British Army in France I ask them once again to accept this expression of my deepest gratitude and heartfelt devotion towards them, and my earnest good wishes for the glorious future which I feel to be assured.

Field-Marshal,
Commanding-in-Chief, the British Army in France.

18th December, 1915.

1st Printing Co., R.E. G.H.Q. 1973

Christmas Message from His Majesty The King.

The following message has been received :—

"Another Christmas finds all the resources of the Empire still engaged in War, and I desire to convey on my own behalf, and on behalf of the Queen, a heartfelt Christmas greeting and our good wishes for the New Year to all who, on Sea and Land, are upholding the honour of the British name. In the officers and men of my Navy, on whom the security of the Empire depends, I repose, in common with all my subjects, a trust that is absolute. On the officers and men of my Armies, whether now in France, in the East, or in other fields, I rely with an equal faith, confident that their devotion, their valour and their self-sacrifice will, under God's guidance, lead to Victory and an honourable Peace. There are many of their comrades now, alas, in hospital and to these brave fellows, also, I desire, with the Queen, to express our deep gratitude and our earnest prayers for their recovery.

Officers and men of the Navy and Army, another year is drawing to a close, as it began, in toil, bloodshed and suffering; but, I rejoice to know that the goal to which you are striving draws nearer into sight.

MAY GOD BLESS YOU AND ALL YOUR UNDERTAKINGS."

GEORGE, R.I.

The following reply has been despatched :—

To :—HIS MAJESTY THE KING,
Buckingham Palace,
London.

The Army in France under my Command desires to be allowed to express its warmest thanks to Your Majesty and to Her Majesty the Queen for the gracious message received. On behalf of the troops I respectfully beg Your Majesties to accept the most heartfelt good wishes of all ranks for Xmas and the New Year and an expression of their firm and lasting determination to prove themselves worthy of the great trust which Your Majesty reposes in us.

From :—SIR DOUGLAS HAIG.

Christmas Day, 1915.

1st Printing Co., R.E. G.H.Q. 2000

FIRST ARMY.

SPECIAL ORDER OF THE DAY

— BY —

GENERAL SIR DOUGLAS HAIG, G.C.B., K.C.I.E., K.C.V.O., A.D.C. GEN.,

Commanding 1st Army.

HEADQUARTERS, 1st ARMY,
19th December, 1915.

On handing over command of the First Army I wish to place on record my high appreciation of the thorough discipline and fine fighting spirit which has characterized all Units in it ever since the Army was constituted a year ago.

I also wish to thank all ranks for the help and support which they have at all times rendered to me. The feeling of mutual confidence and of comradeship which exists between all arms, all services, and all ranks, is the basis of success in war and augurs well for victory.

I look forward to the future with perfect confidence.

D. HAIG, General,
Commanding First Army.

1st Army Printing Section. R.E 769

PROGRAMME
of
CONCERT
CHRISTMAS 1915

THE REST CAMP

M.I.H.

"PROGRAMME OF CONCERT:–"

PART I

1. Song — "Song Birds" — Pte. Gentleman
2. Humorous Song — "servant"
3. The Choir — "Maiden Listen"
   "Sweet + Low"
   "Little Tommy" — Cpl. Smith
4. Violin Solo — C.Q.M.S. Roberts
5. Duet — "Tenor + Baritone" — Sgt. Scott
6. Humorous Song — "The Spaniard who blighted my life" — Pte. Hiltshire
7. Conjuring — by Cpl. Lyne
   Sgt. Gill
   L. Daykin
8. Song —
9. Humorous Song — "When Shadows Gather" — Sgt. Tomlinson
10. Song — "Annie Laurie"
    "Lovely Night"
11. The Choir — "Mulligan Musketeers"

12. Pte. Kitts and a Violin

Accompanists: Lieut. H.E. Martin
Sgt. Hinstow.

PART II

by B. Coy. "Daffodils + Roses" Troupe.

1. Ensemble — "The Suwanee Ritter" — Pte. Haslip
2. Song — "The sunshine of your smile" — Lt. L.W. Emerson
3. Coon Song — "Good Night" — Lt. L.W. Emerson
4. Humorous Song — "Bert down!"
   "You're spotted" — Pte. Brand
   Sgt. Oakley
5. Song — "Sweet Blowing Bells" — The Coys
6. Ragtime Duet — "I want to be in Dixie" — The Brand
7. Humorous Song — "Forget the number" — Cpl. Bridge
   "If my true"
8. Patriotic Song — "We're all under the same flag" — Pte. Haslip
   "Sue" — Lt. L.W. Emerson
9. Coon Song — "The Shot" — Pte. Brand
10. Ragtime Duet — "The Violin" — Pte. Haslip
11. Coon Song — "De Ringtailed Coon" — Pte. Allen
12. Ragtime — "Michigan" — Pte. Bartlett
13. Coon Song — "De Old Banjo" — L. Hiltshire
14. Ensemble — "Ring down the Curtain"

— GOD SAVE THE KING —

"A" Form.
MESSAGES AND SIGNALS.
Army Form C. 2121.

Prefix SM Code /A
Office of Origin and Service Instructions
ZGZ

Words 34

Recd. at 9.15 a.m.
Date 25/12/15
From ZGZ
By Hill C.O.

TO ALL BATTALIONS

Sender's Number: BM4
Day of Month: 25TH
AAA

Christmas and new Year greetings have been received from GOC 8TH DIV 23rd DIV AND CANADIAN CORPS Replies have been sent reciprocating good wishes

From 40th BDE
Time 9 AM

From 1/4 MIDDX

Place 25 R/ Bde
Time 2.30 PM

From 11th SHERWOOD FORESTERS

"A" Form.　　　　　　　　　　　　　　　　Army Form C. 2121.
MESSAGES AND SIGNALS.　　　　No. of Message_____

Prefix SM Code 16A   m. | Words | Charge | This message is on a/c of: | Recd. at_____m.
Office of Origin and Service Instructions. | Sent | | | Date_____
MIG | At_____m. | | _____Service. | From_____
 | To_____ | | | By_____
 | By_____ | (Signature of "Franking Officer.") |

TO　　　1/8TH MIDDX

* Sender's Number | Day of Month | In reply to Number | AAA
  R | 25TH | — |

1/4TH MIDDX thanks 1/8TH MIDDX
for there kind greeting and
please wish them a MERRY
XMAS

From　　　1/4 MIDDX
Place
Time

The above may be forwarded as now corrected.　　(Z)

Censor.　Signature of Addressor or person authorised to telegraph in his name.

Place
Time　　　　　　　　　　　　　　　　　　　　　　2.30 PM

The above may be forwarded as now corrected.　(Z)

From　　　11TH SHERWOOD FORESTERS
Place
Time

The above may be forwarded as now corrected.　(Z)

"A" Form.
MESSAGES AND SIGNALS.

Army Form C. 2121.

No. of Message _____

Prefix S M Code B G F m.
Office of Origin and Service Instructions.
Z Y

Words	Charge

Sent At _____ m.
To _____
By _____

This message is on a/c of:
_____ Service.
(Signature of "Franking Officer.")

Recd. at 3·25 P m.
Date 25/12/15
From Z Y
By Hill C.a

TO 8TH MIDDX RGT

Sender's Number.	Day of Month	In reply to Number	
BM 22	25TH	—	A A A

Very many thanks for your good wishes which I heartily return

From Br General BDF STEVENS
Place 25 ?. Bde
Time 2.30 PM

The above may be forwarded as now corrected. (Z)

Censor.   Signature of Addressor or person authorised to telegraph in his name.
* This line should be erased if not required.

(T1809) Wt. 14142—641. 45000 pads. 4/15. Sir J. C. & S.

From 11TH SHERWOOD FORESTERS
Place
Time

The above may be forwarded as now corrected. (Z)

Censor.   Signature of Addressor or person authorised to telegraph in his name.
* This line should be erased if not required.

(T1809) Wt. 14142—641. 45000 pads. 4/15. Sir J. C. & S.

"A" Form.   Army Form C. 2121.
MESSAGES AND SIGNALS.
No. of Message _____

Prefix S.M. Code ___ m.	Words	Charge	This message is on a/c of:	Recd. at 10.48 a.m.
Office of Origin and Service Instructions.	26			Date 25/12/15
NDL	Sent At ___ m. To ___ By ___		17 H Service. 25/12/15 (Signature of "Franking Officer.")	From 262 By ___

TO — ALL BATTNS

Sender's Number.	Day of Month	In reply to Number	
*	25		A A A

Lt-col H.B. WATSON and all ranks 11th SF send best wishes for Christmas and new year

Reciprocated

From   11th SHERWOOD FORESTERS
Place
Time

The above may be forwarded as now corrected.   **(Z)**

Censor.   Signature of Addressee or person authorised to telegraph in his name.
* This line should be erased if not required.

"A" Form.   Army Form C. 2121.
MESSAGES AND SIGNALS.   No. of Message _____

Prefix SH Code RA m.	Words	Charge	This message is on a/c of:	Recd. at 10.15 m.
Office of Origin and Service Instructions.	29		M I H Service.	Date 27/12/15
YLR	Sent At ___ m.			From 707
	To 25-12-15		(Signature of "Franking Officer.")	By McKinnon
	By			

TO — ALL BATTALIONS

| Sender's Number. | Day of Month | In reply to Number | |
| * | 5th | | A A A |

LT-COL HORNBY and the officers and men of the 8th YORKS and LANCS send Christmas and new year greetings

From 8th YORK and LANCS
Place
Time

From 9TH Y and L
Place
Time

From SEVENTY BDE
Place
Time

"A" Form.
MESSAGES AND SIGNALS.

Army Form C. 2121.
No. of Message _____

Prefix SML Code _____ m. | Words | Charge | This message is on a/c of:
Office of Origin and Service Instructions.

YLRA

Sent At _____ m.
To
By

_____ Service.
(Signature of "Franking Officer.")

Recd. at _____ m.
Date _____
From _____
By _____

TO — 8TH MIDDX R

Sender's Number | Day of Month | In reply to Number | AAA

LT COL J ADDISSON and all ranks 9TH Y AND L regt send best wishes for Xmas and New Year

From — 9TH Y and L
Place
Time
The above may be forwarded as now corrected. (Z)

Censor. Signature of Addressor or person authorised to telegraph in his name.
* This line should be erased if not required.

From — SEVENTY BDE
Place
Time
The above may be forwarded as now corrected. (Z)

Censor. Signature of Addressor or person authorised to telegraph in his name.
* This line should be erased if not required.

Best wishes for Xmas & New Year

"A" Form.
MESSAGES AND SIGNALS.
Army Form C. 2121.

Prefix SM Code A Words 21
Office of Origin and Service Instructions: ZGZ

Recd. at 9.10 A.m.
Date 25/12/15
From ZGZ
By Hill

TO — ALL BATTALIONS

Sender's Number	Day of Month	In reply to Number	
BM3	25	—	AAA

GOC wishes all ranks a MERRY CHRISTMAS and a HAPPY NEW YEAR

Off

From: SEVENTY BDE

```
23rd Inf.Bde.         Div.Train.
25th Inf.Bde.         A.D.M.S.
70th Inf.Bde.         A.D.V.S.
Div.R.A.              Signals.
Div.R.E.              Camp Commandant.
Div.Mtd.Troops.
```

****

Christmas Greetings were sent from 8th Division to the Corps Commander and to 20th and 23rd Divisions.

Christmas Greetings have been received in reciprocation from 20th and 23rd Divisions.

8th Division.
25th Dec., 1915.

P. Neame.
Capt.
General Staff.

8th, Division.

70th, Brigade.

1/8th, Middlesex.

October, 1915.

8th, Division.

70th, Brigade.

1/8th, Middlesex.

January, 1916.

56

1/8 Middlesex Reg.

Jan
Vol VIII

5th Div
76th Bde

Transferred to 167th Bde.
56th Division 5.2.16.

WAR DIARY
or
INTELLIGENCE SUMMARY

Army Form. C. 2118

1/8th BATT. (D.C.O.) MIDDX. REGT

Place	Date	Hour	Summary of Events and Information	Remarks and references to Appendices
STEENBECQUE	1916 January			
	1 Saturday 29 day		Winter Training continued. The C.O. and selected officers and one man attended a lecture and demonstration on "Sniping" by Captain HESKETH PRITCHARD IV Corps. Coys were exercised by their Coy Cdrs. – kit inspection and internal economy. – Showery and boisterous. New Year greetings were received from G.O.C.-in-C. (attached) QMG & 4m to H.T. LOUCH returned from leave.	7.7C.
	2 Sunday 2nd day		H.E. Divine Service "C" Coy under Lieut. ¼ MARTIN went to LA MOTTE and relieved a Coy of 1/5th BLACK WATCH, under orders of C.R.E. III Corps.	7.7C.
	3 30 day		Battalion route march. G.O. & Capt. PEAKE attended a demonstration in the use of daylight free signals. In the final of the Inter-platoon Football Competition the Machine Gunners beat No 4 platoon by 6 goals to 1. – Fine, much wind.	7.7C.
	4 31st day		Attack practice – Coy schemes – in Flagged Attack Course. Bayonet fighting and close order drill. – Showery. Football in afternoon.	7.7C.
	5 32 day		Battalion route march about ten miles. – Fine.	7.7C.
	6 33 day		Flagged Attack course – Company Schemes. Miniature Range. Drill and showery.	7.7C.
	7 34 day		Companies under Coy. commanders. Miniature Range. The C.O. was taken to hospital Stormy.	7.7C.

Army Form. C. 2118

WAR DIARY
or
INTELLIGENCE SUMMARY

(Erase heading not required.)

1/8 Bn. D.C.O. Lancaster Rgt.

Instructions regarding War Diaries and Intelligence Summaries are contained in F.S. Regs., Part II. and the Staff Manual respectively. Title Pages will be prepared in manuscript.

Place	Date	Hour	Summary of Events and Information	Remarks and references to Appendices
STEEN BECQUE	1916 January 8		Winter Training. Officers attend a demonstration kitchen on the use of coloured flares. Kit inspection and preparation for move. Canadians inspect the Btn. from Grenadier School. Lt Col. INGPEN went on leave. Major A.H. WOODBRIDGE assumed command of the Btth. – Fine	7. P.C.
	9		Sunday. Divine Service. – Fine. C'ing upon the Battn.	7. P.C.
VIEUX BERQUIN	10		1st day of Divisional Return to trenches. The Bn. marched in Bde and billeted at VIEUX BERQUIN. Fine	7. P.C.
SAILLY-SUR -LA-LYS	11		The Bn. went into billets in Bde Reserve at Sheet 36. square G.36. — ROUGE DE BOUT. Fine	7. P.C.
	12		Companies Trained under Coy Cmdrs	
	13		R.E Working Parties. 3 officers 130 O.R. Training of "Observers". Miniature Range etc. – Fine	
	14		R.E. Working Parties 5 officers 183 OR Training continued. Fine. Lieut. H. BLOOD reported for duty.	7. P.C.
	15		R.E. Working Parties. 4 officers 185 OR. Fatigues. Cargo under Coy Cmdrs. Miniature Range – Dull. 2Lieut. R.W SMART appointed for duty, also 2Lieut. A.C. BATHO.	7. P.C.
	16		Sunday. R.E. Working Parties. 6 officers 183. O Ranks. Divine Service. Lieut. E.J. HORLEY reported for duty.	7. P.C.
	17		R.E. Working Parties. 8 officers 295. Other Ranks. – Fine	7. P.C.
	18		R.E. Working Parties 8 officers 400. O.Rks. Owing to many men being on leave most men had to attend both day and night working parties. Lt Col P.L. INGPEN Cmdg. returned from leave.	7. P.C.
	19		R.E. Working Parties 4 officers 200. O.Rks. – Fine. Capt. T.D WHITE. 2 offs. 50 O.Rks went into trenches to attend relief of a platoon of 8th Bn. K.O.Y.L.I withdrawn temporarily for special duty.	7. P.C.

Army Form C. 2118.

1/8" Bn. D.C.O. MIDDLESEX R.

WAR DIARY
or
INTELLIGENCE SUMMARY.
(Erase heading not required.)

Instructions regarding War Diaries and Intelligence Summaries are contained in F.S. Regs., Part II. and the Staff Manual respectively. Title pages will be prepared in manuscript.

Hour, Date, Place	Summary of Events and Information	Remarks and references to Appendices
SAILLY-SUR-LA-LYS. 1916. January		
20th	R.E. Working Parties 6 officers 195 O.Rks. — German field gun fired about 12 H.E. shells around the cross roads at Bn. Hqrs. ROUGE DE BOUT at 4.30 p.m. — Fine.	7.7C
21st	R.E. Working Parties. 5 officers. 195 O.Rks. — Bell.	7.7C
22nd	R.E. Working Parties 5 officers 200 O.Rks. In the afternoon "B" Coy billet was shelled. There being three casualties.	7.7C
23rd	R.E. Working Party. 5 ORks. — Divine Services — Fine.	
24th	R.E. Working Party 5 offs 245 O.Rks. — Fine. At midday some shells fell around Bn. Hqrs.	7.7C
25th	R.E. Working Parties 6 offs 295 O.Rks — Fine. "Lieut. R.A. WIDDUP was struck by a piece of shrapnel whilst on working party, bruised leg.	7.7C
26th	R.E. Working Parties. 1 off. 45 ORks. The Battn was relieved by 2nd Bn "TYNESIDE SCOTTISH" (NORTHUMBERLAND FUSILIERS) and went into billets in Divisional Reserve around BAC-ST-MAUR. "O" WINDER to hospital.	
BAC-ST-MAUR 27th	R.E. Working Parties 5 offs 250 O.Rks — Fine.	
28th	R.E. Working Parties 7 offs 295 O.Rks.	

Army Form. C. 2118

WAR DIARY
or
INTELLIGENCE SUMMARY

1/8th Bn. D.C.O. Middlesex Regt.

(Erase heading not required.)

Place	Date	Hour	Summary of Events and Information	Remarks and references to Appendices
BAC-ST-MAUR	1916 January 29th		No working parties were required. Fine. Officers visited various "Posts" in the area, which might have to be occupied.	
	30th		Divine Service. R.E. Working Parties 7 Officers 215 O.Rks. Officers visited Posts in the Bn. played 11th Bn. SHERWOOD FORESTERS at Football. Won 3 goals to 1. 5th Group Division of Cav. Reserve area.	
	31st		R.E. Working Parties. 5 officers 250 O.Rks. Officers visited "Posts" in the Reserve area.	

P.L. Inglis Lt. Colonel,
Commdg. 6th "I.S.B." (Middx. Regt) T.F.

| "A" Form. | Army Form C. 2121. |
| MESSAGES AND SIGNALS. | No. of Message |

| Prefix SM Code FEP m. | Words 15 | Charge | This message is on a/c of: | Recd. at 5.50 P m. |
| Office of Origin and Service Instructions. 262 | Sent At ___ m. To ___ By ___ | | Service. (Signature of "Franking Officer.") | Date 1/1/16 From 262 By Knight |

TO   8th MIDDX REGT

| Sender's Number. SC 11 | Day of Month 1st | In reply to Number | A A A |

3rd Corps wires that the following greetings have been received from Sir Henry Rawlinson AAA Begins Sir Douglas Haig wishes all Units of the (first) army every possible success and good fortune in 1916 Ends.

From
Place   SEVENTY BDE.
Time   5.15 PM

The above may be forwarded as now corrected.   (Z)

Censor. Signature of Addressor or person authorised to telegraph in his name.
* This line should be erased if not required.

(T1809) Wt. 14142—641. 45000 pads. 4/15. Sir J. C. & S.

23RD DIVISION
70TH INFY BDE

8TH BN K. O. Y. L. I.
~~AUG - OCT 1915 &~~
~~JUN 1916 - FEB 1919~~

1915 AUG - 1917 OCT

TO ITALY

70/8

Sir Bm

Noyli

June 1916

File 5

HISTORICAL SECTION
MILITARY BRANCH.

EGYPT & PALESTINE
VOL. II
Map Q.
The Defence of JERUSALEM.

Army Form C. 2118.

WAR DIARY of 2/KRRC

INTELLIGENCE SUMMARY. 26/8/15 to 8/10/15

(Erase heading not required.)

Instructions regarding War Diaries and Intelligence
Summaries are contained in F. S. Regs., Part II.
and the Staff Manual respectively. Title pages
will be prepared in manuscript.

Place	Date	Hour	Summary of Events and Information	Remarks and references to Appendices
BORDON CAMP HANTS	26/8/15		Moved by train from Bordon Camp to Southampton. AJC.	
HAVRE	27"		Arrived at above. AJC	
	28"		Moved by train from Havre to Guethegnet via Rouen. AJC	
NT BERGUE	29"		arrived Guethegnet detained at eternisig. AJC	
	30"		Battalion Training. AJC	
	31"		Battalion & Company Training. Tactical Scheme for C.O. & 2nd in C. Officers at Wagon AJC	
	1–9/15		Divisional Training at Nortegnes AJC	
	2 "		Battalion & Company training AJC	
	3 "		" " "	
	4 "		Rained all day. AJC	
	5 "		Army from Sir D. Haehad said good bye to all Ranks AJC.	
	6 "		Orders for move to Compagne. AJC	
WAGNE	6 "		Marched to Compagne, very hot day. Boor Billets. Sent Sahtr to field ambulance AJC	
WILTESTEEN	7 "		" Cultivation very hot day distance about 20 miles AJC	
	8 "		Inspection by Brigr-Gen Sir W.P.Anthony at 9.15 am AJC	
			Battalion and Company Training AJC	
	10		do do AJC	

2353 Wt. W2544/1454 700,000 5/15 D. D. & L. A.D.S.S./Forms/C. 2118.

WAR DIARY of 8th K.O.Y.L.I.

INTELLIGENCE SUMMARY

Army Form C. 2118.

Sept 1915

Place	Date	Hour	Summary of Events and Information	Remarks and references to Appendices
R. VIERSTRAAT	11 9/10		Kit Inspection in morning, no work in the afternoon. 8JC	
ARMENTIERES	12		Travelled to ERQUINGHEM-LA-LYS, C o D Cys to billets, A o B Cys to trenches.	
"	13		Pte Goodeare drowned while bathing. 8JC	
"	14		C o D Cys relieved A o B in the trenches. 8JC	
FME DE BIEZ	15		A o B & HQ moved into the trenches No 63-66 inclusive, HQ Farm de BIEZ. 8JC	
"	16		In the trenches, very bad sniping in the evening round Battn Hqrs etc. 8JC	
"	17		In the trenches, Genl Bulfin visited the trenches. Heavy bombardment by own artillery in the evening. 8JC	
9/27 2B HQ C o D Cys	18		In the trenches. First Casualty Pte Wade A Cy wounded in the chest, contained Bombardment by our artillery. 8JC	
"	19		Moved to billets in L'ARMÉE and neighbourhood. Two men in C Cy wounded. 8JC	
"	20		Rested in billets, found large working party. 8JC	
"	21		Pte Goodeare found and buried. 8JC	
"	22		Shrapnel burst at 8.10 am killed 3 and wounded 17 men of C Cy. 8JC	
FME DE BIEZ	23		Returned to the trenches. 8JC	
			Heavy bombardment by our artillery. Thunder-Storm in the evening. 8JC	

WAR DIARY of 89[C?] O.Y.L.I.
or
INTELLIGENCE SUMMARY.

Army Form C. 2118.

(Erase heading not required.)

19/5

Place	Date	Hour	Summary of Events and Information	Remarks and references to Appendices
Tr. S.W. DE 31 E 2049-15	25/9/15		We made a feint attack which caused considerable loss to the enemy (vide Intelligence Summary) H.I.W. made another feint attack under cover of smoke bombs. Very heavy artillery bombardment.	H.J.C.
	26		Very quiet day, were relieved by 9/Rsl and moved back to billets. Shrapnel burst over D. Coy's billets on men seriously injured.	H.J.C. H.J.C.
H.F. 0.6.8.	27		Very quiet day. Dug Dugouts for HQ in case of bombardment.	H.J.C.
	28		Baths for all men and drew 60 Short Rifles.	H.J.C.
	29		Return to trenches very quiet day.	H.J.C.
Tr. DE 31 E 2	30		Very quiet day to the trenches on both fronts on both fronts.	H.J.C. H.J.C.
	1 Nov			
	2			
	3		Saturday. Very quiet except for a light shell they were on both sides.	H.J.C.
	4		Very quiet during the day. Moved into the ORCHARD in the evening.	H.J.C.
Tr. N.A.20	5		Other Coy bays in the morning and a good deal of artillery activity about midday 2 Lt H.T. Cork died of wounds at 12.30 p.m. our FLBC	H.J.C.
	6		Very quiet day	H.J.C.
	7		Very quiet day. Heavy bombardment on our Right.	H.J.C.
	8		Returned to Tr. DE 31 E2 in the evening.	H.J.C.

APPENDIX "A"

DISPOSITION OF BOMBING PARTIES

Each party consists of 1 N.C.O. and 7 Men.
The following parties are detailed :-
        12 for Trench Clearing Parties.
         4 " Reserve Parties with O.C. Coys.
         1 "   " Party, Battn. H.Q.
         4 " Carrying Parties.
Total   21 Parties.

2 Parties per Coy. will go forward behind the first wave in each Coy. to clear and collect prisoners in 1st and 2nd and 3rd German lines and communication trenches.

Every part of the Battalion front up to the third German line will be cleared by the Bombing parties.

Two parties have been detailed to get in touch with the 8th Bn. York & Lancaster Regt. on our left and the 2nd Bn. Lincoln Regt on our right flank in each line occupied by the Battalion.

In each line prisoners will be placed under a guard (proportion of 1 Man to 15 Prisoners) until handed over to the 9th Bn. York & Lancaster Regt. who are the Supporting Battalion.

Parties have been told off for certain sections of fire trenches and communication trenches.

1 Bombing party per Coy. will go forward with the 2nd wave. These parties are detailed for different sections of the first objective and communication trenches.

Those parties going forward with O.C. Coys. are available for any work required - e.g. Machine Guns, Batteries, Arrowhead trenches, replacing Casualties, etc:.

The party accompanying Battalion Headquarters act as escort to the Commanding Officer.

The carrying parties will go forward with the 3rd wave of each Coy. and will probably refill the buckets of bombing parties at the first position to be consolidated.

Copy No 1.

S E C R E T.

8TH K.O.Y.L.I. OPERATION ORDER NO. 37.

GENERAL IDEA. 1. The Battalion will assault the German Trenches from a frontage of about 300 yards, from assembly places as before detailed, between LONGRIDGE STREET and SAP 2 (North of BAMBER BRIDGE STREET). The 2nd Bn. Lincoln Regt. (25th Inf. Bde.) on its right, and the 8th Bn. York & Lancaster Regt. on its left.
The assault will take place on "Z" day at Zero hour.

OBJECTIVE.
(a) **1st objective** – From X.2.b.6.2. to about X.2.b.4.5.
(b) **2nd objective** – From R.33.d.8.5. – 78 to R.33.b.6.1.
(c) **Divisional objective** – From R.34.a.9.12 – R.34.a.8.9
    to R.34.a.6.5.   6.1.2

2. **DISTRIBUTION.**
Each Company is allotted a frontage of about 80 yards and will attack on a platoon frontage in 4 waves, the order of Coys. being from the right, "A","B","C","D". Bombers, Lewis Gunners, and Signallers, are shewn in Appendices "A", "B", and "C".
The advance is covered and assisted by the 70th Bde. M.G. Coy, vide 3 (i).
4 Guns 70th Bde. L. T. Mortar Battery accompany the Battalion.

3. **GENERAL PRINCIPLES OF THE ATTACK.**

1st Objective. (a) Before the Zero hour O.C. Companies will move their two leading waves to a position about 200 yards from the German Trench, at a distance of 50 to 100 yards between the two waves. This position will be previously selected and each platoon frontage will be marked by stones, sandbags, or other means. The two rear waves of each Company will be in our own front Trench. Completion of this move to be reported to Battalion Headquarters 10 minutes before Zero hour.

O Hour. (b) At Zero hour the first two waves of each Company will advance, the third and fourth waves similarly moving out from our front line trench, at a distance of about 50 yards from one another.
The assault will be carried out over the open, the 1st and 2nd waves of each Company pushing on to the line 28 – 20 – 03 without stopping in the trench. The

0.5. 3rd and 4th waves of each Company will push on to the line 85 – 66 – 88 – 81.
It must be understood that the trenches will be cleared by Bombing and Blocking parties specially detailed, for whom separate instructions are attached.

0.30. At 0.30 (at which hour the barrage lifts from the first position to be consolidated) the two leading waves of each Coy. will push on to the line 62 – 44 to about X.2.b.4.5. The 3rd and 4th waves simultaneously advancing to the line 28 – 20 – 03.

1.

3. **GENERAL PRINCIPLE OF THE ATTACK. (Continued).**
(b) - Continued

In the advance to the first objective "A" Coy. will move on points 11 - 85 - 28 - 62 and will be responsible for keeping in touch with the 2nd Bn. Lincoln Regt. and for clearing trenches from points 62 - 90 - 40. The left of "D" Coy. will move on points 37 - 81 - 03 to about X.2.b.4.5. This Coy. will be responsible for keeping in touch with the 8th Bn. York & Lancaster Regt.

On arrival at this first position it will be necessary to clear all the first system of trenches and Bombing parties will be despatched at 0.48 to clear the network of trenches which constitute the remainder of the German 1st line system.

2nd Objective. 1.10.
(c) At 1 hour 10 minutes after Zero, Coys. will again advance in 4 waves to the second objective, the right of "A" Coy. moving on points 90 - 40 - 30 - 53 - 84 - 85, the left of "D" Coy. from 78 to 61.

In this advance leaders of waves must take every opportunity of utilising folds of ground with regard to cover from Machine Gun fire, and if necessary lie down, and push on again as early as possible. It must be realised that the 1st Bn. Royal Irish Rifles will be coming through the 2nd Bn. Lincoln Regt. on our right and that it is necessary to go forward with them as far as possible. No parties from waves are to be left behind to deal with guns encountered, the one object being to take the second line system of trenches names as rapidly as possible.

Scouts will be sent forward to determine the condition of the wire in front of this second position, and if necessary the Light Trench Mortars will be sent up to deal with it.

On arrival at the second position, the adjacent trenches will be cleared. Coys. will be reformed and preparation made for taking the 3rd position.

2.35 Divisional objective.
(d) At 2.35 the Battalion will again advance in 4 waves to the Divisional objective, the right of "A" Coy. moving on points 95 - 27 - 48 - 91 - 12, the left of "D" Coy. moving on points 13 - 34 - 65.

In this last assault waves will be reformed and O.C. Coys. will determine in what order they should proceed to attack. It is of the utmost importance that no reinforcements should be asked for which will overcrowd the trenches.

2.45
On arrival at the third position all available stores will be at once obtained for the purpose of consolidation. Wire will be placed in position from rear to front, dumps of ammunition formed, sentries posted, and the men generally warned that they may have to deal with a counter-attack very speedily.

It is on the rapidity and efficiency of this consolidation that the success of the operations may depend.

(e) Battalion Headquarters will advance according to the development of the attack, and if successful as follows :- On the report that the second and third German lines have been taken, to a point in German 2nd line trench about 67 - 77. On the first position to

3. **GENERAL PRINCIPLE OF THE ATTACK. (Continued).**

(e) - *Continued*
be consolidated being reported taken, to a point about 20 in the German third line.
O.C. Coys. and Specialists will be informed of any further advance according to the situation.
Communication of every detail of the progress of the assault to Battalion Headquarters is of great importance with regard to Artillery co-operation and the bringing up of stores and reinforcements.
The attention of all Officers is directed to G.H.Q. No. O.B. 1656, viz: pamphlet regarding Infantry and Aircraft liaison.
As each trench is captured flares will be lit and the red and green flags carried by waves will be hoisted.
Two riflemen orderlies to be told off to each Wave Commander.
Four riflemen Orderlies to be told off to the Company Commander.
Appendix "C" deals with action of Battalion Signalling Section.

(f) <u>Supports.</u>
The Battalion will be supported by the 9th Bn. York & Lancaster Regt., which moves into our front line as the Battalion moves out.
The 11th Bn. Sherwood Foresters is in Divisional Reserve and occupies our first line trenches as soon as the 9th Bn. York & Lancaster Regt. advances.
The 9th Bn. York & Lancaster Regt. and 11th Bn. Sherwood Foresters both advance in 2 waves. The first wave of the 9th Bn. York & Lancaster Regt. moves into German first line trench as the Battalion advances to the capture of the 1st objective.

(g) <u>Artillery.</u>
Maps and diagrams showing Artillery barrages and lifts as far as the Battalion is concerned have been issued to O.C. Companies and Specialists, who will instruct all ranks under them in this subject.

R.E. (h) Immediately the first objective is captured parties of 2nd Field Coy. R.E. will be sent on to consolidate some of the following points X.2.b.6.2., X.2.a.8.1., X.2.b.2.0., X.2.c.2.4.
What points are to be consolidated will depend on the tactical situation, ground, etc:.
One section of pioneers will be accommodated in STANLEY STREET and will open up a communication trench from STANLEY STREET to point X.2.c.3.9. immediately the hostile front line trench is captured.

BRIGADE MACHINE GUN COMPANY (i) No. 3 Section (4 guns) will be in position in ROCK STREET about X.1.a.2.3. They will be on higher ground than our Troops and will fire direct on enemy's second line from Zero to 0.1 min., then on 3rd line until 0.2., they will then sweep the crest of the ridge until 0.6 mins. This section will then proceed to Point 20 and will push on to Point 62 and consolidate with the R.E.
At 0.45 two guns will be sent to Point 94 to assist the advance.
No. 4 Section (4 guns) 2 guns in CONISTON STREET and 2 in BAMBER BRIDGE STREET. These guns will fire direct on enemy third line from Zero for 2 minutes.

3. **GENERAL PRINCIPLE OF THE ATTACK. (Continued).**
(i) - Continued.
They will then lift and sweep the crest of the ridge until 0.30 mins. when they will cease firing.
When the second position to be consolidated has been captured No. 3 Section will move forward to consolidate Points 85 - 78 - 87.
(j)

L.T.M. BATTERIES.
(I) Immediately prior to the assault there will be
    4 Guns at CROSS ROADS, X.1.d.0.8.
    2 " at Sap 3.
    2 " at Sap 2.
At three minutes before Zero these guns will open a hurricane bombardment on German front line trench. This will cease as soon as our Troops are within 100 yards of the German front Trench.
(II) After the assault has begun 4 guns will go forward with the Battalion to the 3rd German Trench, and until 0.30 will bombard the first objective.
(III) When the Battalion is halted in the first objective 4 guns will be with it and will assist in clearing the maze of trenches to the front.
(IV) The employment of these 4 Light Trench Mortars in the advance to second and Divisional objective will depend on development of attack.

DRESS.
4. Haversack on back (to contain iron ration and unconsumed portion of days ration), waterproof sheet, 2 smoke helmets and Lachrymatory goggles, two bandoliers of S.A.A. in addition to equipment ammunition, two Mills bombs, one in each Tunic side pocket, Waterbottle (full), Two sandbags per man. Bombers and Lewis Gunners carry one bandolier S.A.A. The following will be carried by selected men :-
    16 Billhooks per Company.
    25 Hedging Gloves.
    100 Flares.
    12 Bridges.
    Wire-cutters.
    S.A. Wire-breakers.
    Every 3rd or 4th man a pick or shovel, 1 pick to every 4 shovels.
    Traversor Mats.

MEDICAL.
5. Advanced Dressing Station - LOWER HORWICH STREET, X.7.a.4.9.
First Aid Post at X.7.b.1.9. (between LONGRIDGE STREET - QUARRY BRAE STREET).
It cannot be too strongly impressed upon all ranks that no man is to remain behind to attend to casualties. This is the duty of the Stretcher Bearers.

ADMINISTRATIVE
6. The following dumps have been formed :-
(A) FOOD.
    Rations - QUARRY POST Cookhouse,   8,000.
            Tram Base, W.22.c.5.1.   24,000
            W.22.d.8.1.   12,000.

ADMINISTRATIVE 6. (Continued).
  (B) WATER

QUARRY POST	200 Gallons.
Cookhouse GLASGOW ROAD	1,500 "
In Petrol Tins " "	1,680 "
Battn. H.Q.	100 "
Bde. H.Q.	100 "
CONISTON POST,	100 "
First Aid Post,	50 "
Dressing Station,	100 "

These Ration and Water dumps will not be used prior to the assault except by O.C. Battalion's order.

(C) BOMBS AND S.A.A.

Advanced Battalion Stores.
  I. Junction LONGRIDGE STREET and front line.
  II. Half-way between LONGRIDGE STREET and QUARRY BRAE.
  III. Trench end of QUARRY BRAE STREET.

These Stores will each contain :-
  600 Mills Grenades.
  100 Rifle Grenades.
  50 Boxes, S.A.A.
  300 T. M. Bombs.

The extra ammunition and the bombs required for the assault are not to be taken from these Advanced Stores.

TRANSPORT 7. Is divided into two Echelons, viz:
1st Line.
ECHELON "A". - under the Quartermaster.
  8 Pack Mules for S.A.A.
  2 Water Carts.
  Medical Cart.
  2 Tool Wagons.
  2 Lewis Gun Limbers.
  4 Field Kitchens.
  Officers' Mess Cart,
will be parked in the LONG VALLEY.
ECHELON "B".
Remaining Transport at HENENCOURT WOOD under the Transport Officer.
Detailed instructions as regards men employed with these 2 Echelons have been issued.

MISCELLANEOUS 8.

Orders & Papers carried

Water

Bearings

Distances

APPENDIX "B"

DISPOSITION OF LEWIS GUNS.

No. 1 Team with 2nd Wave "D" Coy.

No. 2   "   "   3rd   "   "D" Coy.

No. 4   "   "   2nd   "   "C" Coy.

No. 5   "   "   2nd   "   "B" Coy.

No. 6;   "   "   2nd   "   "A" Coy.

No. 8   "   "   3rd   "   "A" Coy.

Nos. 3 and 7 Teams in reserve with 4th wave of "B" Coy. and "C" Coy. in Battalion Reserve.
Nos. 1 and 6 Teams will move on the flanks of "D" and "A" Coys.' first waves when they go to their positions of assembly in "NO MAN'S LAND" prior to assault.
These guns are NOT to fire except for covering purposes.
Nos. 1 and 2 men of each Team will NOT carry a rifle.

SECRET.

O.C. Companies,
  8th Bn. K. O. Y. L. I.

1. If the wind is favourable Rogers will probably be liberated this evening at a time denoted by Zero.

2. The Rifle Brigade on our right will carry out a raid afterwards as follows on German Trenches X.7.b.9.6. to X.7.b.9.9.

0.	Rogers.
h. m.	
1. 20	Last cylinder.
1. 55	R.B. assemble outside German wire.
2.	Artillery bombard.
2. 16	Crawl forward.
2. 20	IN.
2. 45	HOME.

3. The R.B. will cut their own wire prior to Rogers. All ranks in "C" & "D" and hald "B" Coys. (front 2 platoons) will wear gas helmets rolled on their heads from O hour.

4. The raid will start from junction of our right and R.B. left (LONGRIDGE STREET).

5. On returning to our Trenches should any of the R.B. come home in our lines they will give the password "ORANGES". No rifle is to fire from 2.20 to 2.55 and every assistance is to be given to men of the R.B. returning from their raid.

6. During the discharge of Rogers rapid rifle and M.G. fire will be continued for 2 mins: before and 1 min: after O hour from our front line.

7. The 2 left Lewis guns in front line will fire occasional rapid bursts of fire on enemy front line trenches in a N.E. direction from our line during the time of the raid but no rifle or L.G. fire will take place for 40 mins after Zero & 1 min:.

   H.R.Trevor
   Lt. Colonel,
   Commanding 8th Bn. K. O. Y. L. I.

   Issued to :-   O.C. Coys.   L.G. Officer.
                  Bombg: Officer.   Officer i/c Sigs:
                  Hd.Qrs. 70th Inf. Bde.)
                  O.C. 2nd Rifle Brigade.) For information.

   NOTE - Should this raid take place no patrols or wiring parties will go out between 11.30 P.M. and 1.30 A.M., and rations will arrive at a time to be stated later. The warning for the raid to O.C. Coys. will be Time of Zero followed by word "LEMONS".

APPENDIX "C"

COMMUNICATION

(A) <u>Distribution.</u>
The Signal Section is composed of 1 Officer and 33 Other Ranks.
<u>Stations.</u>
1. Headquarters.
   - 1 Officer.
   - 1 Sergeant in charge of Station.
   - 2 Operators - carry D3 ~~Mark III~~ Telephone.
   - 3 Men - carry and work with Shutter Disc.
   - 2 Men - carry ground sheet and shutter for communication with Aircraft.
   - 4 Linesmen - carry 1 reel D cable each.
   - 1 Man remains at Battalion Headquarters in charge of lamps and wire.
   - <u>14</u>

2. All Companies.
   - 1 N.C.O. - carries shutter or disc.
   - 1 Operator - carries D3 ~~Mark III~~ Telephone.
   - 2 Linesmen.
   - <u>1 Signaller to remain with Coy. Commander.</u>
   - <u>5</u>

(B) <u>Communication between Coys. and Battn. H.Q.</u>
During attack, communication will be maintained between Coys. and Battn. H.Q. by :-
   1. Telephone.
   2. Visual methods.
   3. Orderlies.

<u>1. Telephone.</u>
With each successive advance as far as the first line to be consolidated, a fresh system of telephone wires will be laid.
Each Coy. Station will advance with the 4th wave in the Company, and will fix its station in the trench occupied by this wave after each advance. As they advance they will reel out the lines, and when they halt the Stations will be connected up by a lateral line. In addition H.Q. linesmen will lay cables in advance between one Battn. H.Q. and the next. Thus, after the first advance, Coy. Sigs. Stations will be in the trench 85 - 66 - 81 connected to Battn. H.Q. by 5 distinct lines. Similarly after the second advance, Coy. Stations will be along the line 28 - 20 - 03. One man per Coy. Station is told off to convey messages from the Coy. Commander to the Coy. Signal Station.
In the advance from the 1st to the 2nd lines to be consolidated, telephone wires will be laid from Point 20 (Battn. H.Q.) and will follow the line Points 62 - 90 - 26 - 78 keeping up as close as possible with the advancing Companies.

1.

APPENDIX "C" - COMMUNICATION. (Continued).

(B) Communication between Coys. and Battn. H.Q. (Continued).
2. Visual.
Shutter discs and flags will also be used according to circumstances to communicate with Battn. H.Q. and with Bde. O.P's in BURY AVENUE and CONISTON AVENUE. In the advance from 1st to 2nd lines to be consolidated Points 40 and 09 will be occupied as Visual Stations. By night these Stations will attempt to communicate with the Divl. O.P. in LAVIEVILLE.
3. Orderlies.
In the event of communication, telephonic and visual, breaking down, Signallers will act as Orderlies between Coys. and Battn. H.Q.s.

(C) Communication with aircraft will be maintained :-
(a) By means of flares which will be lit in every German line as soon as it is captured. 415 flares will be carried for this purpose.
(b) By means of the semi-circular ground sheet representing Battn. H.Q.
(c) By means of the ground shutter, which can transmit short and urgent messages from Battn. H.Q. to the Aeroplane.
2 Men are detailed for this duty.

(D) Communication with H.Q. 70th Inf. Bde.
Direct telephonis communication will be maintained from Battn. H.Q. to H.Q. 70th Inf. Bde. by the 70th Bde. Signal Section.
Communication with the Battalions on the right and left, other than by Orderly can only be obtained through the Brigade.

(E) Communication with Artillery will be maintained through the liaison Artillery Officer, who will be in telephonis communication with Batteries in Support.

(F) Carrier Pigeons.
2 Carrier Pigeons will be with Battn. H.Q.s under an expert. These will only be used to convey the most urgent information. The pigeons fly to WARLOY, and from there the information will be telephoned to its destination.

Confidential

WAR DIARY or **INTELLIGENCE SUMMARY**

Army Form C. 2118.

8th Bn. K.O.Y.L.I. Vol VIII

Instructions regarding War Diaries and Intelligence Summaries are contained in F.S. Regs., Part II. and the Staff Manual respectively. Title pages will be prepared in manuscript.

(Erase heading not required.)

Place	Date	Hour	Summary of Events and Information	Remarks and references to Appendices
ALBERT	1/6/16	—	Billets in Bde Reserve.	J.V.I.
	2/6/16	—	Billets in Bde Reserve.	q.v.i.
	3/6/16	—	Billets in Bde Reserve.	q.v.i.
HENENCOURT WOOD	4/6/16	—	1 a.m. Enemy Lachrymatory shell fell in ALBERT. 2 inches S.E. of ALBERT. Relieved by 2nd Middlesex Regt. To No 3 Camp HENENCOURT WOOD & took over from 2nd Berks Regt Relief complete 12.7am	q.v.i.
	5/6/16	—	Cleaning up at No 3 Camp. B&D Companies to Baths HENENCOURT.	q.v.i.
	6/6/16	—	ROUTE MARCH - HENENCOURT - AMIENS - CRESSY ROAD - C.H.Q. & G - CONTAY - WARLOY - CAMP.	q.v.i.
	7/6/16	—	2 Officers joined for duty. Training.	q.v.i.
	8/6/16	—	Brigade Training at TREVILLERS. Bde attack on fixed cover &	q.v.i.
	9/6/16	—	do - do - do	q.v.i.
	10/6/16	—	Weather made outdoor training impracticable. Lectures on Infantry as applied to this front.	q.v.i.
	11/6/16	—	do - do - do - do. Lectures on "Role of Bnduon and Supply of bombs in the attack".	q.v.i.
	12/6/16	—	Demonstration of Stokes Mortars.	q.v.i.
	13/6/16	—	Bugade training at TREVILLERS. Evening: Relieved by 2nd Middlesex R. and took over No 5 Camp from 15th R.R.	q.v.i.
	14/6/16	—	No 5 Camp. Interior Economy.	q.v.i.
	15/6/16	—	do. Heavy working parties.	q.v.i.

Army Form C. 2118.

WAR DIARY
or
INTELLIGENCE SUMMARY.
(Erase heading not required.)

Instructions regarding War Diaries and Intelligence Summaries are contained in F. S. Regs., Part II. and the Staff Manual respectively. Title pages will be prepared in manuscript.

Place	Date	Hour	Summary of Events and Information	Remarks and references to Appendices
HENENCOURT WOOD	15/6/16	—	Weather clearing. Working parties. qv.	
LONG VALLEY	16/6/16	—	Bttn into Bivouac in Long Valley M.24.a9. Battn HQ MILLENCOURT. qv.	Rf 57 D.S.E
	17/6/16	—	Bivouac. Heavy working parties. qv.	
	18/6/16	9 a.m.	6 German Aeroplanes flew over from East. Engaged by our machines without result. To No 5 Camp HENENCOURT WOOD qv.	
	19/6/16	—	6 officers joined for duty. No 5 Camp. qv.	
"HENEN (continued)				
	20/6/16	—	No 5 Camp. 1 officer joined for duty. qv.	
	21/6/16	—	No 5 Camp. Working parties. General preparations. qv.	
	22/6/16	—	The Bttn paraded at 4.30 p.m. to witness the decoration of No 13680 Sergt. J.T. WALDRON 2nd KOYLI with the Distinguished Conduct Medal. Major General H HUDSON CB CIE Cmdg the 8th Divn performed the ceremony, assisted by Brigadier General H. GORDON D.S.O. Cmdg 70th Inf Bde. Major General Hudson addressed the following short Speech to the Battalion:— "Colonel TREVOR, Officers NCOs and Soldiers of the Yorkshire Light Infantry, "I have asked you to come here this afternoon on the occasion of my presenting to Sgt T.T. WALDRON the ribbon of the Distinguished Conduct Medal which he has earned and which I hope he will shortly receive at the hands of his King. I should like to say how satisfied I am, as also are his Corps Commander and your own Brigadier, with the way the Bttn	

Army Form C. 2118.

WAR DIARY
or
INTELLIGENCE SUMMARY.
(Erase heading not required.)

Place	Date	Hour	Summary of Events and Information	Remarks and references to Appendices
HENENCOURT WOOD	27/6/16		has looked sick the day it joined this Division. You have always volunteered and shewn the fullest keenness and efficiency in patrol work, and sedentary labour you have done well and cheerfully. The fruits of this labour we shall see in a few days. I know what a fine spirit animates all ranks of this Battalion and I have the utmost confidence in you because I know that every man will go straight to his front. Don't forget that the weapon of the infantry soldier — and you in infantry soldiers are the crème of all soldiers — don't forget that your weapon is the rifle and bayonet. You may carry bombs, but bombs are troubles, your weapon is the bayonet. Remember that the Russians are doing splendidly & shewing what Russian soldiers can do, and what the French have done at Verdun. What Russian & French soldiers have done, British soldiers can — and will do. You have a fine example in Sgt Walden and, if you follow his lead, you cannot but do well. W.	

Army Form C. 2118.

WAR DIARY 5th Bn. K.O.Y.L.I.
or
INTELLIGENCE SUMMARY.

(Erase heading not required.)

Instructions regarding War Diaries and Intelligence Summaries are contained in F. S. Regs., Part II. and the Staff Manual respectively. Title pages will be prepared in manuscript.

Place	Date	Hour	Summary of Events and Information	Remarks and references to Appendices
TYLERSREDOUBT	23/6		Battalion moves into trenches in front of Authuille Wood	q.v.
AUTHUILLE WOOD	24/6		Our heavy Bombardment	q.v.
	25/6		do - do - do -	q.v.
BOUZINCOURT DEFENCES	26/6		Battalion moves into Bouzincourt trenches	q.v.
	27/6		do - do - do -	q.v.
	28/6		do - do - do -	q.v.
AUTHUILLE WOOD	29/6		do - do - do -	q.v.
	30/6		Battalion moves into trenches in front of Authuille Wood	q.v.
	1/7			q.v.

Casualties during June 1916. Officers wounded 1.
Other ranks -do - 13
Total 14   q.v.

3rd July 1916.

2333 Wt. W2544/1454 700,000 5/15 D, D.& L. A.D.S.S./Forms/C. 2118.

SECRET —   Q/5

H.Q.
    70th Inf Bde
    ―――――――

Herewith a draft copy of Bn
Operation orders for the Assault.

Spaces are left blank under
Miscellaneous and amounts of material
carried by men. — These will be
filled in later.

It is thought that perhaps the C.O.C. W.
care to look through these orders before
the Bde conference this afternoon.

                        H E Trevor Lt Col.
22/6/16   Comdg 8th Bn K.O.Y.L.I.

70th Inf.Bde.
23rd Div.

Battn. with Bde.
rejoined from
8th Div. 17.7.16.

8th BATTN. THE KING'S OWN (YORKSHIRE LIGHT INFANTRY).

J U L Y

1 9 1 6

Army Form C. 2118.

WAR DIARY
or
INTELLIGENCE SUMMARY.
(Erase heading not required.)

Place	Date	Hour	Summary of Events and Information	Remarks and references to Appendices
TRENCHES NEAR OVILLERS	1/7/16		The battalion attacked at 7.30 am, being on the left 8th Yorks middle right and Lincolns in support to our battalion were the 11th S.F's. Below is set forth copy of statement made consequently on reporting action to 70th Brigade "During the preliminary bombardment our losses from shell fire were considerable. Probable strength when ad 10% of the whole strength the first wave moved leaving our trenches just before 7.30 am, reached the German lines with only slight loss. The second wave lost heavily on no mans and from M.G. fire from LAM flanks, I understand that also before they reached the German front line at least ½ of the casualties occurred from our own artillery, the German were silent no doubt. Our men were semi-missed up with both 8th Yorks the 8th Yorks, 9th Yorks, 11th S.F. & sent snipers skilled fighting took place for the next German lines, which second line was moved thanks several of our own hundreds along line the 11th 8rd line. On the second return line no were held up by machine guns. The enemy also stopped entirely on trench lines & bombs & rifle & bayonets. At about 8.30 am the 11th M.F. were forced round possibly evacuating from the enemy & were seventy opened on them by officer I told himself at am N.7.c.6.8 considering by every returned by the attack time 9 Yrs sent back fighting for the second British lines. The last company which tried were but had to lose the German trenches to off at about 6 pm, when though they were	

WAR DIARY
or
INTELLIGENCE SUMMARY.

(Erase heading not required.)

Army Form C. 2118.

Instructions regarding War Diaries and Intelligence Summaries are contained in F.S. Regs., Part II. and the Staff Manual respectively. Title pages will be prepared in manuscript.

Place	Date	Hour	Summary of Events and Information	Remarks and references to Appendices
			(cont)	
LONG VALLEY	3/7/16		Some of our men swamp them in the German second line. Very few of our officers reached the German trenches. The Germans gave many times stronger enemy. Standing out remained. Our Battalion went into action with 25 officers & 659 other ranks. Of these the K.O.Y.L.I. Bn casualties are reported to be the Battalion. The whole strength of the Bn but together from various bases their N.C.O. return only 150 officers & 10 men of the Battalion left. Capt. J.L. Ryan, Captain (unreadable) & 2nd Lt K.O.Y.L.I. During the night the Battalion was withdrawn to LONG VALLEY. qv.	
	4/7/16		(unreadable) In Bivouac. Col 10.15 p.m. marched to DERNANCOURT STATION. By Col H.C. troops in front qv.	
	5/7/16		Entrained at 5.30 a.m. Arrived AILLY-LE-SOMME 6 a.m. marched to ARGOEUVES qv	
6/7/16			At ARGOEUVES. At 10 L.t Carver left to command 103rd Inf. Brigade. qv	
7/7/16			Marched to SAISSEVAL & billeted there. Training	
8/7/16			(unreadable) At 3 p.m. Brigadier-General H. Gordon assumed the situation. He spoke to the Battalion. That also spoke hastily on the recent operations congratulating that it had held trenches won for several months. Held up the 4th Divisions of the Regiment	

WAR DIARY
or
INTELLIGENCE SUMMARY.

(Erase heading not required.)

Army Form C. 2118.

5th K.O.R.L

Place	Date	Hour	Summary of Events and Information	Remarks and references to Appendices
	6/7/16		it is always known that these trenches had been safe up to tupping, but the information had been more than received in the estimate amount by Apl Lisle the lieutenants regret with Coys forming reporters. Bonhomme Confirmed had all done well and the deaths	
	7/7/16		Piecers but that this daily goods they had lost many comrades and all the officers were extremely proud of. In addition the Banshing counter-attack think the Africans it could not keep the normys comrades it had just. they had also they had paid the way	
	8/7/16		covered each man this dusk was being guard	
			Entrained at SALEUX and ee-entrained at BRIAS. Marched to BRUAY to billet.	
	9/7/16		Billeted at BRUAY. Training.	
			Billets at BRUAY.	
	10/7/16		Billets BRUAY. Training.	
			Congratulations BRUAY. Brigade G.H.M., Gen.Lnt. Trey DSO 1st Bnt Chemodie K.A. Hort	
			the command of Battalion - Major N - Genel H Wilson, G.O.C. 8th Division approved	
			the Battalion & congratulated it on the manner in which it had done its duty. He thanked	
			all ranks for the gallant & skilful way in which they had supported him.	
	11/7/16		Billets BRUAY. Training.	

WAR DIARY or INTELLIGENCE SUMMARY

Army Form C. 2118.

(Erase heading not required.)

Place	Date	Hour	Summary of Events and Information	Remarks and references to Appendices
Bellers BRUAY	2/7/16		Training.	
Billets BRUAY	3/7/16		Training.	
Billets BRUAY	14/7/16		Training.	
Billets BRUAY	15/7/16		Training.	
Entrained HOUDAIN. Detrained LONGEAU (near AMIENS). Marched to POULAINVILLE & billets.	16/7/16			
Moved to MIRVAUX to Billets. Capt. Armitage joined.	17/7/16			
Billets MIRVAUX	18/7/16		Training.	
Billets MIRVAUX	19/7/16		Training. Lieut Hornby & 2/Lt Westmate joined.	
Billets MIRVAUX	20/7/16		Training.	
Marched to BAZIEUX WOOD & bivouached.	21/7/16			
Bivouacs BAZIEUX WOOD	29/7/16		Training. A party of Officers reconnoitred ground recently attacked in vicinity of CONTALMAISON	
Bivouacs BAZIEUX WOOD	30/7/16		Training.	

"In obedience to command the 103rd Infantry Brigade I wish to place on record some of the 8th Bn K.O.Y.L.I. on their recent advance against the enemy 6 guns the [?] of company of the battalion one of the heaviest [?] on my [?]. Very many [illegible] to men I am associated with in Fine of Battalion which has always maintained the best...

WAR DIARY or INTELLIGENCE SUMMARY

Place	Date	Hour	Summary of Events and Information	Remarks and references to Appendices
(K.O.Y.L.I.)	24/7/16		Speaking of the Regt. a feature it will continue to keep up throughout was of battle to day.	
	25/7/16		Though you all lost about ½ the best of luck. A witness said I caught sun them afront. K.O.Y. Knox, Bgd. Genl. Comp. issued Bgde. order. In the field 14/7/16. Capt. O.C. Goldman, K.O.Y.L.I., Lieut. Q. to 8 Black Royl. 9/S/6, 2nd Lieut. G.B. Shearman, M. Gilbert 2/Z.L. Pigeon F.S.L. bylo Herron, to 2 Lieut. at D.C.L.I. 9/9/6 Service Battn. q.v.? Transport. Buried BAZENTIN WOOD	
	26/7/16		Marched to trenches immediately left of BAZENTIN-LE-PETIT WOOD. Becoming support Battalion to Brigade. Relieved 2nd Black Watch q.v. In trenches. Capt. Q.F. Simmons Q.S.I. August 4/L.A.Ll. A.H. Derwood, c/o 9A.A. Shaw, all K.O.Y.L.I. Joined q.v.	
	27/7/16		In trenches q.v.	
	28/7/16		In trenches q.v.	
	29/7/16		In trenches q.v.	
	30/7/16		In trenches q.v.	
	31/7/16		Marched to shelter trenches immediately on rear of Brigade H.Q. (Aberdeen Wood). Becoming Reserve Battalion to Brigade. Were relieved by 11th N.F.S. q.v.	

Army Form C.2118.

WAR DIARY
of
INTELLIGENCE SUMMARY.
(Erase heading not required.)

4th KOJRI

Place	Date	Hour	Summary of Events and Information	Remarks and references to Appendices

Casualties during the month of July 1916.

Officers:-
- Wounded, Shell Killed — 11
- Died of wounds — 1
- Wounded — 3
- Missing assumed — 10 Off. 1
- Wounded —

Other Ranks:-
- Killed (this above reported) — 13
- Died of wounds — 15
- Accidentally killed — 1
- Wounded — 356
- Missing — 314   O.R. 1

23rd Division
70th Brigade

1/8th BATTALION

KING'S OWN YORKSHIRE LIGHT INFANTRY

AUGUST 1 9 1 6

WAR DIARY
or
INTELLIGENCE SUMMARY.

Army Form C. 2118.

1915 Aug-Dec
8. KOYLI

Vol 12

Place	Date	Hour	Summary of Events and Information	Remarks and references to Appendices
SOMME SECTOR	1/8/16		Battalion moved from Buffed Trenches near Bazentin wood to reserve lines behind Shelter Wood.	
	2/8/16		In reserve lines behind Shelter Wood. Working parties to Bazentin Dumps. Specialists Training.	
	3/8/16		Ditto	
	4/8/16		Working parties to Bazentin trenches. Specialists training.	
	5/8/16		Ditto	
			Cleaning up. Lieut H.A. Dingdale with 50 O.R. (other ranks) + Lieut Hirst O.A. in conjunction with 9th South Staffs Regt dug a trench to connect our first line at Bazentin Wood with the German front line. Bivouacked L.I. Bty ready to support if required by the supports on right.	
			The Bomb and L.G. Coy (Lewis Gun) were sent to N.E. corner of Bazentin Wood to await such orders.	
			Remainder of Bn sent to shelter trenches near Shelter Wood. Without further specialist training	
	6/8/16		Ditto	
	7/8/16		Marched to billets in Franvillers.	
FRANVILLERS	8/8/16		Billets. H.Q.R. passed from S.O. Y1-4. Training	
	9/8/16		Billets. Bn passed from 9th Y14. Training	
	10/8/16		Billets. Training	
	11/8/16		Marched to Taffencourt & entrained there. Detrained Longpré & marched to billets in Francières	
	12/8/16		Moved to Pont Rémy & entrained there.	

Army Form C. 2118.

WAR DIARY
or
INTELLIGENCE SUMMARY.
(Erase heading not required.)

Instructions regarding War Diaries and Intelligence Summaries are contained in F. S. Regs., Part II. and the Staff Manual respectively. Title pages will be prepared in manuscript.

Place	Date	Hour	Summary of Events and Information	Remarks and references to Appendices
	1/8/16		Entrained BAILLEUL & marched to billets near MORRIS qℓs	
	10/8/16		Marched to billets near STEENWERCK. Maj. Gen¹ (Acting Surgeon) J. T. Johnson (N° 16000) & Private C. Jackson (N° 7907) awarded the MILITARY MEDAL. New O.C's commanders qℓs	
	13/8/16		Marched to trenches in RUE DE SAC. Cap¹ A. E. R. Mortromes & 2nd Lieut P. M. Powell admitted to hospital, sick.	
RUE DE SAC	16/8/16		C.O. visits trenches ST YVES trenches qℓs. Billets. Training Company Signals near ST YVES trenches. Cadet C. Lucas (acting Adjutant) and 2nd Lieut J.B.? Marshall admitted to hospital, sick. Lieut R.C.T. Kenn takes over duties of Adjutant.	
	17/8/16		Private G.L. Angle (N°. 1595) & A. Howard (N°. 1529) awarded the MILITARY MEDAL by Lieut Commander 4th Division (N°. 1476 & 1277). B in support, relieving 26th Royal Fusiliers. 2nd Lieut T. Wright & 2nd Lieut Cotchie joined for duty qℓs	
ST YVES T.R.	18/8/16		On line Lieut C.W. Baskot to duty at Brigade Office qℓs	
"	19/8/16		Lieut Shord took on duty gong dish. Conscript Paul Aug. of Conscripts to H.Q. Division qℓs	

Army Form C. 2118.

WAR DIARY
or
INTELLIGENCE SUMMARY.
(Erase heading not required.)

Instructions regarding War Diaries and Intelligence Summaries are contained in F.S. Regs., Part II. and the Staff Manual respectively. Title pages will be prepared in manuscript.

Place	Date	Hour	Summary of Events and Information	Remarks and references to Appendices
			Following awards by Commander-in-chief notified.	
			Lieut. J.E.J Greenlay - MILITARY CROSS	
			Capt. B.A. Newby - MILITARY CROSS	
			N° 12489 Sec Cpl G Mugford - D.C.M.	
			N° 16764 Sgt S. Priestley - D.C.M.	
			N° 14534 Sec Cpl A. Moir - D.C.M. Q.M.	
ST YVES. 7a.	24/5/16		In line. Special work on new front trench.	
			Coys. H. 5. OC. Q.A.	
			Front line H.Q. dismantle & sec O.A. crossed R.E. (10 past 1st) tapes laying ready for further new trenches.	
	25/5/16		In line. Special work on new front trench.	
			Front line H.Q. dismantle & Breastwork O.A. exceed the work of 350 yards then taking left or new	
			trench & sent to 9th North Staffs Regt to arrange same. Q.M.	
	26/5/16		In line. Special work on new trenches. New trench reg. 4/8/16. Led by Lieutenant J. C. & D. Coys. Q.M.	
			In line. Ditto. Capt. W.C.B. Bull assumed O.C.M. command of A. Coy. Q.M.	
	27/5/16		In line. Ditto. Battalion extended H.Q. frontage to the right, taking over O.A. 123 a	
			Head Qtrs. 122, behind B Coy. occupied, Bn. H.Q. taking over our support trenches. Q.M.	

WAR DIARY
or
INTELLIGENCE SUMMARY.

(Erase heading not required.)

Army Form C. 2118.

Place	Date	Hour	Summary of Events and Information	Remarks and references to Appendices
HAZEBROUCK	25/8/16		Relieved by 9th Black Watch Regt. and marched to billets in HAZEBROUCK. qv. Billets. Training.	
"	26/8/16		Co. Sgt. (Act. aft. Sergeant) H. Black (N°13507) awarded the MILITARY MEDAL by Corps Commander. qv. Billets. Church Parades. Night covering parties to guard line with gas cylinders qv.	
"	27/8/16		Billets. Training. Afternoon moving parties under C.O. 162nd F.C.R.E. Experts.	
"	28/8/16		Night parties to Belgian Camp reconnoitred by Supper party of 9 platoon D.S.O. works Battalion as steering night covering parties to guard line with gas cylinders. qv.	
"	29/8/16		Billets. Training. 4 O.R. received final issue from Regt. in orient "See also" given in new qv. Billets. Training.	
"	30/8/16		C.O. accompanies other time members of right battalion & right brigade on reconnaissance from guard line during the night.	
"	31/8/16		Following awarded the MILITARY MEDAL by Corps Commander N° 18605 Sergeant F. Munden (attached 27?? battery) N° 13567 Sgt A. Withey (attached 2nd T.M. Bty) N° 14351 9/Cpl. C.H. Jones and N° 15434 Pte W. Corner qv.	
"	1/9/16		Billets. Training. Company Commanders visit front trenches taught Esher Junct. Right Brigade qv.	

… WAR DIARY
or
INTELLIGENCE SUMMARY. 8th Bn L⁰ Yorkshire R
(Erase heading not required.)

Army Form C. 2118.

Vol.

Place	Date	Hour	Summary of Events and Information	Remarks and references to Appendices
POE DE SAC	1/9/16		Billeted in POE DE SAC during. Officers received tuition of night battle & night signals, with F. ARMENTIERES gd.	
	2/9/16		Marched to FLETRE & billeted there gd.	
	3/9/16		Marched to STAPLE & billeted there gd.	
	4/9/16		Marched to ARQUES & billeted there gd.	
	5/9/16		Marched to 3¹ DADSROES & billeted there gd.	
	6/9/16		Battalion company gd.	
	7/9/16		Training.	
	8/9/16		[illegible]	
	9/9/16		[illegible]	
	10/9/16		Morning. Officers & NCOs attended lecture on war practicals (small) at ... 2.5. pl. E.O. 2pm at MENINCOURT. Brig-General J M Babington, C.B C.M.G. addressed the battalion. The General told the Battalion that it was returning to the Somme area. He did not know what he should be required to do there, but he made it quite clear however, known to him, that what he could hand to ask of the Battalion to do would at some time the Battalion had taken in July last ... officers and men probably in fighting around BAZENTIN. What he could rely on them & knew that any work entrusted to it would be done by it as well as any troops could do it. he ended the ...	

Army Form C. 2118.

WAR DIARY
or
INTELLIGENCE SUMMARY.

8th Bn. K.C. Yorkshire L.I.

(Erase heading not required.)

Place	Date	Hour	Summary of Events and Information	Remarks and references to Appendices
BIDAUQUES	5/9/16		Battalion the best of luck. gdP	
	6/9/16		Marched to ST OMER & entrained that. hand g.N.J Bombay 2 9.21 O.H. Entrainment gdP	
	7/9/16		Detrained at LONGEAU & marched to ACONVILLE & billeted there. gdP	
BAESLE	8/9/16		Marched to BAESLE & billeted & bivouaced there. gdP	
	9/9/16		In billets. Training. today to officers inc cos by Brig. General & Group. D.S.O. on the	
	10/9/16		attack & c. Schools of instruction and. gdP	
	15/9/16		In billets. Training. gdP	
	18/9/16		Marched to trenches at BLACK WOOD. gdP	
BLACK WOOD	19/9/16		In trenches. gdP	
	20/9/16		In trenches. Much casualties. Cooking at ALBERT gdP	
	21/9/16		Marched to trenches around PEAKE WOOD, relieving 12th H.L.I. gdP	
PEAKE WOOD	22/9/16		In trenches. gdP	
	23/9/16		Marched to trenches near LOZENGE WOOD. gdP	
LOZENGE WOOD	24/9/16		In trenches. Working parties. gdP	
	25/9/16			
FRICOURT	26/9/16		Marched to GODFLEY trench, relieving 12th D.L.I. in SUPPORT BRIGADE area. gdP	
	27/9/16		In trenches. Working parties gdP	

WAR DIARY
or
INTELLIGENCE SUMMARY.

(Erase heading not required.)

Army Form C. 2118.

8th Bn. K.O. Yorkshire L.I.

Place	Date	Hour	Summary of Events and Information	Remarks and references to Appendices
CUINCHY	24/8/15		No change. Strong patrols out	
"	25/8/15		No change. Strong patrols out	
"	26/8/15		No change. Officers reconnoitred front line in front of MARTIN PUICH. In evening Battalion marched into front line, relieving 12th D.L.I. having ½ld S.E. outskts of Bazentins on left of Batallion. Supplies brought 500 yards towards L.E. sags on some being carried by	
"	27/8/15		By evening Two Companies taken 9 cooks in hand. Our firing front line subject to heavy shell fire. Attack by 9th + y r L. Brigade into trenches around O.B.1. on MARTIN PUICH - EONTALMAISON road failed in the main assault O.B.1 falls	
	28/8/15		In trenches around O.B.1. L.O + post in enemy resistance the outle selected for immediately trenches	
			Relieved DESTREMONT FARM P/L.	

WAR DIARY
or
INTELLIGENCE SUMMARY.
(Erase heading not required.)

Army Form C. 2118.

Place	Date	Hour	Summary of Events and Information	Remarks and references to Appendices
Nr MARTINPUICH	1-x-16		Battalion took up its position in assembly trenches behind DESTREMONT FARM just before dawn. The attack was timed for 3:15 pm and the objective was the two lines of German trenches over a frontage of 300 yards in front of LE SARS. The advance was across 600 yards of open ground. At dawn our position was revealed and the assembly trenches were shelled continuously. About 25% of strength was the lost in casualties before the attack. At 3:15 pm our artillery put up an intense barrage and A & D Companies left their trenches closely followed by C. Coy in support. B. Coy. remained in reserve. The objective was gained easily despite a counter barrage by German artillery and work of consolidation on the two lines began. The objective was held all night against small counter attacks and at 2 am B. Coy. reinforced. At 4 am two companies came up from Brigade Reserve and took over O.G.1. while the remainder of the 8th K.O.Y.L.I. were withdrawn to O.G.1. HQrs.	
	2-x-16		Relieved in O.G.1. by 10th WEST RIDINGS 69th Brigade and marched to bivouac in THE DINGLE. Casualties 1 officer killed, 2 missing, 8 wounded. O.R. 248. The following letter was received from G.O.C. 23rd Div. Date 3-x-16 - My dear Colonel, Will you please tell all ranks of your battalion how very pleased I am at their behaviour on Oct. 1st. I congratulate them most heartily on their success which	

Army Form C. 2118.

WAR DIARY
or
INTELLIGENCE SUMMARY.
(Erase heading not required.)

Place	Date	Hour	Summary of Events and Information	Remarks and references to Appendices
			Was due to their gallantry and the fine spirit they showed. Good luck to you all. Yours ever (signed) J.M. BABINGTON. The following immediate rewards for gallantry were made :- Military Cross - 2/Lieut. O.H. COCKE and 2/Lieut. F. NODDLE. Military Medal - 21148 Sgt. WHITE. 15650 Sgt WHITEHEAD. 12983. L/Cpl LUND. 12291. Pte HOLMES. 17497. Pte CROSSLAND. 3609 Pte SHIELDS. 8359 Pte GOLDSBY. 16415 Pte NORGATE.A. 20089 Pte HALL. 21157 Pte GREGG. Bar to the Military Medal - 15269 Sgt HOLBERRY att. T.M.B. HQRS.	
DINGLE	3-X-16		Rests in bivouac. HQRS.	
"	4-X-16		Working parties. Move to CONTALMAISON CUTTING in Div. reserve. HQRS.	
CUTTING	5-X-16		Carrying parties. HQRS.	
"	6-X-16		Carrying parties. HQRS.	
"	7-X-16		Carrying parties. HQRS.	
"	8-X-16		Relieved by 10th S.R. Entrained at MAMETZ WOOD, detrained at VIVIER MILL and marched to billets at BRÊSLE. HQRS.	
BRÊSLE	9-X-16		Quiet day in billets. Kit inspection etc. Warning order recd for move to new area. Lieut Col IMBERT-TERRY D.S.O. went on 10 days leave to ENGLAND. HQRS.	

Army Form C. 2118.

WAR DIARY
or
INTELLIGENCE SUMMARY.
(Erase heading not required.)

Instructions regarding War Diaries and Intelligence Summaries are contained in F. S. Regs., Part II. and the Staff Manual respectively. Title pages will be prepared in manuscript.

Place	Date	Hour	Summary of Events and Information	Remarks and references to Appendices
BRÊSLE	10-X-16		Quiet day in billets.	HQHR.
	11-X-16		Batt. inspected by the Corps Commander. Draft of 7 Officers and 10 O.R. joined for duty. Lieut. E.V.M. BRADLEY rejoined from Hospital. Advance party of 1 Officer & 1 O.R. left for FRANCIÈRES	HQHR.
"	12-X-16		Batt. marched to ALBERT and entrained for LONGPRÉ. Advance party left for POPERINGHE.	HQHR.
IN THE TRAIN	13-X-16		Batt. detrained at LONGPRÉ & marched to billets in FRANCIÈRES.	HQHR.
FRANCIÈRES	14-X-16		Marched to ARGENVILLERS and billeted. A/Lieut. actg Adjt. J.E.A. MANN admitted to Hospital. Sick.	HQHR.
ARGENVILLERS	15-X-16		Church parade. Batt. left at 6 pm, marched to S. RIQUIER and entrained for PROVEN.	HQHR.
POPERINGHE	16-X-16		Batt. detrained 6.a.m. and marched to Rutmarck nr OUDERDOM. Draft of 99 O.R. joined for duty.	HQHR.
OUDERDOM	17-X-16		Entrained for YPRES. Detrained & billeted in THE BARRACKS.	HQHR.
YPRES	18-X-16		Relieved 16th Batt. A.I.F. in front line about SANCTUARY WOOD. HQ. Qrs. DORMY HOUSE. C. & D. Coys in front line. A & B in support.	HQHR.
ZILLEBEKE	19-X-16		Quiet day in line. 1 casualty (accidental)	HQHR.
"	20-X-16		Quiet day. Much work in draining & improving trenches.	HQHR.
"	21-X-16		Relieved by 8th Y & L. Marched to YPRES BARRACKS.	HQHR.
YPRES	22-X-16		Batt. in working parties. 2 Offrs. & 60 O.R. doing special wiring in front of 8th Y&L by night.	HQHR.
"	23-X-16		Working parties and bathing.	HQHR.

Army Form C. 2118.

WAR DIARY
or
INTELLIGENCE SUMMARY.
(Erase heading not required.)

Instructions regarding War Diaries and Intelligence Summaries are contained in F. S. Regs., Part II. and the Staff Manual respectively. Title pages will be prepared in manuscript.

Place	Date	Hour	Summary of Events and Information	Remarks and references to Appendices
YPRES	24-X-16		Working parties & bathing. 1 O.R. wounded. Major G.L. PYMAN went on 10 days leave to ENGLAND.	HQMS.
"	25-X-16		Working parties. Firing of small arms respirators and bathing.	HQMS.
"	26-X-16		Relieved 8th Y. & L. in front line. A & D. Coys in front line. B Coy in STAFFORD TR. C Coy in THE BUND.	HQMS.
ZILLEBEKE	27-X-16		Quiet day. Casualties nil. Capt. M.G. DONAHOE went on 10 days leave to ENGLAND.	HQMS.
"	28-X-16		Left Coy. shelled with minenwerfers. Artillery effectually retaliated.	HQMS.
"	29-X-16		Relieved by 13th D.L.I. 69th Bde. 1 Casualty.	HQMS.
POPERINGHE	30-X-16		Entrained YPRES siding 2 am. Detrained POPERINGHE & Bn. over billets in Corps Reserve.	HQMS.
"	31-X-16		Bn. inspected by Army Commander. Large working party to trenches.	HQMS.

Army Form C. 2118.

8th Battn. W. Yorkshire Regt. T.I.

WAR DIARY
or
INTELLIGENCE SUMMARY.
(Erase heading not required.)

Vol/5

Instructions regarding War Diaries and Intelligence Summaries are contained in F. S. Regs., Part II. and the Staff Manual respectively. Title pages will be prepared in manuscript.

Place	Date	Hour	Summary of Events and Information	Remarks and references to Appendices
POPERINGHE	1/7/15		Billets in the town. Training, Working parties to trenches. q.v.	
"	2/7/15		Billets in the town. Training. q.v.	
"	3/7/15		Billets in the town. Training q.v.	
"	4/7/15		Entrained at POPERINGHE, detrained at YPRES SIDING, and relieved 10th East West Riding Regt in Casual Place, at YPRES INFANTRY BARRACKS. q.v.	
YPRES	5/7/15		Billets in Barracks. Church Parades. Working parties to trenches q.v.	
"	6/7/15		Billets in BARRACKS. Carrying an extra ration among working parties to trenches. C.O. & Coy.Comd^{rs} vis^d trenches of L^t/ Brigade area q.v.	
"	7/7/15		Billets in BARRACKS. Training on subject usual. Working parties Officers reconn^d trenches q.v.	
"	8/7/15		Billets in BARRACKS. Training in extras usual. Advance parties & specialists & working parties q.v	
"	9/7/15		Billets in BARRACKS. Bathing & working as ordered usual. Working parties q.v.	
"	10/7/15		Marched into trenches of L^t/ Battalion of L^t/ Brigade area, relieving 8th B.W. Regt & towards Coy Battⁿ H.Q. HALF WAY HOUSE q.v.	
TRENCHES	11/7/15		In trenches. Building new traverses to left, on L Line + All the Linders, L.O.s. q.v.	
"	12/7/15		In trenches. q.v.	
"	13/7/15		In trenches. q.v.	
"	14/7/15		In trenches. q.v.	
"	15/7/15		In trenches. q.v.	

8th Batt: K.O. Yorkshire L.I.

Army Form C. 2118

WAR DIARY
or
INTELLIGENCE SUMMARY.
(Erase heading not required.)

Instructions regarding War Diaries and Intelligence Summaries are contained in F. S. Regs., Part II. and the Staff Manual respectively. Title pages will be prepared in manuscript.

Place	Date	Hour	Summary of Events and Information	Remarks and references to Appendices
INDIA TRENCHES	16/7/15		Relieved by 13th Batt: Durham Light Infantry, entrained YPRES SIDING, detrained at VLAMERTINGHE & marched into MONTREAL CAMP.	
MONTREAL CAMP	17/7/15		In camp. Cleaning up.	
"	18/7/15		In camp. Cleaning & bathing.	
"	19/7/15		In camp. Church parade.	
"	20/7/15		In camp. Training.	
"	21/7/15		In camp. Training.	
"	22/7/15		Training. Lt. Col. C.H.D.N. Lecky TD, DSO left to take command of Divisional school. Major O.R. Devine assumed command of the Battalion. Orders for him to handover written. 2/Lt Rottelin & Light Brigade G.H.Q.	
"	23/7/15		2/Lt Gwynn transferred Railway Control Returns to Pte A Risley & Pte E Graham. G.O.C. Divisional Brigade, Battalion m.a. DORM HOUSE, went this evening with orders of employing VLAMERTINGHE, detrained YPRES SIDING & relieved 10th Batt: their employments in the line system, 4/5 Battalion & 11/13 Brigade, & Maple Copse and on of the BOND. Q.R.	
TRENCHES	23/7/15		On arrival at MAPLE COPSE and on of the BOND Q.R.	
"	24/7/15		In trenches. Enemy front mostly active Q.R.	
"	25/7/15		In trenches. Enemy front mostly active effectually silenced by our batteries Q.R.	
"	26/7/15		In trenches. Day of the BOND carried up into new dugouts in WINNIPEG ST, REDAN & dugouts in SANCTUARY WOOD Q.R.	
"	27/7/15		In trenches Q.R.	
"	28/7/15		In trenches Q.R.	

2353 Wt. W3141434 700,000 5/15 D. D. & L. A.D.S.S./Forms/C. 2118.

8th Battn. K.O. Yorkshire L.I.

Army Form C. 2118.

WAR DIARY
or
INTELLIGENCE SUMMARY.
(Erase heading not required.)

Instructions regarding War Diaries and Intelligence Summaries are contained in F.S. Regs., Part II. and the Staff Manual respectively. Title pages will be prepared in manuscript.

Place	Date	Hour	Summary of Events and Information	Remarks and references to Appendices
TRENCHES	28/11/15		In trenches q.v.	
	29/11/15		Relieved by 8th Batt. York & Lancasters. Kept amused to billets in YPRES, H.A. HOSPICE, in Convent Annex. q.v.	
YPRES	30/11/15		In billets. Indirect firing, working parties. Practice at Rifle range near Sally Port q.v.	
			Casualties during the Month	
			1 officer wounded	
			1 O.R. killed	
			7 O.R. wounded q.v.	

SECRET.

8TH K.O.Y.L.I. OPERATION ORDER NO. 71.

15th November 1916.

1. The Battalion will be relieved by the 13th Bn. D.L.I. on the night of 16/17th November.

2. 4 Guides per Coy. and 1 for Bn.H.Q. will thoroughly reconnoitre the route from LILLE GATE by night tonight. These guides will parade at Battalion Headquarters tomorrow 16th inst: at 2.30 P.M. under 2nd Lieut: F. Noddle.

3. All kits, chop-boxes, etc., will be sent to the usual dumps by Coys. as soon as it is dusk.

4. All Trench stores, defence schemes, etc., will be handed over to the incoming Battalion. Receipts will be exchanged, and duplicate copies of lists of trench stores handed over to be submitted to Orderly Room by 9 A.M. on the 17th inst:
All gum-boots will be taken out of the trenches by Coys. in the line. These will be collected when the Battalion arrives in MONTREAL CAMP.

5. Advance parties of 1 N.C.O. and 1 man per Company and 1 N.C.O. from Headquarters will report to 2nd Lieut: H. A. Dinsdale at Bn.H.Q. at 9 A.M. 16th inst:.

6. The Battalion will entrain at YPRES SIDING at 12.30 A.M. 17th inst:. Companies will march there independently, and await further instructions. There will be no smoking, and no lights will be shewn, in the train.

7. Officers' chargers will be at VLAMERTINGHE Station at 1 A.M. 17th inst:, and await arrival of the train.

O.C.
8. Companies will report to Bn.H.Q. when Companies are settled in billets, and if the billets were taken over clean.

XXX Lieutenant, Colonel,
Commanding 8th Bn. K. O. Yorkshire L. I.

Issued to :-

H.Q. 70th Inf. Bde. - For information.
O.C. Companies.
Transport Officer.
L. G. O.
A/Quartermaster.

Army Form C. 2118.

Battn H.Q. Yorkshire L.I.
8th

WAR DIARY
or
INTELLIGENCE SUMMARY.
(Erase heading not required.)

Instructions regarding War Diaries and Intelligence
Summaries are contained in F. S. Regs., Part II.
and the Staff Manual respectively. Title pages
will be prepared in manuscript.

Place	Date	Hour	Summary of Events and Information	Remarks and references to Appendices
CAMP	23/9/16		On road to Ypres 9.30 am	
			On road training 9 am	
			March through YPRES 11 AM en route of YPRES to DUG. OUT BARRACKS	
YPRES	24/9/16			
			In BARRACKS Working parties Potizer Corner 9 P	
	25/9/16		In BARRACKS Working parties Potizer Wood Ecole 9 P	
	26/9/16		In BARRACKS Working parties Potizer Crossing 9 P	
	27/9/16		Relieved 8th Y.L.R. Right sub sect in RAILWAY DUGOUTS via HALFWAY HOUSE 9 P	
	28/9/16		In trenches	
	29/9/16		In trenches	
	30/9/16		In trenches	
	1/10/16		Relieved by 9th Y.L.R. to BARRACKS in Infantry Barracks 9 P	
	2/10/16		In BARRACKS Working parties & misc. 9 P	

Army Form C. 2118.

8th Batn. H.C.Oyuls.

WAR DIARY

INTELLIGENCE SUMMARY.
(Erase heading not required.)

Place	Date	Hour	Summary of Events and Information	Remarks and references to Appendices

8th Battalion Yorkshire L.I.

70/23

Army Form C. 2118.

WAR DIARY
INTELLIGENCE SUMMARY.
(Erase heading not required.)

Instructions regarding War Diaries and Intelligence Summaries are contained in F. S. Regs., Part II. and the Staff Manual respectively. Title pages will be prepared in manuscript.

Place	Date 1917	Hour	Summary of Events and Information	Remarks and references to Appendices
MONTREAL CAMP.	Jan 1.	—	In Corps Reserve Montreal Camp. 'Xmas Festivities. Captain Bull → 2/Lt Hope-Hernon go on leave. J.S.7pm.	
"	2.		Baths at Poperinghe. Working parties. J.S.7pm.	
"	3.		Working parties. Captain Poyser awarded D.S.O. A Coy to Bde School, 16 train for maid under 2/Lts Horwood & Dinsdale. J.S.7pm.	
"	4.		Working parties. J.S.7pm.	
"	5.		Lt. & Adj. E.B.B. Speed rejoined for duty. Major F.L. Pyman mentioned in Despatches.	
"	6.		Corps Commander visits Camp. 2/Lt Polgreen on Gas course. J.S.7pm. Lt. Speed took over duties of Adjutant from Lt J.E.F. Mann.. Lt Martin & 2/Lt Martindale go on leave, 2/Lt Noddle returned from leave. J.S.7pm.	
"	7		Church Parade. Working parties. J.S.7pm.	
"	8.		Battalion relieves (lost Company) relieved 10th W. Ridings in Ypres, becomes "D" Battalion in Divisional Reserve. B Coy in Bund, C. Coy at Cavalry Bks. & D Coy at Infy Bks. J.S.7pm.	
YPRES	9		Bn. Hqrs moves at 2.0 a.m. from Hospice, Ypres, to Bund. Working parties. Captain B.H. Horsley rejoined for duty. 2/Lt Stevenson to Hazebrouck to interview R.F.C. officers. J.S.7pm. Bn in Reserve. Captain B.H. Horsley takes over command of D. Coy.. Lt. E.J. Priddy. J.S.7pm.	
"	10		2/Lts W Dowland & Riley joined for duty. J.S.7pm.	
"	11		Bn in Reserve. Working parties. Lt J.E.F.Mann goes on leave. Draft of 156 O.R. at Reinforcement Camp. J.S.7pm	
"	12		Relieved 8Y&L. & became B. Battalion in Left Sector Right Bde. A Coy rejoining from Bde School. J.S.7pm. HdQrs Dormy House	

8th Battalion A.G. Yorkshire R.

Army Form C. 2118.

WAR DIARY
or
INTELLIGENCE SUMMARY.
(Erase heading not required.)

Instructions regarding War Diaries and Intelligence Summaries are contained in F. S. Regs., Part II. and the Staff Manual respectively. Title pages will be prepared in manuscript.

Place	Date	Hour	Summary of Events and Information	Remarks and references to Appendices
TRENCHES	13		In Trenches. Draft of 117 O.R. arrived ABEELE. 2/Lt HOUGHTON to L. Gun Corps ETAPS. 9/Jm	
"	14		Captain BULL & 2/Lt HOBE-HERNON return from leave. 2/Lts SETON & AKEROYD to Training Camp, STEENVOORDE. Draft of 37 O.R. arrive ABEELE. 9/Jm	
"	15.		In front line. 2/Lt RILEY to 126th Field Coy R.E. vice 2/Lt LEE on leave 16.2. 2/Lt E.V.H. BRADLEY promoted Captain whilst commanding a Company. 9/Jm	
"	16.		2/Lt A.S. LEE goes on leave. Relieved in trenches by 8 Y & L. & become D. Battn. in reserve.	
"	17.		H.Q. at BUND with D. Coy, B & C. Coy, YPRES, & A. Coy at Bde School. 9/Jm	
"	18		Divisional Reserve. Lt. Col. OWEN to Bde School	
"	19		Divisional Reserve. Working parties. # Captain G.T. Simmons struck off the strength. 9/Jm & A. Coy in training. 9/Jm	
"	20		2/Lt A.L. CHADWICK returns from Divisional Course. 2/Lt P.K. POWELL to course at Div School. Bn relieves 8 Y & L 92 Regt. in left sector, left Brigade. H.Q. DORMY HOUSE. B.C. & D. Coys in front line. A. Coy remains at Bde School. 9/Jm	
TRENCHES	21.		A. Coy rejoin Bn in line from Bde School. 9/Jm	
"	22		In front line trenches	
"	23.		At 9.0 p.m. after a short but very intense barrage a party of 3 officers & 120 O.R. (A. Coy. a 1 platoon of D. Coy) raided the enemy's trenches between J.19.c.00 & J.19.c.06.10., successfully entering the enemy trenches, which they remained 15 minutes. The enemy had evacuated his trenches which he bombarded heavily. No prisoners were taken. Casualties. 1 O.R. killed, 7 O.R. m'ing, 9 & 9 O.R. wounded. All three officers were wounded, viz. Captain H.C.H. Bull (slightly at duty), 2/Lt DINSDALE & 2/Lt HORWOOD. 2/Lts T.S.H. Dr. P. STEPHENS, E.G. PEABODY & A. WILLIAMS join for duty. 9/Jm	

Army Form C. 2118.

9th Battalion H.O. Yorkshires L.

WAR DIARY
or
INTELLIGENCE SUMMARY.
(Erase heading not required.)

Instructions regarding War Diaries and Intelligence Summaries are contained in F. S. Regs., Part II. and the Staff Manual respectively. Title pages will be prepared in manuscript.

Place	Date	Hour	Summary of Events and Information	Remarks and references to Appendices
TRENCHES	24		CAPTAIN M.G. DONAHOO wounded. 2/Lt W.H.BRYNING joins for duty. Bn. relieved in trenches by 11 N.Fusiliers, entraining at YPRES at 2.0 a.m. (25th), detraining at VLAMERTINGHE & marching to MONTREAL CAMP where in CORPS RESERVE. 9.9.p.m.	
MONTREAL CAMP	25		Corps Reserve. Lieiner Ceremony. MAJOR G.L. NEWSOME returned from hospital. LT. JEF. MANN & 2/Lt MARTINDALE return from leave. 9.9.p.m.	
"	26		G.O.C. Bde inspects "C" Coy under new organisation. G.O.C. Division inspects training party. Close order drill. Major G.L. Pyman goes on leave. Major NEWSOME to TANKS. 9.9.p.m.	
"	27		Working parties. Training. 2/Lt CHADWICK to hospital. 9.p.m.	
"	28		G.O.C. Brigade inspects "C" Coy. Captain E.V.H. BRADLEY to II Army Course at WISQUES. 2/Lt NODDLE takes over command of C Coy. 2/Lt MARTINDALE to hospital. 2/Lt HOUGHTON returned from L.G. Course. 2/Lt STEVENSON (D.C.L.I.) to R.F.C. to air observer and struck off Bn strength. 2/Lt RILEY under close arrest. 9.p.m.	
"	29		Training. 9.p.m.	
"	30		Bn. HQ. Mess (3 Armstrong huts) burnt down 3. Bales. Gas attack practiced at Gas School. 9.p.m.	
"	31		Battn. Training. Corps Commander visits camp. 2/Lt RILEY under open arrest. 2/Lt HOUGHTON to M.G. Corps. Captain M.G. DONAHOO died of wounds No.10 C.C.S. POPERINGHE. 9.p.m.	

Casualties for month:— Officers: Died of Wounds. 1
Wounded 3
—
4

O.R. Killed 3
D.of W. 4
Missing 7
Wounded 56
—
Total 70

J.P. Mann
J.R. Reid V.

Army Form C. 2118.

Confidential.

WAR DIARY
8TH (SERVICE) BATT. K.O.Y.L.I.
INTELLIGENCE SUMMARY

(Erase heading not required.)

Vol/8/1.

Instructions regarding War Diaries and Intelligence Summaries are contained in F. S. Regs., Part II. and the Staff Manual respectively. Title pages will be prepared in manuscript.

Place	Date	Hour	Summary of Events and Information	Remarks and references to Appendices
YPRES.	1/2/17		Battalion relieved 11th W.Yorks Regt. Becoming C Batt in Brigade Reserve. INFANTRY BARRACKS.	Eng.
"	2/2/17		Brigade Reserve. Working parties. G.H.Q. 2nd LINE	Eng.
"	3/2/17		Brigade Reserve. Working parties. Physical drill + rifle exercises during morning	Eng.
"	4/2/17		Brigade Reserve. Working parties. " " "	Eng.
"	5/2/17		Relieved 8th Batt. Y.L. Regt. in trenches becoming A. Batt. of left Brigade Headquarters TUILLERIES.	Eng.
"	6/2/17		Four platoons in front line. Eight platoons in support + four platoons in reserve.	
"	6/2/17		Trenches. Battalion Headquarters moved to DORAN HOUSE. Very clear day, quiet	Eng.
"	7/2/17		Trenches. quiet day. Batt HeadQuarters shelled 5.0 pm.	Eng.
"	8/2/17		Trenches. quiet day. Considerable shelling on to left of MENIN ROAD at 7.15pm.	Eng.
"	9/2/17		Trenches. Relieved by 8th Batt. Y.L. Regt. moved into Brigade Reserve INFANTRY BARRACKS. YPRES.	
"	10/2/17		Brigade Reserve. Small working parties. Capt. G. 82 O.R.Jones, "B" Company Sationer, economy. Capt. H.C.H. Bell and 2/Lieut. H.A.DINSDALE awarded MILITARY CROSS and 1/10 21128 Sgt. R. White awarded D.C.M. for gallantry during raid on enemy trenches on Jan. 23, 1917.	Eng.
YPRES.	11/2/17		Brigade Reserve. Working parties. B. Coy on miniature Range at SALLY PORT. C.D. Coys Battns.	Eng.
"	12/2/17		Brigade Reserve. Working parties. C. Coy on miniature Range. A + B Coys Battns.	Eng.

Confidential

Army Form C. 2118.

WAR DIARY
or
INTELLIGENCE SUMMARY.

(Erase heading not required.)

8TH (Service) BATT.
K.O.Y.L.I.

2

Instructions regarding War Diaries and Intelligence Summaries are contained in F. S. Regs., Part II. and the Staff Manual respectively. Title pages will be prepared in manuscript.

Place	Date	Hour	Summary of Events and Information	Remarks and references to Appendices
YPRES.	13/2/17		Brigade Reserve. Bom relieved 8th Batt H.L.Regt in front line trenches BATT HQ ZILLEBEKE BUND. PNY.	
"	14/2/17		Trenches. Bom H.Q. moved to TUILLERIES. Junior Offr. ZILLEBEKE Started with H.E.Shrapnel at 1.0pm. PNY.	
"	15/2/17		Trenches. Quiet day. PNY.	
"	16/2/17		Trenches. Quiet day. PNY.	
"	17/2/17		Trenches. Quiet day. Relief by 12th Batt. D.L.I. Commenced at 9.0pm. misty in morning clear late. PNY.	
OUDERDOM. (MONTREAL CAMP.)	18.2.17		Relief by 12th Batt. D.L.I. completed by 5.30 a.m. marched to MONTREAL CAMP in Corps Reserve by Platoons in daylight. Trek mist. Last platoon reached camp by 9.0 a.m. PNY.	
"	19.2.17		Batha CORPS RESERVE. MONTREAL CAMP. Interior Economy. PNY.	
"	20.2.17		Corps Reserve. Squad, Section, Cempt. Platoon drill. Very wet. PNY.	
"	21.2.17		CORPS RESERVE. Baths at OPERINGHE. Small working parties. PNY.	
"	22.2.17		Corps Reserve. Training. Small working parties. PNY.	
"	23.2.17		Corps Reserve. Training. Lt.Col. C.H.M. IMBERT-TERRY. D.S.O. rejoined the Battalion, taking over command from Lt.Col. T.H.Burton. PNY.	
"	24.2.17		Corps Reserve. Battalion was relieved by 12th Batt. The Royal Sussex Regt marched to POPERINGHE, entraining for BOLLEZEELE. Arrived BOLLEZEELE 6.30 pm. billeted for the night. PNY.	
BOLLEZEELE	25.2.17		Batt left BOLLEZEELE at 10.45 am marched to WATTEN. Arrived WATTEN 1.0pm. billeted for the night. PNY.	

Confidential

Army Form C. 2118.

WAR DIARY 8TH (Service) BATT.
or
INTELLIGENCE SUMMARY. K.O.Y.L.I.

(Erase heading not required.)

Instructions regarding War Diaries and Intelligence Summaries are contained in F.S. Regs., Part II. and the Staff Manual respectively. Title pages will be prepared in manuscript.

Place	Date	Hour	Summary of Events and Information	Remarks and references to Appendices
WATTEN.	26.2.17		Battalion left WATTEN at 10.15 am and marched to billets at MENTQUE. in the NORDAUSQUES training area arriving MENTQUE. 12.30 pm. "A" Company billeted at LA RONVILLE. B and C Companies at MENTQUES. D Company at INGLINGHAM. PH7.	
MENTQUE.	27.2.17		Drill. British economy. Physical drill + close order drill & platoon. PH7.	
MENTQUE.	28.2.17		Drill. Shooting 7am to 2 noon 400 yard Range. Afternoon organised recreation, football. PH7.	
			Casualties during February. 1917. Killed. 3. Other Ranks. Wounded. 4 other ranks. PH7.	

WAR DIARY or INTELLIGENCE SUMMARY

Army Form C. 2118.

Vol IV 8th (S) Bn. K.O.Y.L.I.

Place	Date	Hour	Summary of Events and Information	Remarks and references to Appendices
MENTQUE	1/3/17		Lt-Col. D. Quirk D.S.O. (8th Y.L.) takes over Command of the Bn.	
"	2/3/17		Training. Musketry. Recreational training. 3pm.	
"	3/3/17		Lt-Col. Intuit-Terry D.S.O. goes to Divisional Headquarters. 9am. Draft of 175 O.R. join from Divisional Training Camp. Training. 2/Lt. Pelgreen rejoined from hospital. Recreational training. 3pm.	
"	4/3/17		Church parade. 9.30am.	
"	5/3/17		Bn. practice the Attack.	
"	6/3/17		Training. C.O. attends Corps (XVIII) Commander's Conference at ST OMER. 3pm.	
"	7/3/17		Training. Officers & N.C.O.s attend Rapid Wiring demonstration at TOURNEHEM. 3pm.	
"	8/3/17		" " G.C.M. of 2/Lt RILEY at Bde H.Q.s. Recreational training. 3pm.	
"	9/3/17		Brigade Field day. 9pm.	
"	10/3/17		Training. Army Commander visits MENTQUE + inspects bayonet fighting training. Recreational training. 3pm.	
"	11/3/17		Church parade. Recreational training; HQ win football v "A" Coy. bomb throwing competition. 3pm.	
"	12/3/17		Training. Rapid construction of a strong point. Recreational training. 3pm.	
"	13/3/17		Artillery formations practiced. 2/Lt L. Wright rejoined. 3pm.	
"	14/3/17		Rifle Range. Captain B.H. HORSLEY to hospital. 3pm.	
"	15/3/17		Training. 3pm.	

Army Form C. 2118.

WAR DIARY
or
INTELLIGENCE SUMMARY. 8th (S) Bn. K.O.Y.L.I.
(Erase heading not required.)

Instructions regarding War Diaries and Intelligence Summaries are contained in F. S. Regs., Part II. and the Staff Manual respectively. Title pages will be prepared in manuscript.

Place	Date	Hour	Summary of Events and Information	Remarks and references to Appendices
MENTQUE	16.3.17		Training. Night march by compass. Recreational training.	JSpn.
"	17.3.17		Outpost scheme. Recreational training. — D. Coy. won Cross-country in Bde competition.	JSpn.
"	18-3-17		Training " — H.P. win football & A Coy Rowing Coy —	JSpn.
			Capt. T. Brearley rejoined. 2/Lt L.J. Wood joined.	JSpn.
MOULLE	19-3-17		Bn. marches to MOULLE.	JSpn.
BOLLEZEELE	20-3-17		" " from " to BOLLEZEELE.	JSpn.
HOUTKERQUE	21-3-17		" " BOLLEZEELE to 'Cleeb at HOUTKERQUE.	JSpn.
"	22-3-17		Rations. Interior economy.	JSpn.
"	23-3-17		Trench to trench attack.	JSpn.
"	24-3-17		Training. Open order. Recreational training — Bn. defeat MSC in football.	JSpn.
"	25-3-17		Church Parade. — Bde H.Q. "	JSpn.
"	26-3-17		Training. 2/Lt TUFNELL joined for duty.	JSpn.
"	27-3-17		Bn. Route march.	JSpn.
"	28-3-17		" " "	JSpn.
"	29-3-17		Training.	JSpn.
"	30-3-17		" — Route march.	JSpn.
"	31-3-17		P.T. inter Gymnastic instructors. 2/Lt. L. WRIGHT to hospital.	JSpn.
			[2/Lt J.L RILEY dismissed from the Service]	
			[by sentence of G.C.M.]	JSpn.
			Casualties during month :— 10 O.R. died.	

J Spurr
Lieut. for
O.C. 8th K.O.Y.L.I.

WAR DIARY
or
INTELLIGENCE SUMMARY.
(Erase heading not required.)

Army Form C. 2118.

Instructions regarding War Diaries and Intelligence Summaries are contained in F. S. Regs., Part II. and the Staff Manual respectively. Title pages will be prepared in manuscript.

Vol 20 7⁰/₁ 7/23
8ᵗʰ S. Bn K.O.Y.L.I

Place	Date	Hour	Summary of Events and Information	Remarks and references to Appendices
HOUTKERQUE	2/4/17		Recreational training. Church Parade.	
-	3/4/17		Route march & recreational training. 2/Lt J.T. HALL (from 15th W.Yorks) joined for duty. Major T.M. OWEN to 11th N.F. as 2 in command.	
-	4/4/17		Lieut T.V. MEDLEY and Lieut H.A. SPEDDING joined for duty from 8th Yorks.	
-	5/4/17		Training.	
WINNIPEG CAMP	6/4/17	10am	Battalion marched to WINNIPEG CAMP near OUDERDOM arriving about 3.30pm. Major S.D. RUMBOLD, MC (8th Yorks) joined for duty.	
-	6/4/17		Bn in WINNIPEG CAMP. Training.	
-	7/4/17		Training. C.O. 2 i/c & Coy Cdrs visited trenches.	
ZILLEBEKE BUND & RAILWAY DUGOUTS	8/4/17		Battalion marched to Support positions in front of YPRES relieving 1/20th London Regt. HQ to Capt "Railway Dugouts". Remainder ZILLEBEKE BUND.	
	9/4/17	6pm	Heavy bombardment by enemy on front line & light of railway in rear of ZILLEBEKE BUND. Bombardment increased in intensity and spread to back areas. Near dusk enemy shelled front line trenches of the Bde front. Casualties 2 OR wounded.	
-	10/4/17	8pm	C Company relieved a company of 11th S.F. at BATTERSEA FARM. Casualties Nil.	
FRONTLINE TRENCHES	11/4/17	8pm	Relieved 9th Yorks in Left Subsector of Bde Front (the 60 subsector). At D Coys front line B Coy support. C Reserve. HQ Rudkin House. Casualties 10 OR wounded.	
-	12/4/17		2nd Lieut A WILLIAMS rejoined from Sniping Course at 2nd Army School. Casualties Nil	
-	13/4/17		Relieved by 8th Yorkshires and moved into Reserve at SCOTTISH LINES near BUSSEBOOM by train from YPRES to BRANDHOEK. Casualties 2 OR wounded.	
SCOTTISH LINES	14/4/17		2/Lt B.T.M.R. POYCE, J.M. CATER, T.C. FAWCETT joined	

WAR DIARY
or
INTELLIGENCE SUMMARY.
(Erase heading not required.)

Army Form C. 2118.

Place	Date	Hour	Summary of Events and Information	Remarks and references to Appendices
SCOTTISH LINE	15/4/17		Lt Colonel D. QUIRK. DSO. C 2nd Army Central School. Capt. T. BREAKEY. on a 3 days Corps Staff tour.	
—	16/4/17		2 huts at Qm Stores destroyed by fire. In lieu Seconomy. 2nd Lieut G. WHEELER + H.W. FRANKS.	
—	17/4/17		Lieut P.V. Medley have to U.K. Bathing at WINNIPEG CAMP P.	
—	18/4/17		Capt H.C. BOWEN joined for duty.	
—	19/4/17		B C & D Coys proceeded to Railway Depots for working parties. Remainder training.	
—	20/4/17		12844 LATTAN, T. (A Cpl) presented with military medal ribbon by Corps Cmdr. Capt Brealey returned from Course.	
—	21/4/17		Lt Colonel Quick DSO. returned from above course. 2/Lieut G. NYE. joined for duty. Trenches reconnoitred by Coy Cmdrs etc.	
Frontline Trenches	22/4/17		Relieved 10th West Riding Regt in Right sector of Brigade front. B & C Coys front line. D Coy support. A Company reserve. HQ SPOIL. Major G. T. Newsome returned from leave. Casualties 1 OR. wounded.	
—	23/4/17		Lieut J.B.J. Mann to 2nd Army Signal School for 6 weeks course. 2nd Lieut P.K. Powell to bombing Course TER DE GHEM. Casualties 5 OR wounded. 1 OR shell shock.	
—	24/4/17		Casualties 1 OR D/W. 7 OR wounded.	
—	25/4/17		Front line Hn HQ heavily shelled during day. 2/Lt Tuffnell returned from Course at Brigade School. Lieut W.M. Lieutenant and 2/Lt T. Thorpesvale returned from leave. Casualties 2 OR killed 4 OR wounded.	
Railway Dugouts	26/4/17 27/4/17 28/4/17 29/4/17 30/4/17		Casualties nil. Relieved by 9th Loyal and Green Support Bn in Railway Dugouts — 3 working parties.	
	3/4/17		Capt F.W. BRONKER RAMC detached from Bn. Lieut W.F. Johnstone RAMC joined. Casualties 1 OR wounded. Relieved Mtr S.F. in Centre Subsector. A & D. Frontline, B support C Reserve HQ LARCHWOOD	

Signatures

Army Form C. 2118.

WAR DIARY
or
INTELLIGENCE SUMMARY.
(Erase heading not required.)

8TH K.O.Y.L.I.

Vol 21

HEADQUARTERS
-4 JUN 1917
70TH BRIGADE

Place	Date	Hour	Summary of Events and Information	Remarks and references to Appendices
FRONT LINE TRENCHES	1/5/17		Hill 60 Sub sector. A & D Coys in front line. C in reserve. B in support. Situation. 1 O.R. wounded. Other ranks.	
BULLETS (WATOU)	2/5/17		B. relieved by 10th Worcester Regt. marched to town. Retrenched.	
	3/5/17		A & M.D. relieved by train to Watou 5:10AM. 9 marched to Hill 60. B. to first line position near Watou. Retour company.	
	4/5/17		transport inspected by B.O.C. Division at 12 noon. T.M.B. 1 Platoon of "C" attached to 66th batt. 1 Platoon of "D" trained to be attacked. 10? at Field by R.F.M. Pilots over Watou. French Pilots. Capt. Pollards returned from 2nd Army of Course Ecole.	
	5/5/17		B. exercised in the attack. "C" Coy fighting at our B. Platoons exercised or rapid loading. "D" Coy 9 Lord Weatherby M.P. Coy No. 12 exercised on the assault. Divisional football final, won by 69 Bde. 2-1. 74.	
	6/5/17		An excursion in close order & unusual drill. Specialists were generally officered. "B" Coy Commanders went to front line trench. Br. inspected by P.C. 70 Inf Bde.	
			M.Collin 2nd Lt B.T.O. 8 KOYLI

WAR DIARY
INTELLIGENCE SUMMARY

(Erase heading not required.)

Army Form C. 2118.

Instructions regarding War Diaries and Intelligence Summaries are contained in F. S. Regs., Part II. and the Staff Manual respectively. Title pages will be prepared in manuscript.

Place	Date	Hour	Summary of Events and Information	Remarks and references to Appendices
SCOTTISH LINES	11/5/17		Bn. proceeded by march route to SCOTTISH LINES arriving in camp at 6 P.M. The lines	
	12/5/17		Bn. proceeded to front line trenches & relieved 6th Bn. Wilts Regt. becoming Bn. in Bde. Res. A, B, C Coys in front line & D in reserve. Hd.qrs. DORMY HOUSE	
FRONT LINE	13/5/17		Lt. SPALDING proceeded on 2nd Bchaly Course WISQUES. Casualties 3 O.R. wounded.	
	14/5/17		Bn. relieved in front line trenches by 5th (Reserve) & proceeded by train to ABEELE	
BILLETS (WATOU)	15/5/17		arriving at 1 A.M. march route to billets near WATOU. The Draft of 43 O.R. joined Bn from 2nd & 4th Bns. HALL & FAWCETT proceeded on leave.	
	16/5/17		Close order drill, musketry & physical training.	
	17/5/17		En route to BOESCHEPE training area. 2nd Lt. STEPHENS to Cross at ETAPLES. Lt. Col. BIRK returned from leave.	
	18/5/17		" " " area B for further training on the attack. The	
	19/5/17		" " " " " " training in the attack. Lectures by Platn.	
			commanders on the attack. The	
	20/5/17		Church parades. Bombers under B.O. throwing hand grenades in rapid return.	
	21/5/17		En route BOESCHEPE training area. Draft of 24 O.R. joined Bn. Ell. P.	
	22/5/17		" 7 A.M. till 4.30 P.M. The	
	23/5/17		Bathing under Coy arrangements, cleaning of arms, equipment & clothing etc.	
	24/5/17		Proceeded to RAILWAY DUGOUTS & relieved 1/4 W. York Regt. & became Bn in Bde. reserve by march route to ABEELE & train to Ypres siding M.P.	
RAILWAY DUGOUTS	25/5/17		Bn. in Bde. RAILWAY DUGOUTS Hd.qrs. BUND, Rev. Relieved 11th Bn SHERWOOD FORESTERS on front line HILL 60 SUB SECTOR	
	26/5/17		Casualties 1 O.R. wounded & 1 O.R. killed	

2353 Wt. W2341/1154 700,000 5/15 D. D. & L. A.D.S.S./Forms/C. 2118.

WAR DIARY
INTELLIGENCE SUMMARY.
(Erase heading not required.)

Army Form C. 2118.

Place	Date	Hour	Summary of Events and Information	Remarks and references to Appendices
FRONT LINE TRENCHES	27/5/17		Bn in front line trenches. W.P	
	28/5/17		2nd LT PILGREEN returned from course W13QUES. 2 LTS HALL & PEWCETT returned from Cave. P.P.	
	29/5/17		2nd LT JEF MANN returned from 2nd army school (ZUYTPENE) P.P.	
	30/5/17		Bn in front line trenches. P.P.	
	31/5/17		Bn relieved in front line trenches by 11th Bn S.P.F.9 proceeded by march route to M camp. 6.17.C.	

Mcbain 2nd Lt
R.I.O.
2nd KOYLI

8th Bn. K.O. Yorks. L.I.

WAR DIARY
or
INTELLIGENCE SUMMARY
(Erase heading not required)

Army Form C. 2118.

70/23
Vol 22

Place	Date	Hour	Summary of Events and Information	Remarks and references to Appendices
Camp near OUDERDOM	1-6-17		Intense economy and cleaning up.	DNJ
"	2-6-17		Bathing etc.	DNJ
"	3-6-17		Church Parades	DNJ
Trenches	4-6-17	9.15 P.M.	Bn. moves from M Camp to Battle Concentration Area in ST. PETERS ST Tunnels, commencing 9.15 P.M. Heavy shelling of THE BUND on way up.	
	5-6-17	1.30 A.M.	Relief hindered by gas, mainly by 30th Division. Commencing 1.30 A.M. 4th Mayorks & S. Staffs. & High trees for duty Bns Relief complete 3 A.M. Bn. H.Q. SEBA DUGOUTS. "D" Company relieves 8th Bn Chesh. - Lancaster Garrison in HEDGE STREET SECTOR.	DSNJ PSNJ
	6-6-17		SEBA Dugouts. 2nd Lieut J.W. Butterworth joined for duty.	
	7-6-17	3.10 A.M.	Second army offensive begun by explosion of mines at HILL 60 and THE CATERPILLAR following operations. See copy 82nd I.O.N.Y.S. Operation & Administrative Orders attached and forwarded herewith. Also (Trench) Maps. HILL 60 5,000 and Map 14 10,000. Copies of which herewith.	

General Plan of Operations

1. The 70th Infantry Brigade having been allotted the position of left front of the whole attack. The main objective of the assault in this sector was to wipe out and hold a line astride running track-m/t and permanent French system at the high ground about I.30.d.4.6. should constitute a firm defensive flank to cover the advance further south. The nature of the operation was therefore virtually ≡ a left form form a position facing S.E. to a final position facing N.E. and E.
2. The frontage of the Brigade attack was from I.30.d.4.6. to the right of CANADA ST. at about T.30.a.4.0. The immediate objective being the IMAGE TRENCH and from ILLUSIVE TRENCH on the enemy front line (see MAP 14) and the final objective being IMAGE CRESCENT from about I.30.d.1.4. to where 32gms IMAGE SUPPORT 9r about I.30.c.3.9.3 and thence to ILLUSIVE TRENCH at I.30.b.5.2.

Rich A Shead
Lieut & Adjutant
8th Bn

8th Bn. L.N. Lancs. L.I.

WAR DIARY
INTELLIGENCE SUMMARY

Army Form C. 2118.

Place	Date	Hour	Summary of Events and Information	Remarks and references to Appendices
Trenches	7.6.17		**3. Stages of the Advance.** The advance to the final objective was divided into two stages, the first commencing at ZERO hour and having for its (purpose) the capture of IMMEDIATE AVENUE and IMAGE RESERVE. The second stage was timed to commence at ZERO + 3 hours 40 min. The objective being IMAGE CRESCENT from I.36.A.1.4 to its junction with IMAGE RESERVE at I.30.d.35.55. The first objective was allotted to the 9th Bn. the York & Lancaster Regt and the 11th Bn. the Sherwood Foresters. The second objective to the (8th Bn.) the York & Lancaster Regt and the 8th Bn. the K.O. Yorkshire L.I. 4. The battalion objective was the left half of the second objective from about I.36.A.55.85. South of the junction with IMAGE RESERVE at I.30.A.35.55. **5. Assembly Position.** Assembly position for the Battalion was the captured enemy trench IMAGE RESERVE (I.30.c.8.4. to I.30.g.35.55.) The Battalion was timed to move to this position at ZERO + 3 hours. 2nd Lieut. R.V. Moore killed in action. The following Officers wounded. 2nd Lieut. L.C. Fawcett, 2nd Lieut. J.A. Holmes, 2nd Lieut. I.D.P. Stephens, 2nd Lieut. H.A. Blands.	Enms Enms Enms
	8.6.17		Bn. in front line trenches.	Enms
	9.6.17		Bn. in front line trenches.	Enms
	10.6.17		Bn. in front line trenches. Relieved on night of 10th/11th June and proceeded to 'L' Camps near OUDERDOM. Total casualties to other ranks for 7th, 8th, 9th and 10th June 250.	Enms
near OUDERDOM	11.6.17		Bn. in 'L' Camps near OUDERDOM.	Enms
	12.6.17		Bn. left 'L' Camps and proceeded by march route to huts and camps near METEREN.	Enms
METEREN	13-6-17		Bn. in huts and camp near METEREN. Interior economy and cleaning &c.	Enms

W.J. Whitehead
Lieut & Adjutant
8 KOYLI

Army Form C. 2118.

8th Bn. Y.C. York L.I.

WAR DIARY
or
INTELLIGENCE SUMMARY.
(Erase heading not required.)

Instructions regarding War Diaries and Intelligence Summaries are contained in F.S. Regs., Part II. and the Staff Manual respectively. Title pages will be prepared in manuscript.

Place	Date	Hour	Summary of Events and Information	Remarks and references to Appendices
near METEREN	14.6.17		Bn. in billets & camp. 'D' Company proceeded to X Corps School at INGHINGHEM for instructional purposes. Also 2nd Lieuts J.H. Cater and A. Knight for course.	SM&S
"	15.6.17		Battalion & close order Drill. Draft of 58 Other Ranks joined from Base.	SM&S
"	16.6.17		Companies on Miniature Range. Lewis Gunners, Signallers, Bombers, etc under Specialist Officers. 2/Lts O.R. & R.E. School for Lewis Gun & Bombing Courses.	SM&S
"	17.6.17		Church Parades. Bathing.	SM&S
"	18.6.17		Companies on Miniature Range. Specialists under Specialist Officers.	SM&S
"	19.6.17		Companies under Bombing Officer for instruction. Bayonet Fighting, Arms drill, Squad drill, etc.	SM&S
"	20.6.17		Lewis Gunners on Miniature Range. Remainder of Battalion. Squad drill, Arms drill, Bayonet Fighting, Musketry, etc.	SM&S
"	21.6.17		Morning - Route march in full order. Afternoon - Coy Comdrs lectures to N.C.Os on maps & Compass reading.	SM&S
"	22.6.17		Lewis Gunners on Miniature Range. Remainder of Battalion. Musketry.	SM&S
"	23.6.17		Companies under Bombing Officer for instruction in mechanism and throwing of bombs.	SM&S
"	24.6.17		Church parade and examination of Individual Mead Forms.	SM&S
"	25.6.17		Companies at disposal of Coy Comdrs - for organization of platoons, Arms drill, Squad drill, etc.	SM&S
"	26.6.17		Left Camp & billets in METEREN area and proceeded by march route to Camp in RENINGHELST vicinity arriving about 11.30 A.M.	SM&S

E.V. Assad
Lieut & Adjutant
8 Y.L.I.

Army Form C. 2118.

WAR DIARY
INTELLIGENCE SUMMARY.
(Erase heading not required.)

8th Bn. R.B. / 69th Bde / 23rd Div.

Instructions regarding War Diaries and Intelligence Summaries are contained in F. S. Regs., Part II. and the Staff Manual respectively. Title pages will be prepared in manuscript.

Place	Date	Hour	Summary of Events and Information	Remarks and references to Appendices
Transloran RENINGHELST	27-6-17		Night of 27/28th June - Proceeded to trenches and relieved 1st Bn. The Royal Fusiliers becoming Bn. in Brigade Support - HILL 60 Sector.	SA/SS
Trenches	28-6-17		Bn. in Brigade Support.	SA/SS
"	29-6-17		Bn. in Brigade Support.	SA/SS
"	30-6-17		Bn. in Brigade Support.	SA/SS
			Awards to Officers N.C.O.s & Men of Battalion for operations of 7th, 8th, 9th & 10th June. Bar to Military Cross - Capt. G.B. Handley, M.C. Military Cross - Captain A.M.R. Becher, 2nd Lieut: W.Durland, 2nd Lieut: G.F. Nye. Distinguished Conduct Medal - 1 Bar to Military Medal - 2 Military Medal - 22.	Mus

E.J.C.M. Oxford
Lieut & Adjutant
8 RB

PRELIMINARY INSTRUCTIONS

and

PLAN OF ATTACK.

8TH. K.O.Y.L.I.

Reference ZILLEBEKE 1/10,000 and attached map.

1. **INTENTION.**
   The 70th Brigade will be the left attacking Brigade of the Xth Corps and will form a defensive left flank facing North, as shewn on attached map.
   There will be a five days bombardment prior to the attack.
   Mines at HILL 60 and the CATERPILLAR will be fired at Zero (time to be notified later).

2. **DISTRIBUTION OF BATTALIONS.**
   The Brigade will attack with two Battalions in the front line and two in support :-
   9th. Y & L. ("A") or Right Front attacking Battalion. Headquarters CANADA STREET.
   11th. Sherwood Foresters ("B") or Left Front attacking Battalion. Headquarters EDGE STREET.
   8th. Y & L. ("C") or Right Support Battalion. Headquarters CANADA STREET.
   8th. K.O.Y.L.I. ("D") or Left Support Battalion. Headquarters SEBA DUG-OUT, WINNEPEG STREET.

3. **BRIGADE OBJECTIVES.**
   "A" & "B" Battalions will capture d consolidate the first objective shewn on the attached map by   line.
   "C" & "D" Battalions will capture and consolidate the 2nd objective shewn on attached map by   line.

4. **BRIGADE BOUNDARIES.**
   The Dividing line between "A" & "B" Battalions in the first objective is TRENCH JUNCTION I.30.d.25.55.
   The dividing line between "C" & "D" Battalions in 2nd objective will be I.36.b.52.85. in IMAGE CRESCENT.

5. **BATTALION OBJECTIVE.**
   The objective allotted to this Battalion is from point I.36.b.52.85. on the right to point I.30.d.25.55. on the left in IMAGE RESERVE.

6. **DIVIDING LINE BETWEEN COMPANIES.**
   The Dividing Line between Coys in the objective is point I.09.d.36.30.
   Should "B" Coy have to move to the right to keep in touch with the 8th. Y. & L., "A" Coy will naturally cross the dividing line and tough up with the left of "B" Company.

7. **DISTRIBUTION OF COMPANIES.**
   "B" Company right front line attacking Company.
   "A" Company Left   do   do   do
   "C" Company Support
   "D" Company. Brigade Reserve Coy.

over

(2).

8. ASSEMBLY POSITIONS PRIOR TO THE ASSAULT.

Night of W/X - The Battalion move from "P" Camp to RITZ STREET & WELLINGTON CRESCENT.

Night of X/Y - Two Battalions Companies (or possibly all four Companies) and Battalion Headquarters will move to TORR TOP dug-outs.
Definite orders on this move will be issued later.

Night of Y/Z - The Battalion will be accomodated in the TORR TOP System of subways from HEDGE STREET to CRAB CRAWL.
Battalion Headquarters will be in SEBA DUG-OUTS in WINNIPEG STREET and will not move until a suitable dug-out is found in the captured system of trenches.

9. BARRAGE LIFTS & TIME TABLE.

Zero plus 1 :- Barrage lifts off enemy front line and goes back gradually at a rate calculated to allow of an advance of 25 yards a minute to the 1st objective.

Zero plus 2g:- Barrage lifts off furtherest point in 1st objective. The barrage line being a straight one, the barrage will naturally clear the part of the 1st objective which bends back to our own line, earlier than this.

Zero plus 3 hours 40 minutes.:- Barrage commences to move back to second (first) objective.

Zero plus 4 hours 10 minutes.:- Barrage clears furthest point in second objective.

10. PLAN OF ATTACK.

At Zero plus 1 minute "A" & "B" Battalions will attack.
As soon as the front line is clear the whole Battalion will move along the tunnel towards HEDGE STREET.
"B" Company will be responsible for seeing that the front line is fairly clear and for giving the order for the Battalion to file out.
"B" Company will file out of the WINNEPEG exit - E 6 - of the tunnel and move down our front line trench to LIVING TRENCH and will get in touch with the 8th Y & L. "A" Company will follow "B" Company.
"A" & "B" Coys will be ready to support the left Battalion (11th S.F.)
On "A" & "B" leaving our front line "C" Company will file out of tunnel along the front line to LIVING TRENCH.
At Zero plus 2 hours "B" & "A" Companies will advance in lines of sections in file to their assembly positions in IMAGE RESERVE as under :-

"B" COMPANY - From I.30.c.80.35. on the right getting in touch with the left flank of the 8th Y & L to point I.30.d.2.3.
An Officer will be detailed by O.C. "B. Coy to ensure that constant touch is kept with the left flank of the 8th Y & L.

"A" COMPANY.- From left of "B" Coy. to point I.30.d.3.5. getting in touch with 11th S.F.'s.

"C" COMPANY.- will then move forward to IMAGE RESERVE in lines of sections in file and occupy the strength from the extreme right to the left of Battalion Assembly Positions - 2 Platoons in support of "B" Coy: and 2 Platoons in support to "A" Company.

O.C. "A" & "B" Company will, if necessary, call on these platoons for reinforcing. The guides sent back by "A" & "B" Coys for reinforcements will act as guides for the same.
Battalion Headquarters will be informed if these platoons are called for..

(3).

10. (Continued)
The objective having been captured, the following Bombing parties will immediately push forward up communication trenches.

Patrols will be sent out - with Lewis Guns if necessary - to cover our front whilst the consolidation of the captured trench is in progress.

If possible, wiring parties will set to immediately and start wiring along the whole front. It is of the utmost importance that as much wire as possible is pushed out and that the consolidation is carried out with all possible speed, ready for any counter attack that may develop.

If "C" Company is not called upon to reinforce the front line and the situation appears to be clear, 1 platoon at a time may be sent back to our original front line for carrying purposes. The remainder of the Company will be employed in colsilidating their trench, IMAGE RESERVE, and at the same time will be prepared to reinforce the front line in the event of counter attacks.

11. ACTION OF RESERVE COMPANY.
When "A" "B" & "C" Companies have moved out of the tunnel "D" coy will move along and occupy that part of the tunnel to which it is near the WINNIPEG exit (E.6.) and be ready to reinforce any part of the line. They will not move forward until order to do so from Battalion Headquarters.

12. CARRYING PARTY.
The carrying party of 30 Other ranks under 2nd Lieut. Franks will be accomodated in the tunnel in a place to be notified later. They will not move forward until the first objective has been taken and then not until ordered to do so from Battalion Headquarters.
The party will work into section of 1 N.C.O. & 14 men each : 1 section of "A" & "D" Companies.
The following is the order in which stores will be sent forward :-

Bombs	Wire.
S.A.A.	Stakes.
Rifle Grenades.	Pick & Shovels

1. Bombs.   5. Stakes.
2. S.A.A.   6. Picks & Shovels.
3. Rifle Grenades. 7. Sandbags.
4. Wire.   8. Water.
             9. Rations.

The position of the Battalion Dumps will be notified later. In addition there will be ammunition etc, placed along the front line trench which may be collected and carried over.

N.B. 2nd Lieut. Franks will be in charge of this party and NOT 2nd Lieutenant. Nye as stated in Administrative Instructions. Men detailed for carrying parties will wear the yellow band on the left forearm under arrangements to be made by O.C. Companies with the Quartermaster.

4.

13. **DOCUMENTS, MAPS, ETC.**

   No papers, documents, maps, or anything which when captured will be of value to the enemy, will be taken into the attack. O.C. Companies will be held personally responsible that this order is carried out.

14. **ESCORTS TO PRISONERS.**

   1 man to every 10 prisoners is sufficient.

15. **DISCARDING OF ARMS & EQUIPMENT.**

   The discarding of arms or equipment by wounded men will be regarded as a serious military crime unless the wound is sufficiently serious to make the man incapable of carrying

16. **COMMUNICATION.**

   All instructions and details with reference to Inter communication will be issued by the Officer l/c Signals. On arrival from the tunnels all Companies will detail 2 reliable runners to report to Battalion Headquarters in SEBA Tunnel.

SECRET. PLAN OF ATTACK.
8TH. K.O.Y.L.I.

Reference ZILLEBEKE 1/10,000 and attached map.

1. **INTENTION.**
   The 70th Brigade will be Left attacking Brigade of the Xth Corps and will form a defensive left flank facing North, as shewn on attached map.
   There will be a five days bombardment prior to the attack.
   Mines at HILL 60 and the CATERPILLAR will be fired at Zero (time to be notified later).

2. **DISTRIBUTION OF BATTALIONS.**
   The Brigade will attack with two Battalions in the front line and two in support :-
   9th. Y & L. ("A") or Right front attacking Battalion. Headquarters CANADA STREET.
   11th. Sherwood Foresters ("B") or Left Front attacking Battalion. Headquarters HEDGE STREET.
   8th Y & L. ("C") or Right Support Battalion. Headquarters CANADA STREET.
   8th. K.O.Y.L.I. ("D") or Left Support Battalion. Headquarters SEBA DUG-OUT, WINNIPEG STREET.

3. **BRIGADE OBJECTIVES.**
   "A" & "B" Battalions will capture and consolidate the first objective shewn on the map already issued by RED line.
   "C" & "D" Battalions will capture and consolidate the 2nd objective shewn on map already issued by GREEN line.

4. **BRIGADE BOUNDARIES.**
   The dividing line between "A" & "B" Battalions in the first objective is TRENCH JUNCTION I.30.d.25.55.
   The dividing line between "C" & "D" Battalions in 2nd objective will be I.36.b.52.85. in IMAGE CRESCENT.

5. **BATTALION OBJECTIVE.**
   The objective allotted to this Battalion is from point I.36.b.52.85. on the right to point I.30.d.25.55. on the left in IMAGE RESERVE.

6. **DIVIDING LINE BETWEEN COMPANIES.**
   The Dividing line between Coys in the objective is point I.30.d.55.30. Should "B" Coy have to move to the right to keep in touch with the 8th Y & L., "A" Coy will naturally cross the dividing line and touch up with the left of "B" Company.

7. **DISTRIBUTION OF COMPANIES.**
   "B" Company right front line attacking Company.
   "A" Company left   do   do   do
   "C" Company in immediate Support.
   "D" Company Brigade Reserve Company.

8. **ASSEMBLY POSITIONS PRIOR TO THE ASSAULT.**
   Night of W/X - The Battalion will move from "M" Camp. Battalion Headquarters, "A", "B" & "D" Coys to ST. PETERS STREET subways "C" Company to RITZ STREET.
   Night of X/Y - "C" Company will move from RITZ STREET into ST PETERS STREET subways.

   Night of Y/Z - No change.

9. BARRAGE LIFTS & TIME TABLE.

Zero plus 1 :- Barrage lifts off enemy front line and goes back gradually at a rate calculated to allow of an advance of 25 yards a minute to the 1st objective.

Zero plus 2 :- Barrage lifts off furtherest point in 1st objective. The barrage line being a straight one, the barrage will naturally clear the part of the 1st objective which bends back to our own line, earlier than this.

Zero plus 3 hours 40 minutes. :- Barrage commences to move back to second (first) objective.

Zero plus 4 hours 10 minutes. :- Barrage clears furthest point in second objective.

10. PLAN OF ATTACK.

At Zero plus 1 minute "A" & "B" Battalions will attack.

As soon as the front line is clear the whole Battalion will move along the tunnel towards HEDGE STREET.

"B" Company will be responsible for seeing that the front line is fairly clear and for giving the order for the Battalion to file out. "B" Company will file out of the WINNIPEG Exit -E.6.- of the tunnel and move down our front line trench to LIVING TRENCH and will get into touch with the 8th Y & L. "A" Company will follow "B" Company.

"A" & "B" will be ready to support the left Battalion (11th S. Fs) On "A" & "B" leaving our front line "C" Company will file out of the tunnel along the front line to LIVING TRENCH.

At Zero plus 2 hours "B" & "A" Coys will advance in lines of sections in file to their assembly positions in IMAGE RESERVE as under :-

> "B" Company -From I.30.c.80.35. on the right getting in touch with the left flank of the 8th Y & L to point I. 30.d.2.3.

An Officer will be detailed by O.C. "B" Company to ensure that constant touch is kept with the left flank of the 8th Y &L..

> "A" Company -From left of "B" Company to point I.30.d.3.5. getting in touch with 11th S. Fs.
>
> "C" Company -Will then move forward to IMAGE RESERVE in lines of sections in file and occupy the Trench from the extreme right to the left of Battalion Assembly Positions &
> 2 Platoons in "B" Coys. frontage.
> 2 Platoons in "A" Coys frontage.

At Zero plus 3 hours and 40 minutes "B" & "A" Coys closely followed in immediate support by "C" Company will advance and capture the Battalion objective, i.e. from point I.36.b.52.85. on the right to point I.30.d.25.55. on the left in IMAGE RESERVE. The objective having been captured, Bombing parties will immediately push forward up communication trenches.

Patrols will be sent out - with Lewis Guns if necessary to cover our front whilst the consolidation of the captured trench is in progress.

If possible, wiring parties will set to immediately and start wiring along the whole front. It is of the utmost importance that as much wire as possible is pushed out and that the consolidation is carried out with all possible speed, ready for any counter attack that may develop.

/2.

10. PLAN OF ATTACK (continued).

If the situation is clear the senior Officer on the spot will order a carrying party, not exceeding 30 men, to fetch wire, grenades, Ammunition or whatever is considered to be most needed at the moment from the Dumps in our present Front Line.

The capture of the Battalion objective must be immediately reported to Battalion Headquarters, SEBA DUG-OUT by runner in order that the Battalion Carrying Party can be sent up with Ammunition, etc, at the earliest moment.

11. ACTION OF RESERVE COMPANY.

When "A" "B" & "C" Companies have moved out of the tunnel "D" Coy will move along and occupy that part of the tunnel to which is near the WINNIPEG exit (E.6) and be ready to reinforce any part of the line. They will not move forward until ordered to do so by Battalion Headquarters.

12. CARRYING PARTY.

The carrying party of 30 Other Ranks under 2nd Lieutenant. Franks will be accomodated in the tunnel in a place to be notified later. They will not move forward until the first objective has been taken and then not until ordered to do so from Battalion Headquarters.

This party will work in two parties of 1 N.C.O. & 14 men each : one party will carry to "B" Company and one party to "A" Company. The following is the order in which stores will be sent forward:-

1. Bombs.
2. S.A.A.
3. Rifle Grenades.
4. Wire.
5. Stakes.
6. Picks & Shovels.
7. Sandbags.
8. Water.
9. Rations.

The position of the Battalion Dumps have already been notified. In addition their will be ammunition etc, placed along the front line trench which may be collected and carried over.

Men detailed for carrying parties will wear the yellow band on the left forearm.

13. DOCUMENTS, MAPS, ETC.

No papers, documents, maps, or anything excepting as laid down which when captured will be of value to the enemy, will be taken into the attack.

O.C.Companies will be held personally responsible that this order is carried out.

14. ESCORTS TO PRISONERS.

1 man to every 10 prisoners is sufficient.

15. DISCARDING OF ARMS & EQUIPMENT.

The discarding of arms or equipment by wounded men will be regarded as a serious military crime unless the wound is sufficiently serious to make the man incapable of carrying.

16. COMMUNICATION.

All instructions and details with reference to Inter communications will be issued by the Officer I/c Signals.

Lt. Colonel,
Commanding 8th. Bn. K.O.Yorkshire.L.I.

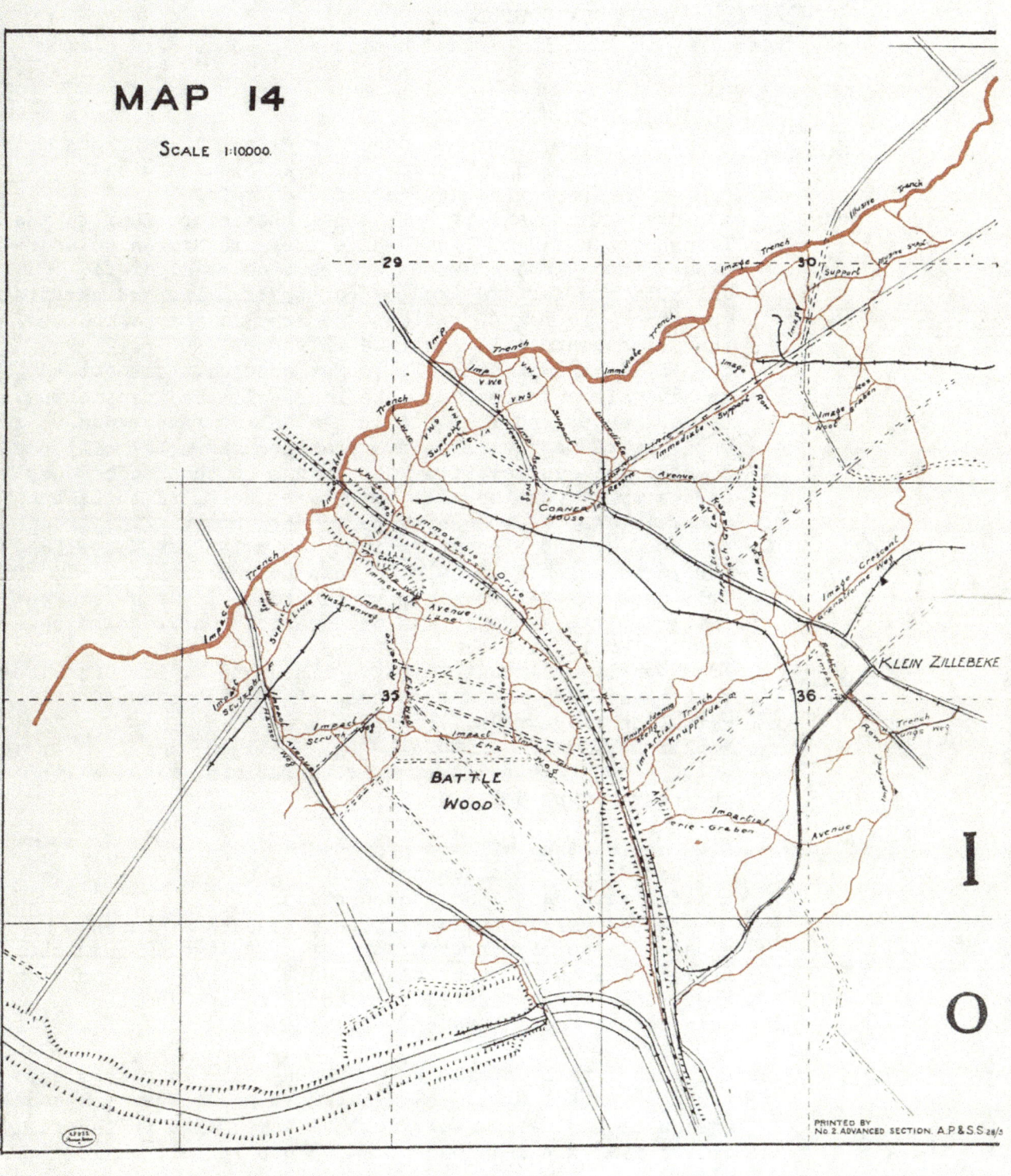

SECRET.   8th. K.O.Y.L.I.   ADMINISTRATIVE INSTRUCTIONS
FOR 2ND. ARMY OFFENSIVE.

1. Disposition of Battalion on various nights.
   (a) W. Day. Camp P., H.13.c.9.5.
   (b) W/X Night. RITZ STREET, and WELLINGTON CRESCENT.
   (c) X/Y Night. TORR TOP.
   (d) Y/Z Night. ASSEMBLY POSITIONS.
   (e) Transport Lines until further notice will be at H.14.c.8.3.

2. SUPPLIES.
   Railhead.- RENINGNHELST SIDING. G.21.a.
   Refilling Point.- Rations will be loaded in detail at Railhead.
                     Trains and platforms must be cleared with 3
                     hours of the arrival of the Train.
   Supplies. are drawn in detail at Railhead. Thence are sent to the
             Transport and wagon lines where they are broken up and
             packed into platoon messes and sent up at night to
             Units in the forward area by carts, tramline and carrying
             parties. In camps, rations are sent to the cookhouses.
             This procedure will continue in force.
             Should it be impracticable to get wheeled transport up to
             the Battalion rendezvous, the loads will be transferred
             to pack mules and taken to the Battalion rendezvous.
             Until extra pack saddles are provided the mules will have
             to make two journeys from the wagons to the rendezvous,
             and carrying parties will have to be detailed to take up
             the remainder of the supplies. When however the troops
             are on P.M. and biscuit rations, 14 mules per Battalion,
             700 strong should be able to take up the rations. In
             this case the ration boxes would probably not be broken
             until arrival at Battalion Headquarters where carrying
             parties would have to meet them.
   Routes.   From Supply Railheads to wagon lines and Transport Lines.
             From wagon and Transport Lines, via YPRES to the
             Battalion rendezvous, viz:-
             VALLEY COTTAGES.   I.33.d.1.5.
             Water arrangements are similar to rations, water carts
             and petrol tins being used.

3. WATER. - A 50 gallon tank will be provided:-
             for Brigade Headquarters.
             for each Battalion Headquarters.
             Two 50 gallon tanks will be placed in a Trench
             alongside the branch tram termini at ARMAGH WOOD which
             will be filled by tanks placed on Tram Trucks. Other
             Tanks and Barrels are to be placed in various places
             between the Front Line and ZILLEBEKE.

             Each Battalion will be provided with 6 carriers each
             taking 4 petrol tins. Two carriers go on the pack saddle
             one on each side. Care must be taken that if the full
             petrol tin is taken away an empty one is left in its
             place.

             Battalions should arrange to improvise funnels so
             as to expedite the filling of the tins, and save wastage
             of water. Arrangements will be made by the Brigade
             as soon as possible to place 670 - 2 gallon Petrol Tins
             in forward dumps.

/over.

3. WATER. (continued)

Location of these and all Tanks and Barrels will be given to Units in due course.

The Petrol tins should be kept as a reserve as long as possible, and not drawn upon unless it is impossible to send for water during the bombardment.

4. RATIONS.- Rations will be drawn normally except for those to be consumed on Y and Z days. For these days complete rations of preserved meat, biscuit, and groceries for all Troops taking part in the Operations, will be drawn by Brigade as soon as possible.

Arrangements are being made by Brigade to send up those for comsumption on Y day to froward dumps, location of which will be duly notified to Units, who will issue them in the Trenches on X/Y night, or Y day.

Rations for comsumption on Z day will be retained by Brigade, and issued in the course of the next week to Units' Transport Lines and will be drawn by the men on W. day and taken up by them in their haversacks.

Personnel in Transport Lines will draw all rations normally.

On Z day rations will be drawn normally for A day and if this is impossible the order may be given by Brigade to use the iron rations on A day.

5. AMMUNITION GRENADE.

Brigade Store will be in MAPLE TRENCH, North of RUDKIN HOUSE. The Brigade will maintain this store, and arrange for forward Dumps, location of which will be duly notified to Companies. These stores must not be used before Z day, excepting the case of great emergency.

When all such stores are completed the Battalion will be responsible for replacing any that are used from the "Brigade Dump".

6. MEDICAL ARRANGEMENTS.

The Regimental Aid Post will be at North end of MAPLE TRENCH where the Aid post of the other three Battalions are situated.

Advanced Dressing Stations.- RAILWAY DUG-OUTS, and ZILLEBEKE BUND.

Evacuations of Stretcher Cases.- By hand carriage from Front Line to Regimental Aid Post MAPLE TRENCH, and thence to Advanced Dressing Station ZILLEBEKE BUND, and thence by Trench Tramway.

Evacuation of Walking Cases.- From Front Line to Regimental Aid Post, MAPLE TRENCH thence via Advanced Dressing Station ZILLEBEKE BUND to Divisional Collecting Station LILLE GATE YPRES.

7. REINFORCEMENTS & FITTING GAS HELMETS.
   1. SITE. The Divisional Reinforcement Camp will remain at ABEELE (CANBERRA CAMP R. 2.b.4.8.)
   2. FITTING GAS HELMETS. Reinforcements on arrival at Railhead will proceed to this Camp where they will be fitted with gas helmets.
   3. GUIDES. Each Inf Bde. 23rd. R.A., 9th.S.Staffs., and A.D.M.S. will maintain a permanent guide at the Camp.

/over.

7. REINFORCEMENTS & FITTING GAS HELMETS. (continued)
   4. NOTICE OF ARRIVAL. Units concerned will be informed of the numbers arriving each day.
   5. BDE. REINFORCEMENT CAMP. Reinforcements will be conducted to the Reinforcement Camps of Bdes. or to transport lines of R.A. R.E. R.A.M.C. and Train Units, under arrangements made by Capt. FRENCH, 1/c Divl. Section Reinforcement Camp.
   6. RATIONS. Reinforcements will be despatched from the Reinforcement Camp with rations for consumption on the day following that on which they joined Bde. Reinforcement Camps.
   7. OFFICERS KITS. G.O.C.'s Bdes. will arrange for transport for conveyance of Officers Kits.

8. ORDNANCE ARRANGEMENTS.
   Trucks with Ordnance Stores will arrive on Supply Train at RENINGHELST SIDING. These are cleared by lorry and the stores sorted at the Ordnance Dump at G.14.b.Central. Units draw their stores from this Dump on the same day and send them up with their rations. Guns and vehicles arriving are removed from Railhead direct by units on notification from D.A.D.O.S.

   Damaged vehicles, field guns, and mortars are taken to Xth Corps Shop near ABEELE. Rifles and Bayonets are also drawn through Armourers Shop.

   Units return unserviceable or surplus stores to the R.O.O. at WIPPONHOEK, where special accommodation is also provided to deal eventually with winter clothing.

   These are the present arrangements which it is not proposed to alter under the scheme.

9. CLEARING THE BATTLEFIELD.
   1 Officer & 30 men per Brigade, will be told off to clear the Battlefield, this Battalion will supply 10 men.
   BURIAL INSTRUCTIONS. Capt H.S.FUSELL, 9th. S.Staffs., has been appointed Corps Burial Officer.
   2nd Lieutenant F.MASON, S.Staffs., has been appointed Divisional Burial Officer, he will be responsible for :-
   (a) Marking the graves.
   (b) Collecting and placing in heaps near a road or tramlines boots, greatcoats, and equipment for salvage.
   (c) Collecting personal effects and custody.

10. TRAFFIC CONTROL POST FURNISHED BY 23RD DIVISION.

No Post.	Men.	LOCALITY AND MAP REFERENCE.	DUTIES.
1.	5.	Road Junction H.13.d.9.2.	Ordinary traffic control.
2.	6.	Road Junction H.14.b.4.8.	Ordinary traffic control. To prevent traffic going east in daylight without a special pass.
3.	5.	Cross roads H.16.d.11.	Ordinary traffic control. To prevent traffic going East in daylight without a special pass.

/over.

10. TRAFFIC CONTROL POST FURNISHED BY 23RD DIVISION. (continued)

No Post.	Men.	LOCALITY AND MAP REFERENCE.	DUTIES.
4.	8.	Road junction H.24.a.9.9.	Ordinary traffic control. To prevent traffic going towards YPRES in daylight with a special pass.
5.	6.	Road junction G.14.d.10.9.	Ordinary traffic control.
6.	4.	RENINGHELST Siding, G.2.a.51.	do.
7.	3.	Road junction G.21.a.6.1.	do.
8.	6.	Cross Roads G.16.c.6.2.	do.
9.	4.	Corps. R.E. Dump. G.21.b.5.5.	do.
10.	6.	SHRAPNEL CORNER I.20.a.6.3.	do.
11.	6.	TRANSPORT FARM. I.21.a.5.3.	do.

NOTES.

1. Traffic control posts furnished by the 47th Division, are located at G.14.c.3.3., G.26.c.4.4., G.24.c.Central., G.32.d.7.3., and by the 24th Division. G.15.b.2.7., G.17.c.6.9. and H.9.a.6.5.

2. Nos. 3 and 4 to split up bodies of troops into parties of not more than three at intervals of 300 yards. And Nos 2,3 & 4 to hold up traffic if there is heavy shelling.

3. No traffic to proceed East of Nos. 3 & 4 in daylight without a special pass signed by the A.P.M.

4. Lamps will be provided by the A.P.M. where necessary in the areas West of the VLAMERTINGHE - OUDERDOM Road.

5. The M.M.P. will patrol both forward and backward areas frequently.

6. CROSS COUNTRY TRACTS. (a) Cross Country Tracts will run from H.13.d.9.2. to H.21.b.8.9.
(b) In 47th Divn. area a trach runs from G.30.b.1.9. to SWAN CHATEAU and DEN GROENEN JAGER CABT.
   As regards (a) The A.P.M. will arrange for these roads to be blocked in wet weather.

7. A Platoon of cyclists will be at the disposal of the A.P.M.

8. A.P.M. will arrange for each post to be provided with 4 days rations.

11. BATTLE TRAFFIC CIRCUITS.

NORTHERN.

Eastwards G.15.c.0.8. - G.15.b.2.6. - BUSSEBOOM G.17.c.6.9. H.8.a.5.3. - H.8.d.7.3. - H.9.a.7.5. - H.16.d.1.3. YPRES - LILLE GATE - SHRAPNEL CORNER - ZILLEBEKE - HELL FIRE CORNER - MENIN GATE - and Westwards by the YPRES - POPERINGHE Roads.

SOUTHERN.

Eastwards G.21.a.6.0. - BUSSEBOOM - G.29.b.5.6. -. H.13.b.1.1. - H.14.b.4.8. - H.16.d.1.2. - CAFE BELGE - VOORMEZEELE. and westwards via CAFE BELGE and DICKEBUSCH.

Traffic on all other roads will follow 2nd Army Traffic Routes. Troops and Traffic may use the road most convenient to them provided the above circuits and traffic routes are adhered to.

/over.

11. BATTLE TRAFFIC CIRCUITS.(continued).

Infantry on the march may use any road in either direction, but the transport must follow the circuit routes.

Motor and Ambulance cars have right of way in either direction on all roads, but should follow traffic circuits as much as possible.

12. ROAD REPAIR.
1. The CAFE - BELGE - ST. ELOI Road is being made into a first class road, and a light railway is being continued from English Wood H.29.d. to VOORMEZEELE.

2. It is intended to repair the track from KRUISSTRAAT to SHRAPNEL CORNER, via Causeway No 14 and to put in an avoiding loop North of SHRAPNEL CORNER ; and also to make a new road from about H. 24.b.1.5. to TROISROIS via Causeway No 16.

13. DRESS.
All ranks taking part in the attack will carry the following:-
1. Steel helmets.
2. Haversack on the back.
3. Waterbottle filled.
4. Entrenching tool.
5. 1 Large Tool on back of every other man, in proportion of 5 shovels to 2 picks, slung on the back by means of twine.
6. Tube Helmet, Box Respirators, Field dressing, 2 sandbags per man tied on the belt.
7. 2 Grenades, in each top pocket of jacket, to be collected by section Commanders, on reaching objective and used to form a reserve.
8. S.A.A. 120 rounds.
9. 2 Flares every third man , one in each bottom pocket.
10 One Iron Ration.
11. One days preserved meat and biscuits.

In addition to the above, each man in Bombing section will carry 12 bombs, 6 in each pouch, either side of the belt.
Each man of the rifle grenade section will carry 12 Hales Rifle Grenades in a bomb bucket, slung over the right shoulder.
Wire cutters, the rate of 48 pairs per Company will be carried these will have a lanyard attached and men carrying same will be marked by white tape on the left shoulder strap.
"A" & "C" Companies will each have 25, M.S.K. lachrymartary Hand Grenades which should be used for throwing into dug-outs.
All Officers must be dressed and equipped same as the men, sticks are not to be carried.

14. CARRYING PARTIES & DUMPS.
2/Lieutenant. Hall and 15 men of "A" "B" & "C" & "D" Companies, will form the Brigade carrying party.
2nd Lieutenant. Priddey will be in charge of ammunition and bombs at the Brigade Store in MAPLE TRENCH, he will see the stores which come up nightly placed in the proper places allotted, and he will be responsible for knowing where everything is.
"B" & "C" Companies will each detail 10 men who will form Battalion carrying party. They will be responsible for ...ving from our original Front Line to the new positions.
...Lieutenant. Nye will supervise the issueing of stores to this

15. The following other ranks will not be taken into the attack.
   In each Company.

   Company Sergeant Major.
   Company Quartermaster Sergeant.
   1 Sergeant.
   1 Corporal.
   1 Lance Corporal.
   4 Rifle Bombers.
   4 Good rifle men.
   8 Lewis Gunners.
   2 Signallers.
   1 Runner.

   In addition to the above :-

   Cpl. Brock, "D" Company.   "Bomber".
   Sgt. Campbell, "C" Company, "Lewis Gunner".
   Lance Cpl. Fawcett, "C" Company. "Lewis Gunner".
   Sgt. Bower, "C" Company.   "Musketry Instructor"
   Sgt. Coupland "A" Company "Musketry & General Instructor".

   Headquarters.

   Regimental Sergeant Major.
   Battalion Gas N.C.O.
   Signalling Corporal.
   2 Signallers.
   2 Runners.

   Officers.

   Major S. D. Rumbold.
   2nd Lieutenant E. V. Bradley.
   2nd Lieutenant I. D. T. Stephens.
   Captain G. F. B. Handley. M.C.
   2nd Lieutenant, G. J. Franks.
   2nd Lieutenant, L. J. T. Polgrean.
   2nd Lieutenant. C. A. Cooke, M.C.
   Lieutenant, J. T. Spalding.
   2nd Lieutenant, Turnell. R.E.
   Lieutenant, J. B. F. Mann.
   Lieutenant, F. Medley.

File

S E C R E T.

Reference - 8th. K. O. Y. L. I.
ADMINISTRATIVE ORDERS

The following alterations will be made :-

For para 4 RATIONS substitute the following:-
(1) Rations will be drawn normally for W - X - & Y days.

(2) Rations for 2 days are already at the Quartermaster
Stores and will be issued on W day and carried on the
man.

(3) Rations for A day will be drawn from the forward
dump in the line.

Reference Para. 6 - The Regimental Aid post for this Battalion
will be at Battalion Headquarters SODA Dug-outs and
not in MAPLE TRENCH.

Reference Para. 11 -
The following will be added :-
(1) Every man will carry a waterproof sheet.
(2) As many very lights and vigilant periscopes as
possible will be carried.

Reference Para. 13 Line 24 - For "A" & "C" Companies read
"B" & "C" Companies.

Reference Para. 16 Line 10 - For 2nd Lieutenant Dye read
2nd Lieutenant Drunk.

Reference Para. 18 - Delete the name of 2nd Lieutenant Drunk.

All ranks taking part in the attack will leave behind
shoulder badges and all papers, etc. likely to give
information to the enemy.
Pay books will be carried

Reference Para. 3 - Delete para (a) and substitute :-
W, Day Coy "A".

Reference Para. 14. - Delete the name of 2nd Lieutenant Hall
as there will not be an Officer required from this
Battalion.

O.C. "D" Company to detail an Officer in the place
of 2nd Lieutenant Wright to keep constant touch with Coy B & A.

2.6.17

To be read in conjunction with Administrative Instructions
for the Attack - 8th K. O. Y. L. I.

SUPPLY.   Dumps in forward areas have been made for S.A.A., Grenades, and
Water as follows :-
   Right forward dump (for use of 'A' and 'C' Bns.) consists of
   slits off CANADA and Living Trenches, gallery entered by saps
   'D' and 'C', and distribution along line (including old Right
   Company's stores).
      S. A. A.   90,000 rounds
      Mills Grenades   3,800
      2 gall. tins drinking water   350
   N.C.O. i/c Sgt. WRIGHT, 11th Sherwood Foresters.

   Left forward dumps (for use of 'B' and 'D' Bns.) consists of
   slits off RUM Tr. and DAVISON LANE, deep dugout in WELLS ST.
   (near Front Line), 'B' drive (entered by E.6) and distribution
   along line (including old left front Company's stores).
      S. A. A.   90,000.
      Mills Grenades   3,800.
      2 gall. tins drinking water   350.
   N.C.O. i/c - L/C ATKIN, 8th York & Lanc. R.

   'A' and 'C' will also have the use of all small stores
   of old right front Company (CANADA) and 'B' and 'D' all small
   stores of old left front Company (WINNIPEG).   The supply
   of 1" Very Lights has been made up to 500 in each case.
   Captain Goldman, 8th K. O. Y. L. I. will supervise both forward
   dumps.

   Brigade Reserve dump consists of slits off MAPLE Tr. with
   subsidiary dumps off ZILLEBEKE St. RUDKIN HOUSE, HALIFAX ST.
      S. A. A.   150,000 rounds.
      Mills Grenades   6,500
      2 gall. tins drinking water   300
      Very Lights 1"   1,000.
         do.   1½"   500.
      Stokes shells,   2,000.
      Ringed cartridges   2,500.
      Green   "   4 Boxes.
      Rifle Grenades No. 23   750.
         do.   24   750.
      P. Bombs,   250.
      Smoke Candles   250.
   Officer i/c - 2/Lt. E. J. Priddey, 8th K. O. Y. L. I.

   The system of supply after Bns. have reached their objectives
   is as follows :-
      They will draw by means of their own carrying parties from
      Right forward Dump and left forward dump respectively.
      The Brigade carrying party under the command of Lieut.
      LONGMUIR, 8th York & Lanc. R. will keep these dumps up to
      strength from Bde. Reserve.   Captain GOLDMAN will
      keep 2/Lt. PRIDDEY advised as to his requirements.

   Flags for denoting dumps, for use in captured system,
   will be issued at once to Bns. as follows :-
      Yellow flags   -   denoting S.A.A. dumps.
      Black flags   -   "   grenade dumps.

It must be clearly impressed upon all ranks that the supply of grenades is strictly limited.

The waste hitherto in offensive operations has been excessive and a scale of allotment has been laid down, which in the opinion of G.H.Q. is more than adequate.

Great difficulty will be experienced in supplying demands during the attack. The Divl. Bomb Store, from which Bde. will have draw when necessary, has only 7,000, with no prospect of increase at present.

DRINKING WATER.
Water will be drawn normally as long as possible. The filled tins mentioned in preceding para must be looked upon as emergency water and should not be drawn upon before 'Z' day, except in case of necessity, and then only by order of an commanding officer.

Water barrels are now in position as below :-
- 1 Brigade Dump ZILLEBEKE.
- 4 VALLEY COTTAGES.
- 1 DORMY HOUSE.
- 2 MAPLE COPSE.
- 2 Regimental Aid Posts MAPLE Tr.

These will not be drawn upon before 'Z' day except in case of absolute need, and then only by order of a Commanding Officer, but they will be drawn upon before the petrol tin supply. A small party has been detailed to keep these barrels filled throughout the operations. Water by pipe is being laid to MAPLE COPSE, and this soruce of supply is nearly ready. Water may also be drawn by pump at DORMY HOUSE. The water from the well in SORREL has not yet been passed by the medical authorities, but it is being examined and in the meantime should be looked upon as a source of supply in great need, and all officers should know exactly where it is.

All ranks should be notified of the fact that the water in the petrol tins may become slightly brown from the rust on the tins, but that this is not harmful.

RATIONS. Rations for "A" day will be drawn on Z/A night from Brigade Dump, OBSERVATORY TR.

REINFORCEMENT CAMP. The Brigade Reinforcement Camp will be at H.13.d.7.8. Captain Carr will be in charge.

Major,
8th Bn. K. O. Yorkshire L. I.

3rd June 1917.

Y.L.I./616.

SECRET.

Headquarters,
8th Bn. K.O. Yorkshire L. I.
3rd June 1917.

To,
O.C. Companies,
8th Bn. K. O. Yorkshire L. I.

Herewith revised Plan of Attack of this Battalion. This cancels the Preliminary Instructions previously issued.

Preliminary Instructions should be destroyed forthwith.

Lt. Colonel,
Commanding 8th Bn. K. O. Yorkshire L. I.

SECRET.

8TH K. O. Y. L. I. ADMINISTRATIVE ORDERS.
(In continuation of Operation Order No. 115)

4th June 1917.

1. All kits for the trenches, dixies, Lewis Guns and 32 Magazines per gun, signalling equipment will be ready on the road in front of the Guard tent by 8 P.M. 1 small box only per Officers' Mess will be carried.

2. All surplus kit will be stacked at the Quartermaster's Stores by 8.30 P.M. Officers' kits will be divided into valises, and surplus kit. The latter will be delivered to the Divisional Surplus Kit Dump, POPERINGHE.

3. 1 Cook per Coy. under L/Cpl. Quirk will proceed to the front line with the Battalion.
All food will come up to the trenches ready cooked. Cooks only duty will be to make tea.

4. Water will be brought to the Dump at VALLEY COTTAGES tonight.

5. There will be a RUM issue before leaving Camp.

6. Lines will be cleaned by 8 P.M.

7. Platoon Commanders will be held personally responsible that every man's water-bottle is filled.

Lieutenant,
Adjutant, 8th Bn. K. O. Yorkshire L. I.

Issued to recipients of O.O. No. 115.

SECRET.   PLAN OF ATTACK.
                           9TH. K.O.Y.L.I.

Reference MILLBEKE 1/10,000 and attached map.

1. INTENTION.
   The 70th Brigade will be left attacking Brigade of the 8th Corps and
will form a defensive left flank facing North, as shown on attached
map.
   There will be a five days bombardment prior to the attack.
   Mines at HILL 60 and the CATERPILLAR will be fired at Zero (time to
be notified later).

2. DISTRIBUTION OF BATTALIONS.
   The Brigade will attack with two Battalions in the front line and
two in support :-
   8th. Y.& L. ("A") or Right front attacking Battalion. Headquarters
CANADA STREET.
   11th. Sherwood Foresters ("B") or Left Front attacking Battalion.
Headquarters HEDGE STREET.
   9th Y.& L. ("C") or Right Support Battalion. Headquarters CANADA
STREET.
   9th. K.O.Y.L.I. ("D") or Left Support Battalion. Headquarters
SHEA DUG-OUT, WINNIPEG STREET.

3. BRIGADE OBJECTIVES.
   "A" & "B" Battalions will capture and consolidate the first
objective shown on the map already issued by RED line.
   "C" & "D" Battalions will capture and consolidate the 2nd objective
shown on map already issued by GREEN line.

4. BRIGADE BOUNDARIES.
   The dividing line between "A" & "B" Battalions in the first objective
is TRENCH JUNCTION I.33.d.35.35.
   The dividing line between "C" & "D" Battalions in 2nd objective will
be I.34.b.52.66. in IMAGE KRESGE CRESCENT.

5. BATTALION OBJECTIVE.
   The objective allotted to this Battalion is from point I.34.b.52.65.
on the right to point I.34.a.25.50. on the left in IMAGE RESERVE.

6. DIVIDING LINE BETWEEN COMPANIES.
   The Dividing line between Coys in the objective is point I.34.c.95.34.
Should "B" Coy have to move to the right to keep in touch with the
8th Y.& L., "A" Coy will naturally cross the dividing line and touch
up with the left of "B" Company.

7. DISTRIBUTION OF COMPANIES.
   "B" Company Right front line attacking Company.
   "A" Company Left   do   do   do
   "C" Company in Immediate Support.
   "D" Company Brigade Reserve Company.

8. ASSEMBLY POSITIONS PRIOR TO THE ASSAULT.
   Night of W/X - The Battalion will move from "B" Camp.
   Battalion Headquarters, "A", "B" & "D" Coys to ST.PETERS STREET subway
   "C" Company to HYDE STREET.
   Night of X/Y - "C" Company will move from HYDE STREET into ST PETERS
   STREET subways.

   Night of Y/Z - No change.

9. BARRAGE LIFTS & TIME TABLE.

Zero plus 1 :- Barrage lifts off enemy front line and goes back gradually at a rate calculated to allow of an advance of 25 yards a minute to the 1st objective.

Zero plus 2 :- Barrage lifts off furthermost point in 1st objective. The barrage line being a straight one, the barrage will naturally clear the part of the 1st objective which bends back to our own line, earlier than this.

Zero plus 3 hours 40 minutes :- Barrage commences to move back to second (first) objective.

Zero plus 4 hours 10 minutes :- Barrage clears furthest point in second objective.

10. PLAN OF ATTACK.

At Zero plus 1 minute "A" & "B" Battalions will attack.

As soon as the front line is clear the whole Battalion will move along the tunnel towards HEDGE STREET.

"B" Company will be responsible for seeing that the front line is fairly clear and for giving the order for the Battalion to file out. "B" Company will file out of the WINNIPEG Exit - N.E. - of the tunnel and move down our front line trench to LIVING TRENCH and will get into touch with the 8th Y & L. "A" Company will follow "B" Company.

"A" & "B" will be ready to support the left Battalion (11th S.Fs) On "A" & "B" leaving our front line "C" Company will ~~advance immediately~~ file out of the tunnel along the front line to LIVING TRENCH.

At Zero plus 2 hours "B" & "A" Coys will advance in lines of sections in file to their assembly positions in IMAGE RESERVE as under :-

"B" Company - From I.30.c.80.85. on the right getting in touch with the left flank of the 8th Y & L. to point I. 30. d. 3. 5.

An Officer will be detailed by O.C. "B" Company to ensure that constant touch is kept with the left flank of the 8th Y & L.

"A" Company - From left of "B" Company to point I.30. d. 3. 5. getting in touch with 11th S.Fs.

"C" Company - Will then move forward to IMAGE RESERVE in lines of sections in file and occupy the Trench from the extreme right to the left of Battalion Assembly Positions &
2 Platoons in "B" Coys. frontage.
2 Platoons in "A" Coys frontage.

At Zero plus 3 hours and 40 minutes "B" & "A" Coys closely followed in immediate support by "C" Company will advance and capture the Battalion objective, i.e. from point I.36.b.52.65. on the right to point I.30.d.25.55. on the left in IMAGE RESERVE. The objective having been captured, Bombing parties will immediately push forward up communication trenches.

~~Reconnoitre~~

Patrols will be sent out - with Lewis Guns if necessary to cover our front whilst the consolidation of the captured trench is in progress.

If possible, wiring parties will set to immediately and start wiring along the whole front. It is of the utmost importance that as much wire as possible is pushed out and that the consolidation is carried out with all possible speed, ready for any counter attack that may develop.

/2.

10. **PLAN OF ATTACK** (continued).

If the situation is clear the senior Officer on the spot will order a carrying party, not exceeding 30 men, to fetch wire, grenades, Ammunition or whatever is considered to be most needed at the moment from the Dumps in our present Front Line.

The capture of the Battalion objective must be immediately reported to Battalion Headquarters, SEBA DUG-OUT by runner in order that the Battalion Carrying Party can be sent up with Ammunition, etc, at the earliest moment.

11. **ACTION OF RESERVE COMPANY.**

When "A" "B" & "C" Companies have moved out of the tunnel "D" Coy will move along and occupy that part of the tunnel to which is near the WINNIPEG exit (E.6) and be ready to reinforce any part of the line. They will not move forward until ordered to do so by Battalion Headquarters.

12. **CARRYING PARTY.**

The carrying party of 30 Other Ranks under 2nd Lieutenant. Pranks will be accommodated in the tunnel in a place to be notified later. They will not move forward until the first objective has been taken and then not until ordered to do so from Battalion Headquarters.

This party will work in two parties of 1 N.C.O. & 14 men each : one party will carry to "B" Company and one party to "A" Company. The following is the order in which stores will be sent forward:-

1. Bombs.   5 Stakes.
2. S.A.A.   6. Picks & Shovels.
3. Rifle Grenades.   7 Sandbags.
4. Wire.   8. Water.
                         9 Rations.

The position of the Battalion Dumps have already been notified. In addition their will be ammunition etc, placed along the front line trench which may be collected and carried over.
Men detailed for carrying parties will wear the yellow band on the left forearm.

13. **DOCUMENTS, MAPS, ETC.**

No papers, documents, maps, or anything excepting as laid down which when captured will be of value to the enemy, will be taken into the attack.
O.C. Companies will be held personally responsible that this order is carried out.

14. **ESCORTS TO PRISONERS.**

1 man to every 10 prisoners is sufficient.

15. **DISCARDING OF ARMS & EQUIPMENT.**

The discarding of arms or equipment by wounded men will be regarded as a serious military crime unless the wound is sufficiently serious to make the man incapable of carrying.

16. **COMMUNICATION.**

All instructions and details with reference to Inter communications will be issued by the Officer I/c Signals.

D. Quirk Lt. Colonel,
Commanding 8th. Bn. K.O. Yorkshire.L.I.

Army Form C. 2118.

WAR DIARY

4th Bn. K.O. Yorks L.I.

INTELLIGENCE SUMMARY

(Erase heading not required.)

Instructions regarding War Diaries and Intelligence Summaries are contained in F. S. Regs., Part II. and the Staff Manual respectively. Title pages will be prepared in manuscript.

Place	Date	Hour	Summary of Events and Information	Remarks and references to Appendices
Trenches	1.7.17		Bn in Brigade Support. (Hill 60 Sector) Left Bgde Support & moved into Front Line relieving 8th York & Lancaster Regt.	
"	2.7.17		Battalion in Front Line trenches.	
"	3.7.17		Bn in Front Line trenches. Draft 21 O.Rks. joined for duty.	
"	4.7.17		Bn in Front Line trenches. Lieut H.G. Houlden joined for duty.	
"	5.7.17		Bn in Front Line trenches. Relieved on night of 5th & 6th June by 13th Bn D.L.I. and proceeded by march route to Micmac Camp (Hubertushoek area).	
Micmac Camp	6.7.17		Bn in Camp. Interior Economy & clearing up.	
"	7.7.17		Bn in Camp. Draft of 21 O.R. joined for duty. Bathing & Entrainment.	
"	8.7.17		Church Parades. Major S.D. Rumbold K.C. Yorks Bn to command 9th York & Lancaster Regt.	
"	9.7.17		Battalion route march & drill order.	
"	10.7.17		Companies in Physical Training, Arms Drill, Squad Drill & Bayonet fighting.	
"	11.7.17		Companies in Physical Training, Musketry, Arms Drill & Squad Drill.	
Steenvoorde	12.7.17		Battalion left Micmac Camp En-trained at Godewaersvelde detrained Steenvoorde and marched to billets in Steenvoorde vicinity arriving about 7.30 p.m.	

Army Form C. 2118.

WAR DIARY
INTELLIGENCE SUMMARY

5th Bn K.O. Yorks L.I.

Instructions regarding War Diaries and Intelligence Summaries are contained in F.S. Regs., Part II. and the Staff Manual respectively. Title pages will be prepared in manuscript.

(Erase heading not required.)

Place	Date	Hour	Summary of Events and Information	Remarks and references to Appendices
Bois Blommerel	13.7.17.		Bn in billets cleaning up billets & equipment	A/R
"	14.7.17.		Companies in Arms Drill, Squad drill & Platoon drill. Specialers in usual C. Gunners Section Etc. Catechie Acrio under M.O. 2 Lieut R J Fawcett joined for duty.	B/R
"	15.7.17.		Church Parade.	C/R
"	16.7.17.		Battalion route march in drill order.	D/R
"	17.7.17.		Close order drill, musketry, Bayonet fighting etc. Officers Commanders & officers proceeded by march route to billets in hilsen	E/R
"	18.7.17.		Left Billets at 2pm & proceeded by march route to billets in hilsen area arriving about 5 p.m. 1 officer + 60 O.R. to 11 Corps School to parade Battalion.	F/R
Hilsen Wieltze	19.7.17.		Bn in billets near hilsen. Interior economy & general cleaning up. 2 Lieuts. R.B. Bracklehurst H.A. Meggett & J. Downer joined for duty.	G/R
"	20.7.17.		G.O.C. Brigade inspected Battn. Runners & Scouts Lewis Gunners on coup. Specialists under Specialist officers. Coy's practice use of Yukon packs.	H/R
"	21.7.17.		Companies practice in employing in the attack. Lewis gun squads practice.	I/R
"	22.7.17.		Church Parade. Battn. M. safai wend	J/R
"	23.7.17.		Battalion & transport inspected by G.O.C. 23rd Divisions	K/R

E Rudder Lieut Colonel
Commanding 5th K.O.Y.L.I

Army Form C. 2118.

WAR DIARY
INTELLIGENCE SUMMARY
(Erase heading not required.)

Place	Date	Hour	Summary of Events and Information	Remarks and references to Appendices
Mar Whinne	24.7.17		Companies on Bullet & Bayonet Fighting Ground. Bomb throwing & Squad drill.	11. O.R. joined
"	25.7.17		Companies on Range. Fire direction control & inoculation of Tayoli.	
"	26.7.17		Battalion route march. Full kit.	
"	27.7.17		Platoons in deploying in artillery formation. Companies on Range.	
"	28.7.17		Coys in Saluting Drill. Guard Mount. General smartening. Bullet & Bayonet	
"	29.7.17		Church Parade.	
"	30.7.17		Battalion on range. Lewis Gunners on range. Men in triggers pressing Running Men.	
"	31.7.17		Range. Specialists under Specialist Officers. Bomb throwing.	

Casualties for month:-
Officers - Nil.
O.R.
Killed 1.
Missing 1.
Wounded 3.

WAR DIARY or INTELLIGENCE SUMMARY.

Army Form C. 2118.

8th K.O.Y.L.I.

Vol 24

Place	Date	Hour	Summary of Events and Information	Remarks and references to Appendices
METEREN	1.8.17		Battalion in Billets. Conferences on Billets & Bayonet fighting grounds. Musketry. Aiming Drill &c.	S.J.P.
"	2.8.17		Scouts on Range. Companies at disposal of Coy Commanders. Report Lt C. Bayne D.S.O. joined.	S.J.P.
"	3.8.17		Batt. Route March. Specialists under specialist Officers.	S.J.P.
"	4.8.17		Route March by Companies. Lecture to all Platoon Commanders by Lewis Gun Officer 2.30	S.J.P.
"	5.8.17		Church Parades. Kits & Gaiters inspection by M.O.	S.J.P.
"	6.8.17		Battalion Route March to Caestre entrained 6pm for Arques. House March & Caestre entrained 6pm detrained at 8pm. Batt in Billets in Arques 9pm	S.J.P.
ARQUES	7.8.17		Battalion proceeded to Bouveligham by March route through Wattinghem. Billets at Bouveligham 7.30pm	S.J.P.
Bouveligham	8.8.17		Outdoor Dinner & tea on line of March. Batt in Billets Conferences of Coy Commanders to Strangy &c	S.J.P.
"	9.8.17		Batt proceeded to Bayenghem-les-Eperlecques. Route Petit Quercamp. Quercamp. Moringhem. Northbecourt. Batt in billets at Bayenghem 12.30pm	S.J.P.
Bayenghem	10.8.17		Battalion proceeded to Swinering Camp St Jans Ter Biezen. March from Bayenghem 6.30 am. Camp 7.30 am. 12 min/KR Division proved Lieut Hopson joins & Lieut C.J. Preddy Lewis & M.O. joins &c	S.J.P. B.J.O.

Army Form C. 2118.

WAR DIARY
or
INTELLIGENCE SUMMARY.

(Erase heading not required.)

Instructions regarding War Diaries and Intelligence
Summaries are contained in F. S. Regs., Part II.
and the Staff Manual respectively. Title pages
will be prepared in manuscript.

Place	Date	Hour	Summary of Events and Information	Remarks and references to Appendices
Annolliers Camp	11.5.17		Companies at disposal of O.C. Companies for clearing up hut inspections	E.J.P.
"	12.6.17		Church Parades	E.J.P.
"	13.5.17		Companies in Rapid loading. Bayonet fighting the Specialists under their own officers	S.J.P.
"	14.5.17		"A" Coy paraded to Brandock for both under Heavy Artillery. B. C. & D Coys in intensive digging by platoons. Baths in afternoon. Lecture by Corps. (K.V.W.) Commandant to all Company Commanders at 4.15 pm	E.J.P.
"	15.5.17		Platoons in 1 hour intensive digging. Specialists under their own officers & after A.Cos view model of country over which Battn is likely to work.	S.J.P.
"	16.5.17		Platoons in intensive digging. Baths.	E.J.P.
"	17.5.17		Company Training. Specialists under their own officers	N.O.R. Jour for duty H Coy Estamo S.J.P
"	18.5.17		"A" Coy at disposal of O.C. Coy. B.C. & D Coys route march by companies. Sub marmer	E.J.P.
"	19.5.17		Church Parades with Q.V.L.	E.J.P.
"	20.5.17		Companies in musketry. digging. Loper Extension into Artillery formation A&B in light order	S.J.P.
"	21.5.17		Companies on musketry range. Extensions in taking Lading fire coering tearlers.	Cr.D. Hiseful took S.J.P.
"	22.5.17		Route march by Companies. Signalling & R.Emoners parade. Delivery	S.J.P.

E.J. Buadey Lieut
A.G.O. 5th K.O. Yorks L.I.

WAR DIARY
INTELLIGENCE SUMMARY
(Erase heading not required.)

Army Form C. 2118.

Place	Date	Hour	Summary of Events and Information	Remarks and references to Appendices
Bruillies Camp	23.8.17		Battalion travelled camp for Dominion Camp by route march arriv[ed] 11. A.m.	E.J.P.
Dominion Cp	24.8.17		Conference at disposal of Company Commander	E.J.P.
"	25.8.17		Batt. leaves Dominion Camp proceeds by Motor Bus to Dickebusch marches by Platoons to Halfway House. Zillebeke Trench Map 1.17.c.4.8.	E.J.P
Field a/c	26.8.17		Batt in Bgde Reserve at Halfway House	E.J.P.
"	27.8.17		Batt. leaves Halfway House for Front line. B&D coys forward trench from J.C.4.1.16. J.14.A.3.2. "C" Coy in support Tunnels at J.13.D.85.80. (Zillebeke) B.HQ at J.13.D.85.80. J.13.A.9.3.	E.J.P.
"	28.8.17		"A" Coy Reserve at J.13.A.9.3. Battalion in front line trenches.	E.J.P.
"	29.8.17		Battalion in Front Line trenches	E.J.P.
"	30.8.17		Batt. in front line Relieved night 30/31 by. 8th K.L. Regt & 10th Chesire Rgt. L.29. L.1.5. (Sheet 2) J.E.	E.J.P.
"	31.8.17		Proceeded to Patricia Lines. Bat in Patricia Lines. General Cleaning up.	E.J.P.
			Casualties for month	
			Officers wounded 1	
			O.R. killed 15. wounded 40.	

E.J. Priestley Lieut
1/B.1.O.
Pr. K.O. Yorks L.I.

WAR DIARY
or
INTELLIGENCE SUMMARY.
(Erase heading not required.)

Army Form C. 2118.

1st K.O. Yorks L.I.

Place	Date	Hour	Summary of Events and Information	Remarks and references to Appendices
PATRICK LINES	1.9.17		Battalion cleaning up. Clothing inspections & inspection of Repellingfront	E.J.P.
"	2.9.17		Shot 27 N.W. A.34. C.H.D.	E.J.P.
"	3.9.17		Battalion proceeded to Bugscheure. Companies and transport to Bugscheure in billets at 7 pm. Repelling front Shot 27. K.32. T.3.7. guns 2th 13 pm	E.J.P.
BUGSCHEURE	4.9.17		Companies at disposal of Company Commanders for arms drill & smartening up.	E.J.P.
"	5.9.17		Companies in attack. Raised Rifleman Sgt. W.C.O's and Cpl R.S. &c.	E.J.P.
"			Officers Reconnaissance front line under Capt Nye M.C.	E.J.P.
"	6.9.17		Companies in new formation for attack, preparing front line under Capt Nye M.C.	E.J.P.
"			Officers visited Bulford Brigade School Lewis guns. officers visited Capt Nye M.C.	E.J.P.
"	7.9.17		Company training. Company Commanders from Reserve to Captured objective, visiting of	E.J.P.
"			Light spinners. Captured ground marred. Both of wounded by Archie.	E.J.P.
"	8.9.17		Battalion training. Both of 51 O.R. Joined	E.J.P.
"	9.9.17		Church Parade Being Inspection	E.J. Preedy Lieut 1.O. 1st K.O.Y.L.I. 21 Sept

Army Form C. 2118.

WAR DIARY
or
INTELLIGENCE SUMMARY.
(Erase heading not required.)

8th K.O. Yorks. L.I.

Place	Date	Hour	Summary of Events and Information	Remarks and references to Appendices
BUSSEBOOM	10.9.17		Brigade Field day. 8 KOYLI & 8th Yorks. attacked in new formations & retired from lines. The Sherwood Foresters & 9th Yorks. retained old new formations & attacked objective on similar purpose to meet counter attack.	S.A.P.
"	11.9.17		Battalion field day. Recovery on capture objectives and of forging attack. New objective & trenches of reverse attacked.	L.A.P.
"	12.9.17		Officers scheme for ZILLEBEKE area. Supervised route to billets in WIPPERS CHURCH and marched from General Sir Arthur Sloggett. Bn. here to RATTONLIEU. Army point out 27 R. 32 a. 7.	2 S.P.
WALKER CAMP	13.9.17		Battalion left billets at RATTONLIEU CAMP & proceeded by march route to CRITERION crossing in billets at 5 p.m. A. 35. d 2.8	
	14.9.17		Bn. C/O Stewart II at 6 p.m. proceeded by march route to DICKEBUSCH area. Bn. moved bivouacs at noon. Inspection of Gen. Ross Raumsford Comdg. 3rd Battalion	6 A.P.
TOLSON	15.9.17		Bn. proceeded to Railway Dugouts and relieved 12 Loyal North Lancs. 60th Battalion	
			Rifle Brigade incoming. Reserve battalion of the Brigade	L.A.P.
		9.25	Working Parties. 2 Lieut Keep wounded. Inbound wounded at summer of today	S.A.P.

E.J. Priddey Lieut K.O.Y.L.I.

WAR DIARY
or
INTELLIGENCE SUMMARY.

Army Form C. 2118.

(Erase heading not required.)

S.K.O. Yorks L.I.

Place	Date	Hour	Summary of Events and Information	Remarks and references to Appendices
Trenches	19.9.17		Plan of Railway Dugouts left vacant by ourselves and "B" & "D" Coys. previous to Bombardment. "A" Coy front line trenches & "C" Coy took up Guards. Bombing "B" Bn. of Brigade. 2nd Lieut. Knott & 10 O.R. joined Bn.	E/P
	20.9.17		B. Bn. now relieved by 11 Northumberland Fusiliers and proceeds to Huskoe Camp.	E/P
Huskoe Camp	19.9.17		Both Coys. who had been out of action reported. Were in platoon formation & were out of gates from time to time. Reconnaissance of "C" Battalion of the Brigade.	
Trenches	20.9.17		Battalion relieved 9 Yorks Regt and took up and B. Coy threw forward positions. Bath took Top Area & threw forward position South Hessian Row.	E/P
	21.9.17		Bath took Top Area. B. Coy threw forward position South Hessian Row.	E/P
	22.9.17		Bath took trench from Top for front line and Reach a relieving Bn. shorter. King's Infantry Regt. Mnr. A Knott & C. Pease were wounded.	E/P
Trenches	23.9.17		Battalion in front line trenches. 2nd Lt. Bison Stewart joined.	E/P
	24.9.17		Bath on Front line trenches relieved by 1st Division & 4 Seaforth Regt & proceeded to Chippewa Camp. Capt Cribbs R.A.M.C. joined for duty.	E/P

E.J. Pudding Lieut.
O/C 5 R O Yorks L.I.

WAR DIARY
or
INTELLIGENCE SUMMARY.

Army Form C. 2118.

(Erase heading not required.)

Instructions regarding War Diaries and Intelligence Summaries are contained in F. S. Regs., Part II. and the Staff Manual respectively. Title pages will be prepared in manuscript.

8 K.O. Yorks L.I.

Place	Date	Hour	Summary of Events and Information	Remarks and references to Appendices
Clifton Camp	25.9.17		Conference at about of O.C. Company Commanding Officers completed. Tools & Rivers & Sketched forms	E.J.R.
	26.9.17		Conference in Barracks was still going on all the	
			Battalion was engaged by Divisional Commander 2.30 p.m.	E.J.R
Havre	27.9.17		Battalion leaves Camp & proceeds by train to Roye & arrived 9 p.m.	
			Belonging to Infantry platoon on leaving positions of the 100th Brigade and	
	28		accompany Right Column of 99th Brigade. "C" Coy disposed	
			two platoons having cover by two sections at head & two sections	
			of "B" Coy later with two platoons "A" & two "D" Coy as Right Rear	
			(6 C of S) Support Coy. Two platoons "D" Coy & 130 18.15. - about Right C	
			10 p.m. & 9 p.m. Two platoons "D" Coy 2ft 14 Support would	
			Battalion in line trenches. had Divisional lights	E.J.R.
	28.9.17		Battalion relieved in front line trenches by the Bedford Group Bria	
	29.9.17		Lancashires Rifle & proceeded to Bedford House Area	

E.J. Friday Lt & K.O.Y.L.I.

S E C R E T.   23rd Division S.G. 62/16/2.

X Corps.

Herewith copies of patrol reports.

[signature]
f. Major-General,

30/9/17.   Commanding 23rd Division.

PATROL REPORT.

Unit.	Strength of Patrol.	Time and Date.	Objective of Task	Remarks and Information.
11th Sherwood Foresters. 'C' Company.	1 officer 4 O.Rs.	11.25 p.m. Sept. 28th/17	Examine ground in front and if possible gt in touch with enemy.	The patrol left our line at J.15.d.5-8. and worked round in front of the marshy ground. Small parties of the enemy were seen going to and from CHATEAU from J.16.c.central. No other trace of the enemy was seen.
'A' Company.	1 officer 3 O.Rs.	11.30 p.m. Sept. 28th.	do	The patrol left our line at J.15.d.5.1. and proceeded towards the enemy. The ground was in good condition. No enemy were encountered. Several of our wounded left by the last Regiment were brought in.

(sd) C.E. HUDSON, Major,
Commanding 11th Sherwood Foresters.

September, 1917.

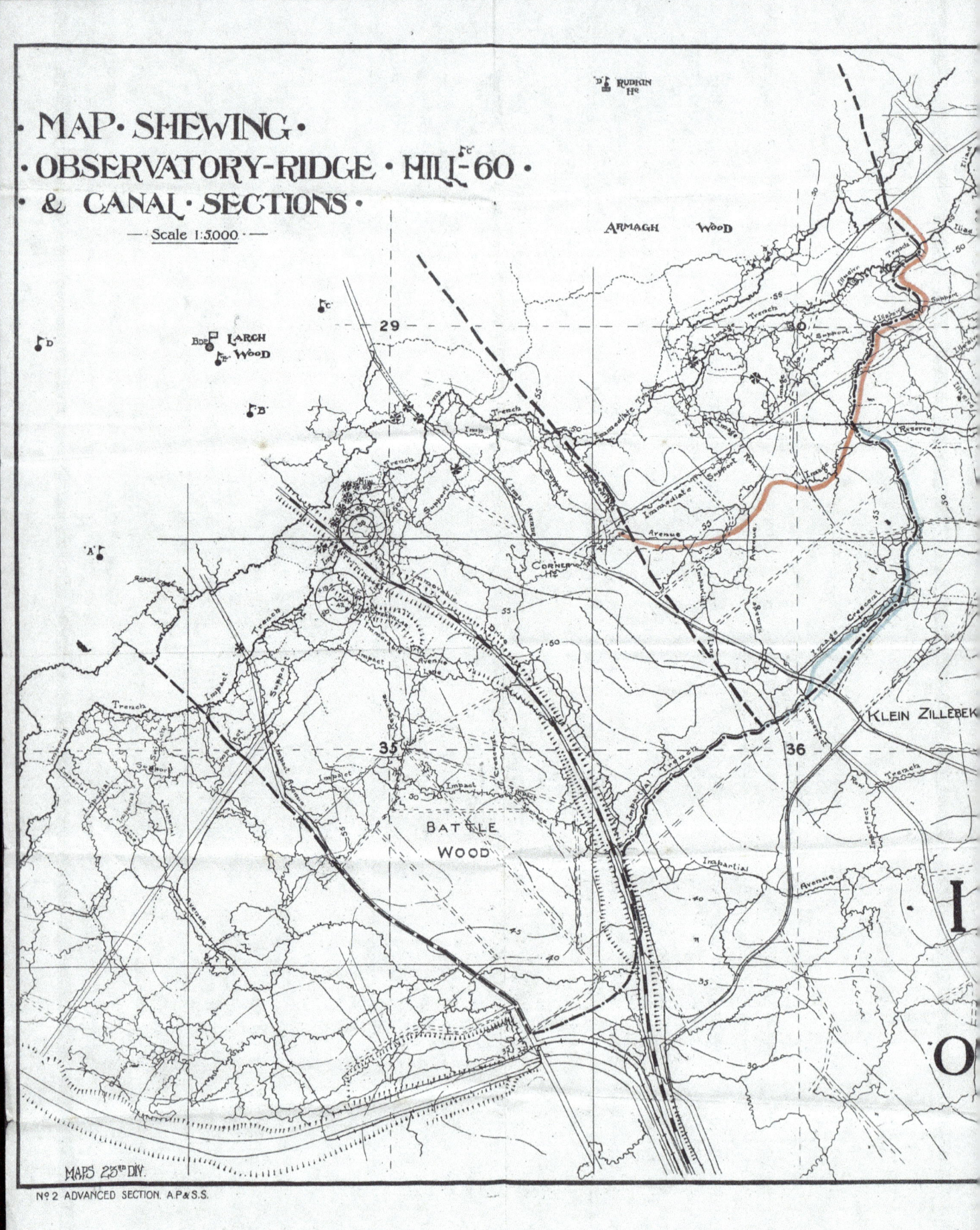

Nº 9.   MESSAGE MAP. Trenches &c. corrected to 10-9-17.

Scale. 1:10,000.

Yds. 500 400 300 200 100 0   500   1000 Yds.

Printed by Nº 2 Advanced Section, A.P. & S.S.

MESSAGE FORM.

To :—　　　　　　　　　　　　　　　　　　　　　　No.

1. I am at........................... {Note :—Either give Map Reference or mark your position by a 'X' on the Map on back.

2. I have reached limits of my Objective.

3. My Platoon / Company is at.............................and is consolidating.

4. My Platoon / Company is at.............................and has consolidated.

5. Am held up by (a) M.G (b) Wire at.....................(Place where you are).

6. Enemy holding strong point............,....

7. I am in touch with.....................on Right / Left at...........

8. I am not in touch with.....................on Right / Left.

9. Am shelled from....................

10. Am in need of :—

11. Counter Attack forming at................

12. Hostile (a) Battery
    　　　(b) Machine Gun　active at........................
    　　　(c) Trench Mortar

13. Reinforcements wanted at ....

14. I estimate my present strength at...........rifles.

15. Add any other useful information here :—

　　　　　　　　　　　　　　　　　　Name..............................
　　　　　　　　　　　　　　　　　　Platoon............................
Time...............m.　　　　　　　Company..........................
Date.............1917.　　　　　　Battalion.........................

　　(A). Carry no maps or papers which may be of value to the Enemy.

　　(B). Give no information if captured, except the following, which you are bound to give :—

　　　　　Name and Rank.

　　(C). Collect all captured maps and papers and send them in at once.

MESSAGE FORM.

To :—   No.

1. I am at.............................. (Note :—Either give Map Reference or mark your position by a 'X' on the Map on back.

2. I have reached limits of my Objective.

3. My Platoon / Company is at........................and is consolidating.

4. My Platoon / Company is at........................and has consolidated.

5. Am held up by (a) M.G / (b) Wire at.....................(Place where you are).

6. Enemy holding strong point................

7. I am in touch with..........................on Right / Left. at............

8. I am not in touch with........................on Right / Left.

9. Am shelled from....................

10. Am in need of :—

11. Counter Attack forming at................

12. Hostile (a) Battery
            (b) Machine Gun   active at........................
            (c) Trench Mortar

13. Reinforcements wanted at..

14. I estimate my present strength at.......... rifles.

15. Add any other useful information here :—

Name.............................

Platoon...........................

Time.............m.   Company.........................

Date............1917.   Battalion........................

(A). Carry no maps or papers which may be of value to the Enemy.

(B). Give no information if captured, except the following, which you are bound to give :—

   Name and Rank.

(C). Collect all captured maps and papers and send them in at once.

C O P Y.

To:- O.C. CAVE.

Patrol Report.

Strength. 1 Officer and 10 Other Ranks.

Objective of Patrol. To reconnoitre Company front and capture a prisonerz

Time of starting. 1.15 a.m.

Remarks. This patrol should have started at 11. p.m. but owing to the S.O.S. going up on our left and gas they started at 1.15 a.m.
They left the front line at J.21.b.50.45. by C.T. and proceeded along C.T. entering trench at J.21.b.60.40. at 'S' in JACKSON TRENCH. This trench was seen to be held early in the evening by lights which were put all along the front. They proceeded 30 or 40 yards along trench and met nobody. The C.T. running towards the two dugouts could not be found and owing to the light the patrol returned by the same route at 2.45 a.m.
Our artillery was firing in front of JACKSON TRENCH about 50 yards, some shells falling short and some in.

9 a.m.   (sd) E.V. BRADLEY, Capt.,
29/9/17.   O.C. 'C' Coy. CAVE.

S.K.ay. L.I

C O P Y.

Report of patrol on the night 28th/29th September.

Owing to S.O.S. and gas I was unable to go out until 1.15 a.m No prisoner was obtained. I found the junction of COMMUNICATION TRENCH at the 'S' in JACKSON TRENCH but no enemy. The trench from this point running parallel to our own was only occupied by a few enemy firing Very lights. The light being rather strong prevented more extensive patrol.

(sd) L. PEBODY, 2/Lieut.

Army Form C. 2118.

WAR DIARY
or
INTELLIGENCE SUMMARY.
(Erase heading not required.)

Instructions regarding War Diaries and Intelligence Summaries are contained in F. S. Regs., Part II. and the Staff Manual respectively. Title pages will be prepared in manuscript.

Place	Date	Hour	Summary of Events and Information	Remarks and references to Appendices
BEDFORD	1.10.17	—	Batt. shown in dug outs in Bedford House — moved at 3pm to Camp No 3	
HOOGE			Pilot wood area. Rifles & pouches Remainder	6/8
RIDGE WOOD	2.10.17		Bat moved from Ridge wood to Busseboom	6/8
NEUREN	3.10.17		Conferences at Dugout of Company Commanders for General Clements at 10am	6/8
			Refitting Rout.	
	4.10.17		Batt. worked at trenches & foregone by various working parties to outside stations	6/8
			entrenching tools & returning near YPRES, no accommodation over 12 in 3rd 9th	
YPRES	5.10.17		Batt in Camp shewn up at Camp etc Returned to Megae. Camp	6/8
	6.10.17		Batt in Camp near YPRES, working parties sent 9 C.R.T. P. laying.	6/9
			2 to Camp in Test Area etc.	
	7.10.17		Batt in Camp worked on R.E. Railways etc. 2 to C.R.T.	6/8
	8.10.17		Batt in Camp work as before, continued raining much	6/8
	9.10.17		Batt. in Camp on WHITE CHATEAU Railway & fatigues, rain 2 C.R.T work of platoon	6/8
			Lts ... to C. Reid & to Jenner joined with 4 other Ranks	6/8
	10.10.17		Batt. in Camp. Work on L.R.I. Railway to R.E. & Cutting building	6/8?
	10.10.17		Batt in Camp of Post fatigues broaden to horseshoe & to Camp wood.	

Army Form C. 2118.

WAR DIARY
or
INTELLIGENCE SUMMARY.
(Erase heading not required.)

S/N R.O. Jones R.E.

Instructions regarding War Diaries and Intelligence
Summaries are contained in F. S. Regs., Part II.
and the Staff Manual respectively. Title pages
will be prepared in manuscript.

Place	Date	Hour	Summary of Events and Information	Remarks and references to Appendices
Scottish Wood	12.10.17		Battalion in Camp. Conference of Officers. Note Coys for supply [?]	
			Interior economy. Battalion w.H. by Troops. Return [?]	
	13.10.17		Conference of Officers. Confn [?] Cmdrs [?]	S.P.
Ypres	14.10.17		Battalion left Camp & Billeted at [?] on Support	
			B.H.Q. Café in Dugouts E.20.f. Polygon Wood. B & C Coys in [?]	
			at [?] [?] to be provided to Rein [?] Coy. [?]	S.P.
	15.10 [?]		Battalion Supplied working parties from line [?]	
			"A" Coy 4 platoons to B.C. Leftsht [?], 1 "B"Coy Supplied 4"C"Coy [?]	
			Supplied 4. Two fort Sidings. Reserves.	
	16.10.17		Battalion in fact time provides [?] OM. D. Bentry & Lieut Coates [?]	
			Joined [?] From two Tunnels	
	17.10.17		About fort by Tunnels. Returned about fort by Ry of Scottish Wood via [?]	
			was moved to provide men. Railway [?] "C" Coy became in effort.	
Scottish Wood [?]	18.10.17		Bat left Railway Dugouts & moved to Camp at Scottish Wood. Coy [?]	
			After rolls were [?] their [?]	S.P.
Scottish Wood	20.10.17		Batt Left Scottish Wood & proceeded by hard route & Knightsgaat Embassy	
			& [?] to Esquenes VES [?] at 7P.M. Esquerdes [?]	S.P.

WAR DIARY
or
INTELLIGENCE SUMMARY.

Army Form C. 2118.

Place	Date	Hour	Summary of Events and Information	Remarks and references to Appendices
ESQUELBECQ	21.10.17		Companies at various places of Employment. Refilling front Escarpments	S.J.R.
	22.10.17		Batt. in same billets. Pt. E. & L.Co's. on similar jobs	S.J.R.
	23.10.17		Batt. in billets. Coys in same areas. A & B. Coys. who were to Regment Lybring	S.J.R.
			& Nev. however to Keep 2 Pls. ready for duty	S.J.R.
	24.10.17		Batt. in billets with the 3 Cos. Sections. Shelling See. Lines Communications	S.J.R.
			Quiet day. Bowers under M.O. organiser amusement. Sporting Sports.	S.J.R.
	25.10.17		Battalion HQ. moved to Hondeghem	S.J.R.
	26.10.17		Officers in Pairs of Bo C Coys or Squad r Bon. Drill.	S.J.R.
	27.10.17		Lectures on Gun Coles Offensive and Defensive. Parade for Officers	S.J.R.
			& men. Received sundry Pamphlets. One hrs. work given to Non Series inspections	
	28.10.17		C.O. ran punt over inspection. (2 hrs. on afternoon)	S.J.R.
			C.O. & O.R. Parade. S. Baths	S.J.R.
	29.10.17		Lectures as before. 2/Lt. E. C. Brown joined Bn. at 10 am.	
	30.10.17		Officers & Coy's details arrive from B.E.F. Ben. the 10 O.R. Marched. S.J.R.	
			to Service from 3 T. O. R. L. training duly to afternoon	S.J.R.
	30.10.17		Company Inspection by Army Commander Officers & men are not to know	S.J.R.

Army Form C. 2118.

WAR DIARY
or
INTELLIGENCE SUMMARY.
(Erase heading not required.)

8th Yorks

Instructions regarding War Diaries and Intelligence Summaries are contained in F. S. Regs., Part II. and the Staff Manual respectively. Title pages will be prepared in manuscript.

Place	Date	Hour	Summary of Events and Information	Remarks and references to Appendices
Bedford House	30.10.17		Batt in Bedford House area	2/Lt M.L. Jones wounded at
			Casualties for month	
			Officers 6 wounded	O.R. 34 Killed
				3 wounded (since died)
				84 wounded
				16 Shell Shock
				___
				137
				___
				8/9
			Capt & Adjt 2nd Lieut (temp Capt) Hume took over Adjutancy in absence of Capt C.H. Clark (Crossmore also for sick leave)	
				E/Pruden Lieut
				8/Yorks Regt

WAR DIARY
or
INTELLIGENCE SUMMARY.

Army Form C. 2118.

8th K.O. Yorks L.I.

Place	Date	Hour	Summary of Events and Information	Remarks and references to Appendices
Esquerdes	31/12/17		Battalion inspected by Commander in Chief at 11am. Pres A.V. Sykes, L.R. Hickson & S.A. Sullivan, Yorkshire Regt.	S.g.B.
			Rem. of Pte. on Coy.	
			Casualties for Month:-	
			Officers Killed 1 Wounded 2	
			Other ranks - 7 31	
			Awards. 15 Military Medals	
			1 D.C.M.	
			Officers 3 Military O.B.E. 2/Lt E.V. Collas	
			Men 6 Military Cross. Capt A.W.P. Blake	
			& Lieut Cooke	

E. Crosby Kent
Lt Col 0. 8th K.O. Yorks L.I.

ATTACHED 8TH DIVISION
70TH INFY BDE 23 DIV

8TH BN K.O.Y.L.I.
OCT 1915 - MAY 1916

8th, Division.

70th, Brigade.

8th, K. O. Y. L. I.

9/10/15 – 30/11/15.

May 1916

8th K.O.Y.L.I.
Vol: 3

121/7624

1K

8th Division

9th Oct & Nov. 15.

WAR DIARY or INTELLIGENCE SUMMARY

Army Form C. 2118.

of 8th K.O.Y.L.I.

(Erase heading not required.)

Instructions regarding War Diaries and Intelligence Summaries are contained in F. S. Regs., Part II. and the Staff Manual respectively. Title pages will be prepared in manuscript.

Place	Date	Hour	Summary of Events and Information	Remarks and references to Appendices
Pt. Ste d'Ez	9-6-15		Very quiet. Major Stockwell admitted to Hospital. Major Owen became 2nd in Comd. 8/Y/C.	
"	10 -		Very quiet - day 8/Y/C	
"	11 -		Returned to JESUS FARM near ESTAIRES near EVERYWHERE. Very good billets 8/Y/C	
TESUS FARM	12 -		Confirmation rest - 8/Y/C	
"	13 -		Whole Battalion had baths at Sailly sur la Lys 8/Y/C	
"	14 -		Rested in billets. Very quiet time. Several shells visited us in the evening 8/Y/C	
"	15 -		Draft of 17 men arrived.	
"	16 -		Inspected by Lt. Gen. Sir Phillips - was very pleased 8/Y/C	
MORBECQUE LONGUEVAL	18 -		Marched to billets about 10 CROIX DES CORNETS 8/Y/C	
"	17 -		Church Parade. 8/Y/C	
"	19 -		Amalgamated with 2 Devon Regt and 8 Platoons went into the trenches 8/Y/C	
"	20 -		Quiet day in billets. 8/Y/C	
"	21 -		" " " " 8/Y/C	
10 WEST TOWN	22 -		Moved into trenches in relief of two Companies 2 Devons 8/Y/C	
"	23		Had 10 Casualties 2 killed in A Coy by shells. Moved to WEATHERCOCK HALL relieved by 8 Devons and relieved 2 Scottish Rifles. 8/Y/C	

Army Form C. 2118.

WAR DIARY
or
INTELLIGENCE SUMMARY.
(Erase heading not required.)

Instructions regarding War Diaries and Intelligence Summaries are contained in F. S. Regs., Part II. and the Staff Manual respectively. Title pages will be prepared in manuscript.

Place	Date	Hour	Summary of Events and Information	Remarks and references to Appendices
WEATHEROCK HOUSE	24-7-15		Moved to FLEURBAIX relieved 2 Rifle Bde. relieved by 2 Lincolns at CRUCIFIX ASYC	
CRUCIFIX MMS	25-7-15		Rested in billets, A & C Coys at LACROIX MARECHAL ASYC	
"	26 -		In billets nothing to report. ASYC	
"	27 -		Moved to billets about COT-DE-SAC relieved by 2 Dy Yorks ASYC	
COT-DE-SAC	28 -		In billets. Divisional Reserve. Route Marching etc. ASYC	
"	29 -		" Training under Company arrangements ASYC	
"	30 -		2nd LT TRENLY Left. Appointed Commandant DUNKIRK ASYC	
"	31 -		Church Parade. at Battn. Hq. ASYC	

12/8/16

A S f (Coventry Lient)
adjutant OK or El for O.C.

Headquarters
8th W.W. Yorkshire Light Infantry
Nov 30th 1915

To The Officer
i/c A.G's Office
3rd Echelon

Strength at T. & 6.2118 for
the month of November

G.S.H Coventry
Lieut
Adjutant 8th KO Yorkshire Light Infantry

Army Form C. 2118.

8th KOYLI

WAR DIARY or INTELLIGENCE SUMMARY.

from Nov 1st 1915 = Nov 30 @ 1915

(Erase heading not required.)

Place	Date	Hour	Summary of Events and Information	Remarks and references to Appendices
CUL-DE-SAC Farm	1-11-15		In billets, short route march about SAILLY. Four new Officers arrived.	
"	2-11-15		Lt. Col. H.E. TREVOR. D.S.O. arrived and assumed Command.	
"	3-11-15		Training under Company arrangements. Nothing to Report.	
WYE FARM	4-11-15		Moved in the evening to WYE FARM, relieved 1st Irish Rifles. 76th Brigade on our right.	
"	5-11-15		In trenches N64 to S.3II.1. very wet. many of the communication trenches being impassable. and got Drainson	
"	6-11-15		Major General Hudson went round the trenches in the morning.	
"	7-11-15		Nothing to Report. Casualties 3 killed 9-4 wounded.	
CRUCIFIX FARM	8-11-15		Came into billets about CRUCIFIX FARM relieved by 1st Irish Rifles	
WEATHERCOCK HALL	9-11-15		Moved into billets about WEATHERCOCK HALL were relieved by 2nd W. Yorks.	
"	10-11-15		Rested in billets	
CUL-DE-SAC	11-11-15		Moved to CUL-DE-SAC Farm relieved 2 W. Yorks and handed over to them.	
"	12-11-15		Training and refitting under Company arrangements.	
"	13-11-15		Short Route March in the morning at disposition of O.C. Coys in the afternoon.	
"	14-11-15		Church parade at CUL-DE-SAC Farm.	
"	15-11-15		Baths for whole battalion at SAILLY.	
"	16-11-15		At disposition of O.C. Coys. Gas Demonstration for all Officers & N.C.O's.	

Army Form C. 2118.

WAR DIARY
or
INTELLIGENCE SUMMARY.
(Erase heading not required.)

Instructions regarding War Diaries and Intelligence Summaries are contained in F. S. Regs., Part II. and the Staff Manual respectively. Title pages will be prepared in manuscript.

Place	Date	Hour	Summary of Events and Information	Remarks and references to Appendices
CUL-DE-SAC	7-11-15		Denonstration by Battalion Grenadiers. Lecture on "French Feet" by Battalion M.O.	
WYE FARM	18-11-15		The following Officers proceeded on leave to England. Lt Col HE Freeman DSO, Lieut's Left F.H. Coverley, Captain H.E. Poyser, Captain H.L. Willey, 2nd Lieut G. Donahoe. The Battalion relieved the 2nd R.I.R. in trenches T 31.1. to N 64 inclusive. The 8th Midd'x Regt was on our left, the 2nd Devon Regt on our right.	
"	19-11-15		Nothing to report.	
"	20-11-15		One man killed.	
"	21-11-15		Bombardment of German trenches near CORDONNERIE, N105.	
"	22-11-15		Relieved about 5.30pm by 2nd Devon Regt and marched to CUL DE SAC Farm	
CUL DE SAC	23-11-15		The 2nd R.I.R. in trenches L 14 c (Sheet 36a)	
"	24-11-15		Marched to billets round NEUF BERQUIN with 10th Brigade into billets near Staenbeeque	
STEEN BECQUE	25-11-15		Preparing for inspection by C in C.	
"	26-11-15		Inspection cancelled. Battalion under Company arrangements. 2nd Lt Spoor DSO returned.	
"	27-11-15		All Officers returned on leave on the 18th returned. Company & Platoon training.	
"	28-11-15		Church Parade	
"	29-11-15		Company Training. School of Instruction for N.C.O's started. Draft of 30 men arrived.	
"	30-11-15		Company Training. Lieut Musehamp went to Signal School 3rd Corps	

F.H. Coverley Lieut a/Adjutant
for Lieut-Col
Comdg 8th K.O.Y.L.I.

8th, Division.

70th, Brigade.

8TH, K. O. Y. L. I.

December, 1915.

8th K.O.Y.L.I.
Vol. 4

121/7824

8th Division

Dec 15

CONFIDENTIAL.

Army Form C. 2118.

WAR DIARY of 8th O.Y.L.I.
Dec 1st–31st 1915.

or

INTELLIGENCE SUMMARY.

(Erase heading not required.)

Instructions regarding War Diaries and Intelligence Summaries are contained in F. S. Regs., Part II. and the Staff Manual respectively. Title pages will be prepared in manuscript.

Place	Date	Hour	Summary of Events and Information	Remarks and references to Appendices
STEENBECQUE	1/12/15		Platoon and Company training. R.E. course for Officers & N.C.O's. A.S.F.C.	VII
"	2/12/15		Platoon and Company training. Night Operations. A.S.F.C.	
"	3/12/15		do. Draft of 50 N.C.O's & men arrived. A.S.F.C.	
"	4/12/15		do. do. A.S.F.C.	
"	5/12/15		Sunday. A.S.F.C.	
"	6/12/15		Close and Open Order Drill. Practise of attack & charge. R.E. class for Officers. A.S.F.C.	
"	7/12/15		Lecture on Air Photography. A.S.F.C.	
"	8/12/15		Battalion Route march. A.S.F.C.	
"	9/12/15		Close and open order Drill. B Company on the 30" Range. A.S.F.C.	
"	10/12/15		" " " " " " A.S.F.C.	
"	11/12/15		Route march by Companies. Lecture on "Gas". A.S.F.C.	
"	12/12/15		D Coy on the 30" Range. Night Operations. A.S.F.C.	
"	13/12/15		Sunday. Sent 2 Lieuts Little & Smith & 2 Sent Boothy went on leave. A.S.F.C.	
"	14/12/15		Company training. D Coy on the 30" Range. Draft of 50 N.C.O's & men arrived. A.S.F.C.	
"	15/12/15		Battalion Route march. A.S.F.C.	
"	15/12/15		A Coy on 30" Range. Remainder Practised the attack on the Hogged out Course. A.S.F.C.	

Army Form C. 2118

WAR DIARY
or
INTELLIGENCE SUMMARY

(Erase heading not required.)

of 2nd K.O.Y.L.I.
Dec 1st – 31st 1915

Instructions regarding War Diaries and Intelligence Summaries are contained in F.S. Regs., Part II and the Staff Manual respectively. Title pages will be prepared in manuscript.

Place	Date	Hour	Summary of Events and Information	Remarks and references to Appendices
STEENBECQUE	16/12/15		D Coy on 30" Range. Remainder on the Battalion Flagged out Course. 4SYC	
"	17/12/15		Battalion Parade on Flagged out Course. 4SYC	
"	18/12/15		A.B.D. Coys on Flagged out Course. Inspection of Coys by C.O. in Marching Order. 4SYC	
"	19/12/15		Sunday. Final Preparation for Divisional manoeuvres. 4SYC	
LYNDE	20/12/15		Divisional manoeuvres. Marched to LYNDE and billetted. Lieut Smith & Bradley returned from leave 4SYC	
ENGUINEGATTE	21/12/15		Left billets about 8 am and marched to ENGUINEGATTE where we billetted 4SYC	
CAUCHIE D'ECQUES	22/12/15		Fought a small Rear-guard action about ENGUINEGATTE and then marched to billets in CAUCHIE D'ECQUES. 4SYC	
STEENBECQUE	23/12/15		Left billets about 9am and marched straight back to billets about STEENBECQUE. All routine Regtl. on arrival. 4SYC	
"	24/12/15		General Interior Economy and Cleaning up after Divisional manoeuvres. 4SYC Regtl on arrival. 4SYC	
"	25/12/15		Christmas Day. 4SYC	
"	26/12/15		Sunday. Church Parades. 4SYC	
"	27/12/15		Close and open Order Drill. D Company on 30" Range. Inspection of Coys under Coy arrangements. 4SYC	
"	28/12/15		Battn Parade on Bdge Flagged out Course. 4SYC	
"	29/12/15		Coys practised the attack on the Battalion Flagged out course. A Coy on 30" Range 4SYC	
"	30/12/15		Route March for A.B & D Coys. C Coy on the 30" Range 4SYC	
"	31/12/15		CO & 2/C Coys visited Canada. Demonstration of attack on Flagged out Course, by Major Owen, Captain Bradley, & Lieut Stead went on leave. 4SYC Lieut Col W.H.Hirsch R.O.Y.L.I.

8th, Division.

70th, Brigade.

8th, K.O.Y.L. I.

January, 1916.

Sgt K.O. & L.I. ~70/8 Jan 1

vol 5

Tan'le

2. K
Malick

SECRET

Army Form C. 2118.

WAR DIARY of 8o K.O.Y.L.I

or INTELLIGENCE SUMMARY. from 1/1/16 — 31/1/16.

(Erase heading not required.)

Instructions regarding War Diaries and Intelligence Summaries are contained in F. S. Regs., Part II. and the Staff Manual respectively. Title pages will be prepared in manuscript.

Place	Date	Hour	Summary of Events and Information	Remarks and references to Appendices
STEENBECQUE	1/1/16		Company Training. One Company on 30ᵗʰ Range. Three Companies on flagged out Course. J.S.C.	
"	2/1/16		2ⁿᵈ Lieut. Lefevre Young attached to the Battalion. 2ⁿᵈ Lieut. E. Watford joined for duty. J.S.C.	
"	3/1/16		Company Training as for 1st inst. J.S.C.	
"	4/1/16		Battalion Route March. Lieut M.A.H. Morley went on leave. J.S.C.	
"	5/1/16		Two Companies on 30ᵗʰ Range & two Companies on the flagged out course. J.S.C.	
"	6/1/16		Three Companies on the flagged out course & one on the Range. Captain Todhams J.S.C. R.A.M.C. went on leave. J.S.C.	
"	7/1/16		Captain J.S. Dyson, Lieut B.H. Horsley & 2ⁿᵈ Lieut W.S. Broome went on leave. J.S.C. Route March for Battalion. J.S.C.	
"	8/1/16		Captain T. Bewley & Lieut E.G.O. Speed returned from leave. J.S.C. 2ⁿᵈ Lieut J.O. Holmes & 2ⁿᵈ Lieut d.H. Hank went on leave. J.S.C. Demonstration of Signal flares by the Battalion, as per attached orders. J.S.C. 2ⁿᵈ Lieut Y.F. Jordan attached to 70 Bde T.M. Battery. Church Parades. J.S.C.	
"	9/1/16		March to ESTAIRES and billetted there. 2ⁿᵈ Lieut J.H. Kernaghan & 2ⁿᵈ Lieut	
	10/1/16		J.S. Marshall & Lieut T.J. Williams R.A.M.C. joined for duty. J.S.C.	

Army Form C. 2118.

WAR DIARY
or
INTELLIGENCE SUMMARY.
(Erase heading not required.)

Instructions regarding War Diaries and Intelligence Summaries are contained in F. S. Regs., Part II. and the Staff Manual respectively. Title pages will be prepared in manuscript.

Place	Date	Hour	Summary of Events and Information	Remarks and references to Appendices
ESTAIRES	11/4/16		The whole Battalion bathed in the 8th Divisional baths. Lieut. M.A.W. Darby returned from leave.	
	12/4/16	2.0.pm	Marched to the trenches and over from the 12th K.R.R. trenches N8 & 9.7. to N 10 0,2,6 and became Right Bat^n of the Right Brigade in the front line. 4 Batt^n Grenadier Guards on our Right and 9th York and Lancasters on our Left. Battalion Head-Quarters SPY FARM. 4SYC	
SPY FARM	13/4/16		Major T.H. Ewen returned from leave. Artillery demonstration on our right at 6.0 pm. 4SYC	
"	13/4/16		Very quiet day. 4SYC	
"	14/4/16		Captain G.S. Bryan & Lieut. B.H. Hornby came back from leave. Hostile artillery active in the morning & afternoon. 4SYC	
"	15/4/16		2 Lieut^s A.H. Head & 2 Lieut G. od Holmes returned from leave. 2 Lieut J Nelson wounded. Moved in the evening & became Right Battalion in Brigade Reserve. Head-Quarters at WEATHERCOCK HOUSE. 4SYC	
WEATHERCOCK HOUSE	16/4/16		Sunday. Church Parades. 4SYC	
"	17/4/16		Slight bombardment by our artillery. 4SYC	

Army Form C. 2118.

WAR DIARY
or
INTELLIGENCE SUMMARY.
(Erase heading not required.)

Instructions regarding War Diaries and Intelligence Summaries are contained in F. S. Regs., Part II. and the Staff Manual respectively. Title pages will be prepared in manuscript.

Place	Date	Hour	Summary of Events and Information	Remarks and references to Appendices
WEATHERCOCK HOUSE	18/1/16	—	Slight bombardment by our artillery. 48/C.	
"	19/1/16		Sent officer party returned to J.H.Q. Moved up to trenches in relief of 11th Sherwood Foresters. at 8.30pm a 9.45pm Guards Brigade on our right open artillery, machine gun & Rapid Rifle fire on enemy's trenches. 48/C	
SPY FARM	20/1/16		artillery of both sides active. 48/C	
"	21/1/16		do do do 48/C	
"	22/1/16		Our artillery bombarded enemy's support line & communication trenches, about 12 noon. 48/C	
"	23/1/16		Enemy bombarded our trenches and our Battn Head-Quarters. Moved back to WEATHERCOCK HOUSE in the evening and were relieved by 11th Sherwood Foresters. 48/C	
WEATHERCOCK HOUSE	24/1/16		Hostile artillery active. 48/C	
"	25/1/16		12.2.00 mn went on trent. S.O.S message was received at 11.20am all companies stood to, but it was cancelled at 12 midnight. 48/C	
"	26/1/16		Enemy's artillery very active SPY FARM shelled and burnt down. Our Head Quarters shelled in the morning and again in the afternoon. 48/C	

Army Form C. 2118.

WAR DIARY
or
INTELLIGENCE SUMMARY.
(Erase heading not required.)

IV

Place	Date	Hour	Summary of Events and Information	Remarks and references to Appendices
WEATHERCOCK HOUSE	26/1/16		Moved in the evening to Divisional Reserve in SAILLY, were relieved by 2nd Batt. Bdge. 48YR	
SAILLY	27/1/16		Sent Y' else went on leave. 48YR	
"	28/1/16		All Battalion Bathed at the 8th Divisional Baths SAILLY. 48YR	
"	29/1/16		Two Companies fired on 30° Range. 48YR	
"	30/1/16		Sunday Church Parade. Service by the Archbishop of Armagh. 48YR	
"	31/1/16		D Coy go into the trenches with 2 Rifle Bdge. Remainder on Fatigue Parties. 48YR	

Casualties during January 1916

1 Officer Wounded
5 Other Ranks Killed
16 Wounded
2 Accidentally Wounded

31/1/16

H. Kerr
Lieut-Col.
Cmdg. 2nd K.O.Y.L.I.

C.R.E.,   G.574/4 K.
O.R.A.,
23rd Inf. Bde.,
25th Inf. Bde.,
70th Inf. Bde.,
G.S.O. 1,
G.S.O. 3,
A.D.C. for G.O.C.,
"A".
    ****

1.   Herewith Scheme for Demonstration of Signal Flares to be carried out by 70th Inf. Bde. in Squares I.12, 17 & 18, at 10.30 a.m. tomorrow, January 8th.

2.   Spectators will please keep in rear of the line X, Y.

8th Division,   C.H.L. Nicholson
7th January, 1916.   Major,
                                       General Staff.

Demonstration of Coloured Signal Flares, 8th Jan. 1916.

Reference 1/40,000 Map, Sheet 36.A., and sketch map attached.

GENERAL IDEA.

1. The 70th Inf.Bde is holding the line of trenches X.Y.Z. facing S.W., astride the HAZEBROUCK - THIENNES Railway.

The front portion of the enemy's trenches which lie S.E. of the Railway is about 150 - 200 yards distant.

Orders have been issued for the enemy's trenches to be assaulted at 10.30 a.m. on January 8th.

SPECIAL IDEA.

2. At 10.15 a.m. on the 8th January, the 8th K.O.Y.L.I. are formed up on the front X.Y., ready to assault the trenches on the S.E. of the Railway.

Other Battalions (imaginary) are assaulting on the right and left of the 8th K.O.Y.L.I.

Three successive lines of trenches (A.B. C.D. E.F.) are to be successively carried, and the final objective will be the line G.H.

General direction of advance 228° true bearing.

3. ### Instructions.

(i) The battalion will advance on a front of three companies, with one platoon from each Coy. in the front line.

(2)

(ii) The enemy, represented by one Company of the 8th K.O.Y.L.I., will wear steel helmets and greatcoats. As each enemy line is reached, the attackers will halt until the defenders have cleared the front to their left flank.

(iii) The capture of each line will be indicated by signal flares. The flares will be lit simultaneously in clusters of about half a dozen of the same colour or grouped as close together as can be arranged.

(iv) Smoke bombs will be lighted in rear of the attackers to simulate the effect of bursting shells, in order to test to what extent the flares are visible through smoke, and the comparative value of the different colours.

(v) As it is especially desired in this demonstration to make a smoke screen between the flares and the observers, the direction of the attack will be reversed, should the wind be from the East.

(vi) The O.C. 11th Sherwood Foresters, will detail three officers, one to be allotted to each of the attacking companies, to record the exact times and positions at which the flares are lit.

Observers will also be detailed to remain on the line X, Y, to note the times and apparent positions at which the flares are lit.

(vii) Motor cars and horses of spectators should be kept West of the Railway or East of the road running from LE BAS (I.6.d) to the Canal during the demonstration.

MAP SQUARE I

DEMONSTRATION 31.10.16
Use of flares in attack

Scale 1/10000

6TH BATTALION K. O. YORKSHIRE LIGHT INFANTRY.

DEMONSTRATION OF COLOURED FLARES, 6 - 1 - 16.

1. Smoke bombs will be used over the whole front.

2. Flares will be used at 4 points only during the advance (in clusters of 6).

    (a) At 1st Enemy Trench.
    (b) " 2nd " " .
    (c) " 3rd " " .
    (d) At a line about 200 or 300 yards before reaching final objective which is the house (corner of wood -- to the Railway.

3. Signals:-

    (a) For advance from 1st British line to 1st German line -- 1 "G" on Bugle.
    (b) For advance from 1st German line to 2nd German line -- 2 "G"s" on Bugle.
    (c) For advance from 2nd German line to 3rd German line -- 3 "G"s" on Bugle.
    (d) For advance from 3rd German line to 4th German line -- 4 "G"s" on Bugle.
    (e) Final Assault -- Regimental call on Bugle.

H E Trevor
Lt. Colonel,
Commanding 6th Bn. K. O. Y. L. I.

A.C. Strenthern, Comardos & Strenthern.

To be used to all ranks.

8th, Division.

70th, Brigade.

8th, K.O.Y.L.I.

February, 1916.

XIII

Army Form C. 2118.

WAR DIARY of 8th Bn. K.O.Y.L.I.
INTELLIGENCE SUMMARY. 1st to 29th Feb. 1916.

(Erase heading not required.)

Place	Date	Hour	Summary of Events and Information	Remarks and references to Appendices
SAILLY	1-2-16		Divisional Reserve. "C" Coy on 30" Range. Remainder at disposal of O.C. Coys. 8YC.	
"	2 -		Coys at Disposal of O.C. Coys. R.E. Demonstration at BAC ST MAUR 8YC.	
"	3 -		Cleaning of billets in morning. Moved in the evening to Left Brigade Reserve in FLEURBAIX in relief of 2nd Middx Regt 8YC.	
PERG NA HSE	4 -		Nothing to Report 8YC.	
"	5 -		30" Range allotted to "C" & "D" Coys. 8YC	
"	6 -		Church Parade	
"	7 -		Moved into trenches N.6.1 to N.6.5 inclusive in relief of 11 Sherwood Foresters. 8 York & Lancs Regt on our Right, 11 R W Yorks Regt on our Left. 8YC.	
D'YE. SAP N	8 -		Very Quiet day. Nothing to Report 8YC.	
"	9 -		Batln HQ. Shelled about 1 PM. Bomys artillery very active, billet of our supporting Company heavily shelled. 8YC	
"	10 -		Very quiet day. Nothing to Report 8YC	
"	11 -		Came back into Bdge reserve in the evening, were relieved by 11 Sherwood Foresters. Head Quarters PERGOLA HOUSE, FLEURBAIX. 8YC	
PER GOLA HSE	12 -		Our artillery very active otherwise quiet day, 8YC	

XIV

Army Form C. 2118.

WAR DIARY of 8 K.O.Y.L.I.
or
INTELLIGENCE SUMMARY.
(Erase heading not required.)

Instructions regarding War Diaries and Intelligence Summaries are contained in F.S. Regs., Part II. and the Staff Manual respectively. Title pages will be prepared in manuscript.

Place	Date	Hour	Summary of Events and Information	Remarks and references to Appendices
PERGHIA HOUSE	13.X.16		Sunday. Church Parades. Enemy's aeroplanes very active. 2 Lieut- J.F.P. Bartlett joined. A.S.C.	
"	14 -		A, B & D Coys had baths at SAILLY. A&C.	
"	15 -		Went round to the trenches and relieved the 11 Sherwood Foresters. A & B Coys on the 30" Range in the morning. 2 Lieut F.B. Ernest joined.	
WYE Farm	16 -		Very quiet day in the trenches. A&C.	
"	17 -		do do A&C.	
"	18 -		do do A&C.	
"	19 -		Very quiet day. Came back into Brigade Reserve in the evening, relieved by 11 Sherwood Foresters. A&C.	
PERGHIA HOUSE	20 -		Church Parade in the morning. Heavy bombardment. A&C.	
"	21 -		C Coy on the 30" Range, very quiet day. A&C.	
"	22 -		A & B Company's on 30" Range. Heavy bombardment on our right. A&C.	
"	23 -		Enemy "A Kill 5". Moved in the evening back to the trenches, relieved 11 Sherwood Foresters. A&C.	
WYE FARM	24 -		Very quiet day. Had a gas alarm in the evening, but was cancelled. A&C.	

2353 Wt. W2511/1454 700,000 5/15 D.D.&L. A.D.S.S./Forms/C. 2118.

Army Form C. 2118.

WAR DIARY of 8th K.O.Y.L.I.
or
INTELLIGENCE SUMMARY.
(Erase heading not required.)

Place	Date	Hour	Summary of Events and Information	Remarks and references to Appendices
WYE FARM	25.		Very quiet day. Our Support trenches were shelled in the evening and the Enemy machine guns very active 8SYC	
"	26.		Nothing to report. 8SYC	
"	27.		Slight bombardment by our artillery on the enemy's trenches opposite N 64. 8SYC. Came back into Brigade Reserve FLEURBAIX in the evening, were relieved by 11th Sherwood Foresters. 8SYC	
FLEURBAIX	28.		B & D Coys went to the Divisional Baths at SAILLY. C Coy on the 30" Range 8SYC. 2nd Lieut J. Grant de Longueuil joined. 8SYC.	
"	29.		B Coy on the 30" Range. 8SYC	
			Casualties during February	
			1 Other Ranks Wounded.	

H.R. Trevor Lieut: Col.
Comdg. 8th K.O.Y.L.I.

1/3/16

8th, Division.

70th, Brigade.

8th, K.O.Y.L.I.

March, 1916.

CONFIDENTIAL.

Headquarters,
8th Bn. K. O. Y. L. I.
4th April 1916.

To,
The D. A. G.,
Base.

Herewith Army Form C. 2118 (WAR DIARY) for the Month of March 1916.

                 G H Coventry   Lieutenant, &
                                 Adjutant,
                     For,
                                 Lt. Colonel,
Commanding 8th Bn. K. O. Y. L. I.

Army Form C. 2118.

XVI.

WAR DIARY, 8th Batt. K.O.Y.L.I.

INTELLIGENCE SUMMARY

(Erase heading not required.)

Instructions regarding War Diaries and Intelligence Summaries are contained in F.S. Regs., Part II, and the Staff Manual respectively. Title pages will be prepared in manuscript.

Place	Date	Hour	Summary of Events and Information	Remarks and references to Appendices
FLEURBAIX.	1/3/1916.	—	In Billets in Brigade Reserve, FLEURBAIX. Headquarters "PERGOLA HOUSE". P.Mg.	
WYE FARM (N.E. FLEURBAIX)	2/3/1916.	—	Relieved 11th Batt. The Sherwood Foresters in front line trenches, N.6.1. to N.6.5 inclusive. 34th Division on our left. 8th Batt. Y & L. Regt. on our right. Relief Complete 8.15 p.m. P.Mg.	
"	3/3/1916.	—	Trenches very quiet all day. P.Mg.	
"	4/3/1916.	—	Trenches very quiet all day. P.Mg.	
"	5/3/1916.	—	Trenches quiet day. Support line shelled in afternoon no damage. P.Mg.	
FLEURBAIX.	6/3/1916.	—	Relieved 11th Batt. The Sherwood Foresters in Billets in Brigade Reserve about FLEURBAIX. relief Complete 8.15 p.m. P.Mg.	
"	7/3/1916.	—	In Billets. FLEURBAIX. "A" Company at Baths, SAILLY. "C" Company on 30 yards Range. B & D Companies, Kit Inspections. P.Mg.	
"	8/3/1916.	—	Billets, FLEURBAIX. B & D Companies Baths, SAILLY. "A" Coy. 30 yards Range from 1.0 p.m. P.Mg.	
"	9/3/1916.	—	Billets, FLEURBAIX. C.Os Inspection of Transport and Workshops. Major General Pulteney Commanding 3rd Corps paid a surprise visit to the Battalion and inspected Cooking arrangements. Expressed great pleasure with all arrangements for feeding and comfort of the men. arrived 11.0 am left 11.45 am. P.Mg.	
WYE FARM. (N.E. FLEURBAIX.)	10/3/1916.	—	Relieved 11th Batt. The Sherwood Foresters in front line trenches. relief Complete 8.45 p.m. 16th Batt. The Royal Scots (34th Div) on our left. 8th Batt Y & L. Regt. on our right. P.Mg.	
"	11/3/1916.	—	Trenches. quiet day. Major General Hudson. Commanding 8th Division visited trenches 9.30 am. "C" Company patrol bombed enemy listening posts opposite N.6.3. during the night. P.Mg.	

Army Form C

WAR DIARY 8th Batt. K.O.Y.L.I.
INTELLIGENCE SUMMARY

(Erase heading not required.)

Instructions regarding War Diaries and Intelligence Summaries are contained in F. S. Regs., Part II. and the Staff Manual respectively. Title pages will be prepared in manuscript.

Place	Date	Hour	Summary of Events and Information	Remarks and references to Appendices
WYE FARM (FLEURBAIX)	12/3/16	—	Trenches. C.O. and Adjutant- 12th Service Batt. Royal Sussex Regt. and 2 Companies (39th Division) attached for Instruction. 1st day Individual Instruction	P.M.g.
"	13/3/16	—	Trenches. Enemy shelled our 300 yards support line with about 50 - 77mm Shells. also Gun Positions behind Rue JOHNATHAN. between 3pm and 3.45pm. 2nd day of attachment of Part R.Sussex Regt. Instruction by Sections.	P.M.g.
FLEURBAIX	14/3/16	—	Relieved 11th Batt The Sherwood Foresters in Billets around FLEURBAIX. relief Complete 8.45pm.	P.M.g.
"	15/3/16	—	In Billets, FLEURBAIX, Town shelled in afternoon about 20-4.2 in Howitzers falling in vicinity of the Church, 1 shell fell in garden of Headquarters PERGOLA HOUSE. at 6.30pm. No casualties.	P.M.g.
"	16/3/16	—	Billets, FLEURBAIX, Town shelled around headquarters. 9.0am to 10 am. B and D. Companies bathed at Divisional Baths at SAILLY in morning. A. Company on 30 yards range. Battalion Headquarters removed from PERGOLA HOUSE to YORK HOUSE. (H.21.d.5.5 sheet 36.1/40,000)	P.M.g.
"	17/3/16	—	Billets FLEURBAIX.	P.M.g.
WYE FARM (FLEURBAIX)	18/3/16	—	Relieved 11th Batt. The Sherwood Foresters in front line trenches relief Complete 8.45 pm. 'A' Coy and details B.D.Companies bathed at SAILLY. in morning. 'D' Company 30 yards range in afternoon.	P.M.g.
"	19/3/16	—	Trenches. Quiet day.	P.M.g.
"	20/3/16	—	Trenches. Quiet day.	P.M.g.
SAILLY	21/3/16	—	Batt, relieved in front line trenches by 12th Batt. The Royal Sussex Regt. + moved to Billets in Divisional Reserve about SAILLY. Headquarters at DUMP HOUSE. (G.9.d.4.4½. sheet 36.1/40,000).	P.M.g.

2353 Wt. W2344/1454 700,000 5/15 L. D. D. & L. A.D.S.S/Forms/C. 2118.

Army Form C. 2118.

WAR DIARY 8TH BATT. K.O.Y.L.I.
INTELLIGENCE SUMMARY

XVIII.

Instructions regarding War Diaries and Intelligence Summaries are contained in F.S. Regs., Part II. and the Staff Manual respectively. Title pages will be prepared in manuscript.

(Erase heading not required.)

Place	Date	Hour	Summary of Events and Information	Remarks and references to Appendices
SAILLY	21/3/16	—	In Billets in Divisional Reserve near SAILLY.	PWP
SAILLY.	22/3/16	—	In Billets in Divisional Reserve. Battalion Bathed at Divisional Baths. SAILLY.	PWP
"	23/3/16	—	Billets near SAILLY. Grenadiers, M/Gun and H.Q. padi on 30yd range.	PWP
"	24/3/16	—	Billets — " Company Training.	PWP
"	25/3/16	—	Distinguished Conduct Medal awarded by the C-in-C. to No 13680 Sergeant J.T. WALDRON for Consistent and Excellent and Gallant Conduct on Patrol on the night of 8/9th and 11/12th February 1916.	PWP
"	25/3/16	—	Billets near SAILLY. Company Training.	PWP
CALONNE	26/3/16	—	Battalion marched to CALONNE (near MERVILLE) and Billeted overnight 26/27.	PWP
VIGNACOURT	27/3/16	—	Battalion entrained at MERVILLE, arrived at LONGEAU at 6.0 p.m. whence it marched to VIGNACOURT (9 miles N.N.W of AMIENS) where it billeted. Bn still forming part of the 70th Inf. Bde. 8th Div. 3rd Corps — 1st Army, having been transferred from 1st Army (Sir C. Monro) 3rd Corps.	PWP
"	28/3/16	—	Billets at VIGNACOURT.	PWP
"	29/3/16	—	" " "	PWP
"	30/3/16	—	" " "	PWP
St GRATIEN	31/3/16	—	Battalion marched from VIGNACOURT to Billets at St GRATIEN. B.G.C. 4th Army (Lt H. Rawlinson)	PWP

Casualties during March 1916. Officers. Nil.
Other Ranks. Accidental Killed. 1.
Killed in Action. 2.
Wounded. 6
Draft National Reserve. 1
Total. 10.

2/4/16

H. Tweed Lt Col.
Cmg 8th Bn KOYLI

2353 Wt. W2514/1454 700,000 5/15 D. D. & L. A.D.S.S./Forms/C. 2118.

8th, Division.

70th, Brigade.

8th, K.O.Y.L.I.

April, 1916.

WAR DIARY
or
INTELLIGENCE SUMMARY

Army Form C. 2118.

8th BATT. THE K.O.Y.L.I. Vol VIII

Place	Date	Hour	Summary of Events and Information	Remarks and references to Appendices
ALBERT.	2/4/16.	-	Billets in Brigade Reserve. At 12.30 p.m. a 4.2" Shell fell in Headquarters Billet yard, wounding 3 men.	
"	3/4/16.	-	Billets. Brigade Reserve. Company Officers Reconny. Officers Reconnoitred ALBERT defences.	
"	4/4/16.	-	Billets. Bde. Reserve. Companies Interior Economy. Headquarters moved to RUE MALLY.	
"	5/4/16.	-	Billets. Bde. Reserve. Officers reconnoitred Trenches of Left Battalion in Front line.	
"	8/4/16.	-	Billets. Bde. Reserve. Parties of Officers reconnoitred Trenches of Left Battalion in Front line.	
TRENCHES Nr. ALBERT.	7/4/16.	-	Relieved 11th Batt. The Sherwood Foresters in Front line trenches as Left Battalion of Left Brigade 8th Division. 8th Batt. Manchesters Regt. on our right. 32nd Division on our left. (19th Lanc. Fusiliers). A & B. Coys in Front line. C. Coy in Close Support. D. Coy in Reserve in Billets at ASHDOWN POST.	
"	8/4/16.	-	Trenches. Artillery active on day. 8th Divisional Artillery registering.	
"	9/4/16.	-	Trenches. Brilliant day. Some shelling in morning. Otherwise quiet.	
"	10/4/16.	-	Trenches. Brilliant day. Quiet. 19th Lancs. Fusiliers on our left relieved by 2nd Manchesters Regt. C. Coy relieved D Coy. B Coy in Front line.	
"	11/4/16.	-	Trenches. Quiet day. At 7.30 p.m. Considerable heavy shelling on our right on 25th Bde Trenches opposite to BOISELLE followed by a successful German Raid on the Royal Irish Rifles.	
"	12/4/16.	-	Trenches. Quiet. Very wet all day.	

Army Form C. 2118.

WAR DIARY 8th BATT. K.O.Y.L.I.

or

INTELLIGENCE SUMMARY.

(Erase heading not required.)

Instructions regarding War Diaries and Intelligence Summaries are contained in F.S. Regs., Part II. and the Staff Manual respectively. Title pages will be prepared in manuscript.

Place	Date	Hour	Summary of Events and Information	Remarks and references to Appendices
TRENCHES near ALBERT	13/4/16	—	Trenches, wet. 8th York & Lancaster Regt. on our right, relieved by 9th Batt. York & Lancaster Regt.	P.M.G.
"	14/4/16	—	Trenches, relieved by 11th Batt. The Sherwood Foresters, relief complete 9.0 p.m., moved into Billets "Old Reserve".	Reg.
ALBERT	15/4/16	—	BILLETS, ALBERT. "C" Batt. in Brigade Reserve in HOUSE LOMOUNT-HURTU.	P.M.G.
"	16/4/16	—	Billets in Bde. Reserve. Caporaux Interior Economy. A Coy. Battn. also Details.	P.M.G.
"	17/4/16	—	Billets in Bde. Reserve. B & C Coys. Baths. A Coy. Miniature Range.	Reg.
"	—	—	Relieved by 2nd Bn. Wiltshire Regt. & moved into billets in Division Reserve at MILLENCOURT.	P.T.
MILLENCOURT	18/4/16	—	Companies Interior Economy.	11.35
"	19/4/16	—	Company Training. Baths A Coy. Range A Coy.	A.S.
"	20/4/16	—	do. B Coy. Range B.	A.S.
"	21/4/16	—	do. C Coy. Range C.	A.S.
"	22/4/16	—	do. D Coy. Range D. Party of officers inspected trenches /Right Sub Sector/ Bapaume - D'Ser	A.S.
"	23/4/16	—	Physical Drill and Bands. Sunday Morning service. 2 M. BOISSELLE. Relief by R.I.R. or German trenches	A.S.
"	—	—	D. Coy imp. Sergts shooting competition. Extra Sunday. Holy Communion & Parade Service. Party of Officers inspected Trench & Right and Left Sub. Sector	A.S.
"	—	—	of Right Bde. 3rd Divn.	A.S.
"	24/4/16	—	Coy. Training. Range. Officers interior Economy. Physical Drill and Band.	A.S.

WAR DIARY 8th Bn R. of Yk.L.I.
INTELLIGENCE SUMMARY

Army Form C. 2118.

(Erase heading not required.)

Instructions regarding War Diaries and Intelligence Summaries are contained in F.S. Regs., Part II. and the Staff Manual respectively. Title pages will be prepared in manuscript.

Place	Date	Hour	Summary of Events and Information	Remarks and references to Appendices
Trenches near LA BOISSELLE	25/9/16		Relieved 1st Bn. R.I. Rifles in front line trenches X.20.B. 6 X 20.b inclusive — B.C. & D Coys in front line & supports — A Coy in Reserve. Relief complete 10.30 pm. 10th Bn Yorkshire Regt. on our right, 8th Bn York & Lancaster Regt. up on our left.	A/A T
	26/9/16		Reconnaissance & w/p patrols pushed out during day — quiet day.	
	27/9/16		Our line of advance completed at 10 pm. Operation from extreme left return all right.	
	28/9/16		Barrage started on our right at 4.15 am. Remainder of Bge. normal. Enemy barraged heavily (bombarded our line of front) which lasts 40 minutes and we raided the TAMBOUR (21st Divn. front) unsuccessfully.	
	29/9/16		6.57 am enemy opened concentrated artillery bombardment — which lasted 45 minutes and then attacked front of B Coy but was repulsed without reaching our lines by heavy artillery & m.g. fire. B casualties 8 other ranks killed, 18 O.R. wounded.	
	30/9/16		The Bn. received the congratulations of Bde, Divl. Genl. and Lt-Genl. Genl. Hudson (C.B., C.I.E.) and the Brigadier fr. [C. H. Gordon D.S.O.] for the success.	

Afternoon Lt. Col.
Comdg 8th Bn R. of Yk.L.I.

8th, Division.

70th, Brigade.

8th, K.O.Y.L.I.

May, 1916.

Confidential

Army Form C. 2118.

WAR DIARY
of 8TH BATT. K.O.Y.L.I.
INTELLIGENCE SUMMARY
(Erase heading not required.)

Instructions regarding War Diaries and Intelligence Summaries are contained in F.S. Regs., Part II. and the Staff Manual respectively. Title pages will be prepared in manuscript.

Vol 9 XIII VIII

Place	Date	Hour	Summary of Events and Information	Remarks and references to Appendices
N.E. of ALBERT	1/5/16	—	In Trenches (Right Batt. Right Brigade, 8th Division) quiet day	P.K.9
"	2/5/16	—	In Trenches. Relieved by 11th Batt. the Sherwood Foresters, moved into Brigade Reserve. Headquarters and C & D Companies at DERNANCOURT and 2nd in Command "A & B Companies at BECORDEL-BECOURT CHATEAU defences. Relief complete 1.30 p.m.	P.K.9
DERNANCOURT	3/5/16	—	C & D Companies in Bde. Reserve. Artizan Economy Detachment A & B Coys. BECORDEL-BECOURT CHATEAU def.	P.K.9
"	4/5/16	—	Disposition as for Yeots day 3/5/16. C & D Coys at BATHS.	P.K.9
"	5/5/16	—	Dispositions as for 3/5/16. C & D Coys on miniature Range.	P.K.9
"	6/5/16	—	Dispositions as for 3/5/16. C & D Coys Interior Economy.	P.K.9
"	7/5/16	—	Dispositions as for 3/5/16. C & D Coys Church Parade.	P.K.9
"	8/5/16	—	Batt. relieved in Bde. Reserve by 27th Batt. Northumberland Fusiliers & moved into No.3 Camp HENENCOURT WOOD. (Divisional Rest Camp) 3.30 a.m. Relief commenced 7.45 p.m. Completed 9/5/16.	P.K.9
HENENCOURT	9/5/16	—	No.3 Camp. Battalion Rested.	P.K.9
"	10/5/16	—	No.3 Camp. A & B Companies Bathed	P.K.9
"	11/5/16	—	No.3 Camp. Divisional Training commenced	P.K.9
"	12/5/16	—	No.3 Camp. Divisional Training	P.K.9
"	13/5/16	—	No.3 Camp. Divisional Training. Night working parties to front line 540 men. 6.30 p.m. to 7 a.m. 14/5/16. Rain all day.	P.K.9

Army Form C. 2118.

WAR DIARY
of 8TH BATT. K.O.Y.L.I.
INTELLIGENCE SUMMARY.

(Erase heading not required.)

Instructions regarding War Diaries and Intelligence Summaries are contained in F.S. Regs., Part II. and the Staff Manual respectively. Title pages will be prepared in manuscript.

Place	Date	Hour	Summary of Events and Information	Remarks and references to Appendices
HENENCOURT.	14/5/16	—	No. 3 Camp. Rect. Divisional Band played in Wood. S.O.S Signal 11-20 p.m. Battalion stood to. S.O.S Cancelled at 11-40 p.m. Rain all night.	P.W.Q.
"	15/5/16	—	No. 3 Camp. Divisional Training. ROUTEMARCH 5pm to 7.30 p.m. HENENCOURT - WARLOY-SENLIS-HENENCOURT.	P.W.Q.
"	16/5/16	—	No. 3 Camp. Divisional Training. The Battalion in Attack. All Specialists Cooperating. Night operations 9pm. to 11 p.m.	P.W.Q.
"	17/5/16.	—	No. 3 Camp. Divisional Training. Battalion Drill on A and B. War BRESLE. Night Operation. Engineers in "Consolidation of Trenches". Raiding demonstration. G.O.C. 8th Division was present.	P.W.Q.
"	18/5/16	—	No. 3 Camp. Battalion Baths at Divisional Baths. Specialists on Miniature Range.	P.W.Q.
ALBERT.	19/5/16	—	Battalion relieved 2nd Royal Berkshire Regt. in the ALBERT-BOUZINCOURT defences. Relief commenced 1.15 p.m. Complete 4.50 p.m.	P.W.Q.
"	20/5/16	—	Battalion in ALBERT-BOUZINCOURT defences. 30. 77 mm shells fell in vicinity of working parties 4.00 next morning day.	P.W.Q.
"	21/5/16	—	Batt. in ALBERT-BOUZINCOURT defences. Fine day. Day & night working parties total 400 men.	P.W.Q.
"	22/5/16	—	Batt. in ALBERT-BOUZINCOURT defences. Hot day. Day + night working parties 350 men.	P.W.Q.
"	23/5/16.	—	ALBERT-BOUZINCOURT defences. Working parties day + night total 400 men.	P.W.Q.
"	24/5/16	—	ALBERT-BOUZINCOURT defences. Working parties 350 men.	P.W.Q.
"	25/5/16	—	ALBERT-BOUZINCOURT defences. Working parties 350 men.	P.W.Q.
"	26.5.16	—	ALBERT-BOUZINCOURT defences. Working parties 350 men. About 40 shells fell in vicinity of defences	P.W.Q.

Army Form C. 2118.

WAR DIARY 8TH BATT. K.O.Y.L.I.
or INTELLIGENCE SUMMARY.
(Erase heading not required.)

Place	Date	Hour	Summary of Events and Information	Remarks and references to Appendices
ALBERT. (TRENCHES)	27.5.16	—	Battalion relieved the 1st Bn. The Royal Irish Rifles in front line trenches as right Battalion of the Left Brigade. (Trenches X.13.6. & X.7.8.) relief complete 7.15 pm. 16th Batt. The Royal Scots (2nd Edinburghs) on the right. 8th Batt. The York & Lancaster Regiment on the Left. PWD.	
"	28.5.16	—	Trenches. Quiet day. PWD.	
"	29.5.16	—	Trenches. Trench mortars carried out bombardment of enemy's front & second lines Nr. OVILLERS. at 10.0 am which produced retaliation on our front line damaging parapets. Otherwise quiet day. PWD.	
"	30.5.16	—	Trenches. Quiet day. Wet. PWD.	
"	31.5.16	—	Trenches. Battalion relieved by 11th Batt. The Sherwood Foresters. relief complete 5.0 pm. Battalion moved into billets in Brigade Reserve in ALBERT. PWD.	
			DECORATION. Extract from Routine Orders by MAJOR GENERAL H. HUDSON. C.B. C.I.E. Commanding 8th Division. dated 18th May, 1916. "The Commander in Chief has awarded the Military Medal to the undermentioned N.C.O. N° 19334 Corporal F. Clarke, 8th Batt. The K.O.Y.L.I. for the following act of Gallantry:— Devotion to duty on the night of the 12th April 1916, when in charge of a wiring party in front of the 'NAB' near ALBERT. Heavy machine gun fire being opened on the party, Corporal Clarke would have been justified in withdrawing the party. Knowing, however, the importance of completing the wiring of this portion of the line which had been previously raided by the enemy, Corporal Clarke stuck to his work, and by his initiation, coolness, courage and fine example kept the men working under heavy fire until the wiring was completed. He was finally wounded in the arm." PWD.	

WAR DIARY
8th Batt. K.O.Y.L.I.
INTELLIGENCE SUMMARY

Army Form C. 2118.

Casualties for the month of May 1916.

Killed in Action.   Other Ranks 1.
Accidentally wounded.   "   "   2
Wounded.   "   "   8
                                  ———
       Total Other Ranks. 11.
                                  P.T.O.

H. Trewer Lt. Col.
Cmdg 8th Bn K.O.Y.L.I.

23RD DIVISION
70TH INFY BDE

11TH BN SHERWOOD FORESTERS
~~AUG - SEP 1915 &~~
~~JUN 1916 AUG 1918~~
1915 AUG — 1917 OCT

TO ITALY

70/23 121/7430

XXIII Sir Wiseman

Ellerwood Treaters
Vol I
Aug Sept & Oct 15

Army Form C. 2118.

WAR DIARY
or
INTELLIGENCE SUMMARY.
(Erase heading not required.)

Instructions regarding War Diaries and Intelligence Summaries are contained in F. S. Regs., Part II. and the Staff Manual respectively. Title pages will be prepared in manuscript.

Place	Date	Hour	Summary of Events and Information	Remarks and references to Appendices
BORDON	20.8.15	5 p.m.	Orders received to proceed on active service in France.	
"	21.8.15		Captain Bucklen proceeded to the Rifles in advance.	
"	25.26	midnight	Lieut Hufford & machine gun section L¹ Snelson with transport, 2/Lt Wyatt & Lt Mullen marched to Liphook & entrained at Liphook	
"	26.	12.30 p.m.	Unit then proceeded to France with 70th Bde H. Qrs.	
"	27.	11 am.	Col Wren D.S.O. & C & B Coys marched out & ciphered	
"		4.30pm	Major Mullins & A & D Coy " " "	
	28	11.15am	Batt¹ landed and marched to the 1st Infantry Camp, Captain Bucklen in command Batt.	
	29	12.15am	Batt. marched to Pont de Brigades Dly Station, where we picked up our transport & Mullen	
			& machine gun section. Captain Bucklen & fifty of Batt. & machine gun [Camp]	
			AUDRUICQ. Dly station. Remainder of Batt. arrived 4.30 am	
Avonrucq	29	3.15 pm	Arrived at AUDRUICQ	
CAMPAGNE	6 Sept.		Marched from ZUTKERQUE at 6 am. arriving at 3.30 p.m.	
OUTTERSTEEN	7		Marched from CAMPAGNE at 8 am arriving at 5.7 pm	
"	Sept. 11		Marched from OUTTERSTEEN at 6.30 am arriving ERQUINGHEM Bridge at 12 Noon	
La Chapelle d'Armentières	"		A & B Coys proceeded at 5 pm for trenches in sector La Chaple d'Armentières, C & D Coys billeted with billets	
	12 th		C & D Coys relieved A & B Coys in trenches	
	Sept 13 th		Whole Batt¹ took their place in trenches.	
	1. 9. -		Lieut Jackson returned to Sr. from 1/5 Infantry Bde.	

2353 Wt. W2511/1454 700,000 5/15 D.D.&L. A.D.S.S./Forms/C. 2118.

Army Form C. 2118.

WAR DIARY
or
INTELLIGENCE SUMMARY.
(Erase heading not required.)

Instructions regarding War Diaries and Intelligence Summaries are contained in F. S. Regs., Part II. and the Staff Manual respectively. Title pages will be prepared in manuscript.

Place	Date	Hour	Summary of Events and Information	Remarks and references to Appendices
La Chapelle d'Armentieres			The following casualties occurred in trenches No 16113 Pte E.S. Heads C Coy } wounded 13.5.15. „ 14164 „ S. Allen B Coy } killed 14.5.15 „ 17991 „ J.N. Tinsley D Coy Captain A.C. Russell C Coy No 19196 Pte E.H. Dorn A Coy } wounded 15.5.15 „ 16348 „ J. Ogden C Coy „ 19397 „ J. Hilson D Coy „ 15632 „ A.N. Carey C Coy } wounded 20th init „ 16451 „ A. Sneare D Coy „ 16995 „ E. Jacklin B Coy } killed 22.5.15 „ 16774 „ H. Davis B Coy } wounded 24.5.15 „ 19397 „ J. Hilson D Coy „ 16219 „ Newton A Coy „ 1557 „ N. Clarke C „ } killed 25.5.15 „ 16156 „ C. Ball B „ „ 21780 „ A. Bills C „	died of wounds 1.25.

Army Form C. 2118.

WAR DIARY
or
INTELLIGENCE SUMMARY.
(Erase heading not required.)

Instructions regarding War Diaries and Intelligence Summaries are contained in F. S. Regs., Part II. and the Staff Manual respectively. Title pages will be prepared in manuscript.

Place	Date	Hour	Summary of Events and Information	Remarks and references to Appendices
Armentières	25.9.15		Wounded 16486 Pte H. Bader D Coy	
			30129 " C. Reason C "	
			17772 Cpl A. Lawrence C "	
			17709 Pte P. Robinson C "	
			16066 " H. Coding B " } self inflicted	
			18108 " H.E. Talbot B "	
			15514 L.Cpl T. Sponge C Coy	
	26.9.15		1/3 0685 Pte J. Hathway A "	
			15832 " H. Lee D "	died of wounds 27.9.15
			15112 " Hirst C "	
	27.9.15		Lieut J.S. Cain A "	
	30.9.15		2/Lt. H.L. Willis A "	
	1.10.15		18348 Pte S. Crawford A "	
			18191 Pte S. Radon D "	
	2.10.15		17620 Pte H. Smith D "	
	3.10.15		21767 Pte A. Bruce B "	

8th, Division.

7oth, Brigade.

IIth, Notts & Derby.

Oct & Nov, 1915.

70/ VIII /4 Dr Kirchheim

To Notes: 18 July
Vol: 2

12/
7656

Miss Kellen

N. 2

5. Ocr — Nov 15

Army Form C. 2118.

WAR DIARY
or
INTELLIGENCE SUMMARY.
(Erase heading not required.)

Place	Date	Hour	Summary of Events and Information	Remarks and references to Appendices
Annelenkeuil	5 Oct.		Battn returned to billets in Rue Harle at 6 pm.	
	8 "		Battn returned to trenches in same sector at 6 pm.	
	11 "		Battn returned to billets in divisional area just before at 8 pm.	
Henencourt	18 "		Battn proceeded to billets in Brigade area. Previously awaited Battn and joined with the 2nd Bn. Lincolnshire Regiment, 3 platoons from each Coy. being taken for this duty, this Battn known as 2nd Lincolns under command of Major Bastard ¾ B. whilst the remainder in Bois Grenier sector.	
			On absence from the Battn ½ to include 11th Bn remained in billets under command of Lt Col. Hutton D.S.O.	
Bac St. Maur	22 "		Lu 11th C.O. returned in billets in divisional area	
La Croix sec between 23rd			The Battn proceeded to Brigade area	
Fleurbaix	21 " to		The Battn moved to Brigade area	
Sailly	29 "		Battn moved to divisional area.	
			On leaving France and sick list strength of Bn from late Adv. Jevanifficial twin women.	
			Captain C. Bulcher 27.9.15 Captain E.G.I. Carey 6.10.15	
			2/Lt H.C. Frith 27.9.15 2/Lt H.L. Slim 5.10.15	
			Captain R.J. Mollos 3.10.15	
			Lieut J.D. Martin reported himself for duty + taken on strength of Bn from 22.10.15	

WAR DIARY
or
INTELLIGENCE SUMMARY.

(Erase heading not required.)

Army Form C. 2118.

Instructions regarding War Diaries and Intelligence Summaries are contained in F. S. Regs., Part II. and the Staff Manual respectively. Title pages will be prepared in manuscript.

Place	Date	Hour	Summary of Events and Information	Remarks and references to Appendices
Armentières	8.10.15		Wounded 7057 Pte J. H. Aitken D Coy	
			16735 " T. C. Hudsworth C "	
			19278 " J. Paulson C "	
			17883 " G. Northage C "	
			19091 " A. Cunfe A "	
			16792 " H. Barrows D "	
	9.10.15		Killed 18745 Pte T. Dessman J Coy	
	10.10.15		" Capt A. C. Ruddell C Coy.	
	11.10.15		" 15217 Pte Wellhouse L. A Coy	
			Wounded 7305 Pte E. Hall J Coy	
			" 17939 " J. Storer C "	
			" 16056 " E. Hays C "	
			" 13838 Cpl N. Greatorex A "	
			" 18143 Cpl J. Smith A "	
			" 21107 Pte J. Dorsha A "	
	14.10.15		" 17906 " J. Gilbert A "	Accidently at Bomb School

Army Form C. 2118.

WAR DIARY
or
INTELLIGENCE SUMMARY.
(Erase heading not required.)

Instructions regarding War Diaries and Intelligence Summaries are contained in F. S. Regs., Part II. and the Staff Manual respectively. Title pages will be prepared in manuscript.

Place	Date	Hour	Summary of Events and Information	Remarks and references to Appendices
Bois Grenier	8.10.15		Wounded 16350 Pte A. Simpson A Coy	
	14.10.15		Dropped dead 16120 Pte. S.A. Fields A "	
	22.10.15		Wounded 16147 L.Cpl. R. Conley B "	
	"		18058 Pte Crowder C "	

2353 Wt.W2341/1454 700,000 5/15 L.D.&L. A.D.S.S./Form 2118.

WAR DIARY
or
INTELLIGENCE SUMMARY.
(Erase heading not required.)

Army Form C. 2118.

Place	Date	Hour	Summary of Events and Information	Remarks and references to Appendices
SAILLY	1915 1st Nov		Battalion in billets	
			14591 Pte Kemp R. 19397 Pte Wilson J.N. Struck off Strength 29.9.15 & 28.9.15. To England	
			16213 A/L/C Chappell D. 15732 Pte Lee W. 16350 Pte Simpson A. To England. Struck off Strength 23.10.15.	
	4th Nov		Battalion left billets & to take over WELL FARM, BRIDOUX FORT line of trenches from 7th Battn Middlesex Regt. The trenches were muddy & water in parts in many places, both parapets & dugouts were in a very bad state owing to the heavy rain.	
			19327 Pte Warren J. To England on 17.9.15 Struck off Strength from that date.	
			16245 Pte Hanwell H.E. killed in action	
Trenches	5th Nov		Lieut H. Bosonth 10th 13th Brigade from 14th Batt. Howard Hunter arrived & were taken on the Strength of the Battalion.	
	6th Nov		13502 Pte Nancy G. 460 Wounded in action	
			The Battalion handed over the Trenches to 2nd Battn Royal Berkshire Regt & marched back to billets at FLEURBAIX.	
	8th Nov		17025 (Capt Skinner A. 6645 Sgt Lyscom Broomhead To England 29.10.15. 16085 Pte Caffery J. To England 30.10.15 Struck off Strength from these dates	

WAR DIARY
or
INTELLIGENCE SUMMARY
(Erase heading not required.)

Army Form C. 2118.

Place	Date	Hour	Summary of Events and Information	Remarks and references to Appendices
FLEURBAIX	Nov 8		The following message has been received "The Brigadier regrets that an unfortunate accident has deprived him temporarily from the command of the Brigade. He wishes to thank all ranks for their loyal support during his short period of command & he is convinced that they will at had the same support & his successor will do their utmost to keep up the reputation which the Brigade has already gained." From General Phillips 26th Field Ambulance.	
FLEURBAIX	Nov 9		Branched out from Rifle & Tata, no killed at LA CROIX LES CORNEX from Rifle Brigade. Returned to 70th Infantry Brigade. Brigadier General R.B. Stephens (commanding 25th Brigade) sends the following message to the Officers N.C.O's & men of the Battalion on their return to the 70th Brigade - "I should like all ranks to know that a fort impression I have formed of your Battalion. You have done much toghether wish to the time their greatly approach. The condition have been bad but I have Officers & men able always cheerful & keen. From what I have seen of them, I am sure that when they have enough more active service practice they will acquit themselves with the greatest credit.	

Army Form C. 2118.

WAR DIARY
or
INTELLIGENCE SUMMARY.
(Erase heading not required.)

3

Place	Date	Hour	Summary of Events and Information	Remarks and references to Appendices
LA CROIX LES CORNET	Nov 10th		Extract from the London Gazette 6.11.15. The following Lieutenants with seniority from 28th July 1915. 2nd Lieut P. Hyatt. 2nd Lieut M. J. Vincent-Jackson.	
	Nov 11th		Marched to SAILLY to H ON billets from Scottish Rifles. 13835 Capt: Gustavus W. J. England 25.10.15. 30129 Pte Renorr. C. 27062 Pte Adcock. J. England on 12.10.15. & 11.11.15. Respectively struck off the strength from those dates.	
SAILLY	Nov 13th		16066 Pte Poling. W. To England 3.11.15. Struck off the strength. Regn W. Sankie-Phelan. (Captain.) C.S. Brennan. Lieut L. Halfer & Lieut R. Vincent-Jackson left on leave to England on leave.	
	Nov 18th		Marched from billets and took over WELL FARM – BRIDOUX Line of trenches from 2 Batt: Royal Dublin Fus: = Reached in a half state only & not weather.	
TRENCHES	Nov 19th		16325 Pte Smith L to England 11.11.15. Struck off strength. (Captain F.D. Blandy R.A.M.C. (T.F.) took over the duties of Medical Officer in 16th unit in place of Lieut W.G. Browne transferred. 1642 Pte Wilson J. wounded in action.	

Army Form C. 2118.

WAR DIARY
or
INTELLIGENCE SUMMARY.

(Erase heading not required.)

Instructions regarding War Diaries and Intelligence Summaries are contained in F. S. Regs., Part II. and the Staff Manual respectively. Title pages will be prepared in manuscript.

4

Place	Date	Hour	Summary of Events and Information	Remarks and references to Appendices
TRENCHES	Nov 20th		The enemy shelled between 2pm and 3p.m with field gun & a trench mortar the reported spot for shells & their impact. The following casualties resulted. Killed 16436 Pte L.H.Brown, Wounded 16366 LCpl Cope, Bugler H. 16281 Pte Simpson R. Killed 16091 Pte Bowen W.	
TRENCHES	Nov 22nd		16232 Cpl Dean W. died of wounds received in action. The Battalion handed in the trenches to 2nd Batt. Leicestershire Reg. & marched back to billets at SAILLY which were taken over from the Lincoln Reg.	
SAILLY	Nov 23rd		The Battalion marched from SAILLY at 1p.m en route for (approx.) Road billets at LA COURONNE	
LA COURONNE	Nov 24th		Busses from billets at 9 A.m for STA Pte BELLS near STEINBECQUE. The Battalion accommodated in Huts & billets. Some of the Officers billeted in farm houses.	
STEINBECQUE	Nov 25th		The Battalion commenced individual training & continued till 27th. Captain R.S. Brennan, Lieuts C. Halford & R. Vincent Jackson returned off leave from England on this date.	
	Nov 27th			
	Nov 29th		Major W. Forster Relan reported himself for duty with H.Q. Staff 23rd Division Company training commenced. Major H.L. Espin transferred to England 17.11.10 Street Willesden from that date	

2353 Wt.W25H/1454 700,000 5/15 D.D.&L. A.D.S.S./Forms/C. 2118.

Army Form C. 2118.

WAR DIARY
or
INTELLIGENCE SUMMARY.
(Erase heading not required.)

Place	Date	Hour	Summary of Events and Information	Remarks and references to Appendices
TEMPLEUVE	Nov 29th		2nd Lieut. G.E. McKerrall arrived & was taken on the Strength of the Battalion.	
	Nov 30th		Lieut. H. Gaskell arrived & was taken on Strength of the Battalion. The following report from H.L. Napier as missing believed to drowned in the sinking of S.S. ANGLIA. Extract from the London Gazette dated 26.11.15. Temporary Lieutenant to be Temporary Captain. John S. Carr 23rd September 1915. Charles S. Hudson 11th October 1915. George B. Fylde 30th October 1915. Temporary 2nd Lieutenants to be Lieutenant. Cyril J. Maitland October 1st 1915. Edward J. Russell October 15th 1915.	

8th, Division.

70th, Brigade.

11th, Notts & Derby.

December, 1915.

"The Moths" &c by
[Author of "First] Vol: 3

VIII

N.3

Army Form C. 2118.

WAR DIARY
or
INTELLIGENCE SUMMARY.
(Erase heading not required.)

11th Batt. Sherwood Foresters

Place	Date	Hour	Summary of Events and Information	Remarks and references to Appendices
Steenbecque	1915 Dec 1st		Battalion commenced Company Training. Extract from the London Gazette dated 26.11.15 "Reuters Foresters Temporary Lieutenants to be Temporary Captains. John E. Carr Sept 23rd 1915, Charles L. Pinder Oct 11th 1915, George B. Fydell Oct 30th 1915. Temporary 2nd Lieutenants to the Temporary Lieutenants. Cyril J. Pruitland Feb 1st 1915 Seniors Record Oct 15th 1915. Major J.H.H. Bernard D.S.O. assumed duties Station in the Strength of the Battalion Captain J.O. Blundy R.A.M.C. left the Battalion, no place being taken by Lieut P H Huggins R.A.M.C.	
"	Dec 5th			
"	Dec 5th		Lieut & Parsuits J S Jaques proceeded on leave days leave to England	
"	Dec 10th		Rev R.C.V. Gower arrived from the Base & was taken on the Strength 2/Lieut H.W. Corbin joined his arrival & was taken on the Strength	
"	Dec 15th		Company Training ended	
"	Dec 16		Battalion Training Commenced	
"	Dec 20		The Battalion marched out to Divisional Training, which took place in the area WARDRECQUES, THEROUANNE, ENGUINEGATTE, REBECQ, ROQUETAIRE, BLARINGHEM.	

WAR DIARY or INTELLIGENCE SUMMARY

Army Form C. 2118.

Place	Date	Hour	Summary of Events and Information	Remarks and references to Appendices
	Dec 20		Billeted at BLARINGHEM for the night	
	Dec 21		The Batt. marched to MELLES. Lt Batt. were billeted there for the night they at WESTREHEN	
	Dec 22		The 90th Infantry Brigade formed the Rear-guard & the 8th Division actg. as Light Battalion. In the late billet; finally taking billets at WARNE. 2/Lieut J. P. Tasker arrived was taken on the strength of the Battalion	
Steenbecque	Dec 23		The Brigade Marched back to billets at STEENBECQUE. The weather throughout the journey was most unfortunate. The Battalion Band also returned as the instruments had been sent in here from the depot at Caly. Lieut H. F. Gardner transferred to England on 12.12.15 to stand off the Kings 12 of Regt. Battalion	
"	Dec 24		Each man was been a Christmas Present which was sent out from the Regt by Wilkinson. A special arrangement was made for Suppers, teas whilst there. In spite of the heavy rain which has fallen - dinner went off successfully	
"	Dec 25		2/Lieut R. B. Milford detailed to leave on short trip to England	
"	Dec 27		(2/Lieut G. E. Martin, J. B. Fisher, Lieut P. Boyall & 2/Lieut R L Evans went	

Army Form C. 2118.

WAR DIARY
or
INTELLIGENCE SUMMARY.
(Erase heading not required.)

Instructions regarding War Diaries and Intelligence Summaries are contained in F. S. Regs., Part II. and the Staff Manual respectively. Title pages will be prepared in manuscript.

Place	Date	Hour	Summary of Events and Information	Remarks and references to Appendices
Montigny	Sep 29th		Proceeded on leave to England for seven days	
"	Oct 20		Arrived 17.30 leaving for the Battalion in the TREVESQUE sector and relieved transport Colonel Crofton Cumoll 6 Batt. Manch. relieving & began half of the home Batt. & one Coy A lent to the Battalion. The Gloucester Territorial Brigade being relieved. ISBERGUES.	
"	Oct 30		Brigadier General H. Hulm Pollok with Brig. Major were invited to have all the officers of the Battalion lunch a luncheon being given & ARLD LYNG SYKE followed by the Regimental march as the old Man bade away.	
"	Oct 31		Arthur Green returned from by leave today which was too short accommodation & Lieut. S.L. Hughes (who fame) the battalion from Base in the South	
				N.H. cotton Col

8th, Division.

70th, Brigade.

11th, Notts & Derby.

January, 1916.

n.4

11th Notts Hslsby
Vol: 4

VIII

23rd

Army Form C. 2118

WAR DIARY
or
INTELLIGENCE SUMMARY
(Erase heading not required.)

11th Batt. Kenwick Fusiliers January 1916

Place	Date 1916	Hour	Summary of Events and Information	Remarks and references to Appendices
STEENBECQUE	Jan 1st		2/Lt. H.L. ELLIS rejoined the Battalion from England (on recovering from wounds received in action) & 2/Lt.	
"	Jan 3rd		2/Lt. J.L. Royarko reported his arrival on 31st December 1915. A football team from 6th Batt. Kenwick Fusiliers came over from IJSBERGES where they were in billets to play the Battalion. They were beaten by 1/nil to nothing.	
"	Jan 5th		Captains C. Hudson, J.G. & J. Who, Lieut Hoyell & 2/Lieut Hoppcock returned from leave.	
"	Jan 6th		Marched the Battalion to IJSBERGES to meet the Kenwick Fusiliers Territorial Brigade billeted there. Played football against 8th Batt. Kenwick Fusiliers & after a close game were beaten by 2/nil to 6/1. Marched west in the evening to camp. A draft of 1 Sergt. & 39 men arrived from 13th Batt. Kenwick Fusiliers & were taken on the strength of the Battalion.	
"	Jan 7th		2/Lieut W.E. Short went to England on seven days leave.	
"	Jan 8th		2/Lieut J.B. Melville proceeded to England on seven days leave.	
"	Jan 10th		Marched out from STEENBECQUE & return to chief in the trenches. Billeted for the night at NEUF BERQUIN.	
NEUF BERQUIN	Jan 11th		The Brigade marched up & took in the line held by 20th Division. The Battalion formed Brigade Reserve to the right Battalion 10th Battalion H.L.I. at WEATHERCOCK HOUSE.	
RUE DE GUEVRE	Jan 13th		7029 Sergt. Bancroft H. wounded by a shell	
"	Jan 14th		2nd Lieut W.T.W. GREEN has from a Commission in the Manchester Regt & transferred to 76th Battalion of that Regiment	

WAR DIARY
or
INTELLIGENCE SUMMARY

(Erase heading not required.)

Army Form C. 2118

Place	Date	Hour	Summary of Events and Information	Remarks and references to Appendices
RUE DE GUESNE	Jan 15"		Relieved the 1st Batt KOYLI in the firing line. Head Quarters at RUE DE GUESNE.	
			2nd Lancs Regt on Right, 1st Batt KOYLI on Left.	
" "	Jan 19"		Gnrt Lan Cash Regt on our left. Captain J.S. Carr took on the duties of Adjutant & G' Lt. 2nd The 8th Division schotty of No trenches. 14144 Pte Jarman M.B. Wounded.	
" "	Jan 20"		Handed over the trenches to 1st R. Batt KOYLI & returned to WEATHERCOCK HOUSE. 19279 Pte Buster E. 15352 Pte Guy R. Wounded in action.	
" "	Jan 22"		15996 Sergt Phelan L. 16124 Lc Cpl Foots J. Killed in action. 15327 Pte Brown H. 16355 Pte Town J. Obit. J. Wounds. 15306 Pte Birstill 16208 Pte Barnshaw H. 16736 Rifleman J. 16345 Lc Cpl Brown 135.02 Pte Thomy J. 15474 Pte Burk H. Captain A.F. Bloomer Wounded in action. Lieut (Revd H.T. Hasten DSO. Concussed by land mine.	
IN TRENCHES	Jan 23"		1st Battalion took on the trenches from 1st Batt KOYLI 9. 2/Lieut C.B. Melville Killed in action. 14509 Pte (and P.) 21511 Lc Cpl McC. G.S. 15262 Rifleman 6253 Sgt Buckett. Wounded. Guards Division on right & 8th Batt Lanc Cash Regt on left.	
" "	Jan 25"		6698 Cpl Tompson H. 15114 Pte White T. Wounded in action.	
" "	Jan 26"		2d Batts. was relieved in the front line by the 2d Batt Royal Irish Rifles. 2d Batt. Royal Irish Lancasters Has shelled & moved to the farms. On leaving the trench the Batt. went into Divisional Reserve & took over the billets in RUE DE GUESNE - Remaining in these billets till the end of the month.	

A.R. Liston Lieut Colonel

8th, Division.

70th, Brigade.

11th, Notts & Derby.

February, 1916.

WAR DIARY or INTELLIGENCE SUMMARY

(Erase heading not required.)

Army Form C. 2118

11th Battn. Sherwood Foresters

Place	Date 1916	Hour	Summary of Events and Information	Remarks and references to Appendices
RUE DU BUSNOY. JAILLY	Feb. 1st		Battalion remained in Divisional Reserve. Lieut Colonel H.F. Watson DSO returned from leave.	
	Feb 2nd		The Battalion relieved 2nd Battn Loyal North Lancs Regt in the WELL FARM Line of trenches, 9th Bde 3rd Div. 1st Lancashire Regt on the Right & 23rd Division on the Left.	
TRENCHES	Feb 3rd		Brigade Head Qrs at FLEURBAIX also Brigade Reserve. 1792 L/Cpl Addington W. 17706 Pte Booth C. killed in action - 16218 Pte Cowell T. died of wounds. Lieut Mr. J. Vincent Jackson went out on a patrol in rear of enemy's lines in the opposite CORNER FORT. He was accompanied by 16253 Lance Corpl Howell A. & 16312 Pte Jackson A. & 15336 Pte Lewis J. When about 30 yards from the German line, the patrol was subjected to a severe cross-fire and Lieut Jackson was shot through the thigh. Pte Jackson who was nearest him stopped him back a short distance when Lance Corpl Howell joined them. He noted that Jackson & Lewis (a ulterior assistance while so endeavoring) to lift the wounded officer but was almost immediately hit. Lance Corpl Howell then got Lieut Jackson into his arms but was almost immediately hit. When the Lance Corpl to leave him & go to get	
"	Feb 5"		the same. Lieut Jackson was wounded again & ordered the Lance Corpl to leave him & go to get that he "did no more" - this he did by firing the other two men as they reached our own lines. On the arrival of 3rd O. C. Company then they knew we lost 2 more men & immediately a party went out & were sent under heavy fire with no result (this had been covered). Lance Corpl Howell & Pte Jackson have been recommended for the Distinguished Conduct Medal."	

Army Form C. 2118

WAR DIARY
or
INTELLIGENCE SUMMARY
(Erase heading not required.)

Instructions regarding War Diaries and Intelligence Summaries are contained in F. S. Regs., Part II. and the Staff Manual respectively. Title Pages will be prepared in manuscript.

Place	Date	Hour	Summary of Events and Information	Remarks and references to Appendices
TRENCHES	Feb 5th		7213 Regimental Sej. Mayor Mott was struck whilst on reconnaissance the S/O P Bryant & O.C Battalion round the trenches:	
			15776 Pte Vesey M.V. was wounded & died of wounds suffering from shell shock.	
			17905 Lance Corporal Smith W.S.	
			17813 Pte Hollings G.A. } Wounded in action	
			7274 Pte Withers G.	
			19178 Pte Broadly A	
			6743 Pte Eyre W	
			15283 Lance Corporal Truitt H.	
			16824 Pte Ayre L. Killed in action	
			5743 Pte Pipe W. Died of wounds.	
			15759 Pte Charlesworth P.C. Wounded in action.	
	Feb 6th		Truck car ran into 2 F. Battn A.C.O gates & raised a blaze at 5 L.M.G Bttn.	
FLEURBAIX	Feb 5		7213 Regimental Sej. Major Mott rose from the ranks to become Sej. Maj: His death is a very great loss to the Battn, a long strenuous, loyal & gallant soldier, who upheld all the best traditions of the service in which he was reared, will not only a short time before this was New Zealand, is nearly 25 years service.	
			He had re-enlisted by every Officer, N.C.O & man in the Battalion.	
			In Companies 2 Battn Northumberland Fusiliers were attached to this Batt for two weeks.	
	Feb 7		the Batt 10th Pte the trenches from Batt H.Q.p.J.J. & was accompanied into the trenches by the Co Companies	
TRENCHES	Feb 11		27 Batt Northumberland Fusiliers Major S right & on left to en Feb 5th =	
			2 Lieut C. Bennett reported to avoid relieve of the Battalion on 9th inst.	

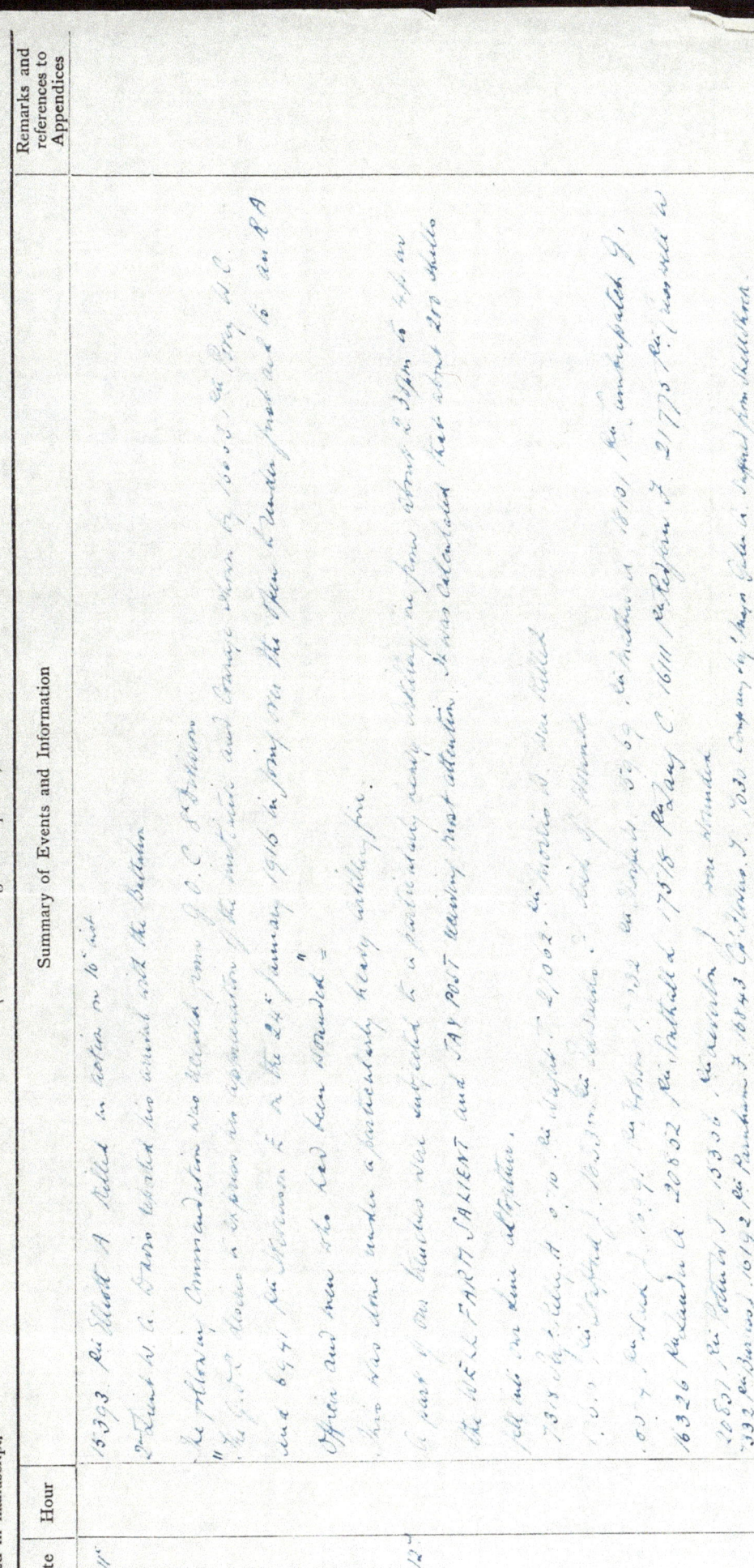

WAR DIARY or INTELLIGENCE SUMMARY

Army Form C. 2118

Place	Date	Hour	Summary of Events and Information	Remarks and references to Appendices
	Feb 14		2/Lt E.S. Rea Ellis & 109.83 Rifleman S. of the Rangers	
			The Bn. (composed of 21st Battn. Northumberland Fusiliers attached for a few days, two troops of our Hussars having surrendered)	
			Lieut. H.L. Harris 2/Lieuts E.H. Brittain & C.W. Bartlett Reported their arrival at 13ʰ.	
			0049 Rifleman Harris E. 17015 C. Batt. S. 0708 Rifleman Worthing wounded in action	
FLEURBAIX	Feb 15 Feb 16 Feb 17		The Battn. marched in from the trenches to the 1st Batt. H.Q. & S. and billeted in FLEURBAIX. 1807 Private T.T. died of wounds received on 12th inst. 6046 Rifleman H. 19337 Rifleman Jack H. wounded in action.	
			The 1st Battalion under Major R. Kershaw was quartered at FORT ROMPU. The Battalion played them at football at Mon Paten 2 goals to one. The Battalion Band played in the Camp of the 1st Battalion & to the 1st Batt. Headquarters in C/Sgts Room. The movements, music and tea of the Bandsmen were lent to them during their visit.	
TRENCHES	Feb 19		The Batt. took over the trenches from 1st Batt. K.O.Y.L.I. The 3rd Batt. York Lancaster Regt. on the right & the 3rd Division on the left.	
			2/Lieut I.T. H.S. 9 men arrived in the Batt.	
	Feb 20		2/Lieut F.A. Reynolds. 15862 A/Cpl Harr. J. 16432 Pte Hangood H. 1619 L/Cpl Bulling W. wounded	
	Feb 22		The Battn. Marched in from trenches to the 1st Batt. K.O.Y.L.I. & billeted in FLEURBAIX. Heavy fall of snow during the day soft & showy, first thaw hindered trenches for transport	
FLEURBAIX	Feb 25 Feb 27		2/Lieut C.H. Rands took a draft of 30 & OR men arrived in the Batt. 2nd Lieut. W.R.D. Carr. The Batt. in rear billeted 1st & 1st Batt. K.O.Y.L. The Bns. moved 700 Rfls new in our left & left.	

Army Form C. 2118

WAR DIARY
or
INTELLIGENCE SUMMARY
(Erase heading not required.)

Instructions regarding War Diaries and Intelligence Summaries are contained in F. S. Regs., Part II. and the Staff Manual respectively. Title Pages will be prepared in manuscript.

Place	Date	Hour	Summary of Events and Information	Remarks and references to Appendices
In TRENCHES	Feb 27		15373 Pte Newton C. wounded in action.	
	Feb 29		One six inch Howitzer opened fire on a part of the enemy's line called THE ANGLE opposite the left of our position.	
	"		5519 Sjt J. Millington to Wounded in action	
			J. Whetton Lieut (Adjt.)	

8th, Division.

70th, Brigade.

11th, Notts & Derby.

March, 1916.

Army Form C. 2118

WAR DIARY
or
INTELLIGENCE SUMMARY
(Erase heading not required.)

11th Batt. (Airborne) Pro tem

Place	Date 1916	Hour	Summary of Events and Information	Remarks and references to Appendices
IN TRENCHES	March 1st		18160 Sgt Percival L. wounded when in front of the parapet working on the wire.	
"	March 2nd		6049 Pte Morris S. & 20811 Pte Bee W.H. Wounded. 1st Battalion relieved in the trenches by the 8th Batt. K.O.Y.L.I. & went into billets at FLEURBAIX	
FLEURBAIX	March 3rd		Snow fell all the morning.	
"	March 4th		2/Lieut R.A. Johnson-Arrival was taken on the strength of the Battalion.	
IN TRENCHES	March 5th		1st Battalion took over the trenches from the 8th Batt. K.O.Y.L.I. 17962 Lance/Cpl Reesby A.W. & 17965 Pte Roots G. were wounded.	
"	March 7th		Snow fell nearly all day. 19462 Pte Roe S. was wounded.	
"	March 8th		There was a heavy fall of snow during the night of 7th/8th.	
"	March 9th		15841 Pte Printo J. 17989 Pte Walker H. & 19304 Pte Penn P were wounded	
"	March 10th		Handed over the trenches to 7th Batt. K.O.Y.L.I. & relieved & billets at FLEURBAIX.	
FLEURBAIX	March 11th		19511 Pte Pinnock N was wounded 13941 Pte Pinto J died of wounds received on 9.3.16. 2/Lieut C.S. Penn Arnison was taken on the strength of the Battalion. Captain H. Fox-Hill on return to England sick was struck off the strength of the Battalion	

Army Form C. 2118

WAR DIARY
or
INTELLIGENCE SUMMARY
(Erase heading not required.)

Instructions regarding War Diaries and Intelligence Summaries are contained in F. S. Regs., Part II. and the Staff Manual respectively. Title Pages will be prepared in manuscript.

Place	Date	Hour	Summary of Events and Information	Remarks and references to Appendices
FLEURBAIX	March 12th		Two (2) Companies of 1st Batt'n Royal Sussex Reg't stationed in 146th Brigade HQrs attached to this Battalion for instruction in trench warfare.	
"	March 13th		A party of FLEURBAIX who lately billeted, & a billet occupied by 9th Batt'n York & Lancaster Reg't near the 11th Batt'n Royal Sussex Reg't hit, wounding a considerable number of casualties.	
"	March 14th		1st & 2nd Batt'n the trenches from the 1st Batt'n R.O.Y.R.S. The Companies of 12th Batt'n Royal Sussex Reg't attached for instruction accompanied the Battalion into the trenches. 2nd Lieut. J.R. Lachan who proceeded when marching into the trenches with his Platoon.	
IN TRENCHES	March 16th		5350 Pte Bradley J killed & 1679.2 Pte Barrows A wounded. 1796.2 Lance Corp Sheeley H.W. wounded & 6 most died of wounds.	
"	March 17th		19023 Pte Battsworth W. Two wounded. The Battalion handed over the trenches to 1st Batt'n R.O.Y.R.S. and marched to FLEURBAIX billets. The 2nd Batt'n Royal Sussex Reg't provided then attachment to this Battalion & marched up to join the other parties of their Battalion in the WELLFARM LINE of trenches.	
FLEURBAIX	March 26th		The 4th Batt'n Hampshire Reg't took over the FLEURBAIX billets from this Battalion, who marched back into Divisional Reserve billets near SAILLY. Head Quarters being at CUL DE SAC FARM.	
CUL DE SAC FARM	March [?]		[?] 1st and 2nd in Command of 17th Batt'n Kings Own (Rifles) killed at LESTAIRES came see here Battalion	

WAR DIARY or INTELLIGENCE SUMMARY

Army Form C. 2118

Place	Date	Hour	Summary of Events and Information	Remarks and references to Appendices
OUL DE JAC FARM	March 22"		A letter was received from Lieut (local Capt) J. Ashton commanding 9th Batt L'pool & Lancaster Regt stating that he wishes to thank 2/F322 Pte Mullens G.R. (Company 11th Battn Kenning) Fusiliers for the very useful & valuable assistance given by him on the behalf of his Battalion in the BATTLE of the 9th Batt L'pool & Lancaster Regt on the 13th March 1916 on the occasion of a RAID by King George's Hills.	
"	March 24		Heavy fall of snow.	
"	March 23		The 15th (Durham) Battalion 16th & 17th Battalions Kenning Fusiliers were all billeted at L'ESTAIRES till this Battalion was billetted within three miles of them. The Battalion ordered to meet the march 6.7". The Battalion & the Kenning Fusiliers marched from OUL DE JAC FARM at 1.15 pm and went into billets at CALONNE for the night	
CALONNE	March 29		Marched out at 3 a.m. & entrained at LESTREM at 5.20 a.m. arriving at LONGUEAU at 4.57 am & went into	
VIGNACOURT	March 28		The Battalion then marched through AMIENS to VIGNACOURT arriving at 10.30 p.m. & went into billets. 2nd Lieuts R.J. Nicholls & J.C. Harrison arrived & were taken on the strength of the Battalion.	
"	March 30		The Battalion left VIGNACOURT and marched to ST GRATIEN where it was billetted for the night.	
ST GRATIEN	March 31		The Battalion marched from ST GRATIEN into billets at ALBERT preparatory to taking over the trenches near AUTHUILLE WOOD. Major Popham A.S.O. Kenning Fusiliers has Bazentin trying to 68th Brigade about the Battn to take over from	

N. Malcolm Lieut Colonel

8th, Division.

70th, Brigade.

11th, Notts & Derby.

April, 1916.

WAR DIARY
or
INTELLIGENCE SUMMARY.
(Erase heading not required.)

Place	Date	Hour	Summary of Events and Information	Remarks and references to Appendices
ALBERT	April 11th		ALBERT. The Battalion marched from Abbotts and took over a portion of a line of trenches from the 16th Bn. Northumberland Fusiliers 96th Bde.	
In Trenches	April 12th		Capt. A. R. Halford wounded & duty No. 16969 Pte Wallace L. wounded to Hospital	
In Trenches	April 12th		No. 22612 Pte Norris H wounded 4.4.16 to Hospital	
In Trenches	April 13th		No. 15079 Pte Rippon died of wounds 5.4.16 received in action some date	
			No. 17997 Cpl Glover H wounded Hospital 5.4.16.	
ALBERT	April 14th		The Bn was relieved in the trenches by the 8th R.O.Y.L.I. and came into Brig. sct. Reserve in ALBERT.	
In Trenches	April 15th		The Bn marched from ALBERT and took over the trenches from the 8th Bn. York & Lanc Regt. became right Bn. left 8th Lept 18th VIII Div.	
In Trenches	April 15th		No. 19474 Pte Stake J. wounded to Hospital 15.4.16.	
In Trenches	April 16th		The Bn was relieved by 2nd Devon Regt & marched into Bde Reserve at HENENCOURT WOOD and took over billets from 2nd Bn West York Regt.	
In Trenches	April 17th		No. 16466 Pte Sturio G. No. 19314 Pte Rainford J. No. 16169 Pte Anthony H. No. 21612 Pte Deakin H. all wounded 16.4.16 to Hospital 17.4.16.	

Army Form C. 2118.

WAR DIARY
or
INTELLIGENCE SUMMARY.
(Erase heading not required.)

Instructions regarding War Diaries and Intelligence Summaries are contained in F. S. Regs., Part II. and the Staff Manual respectively. Title pages will be prepared in manuscript.

Place	Date	Hour	Summary of Events and Information	Remarks and references to Appendices
HENENCOURT	April 18th		No 16468 Pte Shaw W. died of wounds received in action 16.4.16.	
HENENCOURT	April 24th		No 19282 L/Corpl Swann b. accidentally wounded at 76th M.G.Coy. & Hospital	
HENENCOURT	April 24th		No 15625 Pte Noblett R. died from natural causes while on line of march.	
DERNANCOURT	April 25th		The Bn marched from HENENCOURT having one t. and taking over from 2nd B. Rifle Bge — Thorne right reserve Bn right 18th Bde VIII Div.	
	26th		18209 Pte BURGESS wounded while attached to the 2nd Field Coy R.E. 1/5th Hospital accidentally received	
	27th		No 19252 L/Cpl DAWSON died in Hospital from wounds received 17/4/16	
BÉCOURT WOOD	April 28th		No 16580 Pte LEVY, T. wounded and admitted to Hospital 28.4.16	
DERNANCOURT	29th		No 16117 L/Cpl REDFERN, W. wounded, to duty.	

Jville Bernal
Major
1/7th Service Battalion
The Sherwood Foresters

8th, Division.

70th, Brigade.

11th, Notts & Derby.

May, 1916.

Army Form C. 2118.

WAR DIARY
or
INTELLIGENCE SUMMARY.
(Erase heading not required.)

August/16

11 Notts & Derby
Vol 8

Place	Date	Hour	Summary of Events and Information	Remarks and references to Appendices
In the Trenches	2/5/16		The Bn moved from DERNANCOURT and relieved the 8th Bn Y.& L.O.Y. L.I. and became right Bn of right Brigade VIII Divs in the front line trenches. No 22376 Cpl Peake 6. No 17997 Cpl Ghorn & No 16000 Pte Childs wounded & Hospital	
In the Trenches	3/5/16		No 27964 L/Cpl Bulter R. No 15606 Pte Luckworth J killed in action No 17026 Cpl McKern C L° 14574 Cpl Wilkinson B. wounded & Hospital	Mr Chapman
In the Trenches	4/5/16		No 16170 Pte Maw S.A. No 13628 Pte Clarke R. No 19288 Pte Belton G. No 16380 Sgt Hick F. No 16117 L/Cpl Patten C. No 15776 Pte Heyes V. No 16358 Sgt Farncombe R wounded & Hospital	
In the Trenches	5/5/16		N° 15633 Pte Lord S. wounded Hospital	
In the Trenches	6/5/16		N° 7739 Sgt Brockhurst B. killed in action N° 19594 L/Cpl Nathan T. wounded & Hospital The Bn was relieved in the trenches by the 23rd Bn Northumberland Fusiliers & came into Divl reserve	J.B.
HENNENCOURT	9/5/16			
MILLENCOURT	19/5/16		The Bn moved in 6 Divl reserve at MILLENCOURT relieving 2/1s Rifle Brigade	
ALBERT	27/5/16		The Bn relieved 2nd Lincoln Regt in ALBERT and became right of right Brigade VIII Divn in Divn reserve	

Army Form C. 2118.

WAR DIARY
or
INTELLIGENCE SUMMARY.
(Erase heading not required.)

Place	Date	Hour	Summary of Events and Information	Remarks and references to Appendices
In the Trenches	3/5/16		The Bn. moved from ALBERT and relieved the 8th Bn. K.O.Y.L.I. in the trenches becoming Right Bn. Left Bde. Brigade VIII Div. in the front line trenches.	

A.J.Walker Lieut Colonel
11 (Service) Battn.

70/8

11" Bn Sherwoods.

June 1916

File Nº 1

HISTORICAL SECTION
MILITARY BRANCH.

EGYPT & PALESTINE.
Vol. II.
MAP A.

June

Army Form C. 2118.

WAR DIARY
or
INTELLIGENCE SUMMARY.
(Erase heading not required.)

1st Batt. Honved J[?] Fusrs. Vol 9

VII

Instructions regarding War Diaries and Intelligence Summaries are contained in F. S. Regs., Part II. and the Staff Manual respectively. Title pages will be prepared in manuscript.

Place	Date	Hour	Summary of Events and Information	Remarks and references to Appendices
The Trenches	1916. 1st June		A patrol under Lieut E. Russell with an officer R.E. blew up a cart in No Mans Land which was exposed to Apl Shellfire & Sniper.	Miss Brown (?)
		1020	Pte Piper H. Wounded — to Hospital.	
	2nd June		Lieut P. Wyatt with nine men sortied to German wire about 60 yards from our parapet. Seven bombs were thrown into the German advanced trench. One burst falling amongst a party of Germans. The officer firing his shots into the position at them, at a range of roughly 30 yards. The patrol returned to our lines in safety.	T. 9
		6735	Sgt. Grady W. previously reported as missing on 9.10.15. is now reported as killed in action. His body having been found by a patrol & identified by the bottles in the shoulders & his pay book.	
		1640	Pte Bird J. & 16205 Pte. Fell F. Wounded — to Hospital.	
			2 Lieut J. C. Harben is gazetted to have the Suffix of a Lieutenant pending the customary ratification in the London Gazette.	
			Lieut A. C. Watts is gazetted to have the Suffix of Rank of a Captain pending the customary ratification in the London Gazette.	
	3rd June		A patrol consisting of Lieut P. Wyatt, 2 Lieut W.S.R. Short, a Lewis gun & 25 men left our	

WAR DIARY or INTELLIGENCE SUMMARY

Army Form C. 2118.

Place	Date	Hour	Summary of Events and Information	Remarks and references to Appendices
	June 4.		Trenches about 11.40 pm both the intention of engaging the German patrols & if possible capturing a prisoner. Unfortunately the Germans sealed the Battalion on our right about the same time & own them movements which the moved in front of our trenches were drawn upon & fired. They opened a very heavy shrapnel & machine gun fire & his men knelt in no man's line, also firing on them our front line of trenches at far in front of the point at which the patrol had arrived. At 12.30 am the patrol who stayed 4 extra 9 returned to our lines safely with the exception of Lieut. P. Wyatt who was unfortunately wounded so he lies crossing our parapet. This officer has gone out on many patrols & invariably done good work. It is therefore a matter of great regret that he should have been wounded just as he had succeeded in bringing back to hospital from a most unpleasant position, without incurring a casualty. 7320 L/Cpl. Price J. 17753 Lance Corp. Booth W.A. 16710 Pte. Gardner L. 17091 Pte. Simmons P.D. were recommended for the Military Medal for their gallant behaviour in the fights of 2nd & 3rd June. When on patrol & again on 4th. They also took part in the patrol on June 10th. 16457. Pte. Nicholls. A. Killed in action. 21573 Pte. Locker J. 14821 Pte. Nice A. Wounded to hospital. 13521 Pte. Walsh J. Wounded - hospital.	

WAR DIARY or INTELLIGENCE SUMMARY

Army Form C. 2118.

Place	Date	Hour	Summary of Events and Information	Remarks and references to Appendices
HÉNENCOURT	June 8th 9th		Handed over the trenches to 2nd Batl. Devon Regt. marched back to Divisional Reserve at HÉNENCOURT WOOD. 16496 Pte Heaton W. Killed in action. 7273 Pte Bell C. Wounded to hospital on 3.6.16.	
	June 12th		The Batt. marched to FRAMVILLERS to take part in an exercise involving the attack of certain German lines of trenches, shown by flags. The Brigade practised the same attack at FRAMVILLERS in conjunction with the 32nd Division. In the evening the Batt. marched from HÉNENCOURT WOOD to the BOUZINCOURT trenches. This were taken over from the 2/Rifle Brigade. The weather during the stay of the Batt. at HÉNENCOURT had been very fine. Almost continuous rain with cold winds. In the 2 admirzette of June 3rd. 16253 Lce. Cpl. Arnett A. 16312 A.cs Cpl. Jackson A. were awarded the Military Medal for gallantry on 5th February 1915 when in the trenches near FLEURBAIX attempting to bring in Lieut. B. J. Vincent Jackson who had been wounded whilst out on patrol.	

Lieuts R.P. Reeves, J.L. Radford, J.C.M. Jackson, J. Bryers, S.C. Carter, J. Dryhurst, J.H. Woft

Army Form C. 2118.

Instructions regarding War Diaries and Intelligence Summaries are contained in F. S. Regs., Part II. and the Staff Manual respectively. Title pages will be prepared in manuscript.

(Erase heading not required.)

WAR DIARY or INTELLIGENCE SUMMARY

Army Form C. 2118.

Place	Date	Hour	Summary of Events and Information	Remarks and references to Appendices
BOUZINCOURT (DEFENCES)	June 13th		9 H.A. Orrett arrived & now taken on the Strength of the Battn. A draft of 16 other ranks arrived & are taken on the strength. Major G.A. Bond D.S.O. 2/Lieut Humphreys left the Battn. N.C.O.S. 9 men C.S.M.S. Parla & Palin Sergt. Connaughton J, Raw W, Jackson B, Lyman B, Bromley A, Groot H, Bathurst J. Lance Corpl. Hughitt, Sutherland G, Stratton J, Amys A. Private Handley, Lambert, Ruby & Finch, attended the Memorial Service to Lord Kitchener held at MELLINCOURT. These N.CO & men were all chosen as they had all served in the South African Campaign.	
"	June 14th		A Draft of 20 men arrived from 4 Battn. & are taken on the strength. The enemy in France adopted the new front last time 11 p.m. became midnight 14.6.16. N° 1928 Pte Jordan J wounded	
"	June 15th		Capt C.S. Hudson & 2/Lt 22113 R.S.M. Hull J.H. (all ground) led to distinction (Staff mentioned) in the G.O.C-in-C's despatch dated April 30th 1916 An unfortunate accident occurred at the 75th Brigade Bomb School at Long to the following men wounded and admitted to hospital 2/Lieut R.P. Redfern N° 16301 Sergt. Wattley H. N° 14726 Cpl. Perkins D. N° 13621 Cpl. Clarke R.	

Army Form C. 2118.

WAR DIARY
or
INTELLIGENCE SUMMARY.
(Erase heading not required.)

Instructions regarding War Diaries and Intelligence Summaries are contained in F. S. Regs., Part II. and the Staff Manual respectively. Title pages will be prepared in manuscript.

Place	Date	Hour	Summary of Events and Information	Remarks and references to Appendices
B04.21.N(O&R) (DEFENCES)	June 20		N° 15427 Pte Smith J.H. honoured & hospitaled 20.6.16. N° 18120 Pte Bate C died of wounds received in action 20.6.16.	
In the TRENCHES	June 25th		Battn took over Bde front line	
"	27th		Battn were relieved in front line & took of their final position of assembly in GLASGOW Street	
"	28th		Owing to attack being postponed 48 hours the Battn again took over front line. 2nd Lieut F.A. LAWS wounded, 1 Pts killed, 2 Pts wounded.	
"	29th		2nd Lieut R.A. JOHNSON wounded, 2 Pts wounded.	
"	30th		Battn took up final position of assembly for 2nd time. Captain P.H. Lee Donald RFA wounded, 2 Pts killed, 7 Pts wounded	

A. Swinhoe Phelan Major

Comdg 11th (Service) Bn Northumbd Fusiliers

Secret

11th (Service) Battalion THE SHERWOOD FORESTERS
Operation Order No. 6

17th June, 1916.

Reference Map 1/5,000 LA BOISSELLE
For our own Trenches - Reference Map "A".

---

1. Plan

In conjunction with the rest of the Fourth Army the 8th Division will assault the German trenches on the front X.14.a.5.6. to R.31.d.9.0. on the date for the present known as "Z".

Simultaneously the 34th Division will attack the German trenches on the right of this Division, and the 32nd Division on the left of it.

2. Disposition of Division for Attack.

The 8th Division will attack with its three Brigades in the front line; the 23rd Brigade on the right, 25th Brigade in the centre and the 70th Brigade on the left. The Dividing Line between the 25th & 70th Bdes. will be as follows:- X.2.c.1.1. - X.2.c.8.5. - X.2.d.2.6. - X.2.b.6.2.- North Side of Trench to X.2.b.9.0. (trench junction at this point inclusive to 25th Brigade) - North side of trench to Road at X.3.a.4.1. - thence along North side of Road to R.34.a.9.1. (Road inclusive to 25th Brigade).

3. Objective.

The Objective of the 8th Division is a line from X.5.c.0.5. through the Eastern outskirts of POZIERES (about X.4.b.7.5.) - R.34.d.0.9. (inclusive) - R.34.a.9.1. (inclusive) - R.34.a.7.4. - R.34.a.6.5. to about R.28.c.2.0. This line will be consolidated as soon as it is reached. There are in addition to this other intermediate lines which are to be consolidated as soon as captured. These will be known as (a) 1st Position to be Consolidated
      (b) 2nd " " " "
      (c) Divisional Objective.
and are for the 70th Brigade.
    (a) From Z.2.b.6.2., 44, 48, to R.32.d.1.2.
    (b) From R.33.d.8.5., 78, 89, to R.33.b.5.5. to a point about R.33.b.4.7.

4. Distribution of Battalion

The Brigade will attack with two Battalions in the front line, 1 Battalion in Support and 1 in Reserve. These will in future orders be often referred to as "A" "B" "C" & "D" Battalions.
 "A" Battalion front line (right) 8th K.O.Y.L.I.
 "B" Battalion front line (left) 8th York & Lancs.
 "C" Battalion Supporting Battn. 9th York & Lancs.
 "D" Battalion Reserve Battalion 11th Sherwood Foresters.
"A" & "B" Battalions will advance in four waves, "C" & "D" Battalions in two waves.

Sheet 2.

5. Distribution of R.E. and Pioneers.

The 2nd Field Coy. R.E. will work with 70th Bde. This Company will be in assembly places in the rear of Brigade. It will consolidate certain points and trenches in conjunction with the Infantry. Pioneers will open up communication between the German front line and our line immediately the German front line is captured.

Communication trenches will be dug across NO MANS LAND from near STANLEY STREET to X.2.c.3.9.

6. Distribution of Brigade Machine Guns.

Machine Guns of the Brigade will be distributed as follows:-
4 Guns in ROOK STREET X.1.a.2.3.
4 Guns about X.1.b.4.4. in advance of MERSEY STREET
2 Guns in CONISTON STREET X.7.a.3.2.
2 Guns in BAMBERBRIDGE STREET.

7. Patrols.

During the final stages of the bombardment strong Officers patrols will be sent out with a view to seeing what damage has been done, and if possible entering the Trenches and securing a prisoner.

8. Preparation for the Assault.

The assault will be preceded by:-
(a) An Artillery Bombardment lasting 5 days, first day being "U" Day; the Assault to be carried out on "Z" Day.
(b) By discharge of Gas and Smoke. Gas will also be liberated during the night of the V/W on the front of the Brigade on our right.
(c) Smoke will be liberated along the whole Divisional Front for half-an-hour at 6.20 a.m. on "Y" Day. In addition to the above on "Z" Day a Smoke Barrage will be formed by 4" Stokes Mortars of the left of the 70th Brigade, firing from the vicinity of North end of Trench X.1.c.

9. Wire Cutting.

The Battalion will be called upon to continue with the cutting of our own wire when it takes its position in the front line. Care must be taken not to give this operation away. Further instructions will be issued.

10. Preliminary Moves.

The Brigade took over its allotted portion of the Front Line on the night 19/20th June. On the night 26/27th this Battalion will take over the Brigade Frontage from the 9th York & Lancs. On the night 27/28th the Battalion will move from the front line into the position allotted to it prior to the assault; "B" "D" & "C" Coys. in GLASGOW ROAD, "A" Coy. in LOWER HORWICH STREET, Lewis Gun Section & Bn. H.Qrs. QUARRY POST.

11. General Idea of the Attack.

Before the Zero hour, which will notified later, "A" & "B" Battalions will move their two leading waves in front of our wire, their two rear waves will be in our own front line. "C" Battalion will be in readiness to move into our front line as the last two waves of "A" & "B" Battalions move out. Similarly this Battalion will move into our front line as "C" Battalion leaves it.

The leading two waves of "A" & "B" Battalions will move forward above ground without stopping to the Third German Line. The third and fourth waves will then be in the Second German Line. The First German Line will then be occupied by the first wave of "C" Battalion, and

Sheet 3.

and their second wave will be in our front line, while this Battalion will be preparing to move forward into our own front line.

At 0.30 the Artillery Barrage will lift from the first position to be consolidated and the advance of the Brigade will be resumed till the leading two waves of "A" & "B" Battalions have entered the position to be consolidated.

The remainder of the Brigade will still retain its previous distance, so that this Battalion will be formed up in our own front line trench.

On the advance from the first position to be consolidated being begun the first wave of this Battalion will leave our front line, being followed by the second wave when the first wave leaves the first German Line.

O.C. "D" Company will find that, in order to form an Offensive Defensive flank to the left, O.C. "B" Battalion has left Garrisons of Bombers and Lewis Gunners near points 25, 46, 79 & 03. These Garrisons will not be sent forward until O.C. "D" Coy. is satisfied that the situation is clear and has reported it to the O.C. Battalion who will give the necessary orders for these Garrisons to rejoin their unit.

The Artillery Barrage will lift from the second position to be consolidated at 1.25. The leading troops, i.e. "A" & "B" Battalions each supported by two Companies of "C" Battn. will not leave the first position till 1.10. On the arrival of the first wave of "D" Battalion at the first position to be consolidated they will at once proceed to do this. The second wave of "D" Battalion will then be in the German Third Line. On the advance of the leading troops towards the second position to be consolidated the second wave of "D" Battalion will advance in support of them, passing through the first wave, and when these have gone on to the Divisional Objective the second wave of "D" Battalion will consolidate the second position.

12.
Special Idea for "D" Battalion

This Battalion will be the Reserve Battalion, i.e. "D" Battalion.
(a) Movement prior to "Z" Day;
On the night 26/27th the Battalion will relieve the 8th K.O.Y.L.I. in the left section of the trenches and will be relieved by that Battalion in the ALBERT - BOUZINCOURT Defences. No movement will take place till 10 p.m.
"A" Coy. and the Lewis Gun Section will hold the front line from LONGRIDGE STREET to MERSEY STREET both inclusive. This long line will be held by a series of posts.
"B" Company will be in dug-outs in BAMBERBRIDGE STREET and CHORLEY STREET.
"C" Company will be in dug-outs in QUARRY BRAE STREET.
"D" Company will be in dug-outs in GLASGOW ROAD.
Battalion Headquarters will be in QUARRY BRAE STREET.
The patrols referred to in para 7 will be found by "C" Company and the O.C. that Company will submit by 12 noon each day a time table of the patrols he proposes to send out that night, so that the Artillery may be warned against firing on that area.

Snipers are to be kept at work through the bombardment, together with rifle and Lewis Gun fire during the Smoke Barrage.

A Defensive System of Observers will be established and reports sent in of the effect of the bombardment, etc. on the special pro forma which is being issued together with more detailed instructions.

During the discharge of gas and smoke careful note will be made of the system of Barrages established by the enemy.

Further instructions will be issued about gas.

Sheet 4.

The Battalion will be responsible for all repairs to defences and for keeping communication trenches in the Battalion area open; this will be done by "B" & "D" Coys. on receiving orders from the Commanding Officer.
(b) During the night 27/28th the Battalion will be relieved by the 8th Y. & L. and will then move to its position of assembly prior to the assault: "A" Coy. will be in LOWER HORWICH STREET, "B" "D" & "C" Companies in that order from the right in GLASGOW ROAD ~~and the Lewis Gun Section in QUARRY POST~~. Bn. H.Qrs. will remain at QUARRY POST.

read Y/Z

During the night Y/Z 2nd Lieut.J.R.BYERS with 21122 Pte.Woodhouse, 15522 Pte.Wade, 13351 Pte.Godfrey and 18689 Pte.Shorthouse, will report to O.C. "C" Battalion at his Headquarters in our own front line and will act as Liaison Officer between that Battalion and "D" Battalion. He will be responsible for keeping O.C. "D" Battalion informed of the position of "C" Battalion during the advance.

13.
"Z" Day.

"D" Battalion will advance in two waves, each wave being composed of a half Coy. from each Coy. There will be 2 Lewis Guns with "D" Coy. and one with each of "A" "B" & "C" Coys., the remainder will be with Battalion Headquarters.
The Zero hour will be notified later.
O.C. Companies will,arrange that if possible their men have a hot meal before starting.
As the last wave of "C" Battalion is preparing to leave our front line the first wave of "D" Battalion will prepare to move into it by the following routes in the order stated below:-
(1) "A" Company by QUARRY BRAE STREET and "C" Company by CHORLEY & BAMBERBRIDGE STREETS.
(2) "B" Company by QUARRY BRAE STREET and "D" Company by CHORLEY & STANLEY STREETS.
The first wave will move into our own front line as the last wave of "C" Battalion moves out. The second wave will also move forward and take up its position as follows:-
"A" Company in QUARRY BRAE STREET, "B" Company in QUARRY POST.
"C" Company in BAMBERBRIDGE STREET & CHORLEY STREET and "D" Company in STANLEY STREET & CHORLEY STREET.
All movement prior to crossing our own front line will be below ground.
As the first wave moves out of our own front line the second wave will move in.
The order for the first wave to move into our own front line will be given from Battalion Headquarters; subsequent advances of the first wave as far as the first position to be consolidated and of the second wave as far as the Third German line will be made on the initiative of O.C. Coys. on receiving information from their contact patrols to the effect that the wave in front of them is moving forward. Great care must be taken, however, not to lose touch with the Companies on the flanks.
The first wave will move into the first position to be consolidated as "A" "B" & "C" Battalions move forward to the second position to be consolidated. The first wave will remain in and will consolidate the first position.
The second wave will then be in the German third line.
In the advance to the first position to be consolidated "A" Coy., holding from LONGRIDGE STREET inclusive to QUARRY BRAE STREET exclusive, will advance with its right through

Sheet 5.

11, 85, 28, 62 and its left through 24, 56, 67, 88 to 44, exclusive.

"B" Company, holding from left of "A" Company to Sap No.2 (X.1.d.3.5.) inclusive, will advance with its right in touch with "A" Company and its left through 37, 81, 03 to half way between 44 and 48.

"C" Company, holding from left of "B" Company to STANLEY STREET exclusive, will advance with its right in touch with "B" Company and its left through 39, 04, 06, to 30 yards North of 48.

"D" Company, from left of "C" Company to junction of track with our front line at X.1.d.7.9. will advance with its right in touch with "C" Company and its left through 22, 56 to 12.

These points apply to both the first and second waves of "D" Battalion. From the Third German line to the second position to be consolidated the second wave will advance as follows:- Right of "A" Company left through 62, 90, 94, 40, exclusive and onwards in touch with the right of "B" Company. Left of "B" Company will advance through half way between 44 and 48, 78, 61. "C" Company will advance in touch with "B" Company on its right and "D" Company on its left through 30 yards North of 48 and onwards. "D" Company will advance with its right in touch with "C" Company and its left through 12, 86, up trench to R.33.a.1.0. - R.33.b.4½.6½.

The advance of the second wave of "D" Battalion from the third German Line will not be begun till orders are received from Battalion Headquarters. This advance will be carried out in support of the leading troops as stated in para II. No advance will be made in front of the second position to be consolidated unless orders to do so are received from Bn. H.Qrs. as it is the work of the second wave of "D" Battalion to consolidate this position. The leading troops move on to the Divisional Objective at 2.30

During the advance Battalion Headquarters will be stationed as follows:-
    (a) with the second wave
        (1) At "A" Battalions Headquarters when the second wave is in our own front line.
        (2) At 37 when the second wave is in the first German line.
    (b) On the arrival of the first wave at the first position to be consolidated Bn. H.Qrs. will move to the left of "B" Coy.
    (c) On the advance of the second wave to the second position to be consolidated Bn. H.Qrs. - less the Second in Command - will move in rear of the centre of it. The Second in Command will remain at the first position to be consolidated and will take charge of that line.

15. Attached to Bn. H.Qrs.

On "Z" Day the following will be with Bn. H.Qrs. R.S.M., Lewis Gun Section, H.Q. Signallers, 21103 Cpl. Carlin A., 18075 Pte.Copestake A., Regtl.Police, Regtl. Pioneers, Battalion Orderlies, 2 scouts per Coy. as under and H.Q. Bombers as under:-

Sheet 6.

Scouts.
"A" Company 15286 Pte. Taylor,   16126 Pte. Pickworth.
"B" Company 16147 L/C Cowley,   28543 " Newbury
"C" Company 16164 Pte. Smith,   13305 " Dilkes
"D" Company 14981 L/C Hopkinson,   19149 " Marshall.

Headquarters Bombers.
"A" Company 24417 L/C Waterfield, 13863 Pte. Fletcher,
            21583 Pte. Bingham,
"B" Company 18953 " Sutton,   15547 " Trenham,
"C" Company 16022 " Walmsley,   17765 " Walmsley,
             6851 " Morely.
"D" Company 19325 " Smith,   20762 " Harrison.

16. Dress and Equipment, Etc.

Fighting Order. Great coats will be taken into the trenches in addition to Fighting Order. The remainder of the men's kit will be collected by the T.O. during the 25th. Great Coats will be stored by Companies in dug-outs during the night of Y/Z and one man per Coy. will be left in charge of them.

Iron Rations; unconsumed portion of the days rations; water bottles are to be full at the moment of crossing our own parapet; 220 rounds of S.A.A. per man, except that the L.G.S. will only carry 50 rounds per man and Bombers 120 rounds per man; two sandbags per man, 2 bombs per man; every fourth man a pick or shovel in equal proportions.

The following will also be issued when details as to distribution will also be given :- 130 wire cutters with lanyards, 130 wire cutters for fixing on the end of rifles, 64 bill hooks, 120 pairs of hedging gloves, bridges, flares for signalling to aeroplanes in accordance with "Instructions regarding Liaison between Infantry and Aircraft", in the event of the Battalion being pushed forward into the assaulting line, vigilant periscopes for the same purpose as the flares.

Bombing parties of which there will be one per platoon composed of 1 N.C.O. & 7 men carrying the following number of bombs:-

2 Throwers 4 bombs each, 2 Bayonet men 4 bombs each, 2 carriers with 2 buckets each holding 12 bombs in each bucket, 1 spare man carrying 2 buckets each holding 12 bombs. Headquarters Bombing Party will each carry 2 buckets, each holding 12 bombs. Bombs are not to be thrown indiscriminately as they are very hard to replace.

17. Prisoners.

The leading Battalions will pass all their prisoners back to this Battalion. Prisoners will be passed back by Companies to Battalion H.Q. under a guard of one man for every 15 prisoners. The H.Q. Prisoners Party will be composed of :- 6818 Sgt. Slater J., 21765 L/C Legate, 6979 Pte. Bullock, 16178 Pte. Burgin, 22608 Pte. Smith, 18059 Pte. Morely, 19703 " Chambers, 6912 L/S Mettershead, 7280 L/C Bowden, 7286 " Smith, 18175 Pte. Wragg, 16363 Pte. Slack, 18205 " Wilson, 16456 " White, 18196 " Shelton, 14344 " Wickes,.

There will be a prisoners collecting station at the Brickworks W.22.d.6.8. on the ALBERT - AVELUY Road.

Sheet 7.

18. Casualties.

The ordinary casualty report will be rendered daily in writing by 12.15 p.m. During fighting the estimated number of casualties will be forwarded by O.C. Companies to Bn. H.Qrs. every one-and-half hours from Zero Hour. These reports will always include the previous estimated report. Such reports will show numbers only, and no distinction will be made between killed and wounded; Officers will be shown separately and by ranks. These estimated returns may be sent by the best means available. The normal casualty report in writing will be sent in as nearly up to time as possible during fighting.
The reason for estimated casualty returns is to enable the number of reinforcements to be arrived at.

19. Medical.

The Battalion Dressing Station will be at the advanced Dressing Station near QUARRY POST. Stretcher bearers should keep as far forward as possible.

20. Rations. *

The normal method of feeding the Battalion will be continued as long as possible; when this is no longer practicable, from the Dump at QUARRY POST Cookhouse which contains 8,000 Rations. Rations Dumps have also been established at

```
    QUARRY POST Cookhouse      8,000
    TRAM BASE W.22.c.5.1.     24,000
    W.22.4.8.1.               12,000.
```

21. Water. *

Water will be obtained from the Pipe Supply in AUTHUILLE WOOD for as long as possible. When this fails water may be obtained from the following tanks in canvas water buckets under Coy. arrangements

```
    Cookhouse, QUARRY POST       1,500 Gals.
    QUARRY POST                    200  "
    Battalion H.Qrs.               100  "
    Brigade Headquarters           100  "
    CONISTON POST                  100  "
    QUARRY Dressing Station         50  "
    M.O's dug-out, HORWICH St.     100  "
    STANLEY STREET                 200  "
```

22. Bearings.

From 62 to 85 true bearing 59°,
from 85 to 91 " " 59°,
from X.2.b.½.2½. to X.2.b.3½.5½. true bearing 45°,
from X.2.b.3½.5½. to R.33.b.6.1. " " 56°,
from R.33.b.6.1. to R.34.a.6.5. " " 61°,
from R.32.d.1.2. to R.33.a.1½.2. " " 49°,
from R.33.a.1½.2. to R.33.b.4½.6½. " " 65°,
from R.33.b.4½.6½. " R.28.c.2.0. " " 65°.

23. Transport.

Details for transport have already been issued.

X These reserve stores of water and rations are not to be drawn upon without the sanction of the Commanding Officer.

Sheet 8.

24. Reserve Stores.

All receptacles capable of holding water should be collected as additional supplies of water are sure to be wanted. Surplus rations will be collected by the Qr.Mr. for the use of drafts, etc. All guards and caretakers left behind will have four days rations in advance.

25. Maps & Orders.

No papers or orders are to be carried by Officers or men taking part in the attack, except the 1/5,000 LA BOISSELLE, Sheet 1 and the 1/20,000 D. S.E., Edition 2.b.

All messages or reports will refer to one or other of these maps. The numbers on the 1/5,000 Map are only to be used within the III Corps.

All Officers will carry a note book.

26. Captured Arms.

Any guns captured which are in danger of being lost must be rendered useless by damaging the sights and breach mechanism. Methods of doing this with pick axes, bombs, or other expedients will be explained to all ranks.

Machine Guns when captured must be collected or destroyed.

27. Signallers.

21103 Cpl.Carlin A., 18075 Pte.Copestake A. are detailed to be attached to Battalion H.Qrs. No other Signaller will attempt to obtain touch with aircraft unless ordered to do so by the O.C. Battalion.

415 flares will be distributed to the Battalion. These are only to be used by men of this Battalion who have been pushed forward into the Assaulting line. If this happens the flares will be lit
   (a) at each line of enemy's trench captured,
   (b) at five minutes past every fourth hour after Zero.

Flares will be used and fired in a row at three or four paces interval. Fire one flare, $\frac{1}{4}$ minute interval, fire second flare, $\frac{1}{4}$ minute interval, fire third flare.

Special instructions have been issued to the S.O.

28. Distinguishing Marks.

Coloured flags on the scale of two per platoon will be carried by Companies as follows:-
   "A" Company BLUE
   "B" Company RED
   "C" Company CHECK
   "D" Company BLACK

It is hoped that the use of these will enable the whereabouts of Companies to be made out.

29. Very Pistols.

These will be carried by a man detailed by the O.C. Coy. together with the ammunition for them.

30. Scouts.

The following scouts will be attached to Bde. H.Qrs:-
   27765 Pte.Robinson G.   "D" Coy.
   16378 " Page J.   "A" "

Sheet 9.

31. S.A.A., Bombs, Etc.

Dumps have been arranged for Battalion advanced stores as follows:-
No.1 Junction of LONGRIDGE STREET & Front Line.
No.2 Half way between LONGRIDGE & QUARRY BRAE Sts.
No.3 Trench end of QUARRY BRAE STREET.
No.4 Junction of front line and BAMBERBRIDGE STREET.
No.5 Front Line between BAMBERBRIDGE & STANLEY Sts.
No.6 Trench end of STANLEY STREET.

The above each contain 600 Mills Grenades, 100 Rifle Grenades, 50 Boxes S.A.A., 300 Trench Mortar Bombs, Stokes. The Brigade Store in QUARRY POST will contain 1000 Mills Grenades, 1000 Rifle Grenades, 100 Boxes S.A.A., 300 Trench Mortar Bombs, Stokes. The Brigade Store in STANLEY STREET will contain the same amount of Stores.

S.A.A. Dumps will be marked with a RED Flag
Trench Mortar Dumps " " " BLACK "
Bomb Dumps " " " YELLOW "
Divl. Bomb Depot " " " YELLOW & BLACK Flag.

32. Details.

The following will remain with the 1st Line Transport when the Battalion moves into the trenches on the night 26/27th June, in addition to the Transport Officers and Quartermaster's Staff & C.Q.M.S's.

2 Lieut W.S.Spencer Lieut.R.J.Nicolls,   2nd Lieut.H.W.Archer
                      2nd Lieut.G.B.Hayes,   2nd Lieut.R.L.Woodcock
2 Lieut B.W.Bird   2nd Lieut.G.H.J.Swift,   2nd Lieut.C.B.Tomlinson
2 Lieut J.P.Williams 70-30 C.S.M.Galer   7211 Sgt.Mather
                      17030 Sgt.Harman   6645 "   Broomhead
                      20533 "   Jackson,   17785 " Wakefield
                       7404 Cpl.Hopkinson   6950 L/C Herrett
                      20 126 L/C Cooper,   17372 Pte.Varney
                      20865 Pte.Radford   16148 "   Ceney
                       6674 "   Clark   16088 "   Oswin
                       1587 "   Brannan   16810 "   Allard
                      16367 "   Bunting   17545 "   Wdall
                      16255 "   Barlow   6947 "   Savage
                      17956 "   Winfield

Lieut.R.J.NICOLLS will be in charge of the details left behind. and Lieut.G.H.J.SWIFT will assist the T.O. C.S.M.Galer will act as Sergt. Major to Lieut.NICOLLS.

33. Miscellaneous.

(a) Completion of all moves will be reported to Bn. H.Qrs. i.e. (1) Move into trenches on the night 26/27th, (2) Move to position of Assembly on the night 27/28th, (3) Move to final position before leaving our own front line on "Z" Day.

(b) Provided that the situation allows of it the first wave of "D" Battalion will carry over 50 Boxes of S.A.A. & 50 Boxes of Bombs; each Company taking 13 Boxes S.A.A. and 12 Boxes of Bombs. The second wave will carry over 25 Boxes of Bombs per Company. All these boxes of S.A.A. & Bombs will be dumped in the first German Line where they will be collected by O.C. 70th Brigade Bomb School.

The Boxes will be found distributed along our first line trench on the arrival of the waves there.

(c) Instructions will be given to all clearing-up parties to search dead bodies and to forward all correspondence found on them by escorts of prisoners to collection Stations at Brickfields. <u>This order refers to clearing-up parties only.</u>

(d) Important messages sent by runner should be duplicated and two men sent by different routes whenever possible.

Sheet 10.

33.
Miscellaneous
(Continued).

   (e) If iron rations have to be used only 1 tin should be opened between two or three men so that waste may be prevented.

   (f) Battalion Headquarters will be marked by a BLUE Signalling Flag.

   (g) During the advance when R.E. Stores are required two guides will be sent to one of the R.E. Dumps <u>via Battalion Headquarters</u> where the guides will report, after which they will be sent on. The R.E. will supply carrying parties.

   (h) During the bombardment a supply of filled sandbags for repairing damage must be kept in hand; in addition small Coy. R.E. Dumps will be formed. Two shovels and two picks will be found to have been placed in the deep dug-outs; these must be kept there so that if the dug-out collapses the men may have a chance of digging themselves out.

                Captn. & Adjt.

Issued to O.C. Companies.
     Lewis Gun Officer
     Bombing Officer.
     Transport Officer.
     Signalling Officer.
     A.Ds 70th Inf Bde. (For information)
     Second i/c
     War Diary (Two copies)
     Commanding Officer

APPENDIX "A"

The following trenches will be used for "up" traffic only.
  UPPER HORWICH STREET
  QUARRY BRAE STREET
  CHORLEY STREET & BAMBERBRIDGE STREET

The following trenches will be used for "down" traffic only.
  LOWER HORWICH STREET
  THORSEBY STREET.

Other trenches in the left Brigade Area may be used for either up or down traffic.

Trench Police have been detailed and have receiced orders in accordance with the above routes.

Staff Officers can move any way in the trenches, also Brigade Orderlies who will wear a RED rosette tied in the top buttonhole of their tunies.

APPENDIX "B"

General Outline of R.E. Scheme.

Immediately the first position to be consolidated is captured parties of the 2nd Field Coy.R.E. will be sent on to consolidate certain points. These are in or about:-
X.2.b.6.2., R.32.d.1.2., X.2.b.2.0., X.2.b.0.6., X.2.a.8.1. X.2.a.8.5., X.2.c.2.4., X.2.c.3.9..

Only four of the above approximate points will be consolidated. These points will be chosen on the spot. They will be selected in dead ground if possible to allow them to be worked on by day.

The remainder of the R.E. programme depends on the tactical situation.

One section of Pioneers will be accommodated in close proximity to junction of STANLEY STREET & Front Line, and will open up a communication trench from STANLEY STREET to a point in hostile front trench X.2.c.3.9. immediately this trench is captured.

18.6.16.   Captn. & Adjt.

To The Quartermaster
    & Transport Officer.
----

1. Surplus Kit.

    At least 48 hours prior to the commencement of the
Bombardment, all kit and stores surplus to Mobilization
equipment and which cannot be carried on existing Transport
will be stored at MILLECNOURT Salvage Dump (D.5.b.1.7.),
billet No.116.
    Numbers 19372 L/C Cox,   7202 Pte.Read
            7241 Pte.Cotteril, 15663 Pte.Povey
from the Band to be left in charge.
    Battalions will make dumps of great dumps at the last
minute in dug-outs in the forward area and will leave a man
in charge.

2. Supplies.

    Supplies of Infantry units will be delivered to 1st Line
Transport by Divisional Train. The normal method of feeding
troops will be maintained as long as possible. When this no
longer becomes practicable, dumps have been formed as under:-
        QUARRY POST Cookhouse,   8,000
        TRAM BASE, W.22.c.5.1.   25,000
        W.22.d.8.1.   12,000
These Ration Dumps will be common to all troops operating in
the area.

3. Rations.

    O.C. Battalions should collect all receptacles capable
of holding water, as additional supplies of water will sure
to be needed. They should also arrange to collect surplus
rations so that Quartermasters may have a reserve store in
LONG VALLEY for drafts arriving, etc. The Quartermaster
will arrange that all guards and storemen have 4 days advance
rations.

4. Transport.

    Infantry 1st Line Transport will be parked in LONG VALLEY.
    First Line Transport will be as follows:-
    Infantry Battalion -
    S.A.A. Carts Nil, 8 packs animals for S.A.A., 2 water carts,
1 Medical Cart, 2 Tool wagons, 2 Lewis Gun Limbers, 4 Field
Kitchens, 1 Officers mess cart.
    Quartermasters of units will be with the 1st Line Transport
in LONG VALLEY.
    The 2 Lewis Gun Limbers and packs mules from LONG VALLEY
will carry Battalion rations to the trenches. If any additional
Transport is required it will be brought up from HENENCOURT WOOD,
but it must return there to be parked as the water supply in
LONG VALLEY is not sufficient for more than the 1st Line
Transport as already detailed.
    All remaining transport of units will be parked at
HENENCOURT WOOD. The Senior Battalion Transport Officer present
will be in charge of all the remaining Brigade Transport parked
at HENENCOURTWOOD. Supply and forage carts will be with the
8th Divl. Train at BRESLE WOOD. Grenade carts will be with O.C.
Divl. Bomb Depot.
    One cyclist per Battalion (18189 Pte.Hobson H. "D" Coy.)
will report to the D.A.A. & Q.M.G's Office, Divl. H.Qrs. 24 hours
before the day of assault, for the purpose of keeping communication between the Senior Transport Officer and Divl. H.Qrs.

It will be the duty of the Senior Transport Officer to communicate all news to the other T.O's of Battalions and to Qr. Mr's of Battalions.

At least 4 cyclists per Battalion will be with the 1st Line Transport in LONG VALLEY:-

    20714 Pte. Wilson R.   "A" Coy.
    19317 "   Clarke J.   "B" "
    18111 "   Faulkner J.   "B" "
    20855 L/C Wallace W.   "B" "

One cyclist (6954 L/C Palfreyman R. "C" Coy.) will be with the T.O. in HENENCOURT WOOD.

These will be used to meet reinforcements arriving at Railhead, taking messages to Bn. H.Qrs. and maintaining communication between LONG VALLEY & HENENCOURT WOOD. Horses need not be kept inspanned, but should be ready to move at 15 minutes notice.

The Brigade T.O. will be in charge of the 1st Line Transport in LONG VALLEY. The remainder of the Transport in HENENCOURT WOOD will be under the Senior T.O. present.

When the Bde. Transport, prior to the assault, moves into LONG VALLEY they will occupy F.G.H. Areas on the attached map.

The Battalion bivouacked in LONG VALLEY with its transport will water from the LONG VALLEY Supply, or if this runs short from ALBERT.

5. **Moves.**

The Battalion moves into the trenches on the night 26/27th. No movement will take place till 10p.m.
All stores and kit will be collected during 26th inst.

6. C.Q.M.S's will remain with the Transport Lines.

Company Cooks who usually accompany the Battalion in the line will do so on the night 26/27th for cooking in GLASGOW ROAD, where, however, they will remain when the Battalion advances.

7. **Disposal of Kits.**

Your attention is called to the previous orders regarding the disposal of the kits of Officers who have become casualties,; especially as to sealing valises and the completion of the form in para 2 of "Extracts from G.R.O's" (C.D.S.309).

                                Captn. & Adjt.

18.6.16.

To The Signalling Officer.

       Signalling communication with aeroplanes will only be carried out from Battalion Headquarteres unless this Battalion moves into the assaulting line when communication by means of flares and vigiland periscopes as suggested in "Instruction regard Liaison between Infantry & Aircraft" may be carried out.

       Please make sure that Cpl.Carlin and Pte.Copestake ate thwroughly acquainted with the contents of the above mentioned circular, and that they knww the code ih Appendix "A" of that circular by heart.

       Please arrange that the Battalion orderlies have a BLUE Signalling flag to mark Battalion Headquarters with.

       There will be a central visual Signalling Station at LAVIEVILLE (D.10.b.6.9.) which will be in communication with Headquarters of Brigades. This Station can be seen as far as POZIERES and will be on the look out for all signals from advancing troops.

       Details will be issued to you by Brigade S.O.

       Company Signallers will carry telephones but it will be impracticable to use these till hostile positions have been captured and their defence definitely taken up; reliance will therefore have to be placed in visual signalling.

       Carrier pigeons will be issued to the Battalion.

       Brigade Signalling Officer will give you all details on this point.

18.6.16.   Captn. & Adjt.

Reference Operation Order No. 6, para 12 (a)

(a) Night of the 26/27th June 1916.

This Battalion will move into the left section trenches on the night 26/27th June, when it will relieve the 8th K.O.Y.L.I. who will take over the ALBERT - BOUZINCOURT Defences from this Battalion.

Relief will be carried out by Companies at 500 yards interval starting at 10 p.m. in order "A" L.G.S., "B" "C" & "D".

Route - Emergency Road No.2, AVELUY - ALBERT Road - AVELUY - UPPER HORWICH STREET.

Dress - Men to be fully equipped in Fighting Order. Overcoats will also be carried.

Rations for the 27th will be carried on the soldier.

The Officers' Mess cart will take H.Q. and Company mess baskets which must be ready for loading by 9.30 p.m. Three men from H.Qrs. and three from each Company will accompany the Mess cart and will carry the stores in rear of "D" Company.

The 25 additional rations for Trench Police and Trench Caretakers will also be sent up in the Officers' mess cart. Men from H.Qrs. will be detailed to carry them up.

(b) Night of the 27/28th June 1916.

Routes:-
(1) "A" Coy. by LIVERPOOL STREET & by NAB STREET - THORSEBY STREET - LOWER HORWICH STREET.
(2) "B" Coy. by NAB STREET & THORSEBY STREET.
(3) "C" Coy. " " " " " " "
(4) Lewis Gun Teams will join their Companies by the above Routes.

23
/70

11th Bn. Notts & Derby Regt.

July 1916

Appendices see separate
Cover

left 8th Division with
70th Brigade & rejoined
23rd Division 17.7.16&

Index

SUBJECT.

62/E/67.

Liverpool Scottish

No.	Contents.	Date.

Army Form C. 2118.

23 11 Notts & Derby Regt July

WAR DIARY
or
INTELLIGENCE SUMMARY.
(Erase heading not required.)

Vol

Instructions regarding War Diaries and Intelligence
Summaries are contained in F. S. Regs., Part II.
and the Staff Manual respectively. Title pages
will be prepared in manuscript.

70
23

Place	Date	Hour	Summary of Events and Information	Remarks and references to Appendices
In the field	1-7-16		Battalion formed part of the attack near DVILLERS	
			Return of Casualties in Wounded attacked	
	2-7-16		Battalion taken out of the battle and to Bath. was billeted in chapel billy ALBERT	
			Major Jardine Russell returned and took over temporary command.	
			Marched to DERNANCOURT	
	3-7-16		Entrained DERNANCOURT and detrained AILLY-SUR-SOMME, marched to	
			ARGOEUVRES	
	4-7-16		Marched to DISSY	
	6-7-16		Marched to SALEUX & entrained for BRYAY	
	7-7-16		Detrained BRYAS' marched to BRYAY	
			Battalion inspected by G.O.C. 8th Division	
			1st Bat. worked by G.O.C. 1st Army.	
	11-7-16		Roll of 16 men arrived	
	13-7-16		Draft of 111 men arrived	
	15-7-16		marched to midnight, marched to Entrain PERNES at 11 am 16 inst	
	16		Entrained LONGEAU marched to POULAINVILLE	

T2131. Wt. W708—776. 500000. 4/15. Sir J. C. & S.

Army Form C. 2118.

WAR DIARY
or
INTELLIGENCE SUMMARY.
(Erase heading not required.)

Instructions regarding War Diaries and Intelligence Summaries are contained in F. S. Regs., Part II. and the Staff Manual respectively. Title pages will be prepared in manuscript.

Place	Date	Hour	Summary of Events and Information	Remarks and references to Appendices
	17.7.16		Marched to PIERREGOT	
	18.7.16		Inspected by G.O.C. 4th 93rd Divn	
			Draft of 150 men & 7 officers arrived	
	20.7		Marched to BAIZIEUX	
	24.7		Bn left 13 men per Coy to last 14 officers attd	
	26.7.16		Bn marched to vicinity of CONTALMAISON	
	28.7.16		Lt Colonel J.J. Sullivan thrown 15th Bn Cheshire Infantrt ardumsa command.	
	29.7.16		Battn took over trenches NORTH BAZENTIN LE PETIT	
	30.		2/Lt G.S. Curwen killed	
	31.		2/Lt H. Bloxham killed Lt B. Bond wounded to hospital	

Signed J Sullivan Lt Col

T2134. Wt. W708—776. 500000. 4/16. Str J. C. & S.

Account of the part taken

by

11th (Service) Battalion The Sherwood Foresters

in the Operations of 1st July, 1916.

The Battalion took over the 70th Brigade Sector on the evening of the 26th June, being relieved on the following evening when the Brigade took up the final position of assembly.

Owing to the Attack being postponed 48 hours the Battalion again took over the front line on the evening of the 28th and held the Sector until position of assembly was taken up a second time on the evening of the 30th June.

During this time our casualties were comparitively slight, although we were unfortunate in losing 3 Officers including the Medical Officer wounded, and a platoon Sgt.

At 7.45 a.m. on the morning of the Attack, 1st July, a message was received that the German First Line was taken, and shortly after the Battalion was ordered to taken over our front line vacated by the 9th York and Lancaster Regiment. This was done independently by Coys. by pre-arranged routes, under a fairly heavy shrapnel fire.

It had been arranged prior to the assault that the Left Centre Company 1st Wave was to file straight out of a sap and occupy a bank about 70 yards in front of our own front line. After considerable difficulty owing to the congestion of wounded in the sap an attempt to do this was made. A very heavy machine gun fire was brought to bear on this wave from the left flank and the enemy front line which had apparently been re-occupied by use of underground galleries from the enemy 2nd line after the assaulting Battalion had passed over. The same fire was directed on the remainder of the first wave when they attempted to advance from our front line.

The 2nd Wave, lead by Major G.H.W.BERNAL, D.S.O. the second in command, then pushed forward in support hoping to carry forward the 1st Wave.

Casualties along the whole line were very heavy, and a general attempt was made to crawl forward under intense machine gun and shrapnel fire, any available cover being made use of.

Headquarters, lead by Lieut.Col.H.F.WATSON, D.S.O. the Commanding Officer, then advanced, only Headquarters Bombers being left to hold our trenches.

Lt.Col.WATSON walking diagonally across the front collecting men as he went gave a fresh impetus to the advance by his personal example, but the advance died out before the 1st line was reached Col.WATSON himself and other H.Q. Officers being wounded.

Another

Another attempt to reach the German trenches by the sunken road on the right flank was made by about 50 men under Captn.C.E.HUDSON, including the Battalion Bombers and details of other units collected in our line. This attempt was brought to a standstill by heavy frontal and flank fire as they came over the brow of the hill in the last 80 yards.

The casualties sustained by the Battalion during the day amounted to 21 Officers and 508 N.C.O's and men.

The strength of the Battalion on entering the trenches on the 26th June was 27 Officers and 710 men.

W. Sunihoe-Phelan

Major

Commanding 11th (Service) Battalion
THE SHERWOOD FORESTERS

5.7.16.

CASUALTIES IN ACTION JULY 1st, 1916.

WOUNDED

Lieut.Col.H.F.Watson, D.S.O.
Major G.H.W.Bernal, D.S.O.

Captn.G.B.Fyldes, (Adjt).
Captn.L.R.Halford
Captn.H.C.Watts
Captn.H.S.Harris

Lieut.J.C.Harrison
Lieut.E.Russell   (believed killed)

2nd Lieut.W.E.R.Short
2nd Lieut.L.G.Humphrys
2nd Lieut.G.C.M.Jackson
2nd Lieut.J.R.Byers
2nd Lieut.R.W.Clarke
2nd Lieut.H.C.M.Manisty
2nd Lieut.E.H.Brittain
2nd Lieut.W.A.Davis   (Wounded & Missing)
2nd Lieut.S.Longhurst   "   "
2nd Lieut.C.B.Tomlinson   "   "
2nd Lieut.S.C.Carter   (Died of wounds 3.8.16)

Other Ranks

499

in killed, wounded, missing

19

of which were "To duty".

Appendices
to
War Diary
11th Notts & Derby Regt.
- July 1916 -

Index..........

SUBJECT. 62/E/61.

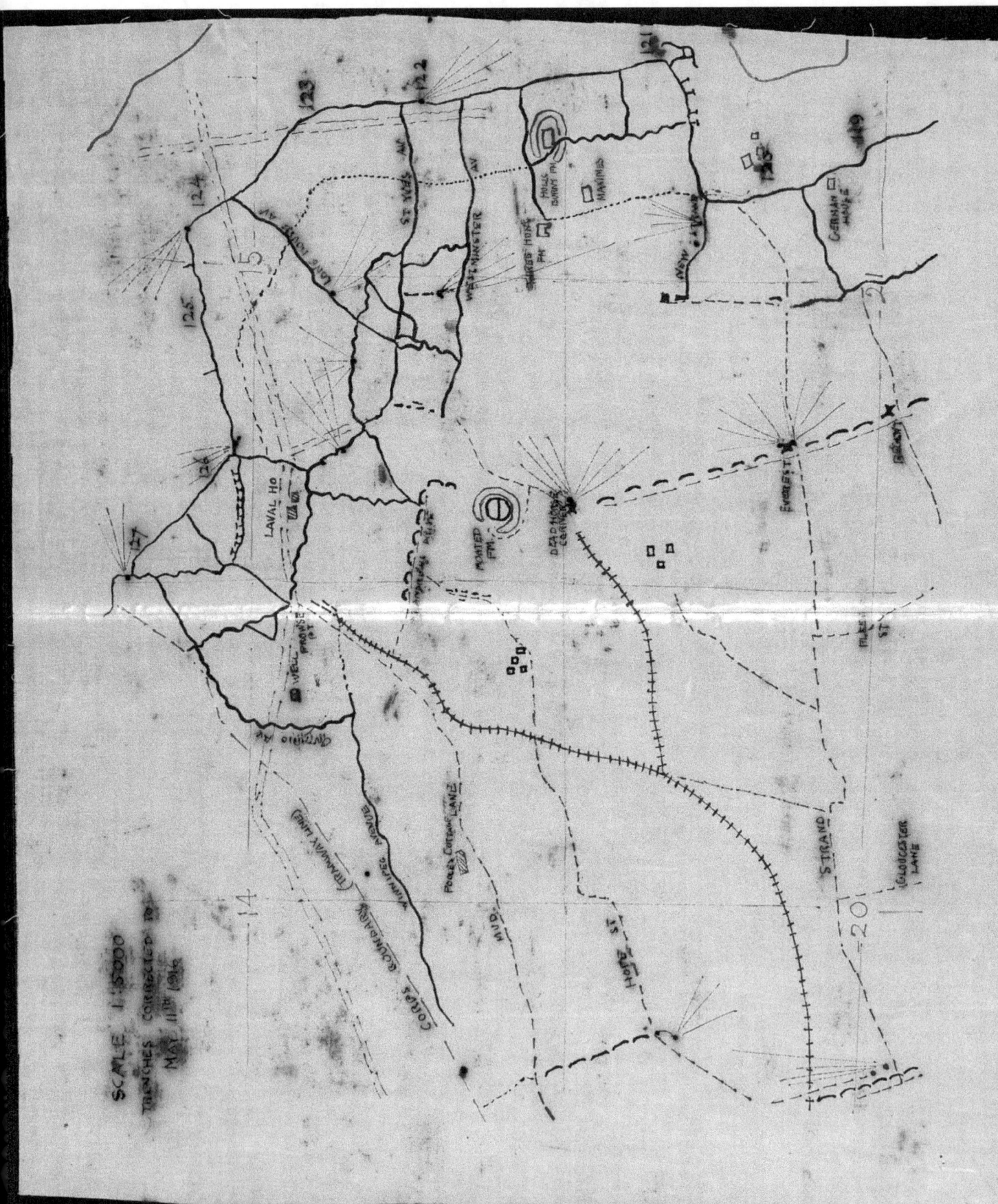

2nd ARMY SHEET 10.
WARNETON
Le Rossignol
La Hutte
St Yves
Bois de Ploegsteert
Le Gheer
Le Pelerin
La Basse-Ville
Au Chasseur Cabaret
Grande Haie
Petite Haie
Pont-Rouge
Deûlémont
Ploegsteert
Touquet Berthe
Laurence Farm
Red House
Keepers Hut
La Douve
La Potterie
Lille
Armentières
Route de
Chemin
When reference is made to numbers, the squares, etc., will always be quoted, e.g. U 28 a 3.
Scale 1:10,000
Trenches corrected to 14th November 1915. (618)
Any trench apparently organised for fire.
Other trenches.
Trenches which appear to be abandoned.
Works which may be dugouts, trench mortar or machine gun emplacements.

B.B.B.B. = 435 yards approx.
D.D.D.D. = 340 yards approx.

GERMAN LINE

Scale 1:5000 approx.

A = FIRST SAP
B = FIRST JUMP
C = SECOND SAP
D = SECOND JUMP

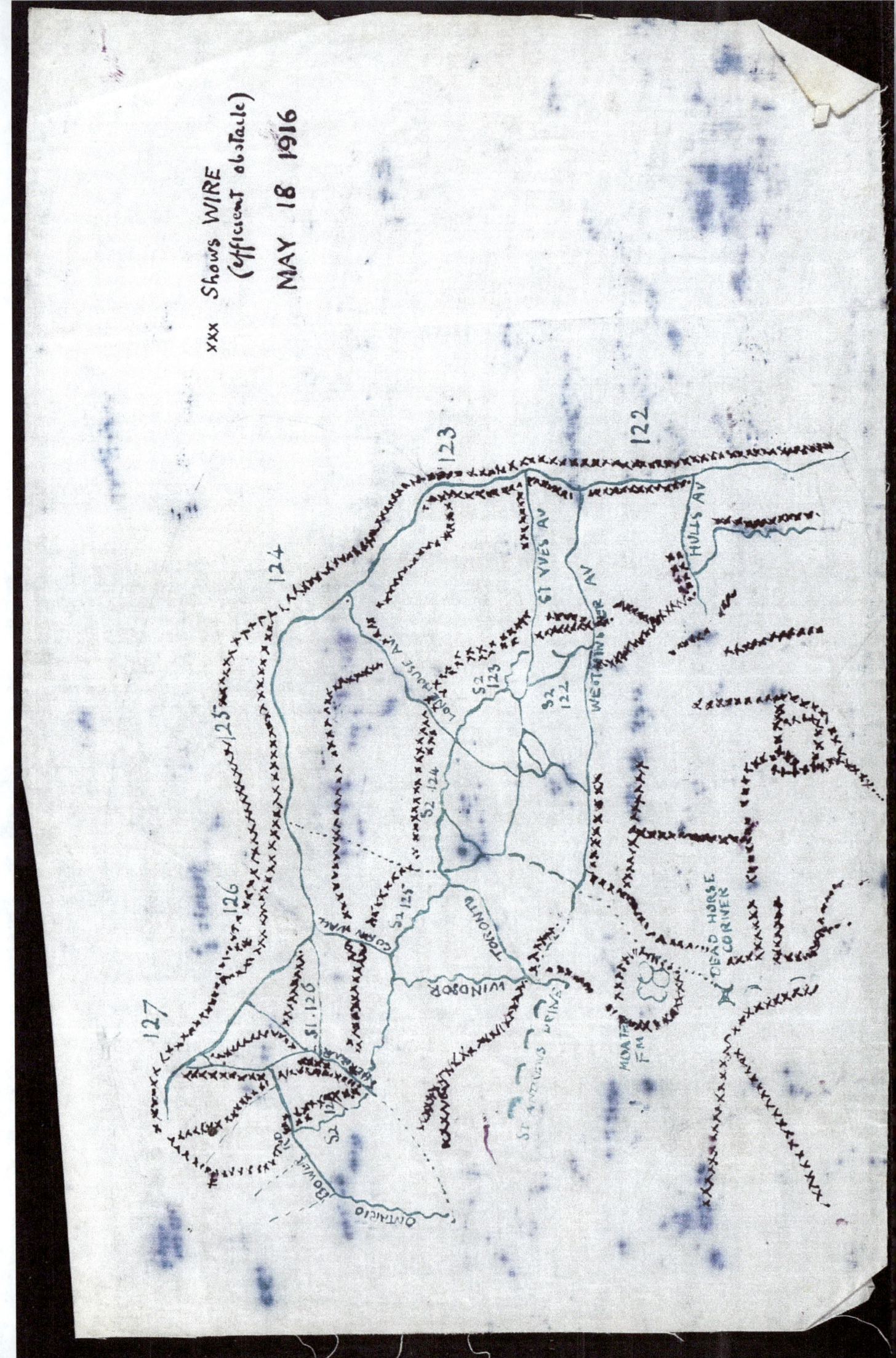

SKETCH MAP.
Showing supposed Location of Enemy's Forces on 31st Aug. 1916.
SECOND ARMY AREA (EAST).

Not to be taken into the trenches.   SECRET.

23rd Division.
70th Brigade

1/11th BATTALION

NOTTS & DERBY REGIMENT

AUGUST 1 9 1 6

23/70

Army Form C. 2118.

WAR DIARY
or
INTELLIGENCE SUMMARY.
(Erase heading not required.)

Aug 16

11th Sherwood Foresters   Vol 11

Place	Date	Hour	Summary of Events and Information	Remarks and references to Appendices
	2.8.16		Battn had relieved in trenches by 13th Bn Durham Light Infantry and took over trenches in support of the front line near MAMETZ WOOD.	
	4.8.16		Lieut R. APPLEYARD Killed ; Lieuts J.F.R.RADFORD and 2nd Lt W.S.SPENCER wounded.	
	8.8.16		Battn was relieved in support trenches by 12th Bn Scottish Rifles and marched into billets at FRANVILLERS.	
	10.8.16		The following officers joined the battn. 2/Lts Stones, Lacey, Drake and Roper, and Cowell	
	11.8.16		Marched to FRENCHENCOURT and thence to LONGPRÉ ; marched to PONT REMY	
	13.8.16		Entrained PONT REMY and detrained BAILLEUL ; then marched to OUTTERSTEEN	
	14.8.16		Marched to STEENWERCK	
	15.8.16		Marched into 9th Army Brigade in vicinity PLOEGSTEERT and relieved 16th Bn K.R.R. in Wulverghem area	7.11
	16.8.16		Remained in reserve billets at PATOT.	
	17.8.16		Battn relieved the 2nd Bn S.A.R.R.C. in front line trenches in front of PLOEGSTEERT WOOD. One O.R. wounded - to hospital. Major G. McPRATT DSO took over temporary command.	
	18.8.16		2 ORs wounded - to hospital	

Army Form C. 2118.

WAR DIARY
or
INTELLIGENCE SUMMARY.
(Erase heading not required.)

Instructions regarding War Diaries and Intelligence Summaries are contained in F. S. Regs., Part II. and the Staff Manual respectively. Title pages will be prepared in manuscript.

Place	Date	Hour	Summary of Events and Information	Remarks and references to Appendices
	19.8.16		One O.R killed in action. 2ⁿᵈ Lt J.P Williams to England - sick	2
	20.8.16		Two O.Rs wounded - to hospital. Major W. Swinhoe-Phelan to England sick	
	21.8.16		Notification received that 2ⁿᵈ Lt E.H Brittain and RSM Moore awarded MILITARY CROSS, 16381 Pte Scott J.J awarded DCM & 16423 Pte Smith E awarded MILITARY MEDAL for gallantry on July 1ˢᵗ 1916.	
	22.8.16		One O.R wounded - to duty.	
	24.8.16		C.S.M Mather J & 4 O.Rs wounded - to hospital	
	25.8.16		One O.R killed in action. Batt'n was relieved in trenches by 8ᵗʰ Yorks Regt and took over reserve billets in Tara.	
	26.8.16		Company and Specialists training started.	
	29.8.16		Draft of 28 specialists arrived and taken on strength.	
	30.8.16		Lt Col T.J O'Sullivan D.S.O left the Batt'n for England on account ill health. Major G.M.D Pratt/3rd assumed command. Notification received that A/C Sgt Dyer R.S awarded MILITARY MEDAL for gallantry on July 1ˢᵗ 1916. 2ⁿᵈ Lt H.C Clarke & 1 O.R wounded - to hospital. 2ⁿᵈ Lt P.C Rogers posted to REC & from 25.8.16	

Army Form C. 2118.

1st Batt. Sherwood Foresters

WAR DIARY
or
INTELLIGENCE SUMMARY.
(Erase heading not required.)

Instructions regarding War Diaries and Intelligence Summaries are contained in F. S. Regs., Part II. and the Staff Manual respectively. Title pages will be prepared in manuscript.

Place	Date	Hour	Summary of Events and Information	Remarks and references to Appendices
PAPOT	1.9.16		Battalion in reserve billets at PAPOT	
	2.9.16		Commenced 9 mile march by 23rd Division to 2nd Army Training Area	
			Marched to ROUGE CROIX.	
	3.9.16		Marched to STAPLE	
	4.9.16		Marched to ARQUES.	
	5.9.16		Marched to SETQUES.	
	6.9.16		Commenced training in 2nd Army Training Area	
	10.9.16		Marched to ST OMER entrained to billets at LONGEAU marched to CAR DONNETTE	
	12.9.16		Marched to BRESLE. Lt Col H.F. Watson DSO rejoined from ENGLAND	
BRESLE	15.9.16		Marched to BLACK WOOD	
BLACK WOOD	18.9.16		Marched to CONTALMAISON. Took over a line of dugouts in The CUTTING 9 in front of CONTALMAISON.	7.12
CONTALMAISON	19.9.16		Spent the day salvaging rifles, ammunition, bombs & equipment which were lying about in great quantities.	
CONTALMAISON	20.9.16		Marched to Bivouacs at LOZENGE WOOD.	

Army Form C. 21

2

11th Batt. Sherwood Forester

WAR DIARY
or
INTELLIGENCE SUMMARY.
(Erase heading not required.)

Place	Date	Hour	Summary of Events and Information	Remarks and references to Appendices
LOZENGE WOOD	Sept 21st		The bodies of 2nd Lieuts H.A. Davis & S. Enghurst 7039 Sergt Connaughton J. 16745 Lance Sergt Pinkington & 16 other Ranks were identified & buried in front of GAUTHVILLE WOOD when they had been killed on July 1st 1916. Captain C.S. Martin relinquished the appointment of Acting Adjutant & took over command of C Company.	
	22nd		2nd Lieut J.H. Bartlett took over the duties of acting Adjutant. Marched back to our lines at the CUTTING at CONTALMAISON. 73145 Pte MORGAN T. Wounded	
CONTALMAISON	25th		The bodies of 2nd Lieut C.B. TOMLINSON and 19 other Ranks were identified & buried in front of GAUTHVILLE WOOD where they had been killed on July 1st 1916. The Battalion relieved the 13th Batt. Durham L.I. (68th Inf Brigade) in the same occupying	
FRONT LINE	26th		a trench sector from M 26 d 5.0. (PUSH ALLEY) to M 33 b 9.1 (PRUE TRENCH). The 152nd Brigade 50th Division were on our right while the 8th Batt. K.O.Y.L.I. were on our left with their left resting on LE SARS. BAPAUME road M 25.C.6.5. The relief was complete by 11p.m. Casualties 2nd Lieut. Other Ranks killed 1 wounded 14 missing 1 Shell Shock 2.	

Army Form C. 2118.

3/
1st Batt. Sherwood Foresters

WAR DIARY
or
INTELLIGENCE SUMMARY.
(Erase heading not required.)

Place	Date	Hour	Summary of Events and Information	Remarks and references to Appendices
FRONT LINE TRENCHES	27th		A hostile trench afterwards known as 26th AVENUE was occupied by C. Company without loss & consolidated. One known being captured. Following Casualties occurred. Other ranks 5 killed, wounded 2nd Lieuts E.O.R. SWAIN & R.D. TREVOR-ROPER. Other ranks 10. Shell shock 3.	
	28th		During the night of 27/28th A patrol was sent to DESTREMONT FARM which was found held by the enemy. One of the enemy was killed. A patrol under 2nd Lieut J.W. BENTON was sent out from 26th AVENUE to gain touch with the Brigade of 50th Division on our right. It was fired on and 2nd Lieut BENTON was killed. Casualties killed 2nd Lieut J.W. BENTON Other ranks 3 wounded other ranks 19. In the evening an attempt was made by Captain A.E. PARLOW with 13 Company to take DESTREMONT FARM which was unsuccessful. 2nd Lieuts H.W. LOMAS and L. DRAKE being wounded. The Battn handed over the line that night to 8th Battn York Lancaster Regt & retired to the support line.	

Army Form C. 2118.

4

11th Batt^n Newf^d Fusiliers

WAR DIARY
or
INTELLIGENCE SUMMARY.
(Erase heading not required.)

Place	Date	Hour	Summary of Events and Information	Remarks and references to Appendices
SUPPORT LINE	29th		16631 Pte Priestly L. Wounded.	
	30th		The Bodies of 7146 Sgt Ford G.H. & 6 other ranks were identified and buried in front of AUTHUILE WOOD having been killed in action on July 1st 1916. The Battalion Remained in the Support Line preparing for the coming engagement next day.	

A J Watson Lieut Colonel
Comm'g 11th Batt^n Newf^d Fusiliers

War Diary

OPERATION ORDER NO. 42 BY MAJOR C.E.HUDSON, D.S.O., M.C.
11th. (S) Battalion THE SHERWOOD FORESTERS.

Reference Sheet 28 N.W.   19th. September 1917.
& ZILLEBEKE.

1. The 23rd. Division will be the left attacking Division of the Xth. Corps taking part in the Second Army Offensive.

2. The 68th. Brigade will attack on the right and the 69th. on the left. The 70th. Brigade will be in reserve.

3. The Attacking Brigade will attack the first objective, the RED LINE at Zero plus 3 minutes. The attack on the second or BLUE Objective will commence at Zero plus 1 hour 28 minutes. The attack on the third or GREEN Objective will commence at Zero plus 4 hours 13 mins.

4. The final protective barrage will be formed 200 yards in front of the GREEN line to enable a line to be consolidated clear of the existing trenches. An outpost line will be established in front of this line to cover its consolidation.

5. In order to notify Infantry when they have reached the RED, BLUE and GREEN lines respectively, the barrage which enable them to reach these lines will contain a proportion of Smoke Shell.

6. Assembly positions and Headquarters of Battalions of the 70th. Brigade will be as follows :-

    A Battalion - 9th. Y. & L.   - BEDFORD HOUSE.
    B   "   - 11th. S.F.   - CANAL BANK.
    C   "   - K.O.Y.L.I.   - RAILWAY DUG-OUTS.
    D   "   - 8th. Y. & L.   - RAILWAY DUG-OUTS.

At Zero hour the 9th. Y. & L., A Battalion, will march to assembly trenches at TOWER TOP.
At Zero plus 1 hour this Battalion, B Battalion, will move via ZILLEBEKE Track to assembly trenches about I.24.b.00.50 vacated by 2 Companies 8th. YORKS Regt. and 1 Company DUKE OF WELLINGTON'S Regt. in the following order :-

    'A' Coy. Move Zero plus 1 hour.
    'B'   "   "   "   "   1 hour 40 minutes.
    'C'   "   "   "   "   2 hours 10 minutes.
    'D'   "   "   "   "   2 hours 40 minutes.
    B.H.Q.   "   "   "   3 hours 10 minutes.

The movement will be carried out by half platoons at 4 minutes interval.

7. Advance parties under Lieut. SWALE, who will allot Company frontages of 1 Officer per Company and 2 guides per platoon will proceed to the assembly positions at Zero minus 3 hours and these will guide half platoons into positions.
Reports will be rendered to B.H.Q. at I.28.b.0.5. on arrival of Companies, by orderly.
Lieut. SWALE and advance parties will proceed to assembly positions at J.13.c. and J.19.a. On their occupants (3 Coys. 10th. DUKE OF WELLINGTON'S and 2 Coys. 8th. YORKS Regt.) leaving he will send two runners at intervals back to O.C. Battalion J.2.b.0.5.
Companies will, on receipt of orders, proceed to these positions. They will be met by guides from Lieut. SWALE's party near JACKDAW DUMP I.24.b.9.9. and be guided into new positions. They will advance in half platoons at 4 minutes distance. On reaching these new assembly positions guides will again report to Lieut. SWALE who will take them forward to CLAPHAM JUNCTION and inform O.C. Battalion when troops have vacated our old front line.

Companies will, on receipt of orders, proceed to take up assembly positions in our old front line.
Lieut. SWALE will arrange for guides to meet Coys. at CLAPHAM JUNCTION.
After each movement forward Coys. will report to Battn.H.Q. Os.C.Coys. will detail one orderly to a company Lieut. SWALE and remain with him.

3. PROBABLE ACTION.

From this point Battalions will probably be called on either :-

(1) To take over the GREEN LINE captured by the 89th. Bde.
(2) To Attack and take the GREEN LINE.
(3) To resist a German counter attack on any part of the 89th. Bde. front.

The S O S Signal (Rifle Grenade) will be a parachute with 3 coloured lights RED over GREEN over YELLOW. The only maps to be carried into action will be the Trench Operation Map, Message Map and ZILLEBEKE 1/10.000
Os. C. Coys. will re-organise as far as possible and forward casualty report at each new position.
Zero hour will be notified later.
Dress - New Fighting Order with packs and shorts and fighting stores.
The Officers, Sergeant Majors and senior N.C.Os detailed to be left behind will accompany the Battalion to CANAL BANK tonight, and will then join the details at MICMAC CAMP.
Watches will be synchronised at 7 p.m. tonight and again at 8 a.m. tomorrow at Battalion Headquarters.

Attack Day will be tomorrow, September 20th. 1917, and Attack Day plus one will be known as Barrage Day. Rations for these two days will be at CANAL BANK and Companies will arrange to draw rations for Attack Day on arrival tonight. Rations for Barrage Day will remain in their present position until further orders.
Breakfast tomorrow will be at 4.30 a.m.

Two Headquarter Signallers will accompany Lieut. SWALE and will endeavour to keep in touch with Battalion Headquarters. Company Signallers will take up suitable positions for visual and get into touch with Headquarters or existing visual stations.
A contact aeroplane will be maintained in the air and will be distinguished by three broad white bands on a dark fusilage and will have a black board attached to the left lower plane.
Flares are only to be lit when a plane of this description calls for them on a Klaxon Horn or by firing a white Very Light.

Lieut. A & A/Adjutant.

War Diary

ADMINISTRATIVE DETAILS.

1. The Battalion's rations for Attack Day, i.e. Sept. 20th. 1917, have been dumped in gun pit at side of road opposite BEDFORD HOUSE at I.26.a.3.4. C.Q.M.S. and Sgt. Bowden (with pioneers to Headquarters) will report to the B.Q.M.S. on arrival in CANAL BANK and draw these.

2. The Battalion's rations for Barrage Day will remain at this dump and be forwarded to a convenient dump later.

3. Os. C. Coys. will arrange to carry forward 1 dixie per platoon. On reaching each assembly position water will immediately be boiled, wood fires being employed, and tea will be brewed if time permits. "Tommys Cookers" or water bottles will not be used without permission from O.C.Coy. west of CLAPHAM JUNCTION.

4. 200 extra Water Bottles will be issued and will be carried by men not carrying picks and shovels.

5. WATER. 2 Water Carts will be available in CANAL BANK.
   00 Tins per Battalion have been dumped with (Barrage) rations. These will not be touched until Barrage Day when they will be sent forward with rations for that day.
   There will be water dumps at :-

   (1) JAM Dump....................J.19.a.5.5.... 80 gallons.
   (2) STIRLING Dump...............J.13.d.9.8.... (from 21st.
   (3) CLAPHAM Dump................J.13.d.9.8....   -
   (4) OBSERVATORY Dump............I.24.d.1.4.... 600 gallons.
   (5) JACKDAW Dump................I.24.d.9.9.... 200 gallons.
   (6) DORMY HOUSE Dump............I.25.a.5.5.... 400 gallons.
   (7) VALLEY COTTAGES Dump........I.23.c.3.6....1000 gallons.
   (8) TOR TOP.....................................1000 gallons.

   NOTE : A.P.M. is issuing instructions to ensure that all water vehicles have a right of way over all roads in either direction whatever direction they belong to.

6. S.A.A. Dumps have been formed as follows :-

   (1) DORMY HOUSE.................I.25.a.5.5.
   (2) JACKDAW Dump................I.24.b.9.9.
   (3) JAM Dump....................J.19.c.5.9.
   (4) STIRLING CASTLE.............J.13.d.2.3.
   (5) CLAPHAM Dump................J.13.d.9.8.

7. CASUALTIES. Companies will report estimated casualties on arrival at each assembly position. Actual casualties will be reported by 12 noon and again every 6 hours after.

   On Attack Day and onwards S.A.A. Wagons of First line Transport will be ready loaded and prepared to move.
   O.C. 193 Coy. A.S.C. will be prepared to give all assistance possible in delivering rations. The B.T.O. will get in touch with him as soon as possible.

2.

8. **BATTLE STRAGGLERS.**

   All Battle Stragglers who are sent back to their Transport Lines will be given a certificate by M.Os at Battle Stragglers Posts. This must be produced to the Officer at the Transport Lines. Loss of this certificate makes a man liable to the charge of desertion.
   This is to be brought to the attention of all ranks.

9. **R.E. DUMP.** ..... VALLEY COTTAGES.

10. **SALVAGE.** Os. C. Coys. will always send ration parties down with empty tins or salvage.

11. VERY LIGHTS)
    BOMBS   ) JACKDAW Dump or
    FLARES   ) DORMY HOUSE.

12. **PRISONERS OF WAR.** @ Battalion Headquarters and on to Birr X Roads. One escort to 10 prisoners will be sent. They will not be searched for papers but they will be disarmed.

13. **WOUNDED.** Should any man be wounded between CANAL BANK and I.24.b.0.5., if walking cases they will go to the RAILWAY DUG-OUT Aid Post or OBSERVATORY Dump, I.24.d.2. . : if stretcher cases they will be carried to OBSERVATORY Dump Aid Post and handed over to the R.A.M.C. Battalion Stretcher Bearers will then rejoin Companies.
    Between assembly position at I.24.b.0.5. and CLAPHAM JUNCTION walking and stretcher cases will go to OBSERVATORY Dump or JAM SUPPORT, I.19.a.5.5. or JACKDAW CRATER J.13.c.5.1.
    East of CLAPHAM JUNCTION all cases to R.A.P. in MENIN TUNNEL at CLAPHAM JUNCTION.

14. For Breakfast tomorrow cooked cold meat will be issued by B.Q.M.S. at Battalion Headquarters at 4.30 a.m. and Companies will make their own arrangements for tea.

15. **COMMUNICATION.** All existing communications will be taken over and maintained, if possible, and visual communication can be established with the visual-stations.

    BEDFORD HOUSE (before ZERO)
    YEOMANRY POST.
    J.19.b.10.23

    The Battalion code name is PEAK and messages should be addressed thus and signed from -- Coy. PEAK.
    In case any Companies are the most forward troops and the contact plane calls for flares, all of which have been used, the waving of a signal flag horizontally will be substituted. A wireless Tank will co-operate with the Division and will be known by a round disc of Blue and White and urgent messages can be sent here to be transmitted by wireless.

    B.W.Bird
    Lieut. & A/Adjutant.

Report on Operations from Sept. 20th. 1917 until 1st. Oct. 1917 in which 11th. (S) Battn. SHERWOOD FORESTERS took part.

On the night of 19/20th. Sept. the Battalion took up assembly positions East of the YPRES – COMINES CANAL in bivouacs. Rain fell heavily during the march up. Rations for ATTACK DAY (Sept. 20th.) and BARRAGE DAY (Sept. 21st.) had been dumped at the Canal Bank and were drawn.

At 5.40 a.m. the two Brigades of the 23 d. Division who were carrying out the Attack went forward. The 70th. Brigade was in reserve. At ZERO hour (5.40 a.m.) the 9th. Battn. YORK & LANCASTER Regt. went forward from their assembly positions and at ZERO plus 1 hour this Battalion started to move forward to its next assembly position east of ZILLEBEKE in half platoons at 5 minutes distance. The distance to be traversed was about 1000 yards. The t ack up was marked by white ringed pegs: shelling was confined to batteries and as this track avoided batteries the Battalion arrived at the next assembly positions intact. The Battalion remained in these positions for about 3 hours during which time there was a little shelling resulting in the loss of one Officer and 6 O.Rs.

Advance parties had been sent forward to the assembly position of the reserve Battalion of the leading Brigade (69th.); on the report of the advance of this reserve Battalion we again moved forward to their vacated positions with Headquarters at STIRLING CASTLE and proceeded to dig in – shelling was intermittent but not heavy. On reaching these positions we came under the immediate orders of the 69th. Brigade for tactical purposes and were to be in readiness to support the Battalions in the newly captured line. The night 23/24th. were ordered to take over the front line from the 69th. Brigade 9th. YORKS on a front of about 500 yards, our right about 100 yards north of the MENIN ROAD and our left about 100 yards south of the REUTELBECK stream, the Australians on our left and onmour right the 9th. YORKS. & LANCS. and the remnants of the 68th. Brigade forming a defensive flank running back from the MENIN ROAD to east of DUMBARTON LAKES, the high ground at TOWER HAMLETS on our right still remaining in enemy hands.

The relief was carried out without incident although shelling was pretty continuous. The old enemy concrete dug-outs and gunpits afforded protection for about half the Battalion. During the 23rd. September the enemy appeared to be moving his guns back.

On the night of the 24/25th. the 33rd. Division relieved us in the line, the 1st. KINGS, 2nd. WORCESTERS and GLASGOW HIGHLANDERS (H.L.I.) took over from the Battalion, each with a Company on a front of 200 yards: the remainder were to dig in in rear. This relief was far too complicated to be successful in intense darkness and heavy shelling. We had to provide no less than 34 guides (one per platoon) and these had only one night in which to study the routes. The 900 yards from B.HQ. to the front line could not be tarversed in daylight owing to sniping from TOWER HAMLETS, there was practically no landmarks and the ground was a mass of shell holes. Tapes were laid through INVERNESS COPSE but these were too broken by shell fire to be of value. By daylight on the 25th. the Battalion had been conveyed to MICROBRIDGE CAMP near RENINGHELST in lorries.

On the morning of the 27th. inst. we were back to BEDFORD HOUSE by 11 a.m. and marched up that night to relieve the same Battalions to whom we had handed over the line. This relief was carried out without difficulty as we knew the ground. Our left rested on the REUTELBECK and our right 100 yards north of the MENIN ROAD. The enemy barraged an area about 100 yards in rear of our line on their old front line west of INVERNESS COPSE almost continuously day and night but appeared to be uncertain both of his own new line and ours. Our patrols encountered no patrols nearer than 300 yards but by the night of the 29th. the enemy had undoubtedly pushed patrols and posts nearer and began to shell the front line. In the meantime a good system of defensive posts had been completed.

On the night of the 29/30th. we were relieved by the 8th. YORK & LANCS. Regt. and went back to TOWN TOP being relieved by the

2.

2nd. K.O.S.Bs (5th. Division). On the 1st. October we marched back to camp near DICKEBUSCH.

Communications throughout presented the greatest difficulty: runners were mostly employed but visual was found useful for sending back news but no orders could be sent forward by this means or replies given to messages. Runner posts were found apt to delay messages considerably. Pigeons were used a good deal pigeon messages being the only means of notifying the Artillery of short shooting on the front line by daylight. The taping of routes was the only means of assuring any party reaching its destination by night.

The frequent moving of supporting platoons' positions was the surest way of avoiding casualties. The ground was very broken and it was easy to dig in in fresh positions each night: picks were not wanted.

A portable tripod for using with a Lewis Gun for Anti-Aircraft work would be useful.

It was found that the greater the distance between platoons or half platoons the less the casualties sustained on the march. These distances had, of course, to be subject to the time allowed for the movement.

The Casualties sustained were :-

Officers :- 3 Wounded.
O. Rs. :- 27 Killed.
        10 Died of Wounds.
      127 Wounded to Hospital.
       13 " " Duty.
        7 Missing.

H.H.Watson Lieut Colonel
11th (SERVICE) BATTALION
SHERWOOD FORESTERS.

4.10.1917

Army Form C. 2118.

WAR DIARY
or
INTELLIGENCE SUMMARY.
(Erase heading not required.)

Instructions regarding War Diaries and Intelligence Summaries are contained in F. S. Regs., Part II. and the Staff Manual respectively. Title pages will be prepared in manuscript.

Place	Date	Hour	Summary of Events and Information	Remarks and references to Appendices
FRONTLINE			The Batt. has returned on the front line & marched back to camp at MONT EDGAR CORNER near DICKEBUSCH Town at rear joined by the Batt. left at BELGIAN chateau on the fighting position Sept 20 to 24 casualties were Officers wounded 3 — ORs killed 28 wounded 165 missing 26	Mr Brown(?) 7.25
DICKEBUSCH			The Batt. lay by L. METEREN and left for the camp at LA MOTTE resting, but on L. VIEUX BERGUIN on the 11th of the men joined the Batt.	
			Major C. E. A. DIEHLEN 11th NORTHUMBERLAND to attend the Bomb. officers course at WISQUES	
			MAJOR THE HON...(illegible)...shamed Bath got sister at...(illegible)...ordered to rural LA MOTTE where he intended for the train near YPRES Sgt...(illegible)...	
			...LT the Batt. moved from camp by a LT...(illegible)... L...(illegible) for military tickets to A.M. reports the Batt	

WAR DIARY
or
INTELLIGENCE SUMMARY.
(Erase heading not required.)

Army Form

Instructions regarding War Diaries and Intelligence Summaries are contained in F. S. Regs., Part II. and the Staff Manual respectively. Title pages will be prepared in manuscript.

Place	Date	Hour	Summary of Events and Information	Remarks and references to Appendices
BILLETS	6.4.17		717835 Pte J GILLULEY, 16287 Sgt G TOMLINSON, 4/7184 L/cpl J LEANHAM, 16995 Pte T SLACK, 23345 Cpl A DAVIDSON, 13163 Pte T REDDINGTON, 28 O.R's Lieut W E CLARKE. M.O. Lt A J Dale. The Regt. Pipers. Jun. Yates & 2 Cooks at SCOTTISH WOODS nr PITTENWEEM. The camp was being made.	
DRKESKINNA	7.4.17		In the morning the Bn marched to GILLIBERRIE BAND. In the afternoon no 2 Coy was in the field (Dummy Landings) & no 3 Coy by rote companies no 2 went by motor wagon & 3 marched and marched back.	
GILLIBERRIE BAND	8.4.17		The Bn marched & Rec' Divine Service as a Bn with 207th Inf Brigade.	
	9.4.17		2/Lt J S Browne reported & posted to no 5 coy. 45787 Pte W Horsley Rejoined from the depot. Byrne to the light Duty, PTE BRENNAN to the S.A. O.T.C. Both took the shilling & are only in the month. the Month & the 4 mentioned reversed.	
			LIEUT J A MCKEE reported & posted & attached R. Army Service dept. Reinforcements to be found. The shed has not completed till this morning & was hardly. the weather has been altered except to increase the strong & nothing could except	

2353 Wt. W3144/1454 700,000 5/15 L. D. & L. A.D.S.S./Forms/C. 2118.

WAR DIARY or INTELLIGENCE SUMMARY

Army Form C. 2118.

Place	Date	Hour	Summary of Events and Information	Remarks and references to Appendices
HALLEBAST CNR			The following ranks suffering from influenza 244983 Sgt W FLINT discharged to duty. 19066 Sgt A HEELIS Bn. & Molly Mehal. 19286 Cpl H ROWLANDS 1865 Cpl G JACKSON 30534 Pte HART 19378 Cpl T WYATT 7302 L/Cpl J H SMITH 30650 Pte MELLOR 7306 Pte GUTTM 23538 Sg E BRONT shilling mehal. The Bath behaviour of DICK ERSHAM 692 m th H/Lancs has been no on at 2.30 p.m. was noticed from there. L/Mt. A SETOUCH. The following other ranks were commended by the E'Officer Commanding on gallantry during the recent 20-24th Sept: 7039 RSM Sgt. R BRESHAM 30528 Cpl MORRICE. 15332 Pte T MURREE. The Batt'n states a cases of Kennep at men attacks especially since 17th minuting. Lieut R BROWNES died of wounds in 14 General Hospital WIMEREUX. The Brigade was inspected by G.O.C. 23 Division. The symptoms all seem to have resulted from Gare.	

Army Form C. 2118.

WAR DIARY
or
INTELLIGENCE SUMMARY.
(Erase heading not required.)

Instructions regarding War Diaries and Intelligence Summaries are contained in F. S. Regs., Part II. and the Staff Manual respectively. Title pages will be prepared in manuscript.

Place	Date	Hour	Summary of Events and Information	Remarks and references to Appendices
SEIGUES	21.3.		Major C E HODSON DSO M.C. (who received a BAR to his DSO for gallantry in the field). The Brigadier was inspected by the Commander-in-Chief who expressed his approval of the way that he men handled their arms & their turned out.	
	22.3.			

A.J Wheaton Lieut (Bvt)
H.Q Brit Reserve Brigade

Secret. Map B   70th Infantry Brigade   Scale 1/10000

Position on Sepr 27th 1916 shown in Blue

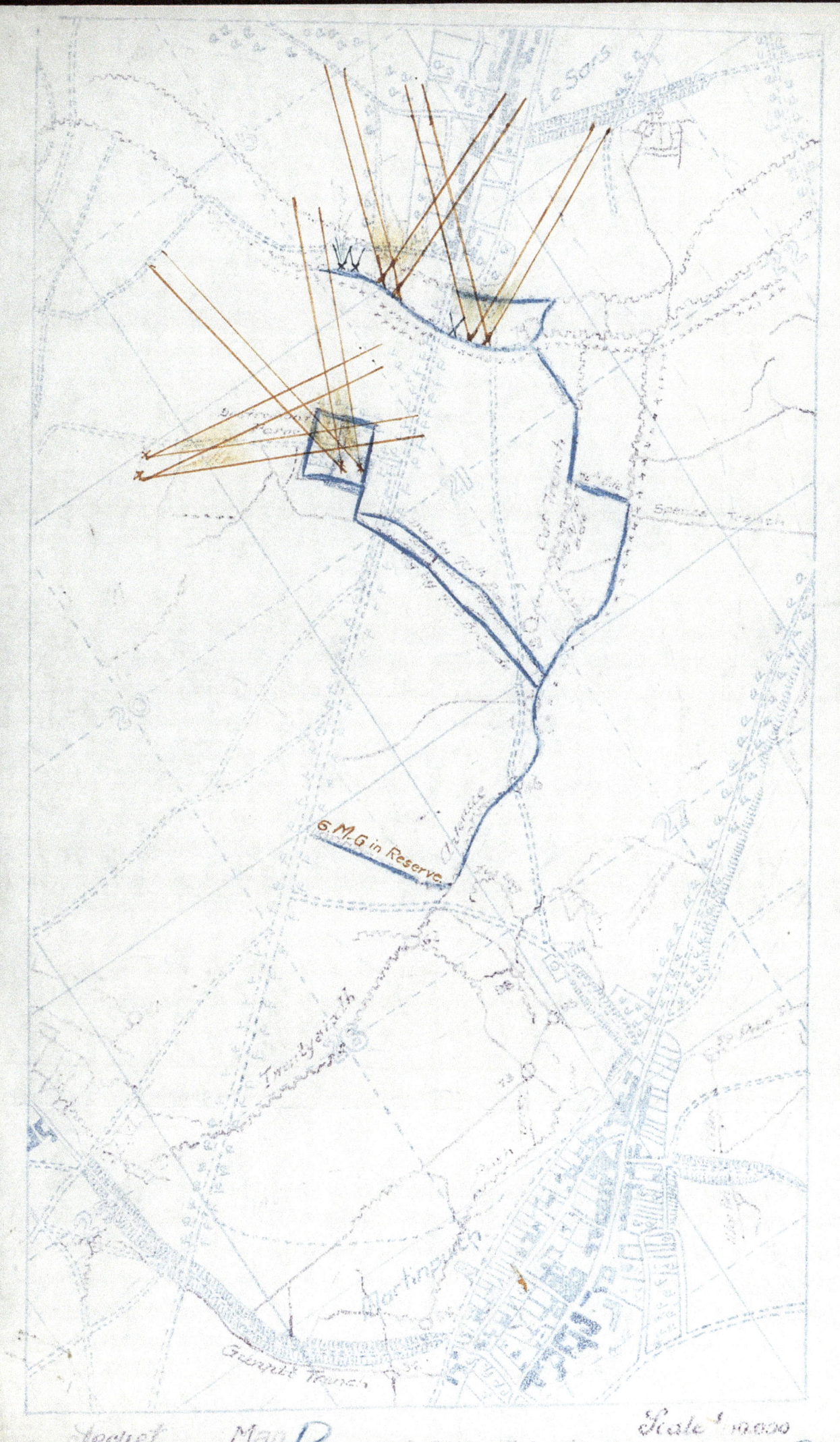

Army Form C. 2118.

War Diary 13

October Diary Martinpuich

11th Batt Newport Fusiliers

n.13

WAR DIARY
or
INTELLIGENCE SUMMARY.
(Erase heading not required.)

Place	Date	Hour	Summary of Events and Information	Remarks and references to Appendices
MARTINPUICH	10/16		The Battalion formed part of a new Army Corps of 23rd & 50th Divisions & captured the FLERS–LESARS line on a front of over a mile with the 50th Division on the right of 23rd Division. The Battalion was the right Battalion of the 70th Brigade being in front with the 50th Division on our right & the 8th Batt KOYLI on our left. The Battalion moved up from trenches in O.G.2 and THE TANGLE at 9.15 am to the Dorothy trenches forming up & the following order A Company on the right, D Company on the left, B Company on the right, C Company in support from M.21.a.2.6 & M.27.a.7.9. which will be known as DESTREMONT TRENCH. C Company on left & B on the right formed up in a second French Chief 50 yards in rear of the others. The objective of the Battalion was our own & hostile trenches in FLERS-LESARS line between the Divisional Boundary M.21.d.8.5 on the right & the main ALBERT –BAPAUME ROAD on the left. The Leading Companies were to pass the 1st Hostile line & take the second, the supporting Company was to take & consolidate the 1st hostile line. At 3.15 pm A & D Company advanced in two Waves under our own Barrage which lifted off the Objective at 3.47 pm. C Company advancing in support in one Wave . B Company following in reserve	Mon Brown

WAR DIARY or INTELLIGENCE SUMMARY

Army Form C. 2118.

Place	Date	Hour	Summary of Events and Information	Remarks and references to Appendices
	October			
			The Objective was taken and consolidated, touch with the Division on our right was kept but the Battalion on our left failed to reach its objective & that flank was left in the air.	
LE SARS LINE	2nd		The Battalion marched from the line during the evening & came back to bivouacs at LOZENGE WOOD. The losses on these two days were Killed Officers Captain R. Luttrell, 2nd Lieut G.S. Bartle, F.L. Henley & 12 Other Ranks, Wounded Captain R. Abbott, 2nd Lieut J.B. Hayes, J.M. Bellamy & 137 Other Ranks, Missing 2nd Lieut E.A. Basevano & 13 Other Ranks.	
LOZENGE WOOD	4th		The O.C. 23rd Division A.C.K. the following letter to the Officer Commanding "Will you please tell all ranks of your Battalion how delighted I am at their behaviour on October 1st & congratulate them most heartily on their complete success & tell them also how gallantly and thoroughly they did their good work & you all. Signed J.M. Babington. 2nd Lieuts J.H. Bellamy & Martin were wounded. The following non-commissioned were made to Brevetral Rowland Orders	

Army Form C. 2118.

WAR DIARY
or
INTELLIGENCE SUMMARY.
(Erase heading not required.)

3

Place	Date	Hour	Summary of Events and Information	Remarks and references to Appendices
	7th		dated 4-10-16. The G.O.C. has conveyed pleasure of awards of the Military Medal by the Corps Commander to the Sergts of the 11th Bn. Sermon Molino 16205 Pte J.R. Pitt 17519 Gunn Cpl of Ronne 15440 L/Cpl B. Boutry 17528 Pte A.H. Pye.	
LOZENGE WOOD	7		The Battalion moved up to GOURLAY TRENCH to support the 68th & 69th Bgdes to who made an attack on LE SARS which was successful	
	8		Marched back to LOZENGE WOOD and then to PRICOURT where he entrained for VIVIER HILL, marched on to BRESLE WOOD CAMP	
BRESLE WOOD	10		The Bodies of Captain H.S. Harris & 8 Other Ranks were identified & buried near AUTHUILLE WOOD having been killed in action on 1st July 1916	
	11		The Brigade was inspected by the Corps Commander.	
	12		Marched to KALBERT. Was met at the station by a draft of 69 men. The Battalion entrained for PICQUIGNY in LONGPRE and marched from there to PONT REMY	
PONT REMY	14		March to GRAPENNES.	

Army Form C. 2118.

WAR DIARY
or
INTELLIGENCE SUMMARY.
(Erase heading not required.)

Instructions regarding War Diaries and Intelligence Summaries are contained in F. S. Regs., Part II. and the Staff Manual respectively. Title pages will be prepared in manuscript.

Place	Date	Hour	Summary of Events and Information	Remarks and references to Appendices
	Oct.			
PONT REMY	14th		The following have been awarded the Military Medal 73176 Pte Compton A 16367 Pte Black Lloyd J. The following Letter has also been received. The Divisional Commander conveys his most sincere appreciation of the gallantry & devotion to duty of all ranks engaged in the late operations. The attack on 26th Avenue, the capture of DESTREMONT FARM (sic) OG 1 & 2 and subsequently the capture of LE SARS are performances of which the Corps may feel justly proud. Since 5th September last the Divisional and other Casualties have been inflicted on the enemy which cannot but have saved his hide and again forced him into inferiority. The Divisional Commander is very proud to be a British Soldier, associated with such gallant comrades as the officers & men of the 23rd Division.	
CRAPENNES	15th		Marched to ST. RIQUIER and entrained for PROVEN, arriving at 3.30 a.m. & marched to OUDERDOM	
OUDERDOM	16th		A Draft of 56 other Ranks arrived for the Battalion	

WAR DIARY or INTELLIGENCE SUMMARY

Army Form C. 2118.

Place	Date	Hour	Summary of Events and Information	Remarks and references to Appendices
OUDERDOM	Oct 16th		15462 Sgt MOLSON F. 35943 Lce Cpl CLARKE Capt NIMMITT 16721 Lce Cpl CARTER G. were awarded the Military Medal. And following extract from mornings state 13th inst. is published. TEMP LIEUT H.C. WATTS to be TEMP CAPT to complete establishment 24th July 1916. TEMP 2 Lieut G.B. HAYES to be TEMP LIEUT 30th July 1916. 2 Lieut Bell & 60 other ranks arrived for the Battalion. The Battalion sent by train to YPRES and took over Bryants Reserve.	5
	18th		Lines at ZILLEBEKE BUND. 11006 Sgt MACKETT J & 16950 Sgt KIRKLAND C. were awarded the Military Medal.	
ZILLEBEKE BUND	21st		Took over the trenches infront of SANCTUARY WOOD from 9th Bn York & Lancaster Regt Rifle. The 47th Division were on our right & the 8th Bn York & Lancaster Regt on our left. Lieut R.S. LYMBERY, 2 Lieut C.D. PRIST, R. GROVES, H. CASSELS, A.D. SWALE, A. BARBER & C.S. TOMLINSON reported on 18th were taken on Strength of the Battn.	
	26th		Heavy bombing to go to 3rd Batt York & Lancasters Regt. The enemy were very active during the last ten days & he kept up persistent Concentration & Shelling active on the trenches other ranks. Killed 2 Wounded 15 Shell Shock 1.	

Army Form C. 2118.

6

WAR DIARY
or
INTELLIGENCE SUMMARY.
(Erase heading not required.)

Place	Date	Hour	Summary of Events and Information	Remarks and references to Appendices
	Oct.			
ZILLEBEKE BUND	27.		Major J. McD. Pratt D.S.O. York and Lancaster Regt. attacked to 2nd in Command to this Battalion left on 29th to assume Command of 11th Batt. Northumberland Fusiliers.	
	29.		Lieut N.W. Coates has assumed the building Crow on a recent forgette. The Battalion moved back to billets in POPERINGHE.	

A.H. Watson Lieut Colonel
11th Batt Northumberland Fusiliers

Army Form C. 2118.

WAR DIARY
or
INTELLIGENCE SUMMARY.
(Erase heading not required.)

Instructions regarding War Diaries and Intelligence Summaries are contained in F.S. Regs., Part II. and the Staff Manual respectively. Title pages will be prepared in manuscript.

1/5 Battⁿ Sherwood Foresters Vol 14

Place	Date	Hour	Summary of Events and Information	Remarks and references to Appendices
	1916			
POPERINGHE	Nov 1st		The Battalion arrived from the trenches afternoon & evening.	
			19066 L/Cpl Shirley - Brixton relieved	Miss Little
	Nov 2nd		The Battalion at POPERINGHE to YPRES by train & route marched	
			Battalion on the up sector of the defences. On the right wing the 6th Brigade on the left the	
			8th Battⁿ York & Lanc^s Reg^t. Battⁿ Head Quarters at the TOWERS	
THE TRENCHES	Nov 3rd		Captain Shepherd O.B.E. Lewis returned from ENGLAND & took over the duties of Adjutant	
			17937 L/Cpl Andlipe H. wounded	
			The Battalion traded over the trenches to the 9 Battⁿ York & Lancs in Reg^t & went into	
			Brigade Reserve with billets in the Barracks at YPRES –	
			Lieut R.E. Jones borrowed & Joined the Royal Hq of Cyclos	
YPRES	Nov 4th		2335 Pte W.H.H. Maitland & sea wounded	
	Nov 5th		7312.28 Pte Lock J. & 24045 Pte Goulbho G. wounded	H.14
			The platoon to billets near Above wounded the Brotherty Return	
			7320 L/Cpl Irvine L. 17223 Cpl Shepherd J.E. 17130 Ollivant Cpl^l Broth W.H.	
			16710 Pte Gosling J.S. 17081 Pte Mason P.R. 16663 Pte Foley R.C. 69211 Pte	
			Newment	

WAR DIARY or INTELLIGENCE SUMMARY

Army Form C. 2118.

4th Battn Sherwood Foresters

Place	Date	Hour	Summary of Events and Information	Remarks and references to Appendices
YPRES	Nov 16		The Bath handed over the billets to 68th Brigade & went back to Brandhoek.	
TORONTO CAMP	Nov 17		Reserve at TORONTO CAMP near ELVERDINGHE. Very cold weather. The camp was composed of very draughty huts with no stoves.	
	Nov 18th		2nd Lieut R. Turner transferred to the Battalion 6th R Battn West Lancash Regt both effective from 29.7.16	
	Nov 22		The Battalion relieved the 1/5th Battn West Riding Regiment at ZILLEBEKE BUND 2nd Lieut J. Allsopp joined the Battalion was taken on the strength from 20/11/16	
ZILLEBEKE BUND	Nov 23		16980 Sgt Richard C has been awarded a bar to his Military Medal.	
	Nov 28		London Gazette dated 22nd November 1916 Temp 2nd Lieuts to be 2nd Lieuts — N.W. Corbet, C.W. Bartlett 2nd Lieut V.G.R. Brough arrived and taken on the strength of the Battn from this unit.	
	29		3rd Batt Ox & Bucks right Battalion, part of the Batt relieved from the Right Sector from the 9th Battn	

Army Form C. 2118.

WAR DIARY
or
INTELLIGENCE SUMMARY.   3.

(Erase heading not required.)

Instructions regarding War Diaries and Intelligence Summaries are contained in F. S. Regs., Part II. and the Staff Manual respectively. Title pages will be prepared in manuscript.

Place	Date	Hour	Summary of Events and Information	Remarks and references to Appendices
			York Lancs in Res. The London Brigade on the right & 6th Batt York Lincoln Reg on the left. In the supplement to the London gazette dated November 25th 1916 Temp Captain C. E. Hudson was awarded the Military Cross.	

A.J. Watson L/Cpl.
11 Batt Sherwood Foresters

ORIGINAL

Army Form C. 2118.

11th Sherwood Foresters

Vol 15

WAR DIARY
or
INTELLIGENCE SUMMARY.

Place	Date	Hour	Summary of Events and Information	Remarks and references to Appendices
TRENCHES	1915 Dec 1/2		On the night of the 1st/2nd December a raid on the German front line from Sap F was attempted. The raiding party consisting of 2 Lieuts Bennett & Gibson with 20 other ranks had been previously trained for a fortnight at the Brigade School. Zero hour was fixed at 12.30 a.m. on 2nd. All went well up to this hour. The whole party being in position as previously arranged. The heavy artillery started fire 2 minutes early. A Box barrage had been arranged to commence at 2 minutes after the zero hour by 18 Pdrs. and by 4" mortars on the flanks of the hostile trench to be attacked on rear from Trench Mortars 47.53 Lieut Cartlidge H 36.753. The raiding party had to suck the hostile trench on our Trans Trench a number of Stokes among the trenches. 4753 Lieut Cartlidge H 36753 R.E. Supt. O. 1932.30 Pte Harring C were wounded and 2nd Lieut Gibson was shot into our Sap. The enemy wire to the Cathedral and started to swing fire from their line. Our artillery continued to shell so the party finding further progress impossible returned. The Artillery Brigade Commander afterwards admitted that one or more of his batteries were entirely to blame. 24264 Pte Yeomans S. Wo. Killed 17537 Lce Cpl Brady J. Wo Killed	

ORIGINAL

Army Form C. 2118

WAR DIARY
or
INTELLIGENCE SUMMARY
(Erase heading not required.)

Instructions regarding War Diaries and Intelligence Summaries are contained in F. S. Regs., Part II. and the Staff Manual respectively. Title Pages will be prepared in manuscript.

2/

Place	Date	Hour	Summary of Events and Information	Remarks and references to Appendices
Trenches	5th Dec		The Battn. was relieved in the front line by the 9th Battn. YORK & LANCASTER Regt. and marched back to support in the ZILLEBEKE BUND. 7253 SERGT LEWIS W. & 165-72 Pte. HAINES. W.J.E. Have awarded the Military Medal. 21783 Pte. SPARR. G. was killed & 16105 L/Cpl. WOOLLEY was wounded.	
ZILLEBEKE	6th Dec		87th YORK & LANCASTER REGT. MAJOR D. BUIRK assumed temporary Command of the Battalion.	
	7th Dec		The Battn. was relieved by the 13th Battn. Durham L.I. & trained back to TORONTO CAMP. Men who had been relieved & the Camp was generally more comfortable.	
TORONTO CAMP	10th Dec		73288 Sergt. WILLIAMS G. 36152 L/Cpl. SWIFT G. 4743 L/Cpl CARTLEDGE 73230 Pte. HURRING. C. 4689 Pte. FARNSWORTH. Have awarded the Military Medal. 2nd LIEUT R.W. CLARK reported his arrival & was taken on the strength of the Battn. He had been wounded on July 1st 1916 when serving with the Battn. The Battn. relieved the 9th Battn. YORKSHIRE REGT in the right Battn. sector Left Brigade front line. Very strong was quiet during the 4 days spent in the line - there were no casualties.	
	15th Dec			
TRENCHES	19th Dec		The Battn. was relieved in the front line trenches by 9th Battn. YORK & LANCASTER REGT. & marched back into support to the BARRACKS YPRES.	
YPRES	18th Dec		MAJOR A.B WAYTE from 1st Battn. joined and took over temporary Command of the Battn. CAPT. H.C. WATTS returned to took over command of B Company.	
	23rd Dec		50146 Pte. WALTERS. S. 57215 Pte. LACEY. J. were killed. 16437 L/Cpl. WING. W. died of wounds. 19487 Pte. ROSE J. 20623 Pte. BURROWS. N. 206363 Pte. TURNER L. 35759 Pte. GIBSON F. were wounded in a working party.	

ORIGINAL

3

Army Form C. 2118.

WAR DIARY
or
INTELLIGENCE SUMMARY.

(Erase heading not required.)

Place	Date	Hour	Summary of Events and Information	Remarks and references to Appendices
YPRES	1916 Dec 23 Sat	3.45 P.M.	The Battalion relieved the 9th YORK & LANCASTER REGT in the HOOGE Trenches. All quiet.	
	Sun 24th		Considerable Aeroplane and Artillery activity on both sides all day - Nothing else to note.	
	Mon 25		Christmas day - Plum puddings were enjoyed by the Battalion, the gift of the Ladies of Nottingham. The day was warm and wet and passed quietly. There was no attempt at fraternising on either side. About 9.30 P.M. Considerable Gunfire was heard in the north which lasted half an hour -	
	Tues 26th		Very fine and clear and Aeroplanes were proportionately busy - an Allied aeroplane was brought down by a German machine about 12 noon. It fell inside our lines some miles to N. At 2.15 P.M. MAJOR C.E. HUDSON was presented with his M.C. ribbon by General BABINGTON Commanding 23rd Division, and Pte P. STOKES B Coy (no 16032) and Pte S. THOMPSON B Coy (no 73050) were presented with Military Medal Ribbons. The ceremony took place at Brigade Headquarters.	
	Wed 27th		All quiet. at 6.45 P.M. the Battalion was relieved in the Trenches by the 9th YORK & LANCASTER Regt. and returned to YPRES Barracks without suffering any casualties.	

ORIGINAL

WAR DIARY
or
INTELLIGENCE SUMMARY
(Erase heading not required.)

Army Form C. 2118

Place	Date 1916	Hour	Summary of Events and Information	Remarks and references to Appendices
YPRES INFANTRY BARRACKS	Dec. Thursday 28th to Sunday 31st		The Battalion was in reserve Billets at the Infantry Barracks. Beyond the usual daily exchange of Shells there has been nothing to write about. On the evening of Sunday 31st Dec the Battalion moved into Divisional reserve at TORONTO CAMP. On that day Lieut Col WATSON D.S.O. returned from leave and resumed command of the Battalion. W.B. Wayte, Major 11th Bn. Sherwood Foresters.	

Army Form C. 2118.

1/17 Sherwood Foresters

N.16

WAR DIARY
or
INTELLIGENCE SUMMARY.
(Erase heading not required.)

Place	Date	Hour	Summary of Events and Information	Remarks and references to Appendices
TORONTO CAMP	1917 Jan 1st		The Battalion arrived here at 10. P.M. last night. The morning was spent cleaning up. We played the York and Lancs at football and drew the match 1 goal all.	
	2nd		This day was a general holiday. At 9.30 A.M. Lieut Colonel Watson who had today received the C.M.G. inspected the Battalion on parade and wished all ranks a happy new year. At 1 P.M. a New Year dinner was provided in the Y.M.C.A. hut, to which everyone did ample justice. In the evening 30 Officers sat down to dinner in the same building. The Regimental Band played a Selection of music during dinner. The toasts were —

The King proposed by Major C. E. Hudson.
The Regiment " " Lieut Col. H. F. WATSON C.M.G. D.S.O.
Absent friends " " Major Hudson.
The Commanding Officer " " Major WAYTE.
A Smoking Concert after dinner brought a very pleasant Evening to a successful ending — | |

Army Form C. 2118.

WAR DIARY
or
INTELLIGENCE SUMMARY.
(Erase heading not required.)

Instructions regarding War Diaries and Intelligence Summaries are contained in F.S. Regs., Part II. and the Staff Manual respectively. Title pages will be prepared in manuscript.

Place	Date	Hour	Summary of Events and Information	Remarks and references to Appendices
	1917			
TORONTO CAMP	Jan 3rd		Parades as in Camp - Putting in Units about.	
" "	4th to 7th		Football Match v. 8th York and Lancaster Regt. We won 3 goals - 2.	
	8th		Putting in Huts.	
			The Battalion returned at BRANDHOEK at 5 P.M. and took over the MOUNT SORREL Trenches, with Headquarters at RUDKIN HOUSE. No 19585 Cpl J. STATHAM was wounded.	
RUDKIN HOUSE HQ	9th		There was much trench mortaring all day by the Germans. Our losses were: Killed nil. Wounded 32604 L/Cpl H Bate, 15482 Pte C Charlesworth, 35605 Pte J. Reddington, 46797 Pte J. Brown, 56451 Pte J Martin 51318 Pte A. Gradon, 15156 Pte J. Carlisle.	
	10th		Artillery very lively on both sides all day.	
	11th		Heavy fall of Snow. The 55th Division did a raid on our left.	
	12th		Bitterly Cold all day. The Battalion was relieved by the 9th YORK and LANCASTER Regt. and went into Brigade reserve at ZILLEBEKE BUND.	

Army Form C. 2118.

WAR DIARY
or
INTELLIGENCE SUMMARY.
(Erase heading not required.)

Instructions regarding War Diaries and Intelligence Summaries are contained in F. S. Regs., Part II. and the Staff Manual respectively. Title pages will be prepared in manuscript.

Place	Date	Hour	Summary of Events and Information	Remarks and references to Appendices
THE BUND	1917 January 13 to Tuesday 16th.		The Battalion was in Brigade Reserve between these dates. There has been nothing to report, and the Enemy's Artillery have been quieter than usual. On the evening of Tuesday 16th we relieved the 9th YORK & LANCASTER Regt. in its Right Sector of Trenches –	
RUDKIN HOUSE	17th		About 4 inches of Snow fell during the night and the Cold was intense. Much damage was done to our Support trenches and the day was spent chiefly in clearing a way through them. The Enemy's "Minnies" were very troublesome all day, and in answer to an urgent message from the C.O. a systematic bombardment of CLONMEL COPSE took place for 2½ hours. Over 1500 shells were sent over, but directly they stopped, the Germans started from HILL 60, and shelled unintermittently through the night.	
	18th		Very Cold all day – Special vigilance was exercised at night and extra strong patrols sent out as a party of Germans, clad in White Suits cut up a post of the 47th Division on our right.	

T2134. Wt. W708—776. 50,000. 4/15. Sir J. C. & S.

Army Form C. 2118.

WAR DIARY
or
INTELLIGENCE SUMMARY.
(Erase heading not required.)

Instructions regarding War Diaries and Intelligence Summaries are contained in F. S. Regs., Part II. and the Staff Manual respectively. Title pages will be prepared in manuscript.

Place	Date	Hour	Summary of Events and Information	Remarks and references to Appendices
	1917			
RUDKIN HOUSE	Jan 19th 20th		Snow still holding. A much quieter day. The Battalion was relieved by the 9th York and Lancaster Regt and returned to Brigade reserve at THE BUND.	
THE BUND	21st to 24th Jan.		In reserve at the BUND. No events of interest. On the evening of 24 Jan we went into divisional reserve at TORONTO CAMP.	
TORONTO CAMP	25th to 31st		We suffered considerable discomfort as every drop of water was frozen and had to be melted and the supply of fuel, of course, was less than usual. Usual cleaning up day - The time in Divisional reserve passed quietly without special incident. On Tuesday 30th Jan a successful Smoking Concert was arranged in the Y.M.C.A. Attached is a list of Casualties for this month Killed in action: 25480 Pte Wheeler A, 50600 Pte Bayes C.H.; 70537 Pte Walker H.N 46280 Pte Murray Fear J. 70556 Pte Ellis T.; Wounded: 18190 Pte Else H.N. 51874 Pte Cubitt W.; 5050 L/c Legard E., 73219 Pte Cheadle R. 28602 Pte Warden G. 21401 Pte Bowler B. 6915 Coy Q.M.S Sadler T. 70558 Pte Ellis T. 58650 Pte Gutton J.H. 6216 Pte Jones J.E.	

A.B. Wayte Major
11th Bn. Sherwood Foresters

WAR DIARY
or
INTELLIGENCE SUMMARY.
(Erase heading not required.)

Army Form C. 2118.

Y/1/17 11th Sherwood Foresters

Y.17

Place	Date	Hour	Summary of Events and Information	Remarks and references to Appendices
HALF WAY HOUSE	1917 Feb. 1st to 5th		The Battalion entrained at BRANDHOEK at 6 P.M. and proceeded to YPRES, thence by foot to the trenches with Bt. H.Q. at HALFWAY HOUSE. All quiet. We have not before been in these trenches which are a great improvement on the right sector and about 600 yds from the Hun. In consequence we were free from "minnies" which made life in the other sector such a burden. On 1st Feb. Lieut Col Watson C.M.G. D.S.O. went to command the 70th Brigade and Major Wayte took over temporary command of the Battalion – Owing to the intense frost, very little engineering work was possible, but the line was well strengthened by barbed wire, and much patrol work done – On 4th February 2nd Lieut LOVETT was hit by a Whizz Bang in the right arm whilst on duty in the Culvert. It is hoped that the wound will not prove serious. On the evening of 5th February the Battalion was relieved by the 9th Y and L. Regt and went into Brigade reserve at Infantry Bks YPRES.	Sir Harri
YPRES BARRACKS	6th –		Clean up day. In the afternoon there was a strafe by the Corps Heavy Artillery just outside Barracks which effectually dispelled any idea of sleep.	

WAR DIARY
or
INTELLIGENCE SUMMARY.
(Erase heading not required.)

Army Form C. 2118.

Place	Date	Hour	Summary of Events and Information	Remarks and references to Appendices
YPRES BARRACKS	February 7th		A draft of 60 men arrived, all men of 2 years service but fresh to this country.	
	10th -14th		The battalion returned to the front line (left battalion of left sector) relieving the 9th Y & L Regt. The front – 500 held and work in the line had to be confined to wiring and carrying stores – 9312 Pte LAWRENCE and 19233 Pte RIGLEY were wounded by gunfire in the CULVERT. Heavy shelling continued on our left throughout our tour culminating in two raids by the division on our left. The enemy included our left company trenches in their retaliation defensive barrage but we suffered no casualties – 2nd Lt LACEY did a very good patrol from the CULVERT up the MENIN ROAD bringing back useful information and a new HUN Cap. MAJOR C.E. HUDSON was awarded the CROIX DE GUERRE by the Commander-in-Chief.	
	14th -15th		The battalion were relieved by the 9th Y&L Regt and returned to Brigade Reserve in the BARRACKS YPRES. during the night the BARRACKS were heavily shelled with 5.9, 8", 4.5 and in fact an hour at a time. A good deal of damage to material but no casualties was the result – 20497 Pte WAINWARD 17019 Pte PRIEST were wounded with the tramspout, which was shelled in YPRES.	

WAR DIARY or INTELLIGENCE SUMMARY

Army Form C. 2118.

Place	Date	Hour	Summary of Events and Information	Remarks and references to Appendices
TORONTO CAMP	18th		The Battalion was relieved and by the 11th N.F. and returned by train to TORONTO CAMP	
	23rd		MAJOR C.E. HUDSON was presented with the CROIX DE GUERRE by GENERAL NIVELLE at ARMY H.Q. The Battalion played the M.G. Coy at soccer winning with easy matches with the 8th and 9th Y&L Regt. resulted in draws as all in each case. "Special Platoon" training was started, one platoon per Coy being told off, all duties and special attention being devoted to their training. This week based to be discontinued owing to an order that we were to do 4 hours a week. MAJOR WAYTE went to the C.O.'s course at the II ARMY SCHOOL and MAJOR HUDSON took over command of the Battalion in his absence. 2nd Lt LOVETT transferred to the R.F.C. One of Miss LENA ASHWELL'S concert parties entertained the troops in the Y.M.C.A. HUT in Camp.	
	24th		The Battalion trained from POPERINGHE to BOLLEZEELE the new small-gauge railway where they billeted the night.	
	25th		The Battalion marched on to WATTEN a distance of 7 miles to billets.	
	26th		Marched on 8 miles to NORDAUSQUES near ZUTKERQUES our first billets in FRANCE. MAJOR WAYTE rejoined and took over command of the Battalion.	

Army Form C. 2118.

WAR DIARY
or
INTELLIGENCE SUMMARY.
(Erase heading not required.)

Place	Date	Hour	Summary of Events and Information	Remarks and references to Appendices
NORDAUSQUES	1917 Feb 27th		The day was spent in settling down in Billets which are very scattered.	
	Wednesday 28th		The Battalion marched to the range to shoot, where, as may be expected, the results were not good. Captain WHYATT rejoined the Battalion, also 2nd Lieut BAYLEY from 13th Battalion.	

Whyte Major
Comdg 11th Bn
Sherwood Foresters.

Army Form C. 2118.

11th Sherwood Foresters   Vol/8

WAR DIARY
or
INTELLIGENCE SUMMARY.
(Erase heading not required.)

Place	Date	Hour	Summary of Events and Information	Remarks and references to Appendices
NAUDAUSQUES	1917 March 1st		The usual training went on. After 2½ years of war, the Higher Command have invented an entirely new form of organization of Battalions and this is giving much food for thought. — We welcome back Captain P. WHYATT, an old 11th Battalion officer who arrived today —	
	2nd		Firing on the Range, about 2½ miles away. As may be expected, the shooting was not good. —	
	3rd 4th 5th 6th		There were various inter-platoon football competitions in the afternoon — Sunday. Church Parade. A real day of rest. — Training all day. Nothing to note — Major A. B. WAYTE was promoted temporary Lieut Colonel whilst in Command of the Battalion. The usual programme of work was carried out on 7th and 8th March.	
	9th		The Battalion took part in a Brigade Field Day. Parading at 7.30 A.M. In a blinding snowstorm (winter has once more returned) we attacked LA COUDRÉE Farm in conjunction with 2 other Battalions. The Divisional Commander (Major-General BABINGTON) was present, and said that the operations were very satisfactory. Considering the small amount of "Open Warfare" practice we have had.	

Army Form C. 2118.

WAR DIARY
or
INTELLIGENCE SUMMARY.
(Erase heading not required.)

Place	Date	Hour	Summary of Events and Information	Remarks and references to Appendices
NORDAUSQUES	1917 MARCH 10th		The Battalion performed another tactical exercise at INGLINGHEM. We took dinner out and as the day was very fine, it was a great success.	
	Sunday 11th		Rest day and very welcome.	
	12th		We were very busy all day practising the new attack.	
	13th and 14th		We did an attack on LA COUDREE Farm in the new formation which went quite well, and 2 Senior Staff officers on the ground said the drill and handling of Arms was exceptionally good. The men are all looking very fit and have already "Lost the Trench Slouch".	
	15th		Musketry on A Range. The Shooting was better.	
	16th		No 13 Platoon was beaten by the K.O.Y.L.I. in the inter platoon football at MENTQUE after a very good game. Both goals were scored in the last few minutes. We did a night march from CULEM.	
	17th		This was a Company day as Everyone was tired and dirty.	
	Sunday 18th		Everyone packing up ready to go tomorrow.	

Army Form C. 2118.

WAR DIARY
or
INTELLIGENCE SUMMARY.
(Erase heading not required.)

Place	Date	Hour	Summary of Events and Information	Remarks and references to Appendices
NORDAUSQUES	1917 March 19.		The 70th Brigade Group marched from NORDAUSQUES at 10. A.M. We were very sorry to leave it & whole and have had a pleasant 8 weeks here. The Divisional Commander congratulated the C.O. on the fine march discipline of the Battalion. We went into billets at HOULLE, a place nearly surrounded by water. The men were billeted in a large brewery and were fairly comfortable.	
	20th		The Battalion left HOULLE at 8 A.M. in a snowstorm and marched through WATTEN and up a long hill through dull little Flemish villages to BOLLEZEELE where we halted, altogether about 10 miles.	
	21st		We left BOLLEZEELE at 9.40 A.M. and marched to HOUTKERQUE, about 14 miles. The Brigade halted in a field for lunch about noon. Not a single man has fallen out on this march of 3 days. The Bn Hqts are about 2½ miles from Headquarters.	
	22nd		A Sports meeting was held and a programme arranged settling down.	
	23rd		Usual parades. The Open Warfare Stunt has given way to trench attack.	
	24th		The Battalion played the 9th YORK & LANCS at HERZEELE and won 6 goals to nine.	

WARY DIARY or INTELLIGENCE SUMMARY.

Army Form C. 2118.

Place	Date	Hour	Summary of Events and Information	Remarks and references to Appendices
HOOTKERQUE	28th		Lt Colonel Doyle granted leave to England. Major Madden took over temporary command of the battalion.	
	29th		Brigade Sports took place, owing to a mistake the morning had to be cancelled and will be run again later on. We were 24 on the signalling, gas and battalion runners Competition missing a 1st and his by a narrow margin.	
	30th		Heats for the battalion sports to morrow, were run off.	
	31st		The Battalion Sports proved a great success in spite of somewhat inclement weather. There were large entries from the units for the open races, mob officers 440, and mule race. "B" Company carried away the largest number of prizes.	

WAR DIARY or **INTELLIGENCE SUMMARY**
Army Form C. 2118.

Vol 19
11th Sherwood Foresters

K.19

Place	Date	Hour	Summary of Events and Information	Remarks and references to Appendices
HOUTKERQUE	2-4-19		The BRIGADE 3 mile approaching rail took place – 50 minutes for train, the King being invited to the mess with all its men in half an hour and numerous places immediately, with the Guest Officer against them. The Battalion although 3 of the last minutes was unable to man the big a number was given and received the finished £10 with which it was decided to purchase medals.	Min Harris
	3-4-19		9260 C.S.M HOULGAN.S. who has been C.S.M G A'cy came to Littleton on Sheriffs Foresters formed at FRENSHAM left for England being posted to Home establishment. The Acting Adjutant 2/Lt H.J CAVELL was promoted to Lieut: The Battalion marched 12 miles to TORONTO CAMP a very trying march for the men along "pavé" roads nearly the whole way but none fell out.	
TORONTO CAMP	EASTER SUNDAY 6/4/19		Went up by train to YPRES and took over the BUND from the 14th HANTS	
BUND.	8/4/19		Took over the central B.Lt Line of the HILL 60 outpost. For 20th LONDON REGT the relief was not complete until 2 am on the morning of the 9th April	
	9/4/19		The enemy raided in a 2 battalion frontage (account and sketch map attached of enemy fighting patrol endeavoured to gain possession of the bridge over the Cutting (an important tactical point) with a strong frightning patrol	
	10/4/19			

WAR DIARY or INTELLIGENCE SUMMARY

Army Form C. 2118.

Place	Date	Hour	Summary of Events and Information	Remarks and references to Appendices
HILL 60	10.4.17		Captain L.R. HALFORD who went with a Platoon and 3 Lewis guns to assist the attack settled a strong point to cover the bridge. This he did with a few casualties. No killed (being shot at a range of 10 yards).	
	11.4.17		The 2nd line DEEP SUPPORT LINE – COMPANY TRENCH was held as the line of resistance and kept was pushed forward into the morning of the 12th its line at night and gradually, after much hard work, and with the assistance of numerous working parties, its old line was dug out and reclaimed, all dispositions and lines being handed over to its incoming Battalion on the early morning of the 15th April. A feat worthy of the finest traditions of the SHERWOOD FORESTERS.	
	12.4.17			
	13.4.17			
	14.4.17			
TORONTO CAMP	15.4.17		Lt Col. WAYTE rejoined the Battalion on its arrival back in TORONTO CAMP and resumed Command on his return from leave.	
	14.4.17		The total casualties during the above 2 days tour in the trenches were: One Officer killed and died of wounds and 6 wounded, 29 ORs killed and 49 ORs wounded 1 died of wounds 3 missing.	

Army Form C. 2118.

WAR DIARY
or
INTELLIGENCE SUMMARY.
(Erase heading not required.)

Instructions regarding War Diaries and Intelligence Summaries are contained in F. S. Regs., Part II. and the Staff Manual respectively. Title pages will be prepared in manuscript.

Place	Date	Hour	Summary of Events and Information	Remarks and references to Appendices
TORONTO CAMP.	1917 15 April.		The Battalion arrived tired out from the Trenches about 6.A.M. where breakfast was waiting after which everyone went to bed. —	
"	16 April.		Cleaning day — a large number of deficiencies were found owing to the recent action.	
"	17 April		The G.O.C. 70th Brigade inspected the Battalion in Mass on Parade at 10.30 A.M. In his speech he said "I am proud to see you looking so fit and smart on parade after going through a bombardment unprecedented; even on the SOMME. The name of HILL 60 which is known through the Civilized World will have fresh lustre added to it by the gallantry of the 11th Batt Sherwood Foresters." The Battalion then marched past the G.O.C.	
"	18th April 19th "		Company Parades &c in Camp. A heavy Snowstorm. The 70th Brigade played 15 68th B.de at football in POPERINGHE. The 70th won 3 goals — 1.	
"	20th April		The Corps Commander (Lieut General MORLAND C.B. C.M.G. D.S.O.) presented Military Medals to Sgt ANTCLIFFE, Pte BAXTER and L/Cpl COOKE on Parade.	

Army Form C. 2118.

WAR DIARY
or
INTELLIGENCE SUMMARY.
(Erase heading not required.)

Instructions regarding War Diaries and Intelligence Summaries are contained in F. S. Regs., Part II. and the Staff Manual respectively. Title pages will be prepared in manuscript.

Place	Date	Hour	Summary of Events and Information	Remarks and references to Appendices
	1917			
TORONTO CAMP	20th April		The Battalion was formed up in a hollow square and received the CORPS Commander with a General Salute, the Band being in attendance. The Divisional and Brigade Commanders were also present.	
	21st April		Quiet day. Company football in the afternoon.	
	22nd April		Church Parade. We were relieved by 11th W. YORKSHIRE Regt and entrained at BRANDHOEK at 9.30 P.M. & returning to HILL 60 on the same sector as last week.	
Tunckes HILL 60	23rd April		There was a heavy strafe by our Corps Artillery which provoked much retaliation. No. 73296 R.S.M. G. W. ROSE was awarded the D.C.M. for gallant work on Easter Monday, also No. 21765 Sgt J. H. LEGATE. This N.C.O. was most tragically killed by a shell at the exact moment that the message containing his good fortune was being handed to him.	
	24th April		Very heavy shelling on both sides all day. Aeroplanes were very active and we saw one of ours fall in flames by the BUND.	
	25th April		The shelling continued all day with fury. The Germans blew up a Sap and killed instantly 3 Australian Officers and buried many men.	

WAR DIARY
or
INTELLIGENCE SUMMARY.
(Erase heading not required.)

Army Form C. 2118.

Place	Date	Hour	Summary of Events and Information	Remarks and references to Appendices
HILL 60	1917 25 April		In a gallant effort to extricate them Captain HALFORD was saved and brought in insensible. Lieut BROWNE was shot through both legs.	
"	26th April		A party of Germans attempted to bomb ALLEN CRATER but were driven out by our Lewis Guns and by a bomb attack led by 2/Lieut LACY. Artillery not so bad today.	
	27th April		We suffered much from trench mortars which did a lot of damage to DEEP SUPPORT. CAPT HALFORD went to Hospital	
	29th and 30th April		Artillery stays resumed. We heard that we were going to be relieved by the 19th Division whose advance parties came up in 'buses and were followed upon by the Hun. on the evening of 30th April the Battalion were relieved by the 8th K.O.Y.L.I. and went into Brigade Reserve at RAILWAY Dugouts near ZILLEBEKE Bund, all very thankful. Our Casualties during the tour in the trenches were: 9 O.Rs killed, 18 wounded to Hospital and 2 wounded to duty.	

A.B. Way Lieut Colonel
Comdg 11th Bn Sherwood Foresters

REPORT ON ENEMY ATTACK ON CENTREBATTALION OF THE HILL 60
SUB-SECTOR ON THE NIGHT OF APRIL 9TH, 1918.

....

At about 9 a.m. in the morning the enemy began a very heavy bombardment of our front line, support and communication trenches, with heavy calibre guns and Trench mortars. The bombardment was also directed on the right and left Battalions - THE GAP I.29.b. was not bombarded.

All communication by wire was cut with the exception of the wire through the tunnel with the Right Company (Left of CUTTING). At 4 p.m. the shelling increased in intensity - at 4.10 p.m. a messenger from the Right Company had to come down over the top and reported Infantry Tunnel under DEEP SUPPORT blown in cutting off the majority of the Company taking cover there from the Company Officer and a few men. The numbers left to defend the Left of the Ri Right front line were at once reduced to a few sentries along the line and the few men with Captn.WATTS, the Company Officer.

At 4.10 p.m. therefore, a message was sent for two platoons at BATTERSEA FARM to reinforce the Right of the line and two platoons from RAILWAY DUGOUTS to take over their vacated positions.

At about 5.45 p.m. the shelling ceased and all men were ordered out of dug-outs. This opportunity was taken to clear two entrances from the Infantry Tunnel into the trench - Captn.WATTS took the remainder of his Company in the line and succeeded in establishing communication along I.29.2. and I.29.3. as far as ALLEN STREET but touch with the Left Company was not gained. Six bombing groups were organised along this frontage.

On the Right, ALLEN CRATER was entirely cut off, containing a bombing post and Lewis gun post and the rest of the line was badly damaged. During the lull, Captn.WHYATT succeeded in reaching ALLEN CRATER and, finding the Lewis gun blown up and two men killed and three wounded, decided to withdraw temporarily and establish a post with a Lewis gun in WANGARATTA trench from which ALLEN CRATER could be covered. Touch with the Company on the Right could not be obtained along either the Front or Second line.

At 6.45 p.m. a very intense bombardment set in followed quickly by the enemy who appeared to come over in two waves. His right rested on ALLEN CRATER and down ALLEN STREET his left on MARSHALL LANE. The few men left untouched on Right of the front line were swamped owing to the proximity of the enemy to the intense barrage. The Lewis gun at the top of BENSHAM was smashed. The enemy thus succeeded in reaching DEEP SUPPORT trench. 2nd Lieut GIBSON, who was posting the Lewis gun team in WANGARATTA trench, to cover ALLEN CRATER, as described above, was able to bring an enfilade fire on the enemy as they came over account for two men - one of the leading wave and one stretcher bearer who ran to his assistance. This Officer then led his platoon up COMPANY TRENCH and bombed the enemy attempting to establish a strong point at the junction of DEEP SUPPORT and ALLEN STREET where the enemy was forming a dump, etc., and had he held would have given him command of all tunnel entrances as far as the CUTTING - no entrance being on his Right of this point.

Of the two entrances cleared from INFANTRY TUNNEL into DEEP SUPPORT one was again blocked by the intense fire and the guard on the other was wounded. The enemy whereupon bombed this entrance in which Captn.WATTS and a few men were, the Corporal in charge of the guard wounded above was killed by his bomb and occupants partially gassed - Captn.WATTS and the others rushed out and bombed the enemy back up SWIFT STREET. Meanwhile the enemy bombing party in MARSHALL LANE had reached and bombed the two entrances and petrol store there. - the guards on which are provided by Infantry attached to the Australians.

At Headquarters, during the lull, all troops had been organised and were "standing-to" at the various entrances and a digging party had been sent to attempt to free the trapped men in the Tunnels.

Hearing rifle fire following the intense shelling the Adjutant, Lieut. CAVELL, was told to send up the S.O.S. He was wounded as soon as he left the entrance and this delayed the S.O.S. However, the Artillery had started on the S.O.S. of the Right Battalion and that of the Left Company.

At about 6.50 p.m. the two platoons from BATTERSEA FARM arrived at the dug-outs in rear of LARCH WOOD. They had lost their Officers and three N.C.Os. These two platoons were able to get up MARSHALL LANE - the enemy retiring - and were placed in extended order along the old Front line, their Right resting on a bombing post on the left of the Bridge. These platoons had to be withdrawn to the new line of resistance along DEEP SUPPORT before daylight. Later, a number of our men who were in shell holes, etc., along the old Front line who had been left out returned and three more platoons from RAILWAY DUG-OUTS and HEADQUARTERS took over the new line - a bombing post being pushed forward during the night.

The casualties sustained during this action were 2 Officers killed, the Adjutant badly wounded, 2 gassed and 3 slightly gassed, 26 O.Rs. killed, 45 wounded or gassed, 4 missing. 31 dead Germans were found in our trenches and a large store of bombs, belts of machine guns, charges for tunnels, gas apparatus, etc., for dug-outs.

15.4.1917.

Lieut. Colonel.
Commdg. 11th (S) Battalion,
THE SHERWOOD FORESTERS.

WAR DIARY or INTELLIGENCE SUMMARY

XI Notts & Derby Y.20

Place	Date 1917	Hour	Summary of Events and Information	Remarks and references to Appendices
RAILWAY DUGOUTS YPRES	May 1st		The Battalion rested and bathed and slept. Captain FYLDES returned from being attached to 70th Brigade and resumed the duties of Adjutant. Much Aeroplane fighting and it was not possible to remain in the open without showers of Anti aircraft splinters making life a burden.	Mr Harris
"	2nd		We were relieved by the 8th GLOUCESTERSHIRE Regt and marched to BRANDHOEK arriving 2.30.A.M. The Y.M.C.A took us in and gave hot Cocoa to everyone which was most reviving. At 6 A.M. we entrained for ABEELE where the train and Captain HALFORD quit it again, not us. A mile walk brought us to very comfortable billets where everyone went straight to tea.	
NEAR ABEELE	3rd		Everyone asleep till late afternoon. Perfect weather and nice quarters.	
"	4th			
"	5		The Divisional Commander inspected the Bn and professed himself very satisfied considering our unwashed and unequipped condition. Cricket states with much enthusiasm. All busy cleaning and re-fitting.	

Army Form C. 2118.

WAR DIARY
or
INTELLIGENCE SUMMARY.
(Erase heading not required.)

Instructions regarding War Diaries and Intelligence Summaries are contained in F. S. Regs., Part II. and the Staff Manual respectively. Title pages will be prepared in manuscript.

Place	Date 1917	Hour	Summary of Events and Information	Remarks and references to Appendices
ABEELE	May 6th		Battalion Church Parade. Cricket Match C Company V. Transport	
	7th		We went out to B Training Area and Practiced open warfare. Nothing to note.	
	8th		Captain OTTOWELL joined from 15th Bn. and took over B Coy. More Cricket in the afternoon.	
	9th		Nothing to note. Training programme carried on.	
	11th		We marched back to TORONTO Camp in lovely hot weather. We accomplished the march without one single man falling out, arriving in at 6 P.M.	
TORONTO CAMP.	12th	10.40 P.M.	We entrained at BRANDHOEK and returned to YPRES where we became Support Battalion of the left Brigade with headquarters at HALFWAY HOUSE. Very long and tedious relief	

WAR DIARY or INTELLIGENCE SUMMARY.

Army Form C. 2118.

Place	Date	Hour	Summary of Events and Information	Remarks and references to Appendices
HALF WAY HOUSE	1917 May 13th.		A quiet day but much Aeroplane fighting -	
	14th.		We were relieved at night by the 1st S. STAFFORDS and returned to our former billets near ABEELE.	
ABEELE	15th.		Cleaning day.	
	16th.		Lieut Colonel WATSON C.M.G. D.S.O. returned from Sick leave and resumed Command of the Battalion.	
	17th.		We marched to near BOESCHEPE and did a preliminary examination of a taped out piece of ground for the forthcoming "stunt". The rain descended in a deluge the whole time; dinners eaten in a field were depressing in consequence.	
	18th.		An exact repetition of yesterdays operations except that the weather was fine.	
	19th.		Rehearsing drill in billets. Cricket in the afternoon -	
	20th.		Church Parade - Cricket at C Company billets afterwards	

Army Form C. 2118.

WAR DIARY
or
INTELLIGENCE SUMMARY.
(Erase heading not required.)

Instructions regarding War Diaries and Intelligence Summaries are contained in F.S. Regs. Part II. and the Staff Manual respectively. Title pages will be prepared in manuscript.

Place	Date 1917	Hour	Summary of Events and Information	Remarks and references to Appendices
ABEELE	MAY 21st		Rehearsing on the Tapes at BOESCHEPE. We did not get back till 4 P.M.	
"	22nd		The same programme as yesterday –	
"	23rd – 24th		Billet day – The Battalion Entrained at 8.30 P.M. at ABEELE and relieved the 8th Bn YORKSHIRE Regt at HILL 60 – A very long relief as the Germans were shelling POPERINGHE and held the train up –	
TRENCHES HILL 60.	25th		Much artillery fighting all day – a rumour (printed) of an impending Gas & attack kept us on the alert at night, but it did not materialize. We were relieved by the 8th KOYLI and retired to the ZILLEBEKE BUND.	
THE BUND.	26th		Quiet day except for much shelling of neighbouring batteries	
"	27th		Quite quiet till night when the Germans blew up an ammunition dump about 200 yards away; killing the Battery Commander, Major SHAW and others: We relieved the 9th Y.L. at RUDKIN HOUSE.	Maye [signature]
RUDKIN HOUSE	29th		Much artillery shelling all day –	
"	30th		Captain MILES was killed to our sorrow – a very keen promising young soldier and one not easily to be replaced –	Sherwood 11 Sherwood Foresters two
"	31st		The expected relief did not take place. LIEUTS LACY and KNIGHT were wounded. Also	

Captn OTTOWELL

COPY NO. 8

The 11th (S) BATTALION, THE SHERWOOD FORESTERS.
....

OPERATION ORDER NO. 15.
--- by ---
LIEUT. COLONEL H.F.WATSON, C.M.G., D.S.O., Comdg.
....

Ref. Maps 1/5,000 Div. map German trenches.   20th May, 1917.

1. PLAN.

In conjunction with the rest of the 2nd Army the 23rd Division will assault the German trenches round HILL 60 and MOUNTSORREL. The 70th Brigade will be the Left of the 2nd Army offensive and will form a Defensive flank. The 69th Inf. Brigade will attack on the Right of the 70th Inf. Brigade. The dividing line between Brigades is shown on the maps which have already been issued, as is also the objective which is to be consolidated, and beyond which no advance is at present contemplated.

2. DISTRIBUTION OF THE BNS. OF THE 70th BRIGADE.

The 70th Inf. Brigade will attack with two Bns. in the front line and two in support.

9th York & Lancs. Regt.   'A' or Right front attacking Bn.
                         Bn. H. Qrs. CANADA STREET.
11th Sherwood Foresters.   'B' or Left front attacking Bn.
                         Bn. H. Qrs. HEDGE STREET.
8th York & Lancs. Regt.   'C' or Right support Bn.
                         Bn. H. Qrs. CANADA STREET.
8th K.O.Y.L.I.   'D' or Left support Bn.
                         Bn. H. Qrs. SEBA DUGOUTS in WINNIPEG STREET.

3. DIVIDING LINE BETWEEN 'A' & 'B' BNS.

(a) In our own front line :
     The junction of the N end of CANADA STREET and the front line.
(b) In German line : I.30.a.87.06. to I.30.c.95.88. to I.30.c.90.82. to I.30.d.03.80. These last three points are the corners of the triangle which compose the strong point, then to I.30.d.20.55. This last point is on the objective and will be the Right of the Bn.

4. POSITIONS AT ZERO - 1 HOUR.

The Bn. will take up the following positions in readiness to advance to the attack.
1st Wave.
No.11 platoon lying in file on the Right flank of the Bn.
Nos.3 & 2 platoons and 2 sections of 'C' Coy. & 2 sections of 'D' Coy. lying in front of our line from Right of Bn. to 50 yards NORTH of 'F' SAP.
Nos.13 & 14 platoons along 'F' SAP - 13 at top - and along a line in prolongation of this sap behind our parados
Nos.5 & 6 platoons in our front line from the Left of 'A' Coy. to the left of the Bn.

2nd Wave.
Nos.1 & 4 platoons in front of LIVING & MAIN TRENCHES on the frontage covered by the platoons of 'A' Coy. in the first wave.
Nos.7 & 8 platoons in our own front line.

3rd Wave.
Nos.10 & 12 platoons (less one section each) in LIVING & MAIN TRENCHES.

4th Wave.
Nos.9, 15 & 16 platoons (less one section each) in LIVING and MAIN TRENCHES. Till Zero these platoons will be in CANADIANS SAPS.

O.C. Coys. of the leading waves will arrange to cover their advance across NO MAN'S LAND by Lewis gun fire directed on the German first & second lines & the STRONG POINT.

5. **MOVEMENT INTO ASSEMBLY POSITIONS IN OUR TRENCHES.**

The following will be the order of march :-

(1)	No.	15	platoon,
(2)	"	16	"
(3)	"	9	"
(4)	"	11	"
(5)	"	1 & 10	"
(6)	"	4 & 12	"
(7)	"	3	"
(8)	"	2	"
(9)	"	13	"
(10)	"	14	"
(11)	"	5 & 7	"
(12)	"	6 & 8	"

With Nos.3 & 2 platoons will go the 3 sections from 'C' Coy. and the 2 sections from 'D' Coy. to be used as "MOPPERS-UP".

6. **BARRAGES, TIMES & ORDER OF ADVANCE.**

At Zero HILL 60 and THE CATERPILLAR, which is SOUTH of HILL 60, will be blown up by mines.

At Zero plus 1 the 1st barrage of 18 pdrs. & Stokes guns lifts off the German front line on to a line about 200 yards in rear of the German front line. The 1st & 2nd waves then begin to advance and are timed to reach 2nd barrage at Zero plus 9 when it will lift on to a line another 300 yards in advance. This 3rd barrage will lift at Zero plus 20 to allow the 1st & 2nd waves to enter their objective; with the exception of the 5 sections of "Moppers-up"; and will remain stationary till Zero plus 3 hours & 40 minutes when the 2nd objective is attacked by 'C' & 'D' Bns.

When the 2nd wave is clear of our original front line trench by 25 yards the 3rd & 4th waves begin their advance and carry on till they reach their objective, but always maintaining the interval of 25 yards between waves.

7. **OBJECTIVES.**

(a) The BATTALION OBJECTIVE which is a Defensive flank facing half Left, i.e., NORTH is from I.30.d.20.55. to I.30.d.36.97, to I.30.b.17.14. along German front line to I.30.b.60.36.

(b) WAVE OBJECTIVES.

(1) 1st & 2nd Waves to Bn. objective except that No.3 platoon will move to & hold the Communication Trench that runs into the

OBJECTIVES (Contd).

extreme Right of the Bn. objective from IMAGE SUPPORT while the five sections of "Moppers-up" will be left in this latter trench and the German front line. The remainder of these waves are allotted to the objective as follows :-

  No.11 platoon to the STRONG POINT.
  Nos.1,2 & 4 platoons from I.30.d.20.55. to I.30.d.35.95. in above order from the Right.
  No.13 platoon the SOUTH half, i.e., the half furthest from our trenches, of the communication trench from I.30.b.87. to I.30.d.35.95. O.C. 'D' Coy. must, however, send forward bombing parties to assist 'A' Coy. in clearing their portion of Bn. objective.
  No.14 platoon to the other half of the above mentioned trench.
  Nos.5,7,8,6 platoons from I.30.b.17.14 to I.30.b.60.36. in above order from the Right.

3rd Wave. Nos.10 & 12 platoons (less one section each) along IMAGE SUPPORT in above order from Right.

4th Wave. No.9 platoon (less one section) to the COMMUNICATION TRENCH between the GERMAN FRONT LINE and the STRONG POINT. 15 & 16 platoons (less one section each) to GERMAN FRONT LINE from Right of Bn. to Right of 'B' Coy. in order from Right as above. These last 2 platoons on reaching their objective must be prepared to reinforce on either flank.

8. BLOCKING PARTIES.

  O.C. Coys. will be responsible for sending bombing parties sufficiently far up all communication trenches that run into the Battalion objective to allow of permanent blocks to be made in rear. O.C. 'C' Coy. being responsible for the two trenches running into objective at the point where IMAGE SUPPORT meets it, i.e., junction of 'A','C' & 'D' Coys.
  Later, 'B' Coy. will be ordered to withdraw to the final line of resistance which will be 'G' SAP and a new fire trench which will be dug in continuation of 'G' SAP to I.30.b.35.37.

9. MOVEMENT OF OTHER BATTALIONS.

  While we are gaining our objective 'A' Bn. will be moving with us to their objective which runs from I.30.c.40.00. to I.30.d.20.55. with whom O.C. 'A' Coy. must always keep in touch. At Zero plus 3 hours & 40 minutes the barrage will lift on to the final objective (stamped on in black on map) & will allow 'C' and 'D' Bns. to enter this at zero plus 4 hours when O.C. 'A' Coy. must at once obtain touch with O.C. Left Coy. of 'D' Bn.

10. MACHINE GUNS.

  4 Vickers guns have been allotted to the support of this Bn. They will cross NO MAN'S LAND about Zero plus half hour and will take up positions near the following points :-
  1. At top of SAP 'H'.
  2. " " " SAP 'F'.
  3. In STRONG POINT.
  4. At I.30.d.20.55.

11. STOKES MORTARS.

  3 guns of the 70th L.T.M. Battery will move up after we have captured our objective for the support of the Bn.

12. ADMINISTRATIVE ARRANGEMENTS.

Administrative arrangements will be issued in a later order.

(signature)
Captain & Adjutant.

Issued to :-

Copy No. 1. O.C. 'A' Coy.
"   "   2. O.C. 'B'
"   "   3. O.C. 'C'
"   "   4. O.C. 'D'
"   "   5. Signalling Officer.
"   "   6.
"   "   7. Office.
"   "   8. 70th Infantry Brigade.)
"   "   9. O.C. 9th Y & L. Regt.   ) For information.
"   " 10. O.C. 8th K.O.Y.L.I.   )

STOKES MORTARS (Contd).

2. EMPLOYMENT.

    ZERO.   All guns will bombard the enemy front line at their maximum rate of fire.

    ZERO plus 1   Guns I to V (inclusive) cease fire. Guns VI to VIII (inclusive) lift not less than 100 yards on to enemy support line.

    ZERO plus 2   Guns VI to VIII (inclusive) cease fire.

From Zero plus 2 minutes onwards, all guns will stand by ready to open fire at once if required.

Guns V to VIII (inclusive) will be re-laid on the enemy trenches to the left of Sap 'H' so as to protect the flank of the attack.

After relaying, guns V to VIII will continue to fire a few rounds at intervals of ten minutes.

In the event of a hostile counter attack, developing against the left flank of the Brigade, guns V to VIII will at once open fire at the maximum rate of fire.

10. MACHINE GUN BARRAGE.

A continuous machine gun barrage will be in operation from Zero hour to dark in 'Z' day covering the objective. After dark, guns will be employed in searching the back areas but on a S.O.S. signal - RED Very Light - they will fire on their barrage lines. This will be in addition to the 4 machine guns allotted to the Battn.

O.C. Coys. will detail 1 man per Coy. to act as a Carrier for M.G.ammunition. They will report to Battn. H.Qrs. on their arrival in HEDGE ST. on Y/Z night. Their names will be submitted at once, please.

11. CONTACT AEROPLANE.

Arrangements for communication between advanced troops and aeroplanes will be as follows :-
(1) A contact aeroplane will be up from Zero (if light enough) till 6 hours after Zero.

The contact aeroplane will be distinguished by three broad white bands on the fuselage and by the attachment of a black board on the left lower plane, thus :-

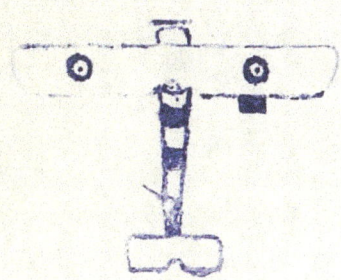

The machine will be furnished with wireless but will only use it for the purpose of reporting a counter-attack or transmitting an infantry signal message calling for barrage.

Contact aeroplane will call for flares by firing a WHITE light and sounding a Klaxon horn.

Leading infantry will light flares approximately at the following times :-
Zero plus 30 minutes.
" " 1 hour.
" " 4 hours 30 minutes.
" " 5 hours.

O.C. platoons must, however, ensure that the aeroplane is calling for flares before lighting up.

It is recognised that during confused fighting it is difficult for bodies of troops to know if they are actually the leading troops, and it must not be assumed that flares show that there are no other troops in front.

Isolated bodies of troops out of touch on their flanks should light flares when called on to do so by aeroplane.

The colour of flares will be GREEN.

2. A wireless aeroplane will be up throughout the day from one hour after Zero for the purpose of looking out for counter-attacks. In the event of a counter-attack developing this machine will call on the artillery by the zone call, and will warn the infantry by flares; a RED flare will signify that the attack is NORTH of the Canal and a GREEN flare SOUTH of the Canal.

The zone call will give the position and direction of movement of the enemy's infantry, and this information will be immediately communicated by the Artillery to the Infantry Brigadier concerned.

This machine will also transmit Infantry messages calling for barrage.

12. MOPPERS-UP.

Every other man detailed as a "Mopper-up" will have one RED and one WHITE flag.

Twenty five M.S.K. bombs will be issued to each of 'A' 'B' and 'C' Coys. These will be carried by Officers and senior N.C.Os.

"Moppers-up" will in every case follow the first line of the leading waves of assaulting Battalions. All mopping-up parties must be strong and thoroughly organised. They must clearly understand their duties and that they are responsible for the clearing of all dug-outs and the silencing of any machine guns passed over by the leading troops.

~~Special mopping up parties will be detailed to the supposed strong point at I.30.c.Central.~~

13. DISTINGUISHING MARKS.

Para. 6 of "Administrative details" is cancelled.

14. BATTALION H. Qrs.

Battn. H. Qrs. will remain at HEDGE ST. A Forward Battn H. Qr. will be established about I.30.d.2.9. but O.C. Coys. will be notified of the move there.

15. WORKING PARTIES.

    Detachments of Tunnellers and R.E. will be sent across as the situation allows. Officers will give these specialists all the assistance they can.

16. STAFF OFFICERS.

    Officers attached to Corps H. Qrs. will wear a small RED & WHITE square on the Left sleeve. Bde. staff wear a BLUE armlet; Divl. staff a RED armlet; Corps staff a RED and WHITE armlet.

17. MISCELLANEOUS.

    Identity discs are not to be removed from dead Germans unless special orders to do so are received.
    Plans of all mining operations are urgently required.
    Four Brigade Observers will be employed to collect documents from the battlefield. These men will wear brassards marked "INTELLIGENCE".
    They will search particularly for documents and correspondence in dug-outs and Headquarters. Dead bodies, especially those of Officers and N.C.Os. will be carefully searched.

18. PRISONERS. (a continuation of para.8 of 'Administrative details)

    Captured Officers and N.C.Os. should be kept separate from their men.
    Escorts must have a statement showing number of prisoners and where they come from.
    Prisoners will now be sent to KRUISSTRAAT I.13.c.2g.5g. and H.24.a.1.1. and not the places referred to in para.8 of Administrative Details.

                                        Captain & Adjutant,
                                        11th (S) Battalion,
                                        THE SHERWOOD FORESTERS.

Issued to :-
Copy No. 1.   O.C. 'A' Coy.
 "   " 2.   O.C. 'B' "
 "   " 3.   O.C. 'C' "
 "   " 4.   O.C. 'D' "
 "   " 5.   Signalling Officer.
 "   " 6.) Office.
      & 7.)
 "   " 8.   War Diary.
 "   " 9.   Headquarters, 70th Inf. Bde.
 "   " 10.   Major C.E.HUDSON, M.C.,
 "   " 11.   Quartermaster.

Copy No. 9

THE 11th (S) BATTALION, THE SHERWOOD FORESTERS.

OPERATION ORDER No. 15.
--- by ---
LIEUT. COLONEL H.F.WATSON,C.M.G.,D.S.O., Comndg.

Ref.Maps 1/5,000 Div.map German trenches.   20th May,1917.

1. PLAN.

In conjunction with the rest of the 2nd Army the 23rd Division will assault the German trenches round HILL 60 and MOUNTSORREL. The 70th Brigade will be the Left of the 2nd Army offensive and will form a Defensive flank. The 69th Inf. Brigade will attack on the Right of the 70th Inf. Brigade. The dividing line between Brigades is shown on the maps which have already been issued, as is also the objective which is to be consolidated, and beyond which no advance is at present contemplated.

2. DISTRIBUTION OF THE BNS. OF THE 70th BRIGADE.

The 70th Inf. Brigade will attack with two Bns. in the front line and two in support.

9th York & Lancs. Regt.	'A' or Right front attacking Bn.
	Bn. H. Qrs. CANADA STREET.
11th Sherwood Foresters.	'B' or Left front attacking Bn.
	Bn. H. Qrs. HEDGE STREET.
8th York & Lancs. Regt.	'C' or Right support Bn.
	Bn. H. Qrs. CANADA STREET.
8th K.O.Y.L.I.	'D' or Left support Bn.
	Bn. H.Qrs.SEBA DUGOUTS in WINNIPEG STREET.

3. DIVIDING LINE BETWEEN 'A' & 'B' BNS.

(a) In our own front line :
    The junction of the N end of CANADA STREET and the front line.
(b) In German line : I.30.a.87.06. to I.30.c.95.88. to I.30.c.90.82. to I.30.d.03.80. These last three points are the corners of the triangle which compose the strong point, then to I.30.d.20.55. This last point is on the objective and will be the Right of the Bn.

4. POSITIONS AT ZERO - 1 HOUR.

The Bn. will take up the following positions in readiness to advance to the attack.
1st Wave.
   No.11 platoon lying in file on the Right flank of the Bn.
   Nos.3 & 2 platoons and 3 sections of 'C' Coy. & 2 sections of 'D' Coy. lying in front of our line from Right of Bn. to 50 yards NORTH of 'F' SAP.
   Nos.13 & 14 platoons along 'F' SAP - 13 at top - and along a line in prolongation of this sap behind our parados
   Nos.5 & 6 platoons in our front line from the Left of 'A' Coy. to the left of the Bn.

2nd Wave.
Nos.1 & 4 platoons in front of LIVING & MAIN TRENCHES on the frontage covered by the platoons of 'A' Coy. in the first wave.
Nos.7 & 8 platoons in our own front line.

3rd Wave.
Nos.10 & 12 platoons (less one section each) in LIVING & MAIN TRENCHES.

4th Wave.
Nos.9,15 & 16 platoons (less one section each) in LIVING and MAIN TRENCHES. Till Zero these platoons will be in CANADIAN SAPS.

O.C. Coys. of the leading waves will arrange to cover their advance across NO MAN'S LAND by Lewis gun fire directed on the German first & second lines & the STRONG POINT

5. **MOVEMENT INTO ASSEMBLY POSITIONS IN OUR TRENCHES.**

The following will be the order of march :-
(1) No.15   platoon,
(2)   " 16   "
(3)   "   9   "
(4)   " 11   "
(5)   "   1 & 10 "
(6)   "   4 & 12 "
(7)   "   3   "
(8)   "   2   "
(9)   " 13   "
(10) " 14   "
(11) "   5 & 7 "
(12) "   6 & 8 "

With Nos.3 & 2 platoons will go the 3 sections from 'C' Coy. and the 2 sections from 'D' Coy. to be used as "Moppers-up".

6. **BARRAGES, TIMES & ORDER OF ADVANCE.**

At zero HILL 60 and THE CATERPILLAR, which is SOUTH of HILL 60, will be blown up by mines.

At zero plus 1 the 1st barrage of 18 pdrs. & Stokes guns lifts off the German front line on to a line about 200 yards in rear of the German front line. The 1st & 2nd waves then begin to advance and are timed to reach 2nd barrage at zero plus 9 when it will lift on to a line another 300 yards in advance. This 3rd barrage will lift at zero plus 20 to allow the 1st & 2nd waves to enter their objective; with the exception of the 5 sections of "Moppers-up"; and will remain stationary till zero plus 3 hours & 40 minutes when the 2nd objective is attacked by 'C' & 'D' Bns.

When the 2nd wave is clear of our original front line trench by 25 yards the 3rd & 4th waves begin their advance and carry on till they reach their objective, but always maintaining the interval of 25 yards between waves.

7. **OBJECTIVES.**

(a) The BATTALION OBJECTIVE which is a Defensive flank facing half Left, i.e., NORTH is from I.30.d.20.55. to I.30.d.36.97. to I.30.b.17.14. along German front line to I.30.b.60.36.
(b) WAVE OBJECTIVES.
(1) 1st & 2nd Waves to Bn. objective except that No.3 platoon will move to & hold the Communication Trench that runs into the

OBJECTIVES (Contd).

extreme Right of the Bn. objective from IMAGE SUPPORT while the five sections of "Moppers-up" will be left in this latter trench and the German front line. The remainder of these waves are allotted to the objective as follows :-

No.11 platoon to the STRONG POINT,
Nos.1,2 & 4 platoons from I.30.d.20.55. to I.30.d.35.95. in above order from the Right.
No.13 platoon the SOUTH half, i.e., the half furthest from our trenches, of the communication trench from I.30.b.27. to I.30.d.35.95. O.C. 'D' Coy. must, however, send forward bombing parties to assist 'A' Coy. in clearing their portion of Bn. objective.
No.14 platoon to the other half of the above mentioned trench.
Nos.5,7,8,6 platoons from I.30.b.17.14 to I.30.b.60.36. in above order from the Right.
3rd Wave. Nos.10 & 12 platoons (less one section each) along IMAGE SUPPORT in above order from Right.
4th Wave. No.9 platoon (less one section) to the COMMUNICATION TRENCH between the GERMAN FRONT LINE and the STRONG POINT.
15 & 16 platoons (less one section each) to GERMAN FRONT LINE from Right of Bn. to Right of 'B' Coy. in order from Right as above. These last 2 platoons on reaching their objective must be prepared to reinforce on either flank.

8. BLOCKING PARTIES.

O.C. Coys. will be responsible for sending bombing parties sufficiently far up all communication trenches that run- into the Battalion objective to allow of permanent blocks to be made in rear. O.C. 'C' Coy. being responsible for the two trenches running into objective at the point where IMAGE SUPPORT meets it, i.e., junction of 'A', 'C' & 'D' Coys.

Later, 'B' Coy. will be ordered to withdraw to the final line of resistance which will be 'G' SAP and a new fire trench which will be dug in continuation of 'G' SAP to I.30.b.35.37.

9. MOVEMENT OF OTHER BATTALIONS.

While we are gaining our objective 'A' Bn. will be moving with us to their objective which runs from I.30.c.40.00. to I.30.d.20.55. with whom O.C. 'A' Coy. must always keep in touch. At Zero plus 3 hours & 40 minutes the barrage will lift on to the final objective (stamped on in black on map) & will allow 'C' and 'D' Bns. to enter this at Zero plus 4 hours when O.C. 'A' Coy. must at once obtain touch with O.C. Left Coy. of 'D' Bn.

10. MACHINE GUNS.

4 Vickers guns have been allotted to the support of this Bn. They will cross NO MAN'S LAND about Zero plus half hour and will take up positions near the following points :-
1. At top of SAP 'H',
2. " " " SAP 'F',
3. In STRONG POINT,
4. At I.30.d.20.55.

11. STOKES MORTARS.

3 guns of the 70th L.T.M. Battery will move up after we have captured our objective for the support of the Bn.

12. ADMINISTRATIVE ARRANGEMENTS.

Administrative arrangements will be issued in a later Order.

Captain & Adjutant.

Issued to :-

Copy No. 1. O.C. 'A' Coy.
"   "   2. O.C. 'B' "
"   "   3. O.C. 'C' "
"   "   4. O.C. 'D' "
"   "   5. Signalling Officer.
"   "   6.)
"   "   7.) Office.
"   "   8. 70th Infantry Brigade.)
"   "   9. O.C. 9th Y & L.Regt.   ) For information.
"   " 10. O.C. 8th K.O.Y.L.I.   )

S E C R E T.   Copy No. 9

2nd ARMY OFFENSIVE.

29th MAY, 1917.

ADMINISTRATIVE DETAILS to be read in conjunction with O.O. 15

1. PRELIMINARY MOVES.

    On W. day the Battalion will be in HALIFAX CAMP.
    During the Night X/Y the Battalion will move to WELLINGTON CRESCENT and MAPLE STREET - Dispositions will be detailed later.
    During the Night Y/Z the Battalion will move to its assembly positions.

2. DRESS. Fighting order. If obtained, the second water bottle will be worn on the Left side. The three sandbags will be hung over the back of the belt. (Runners will not carry sandbags). The unconsumed portion of the day's rations will be in the Canteen, and the other rations in the breast pockets and Haversack.
    Officers taking part in the Attack must be dressed and equipped just as the men. They must not carry sticks.

3. RATIONS.

    Rations for Z & A days will be Preserved Meat, Biscuit and Grocery rations, those for Z day will be sent up by the Brigade to the forward area and will be drawn by the Battn. during the Night X/Y. Those for A day will be carried on the man when the Battalion moves into the trenches during the night X/Y.
    Rations for Y and B days will be drawn normally.

4. WATER.

    Filled petrol tins and water carts will be brought up to the Battalion ration dump at VALLEY COTTAGES every night if possible. Should this supply fail, water may be obtained from tanks placed in the forward area between Front line and ZILLEBEKE and from the two tanks by the branch tram termini at ARMAGH WOOD. Dumps of filled petrol tins will also be formed, these, however, are only to be used as a last resort and on the orders of the O.C. Coy. after, if possible, communication with Battalion H. Qrs. The amount taken must always be reported to Battalion H. Qrs. as soon as possible as the tins will have to be re-filled.

5. MEDICAL.

    The Regimental Aid Post will be at MAPLE TRENCH (North end).
    Advanced Dressing Station will be at ZILLEBEKE BUND.
    Walking cases will proceed by Regimental Aid Post and Advanced Dressing Station to the Divisional Collecting Station at the LILLE GATE, YPRES.
    Regimental stretcher bearers are not to take cases further back than the Regimental Aid Post, they are not to take orders from anyone not in this Battalion. 10 stretcher bearers will be accomodated at Battalion H. Qrs. for the Night Y/Z and will receive orders as to their movements as soon as the situation is clear on Z day.

6. DISTINGUISHING MARKS.

Colour flags will be carried by Coys. as follows :-
Red   'B' Coy.
Black   'C' "
Green   'D' "
Yellow 'A' "

It is hoped that the use of these will enable the whereabouts of Coys. to be made out.

7. CAPTURED ARMS.

Any guns captured which are in danger of being lost must be rendered useless by damaging the sights and breech mechanism. Methods of doing this with pick axes, bombs, or other expedients will be explained to all ranks.

Machine guns, when captured, must be collected or destroyed.

8. PRISONERS.

Prisoners will be passed back to Battalion H. Qrs. as the situation allows of it under a Guard of 1 man for every 15. At Battalion H. Qrs. the Guard will be sent back to rejoin his Coy. From there prisoners will be sent to KRUISSTRAAT BRIDGE and LEVEL CROSSING at I.7.c.3.7.

9. CASUALTIES.

The normal Casualty Report made up to 12 Noon each day will be rendered as soon after that hour as possible, in writing. From Zero hour on Z day until further orders estimated Casualty Reports will be sent so as to reach Battalion H.Qrs by 6 a.m., 12 xxxx, 3 p.m. and xxxxx. Each estimated report will render the numbers in the previous report and will only give numbers of O.Rs. e.g., 'A' Coy. total estimated casualties from Zero 2nd Lieut.A, 2nd Lieut.B. and 45. No distinction will be made between Killed and Wdd. Punctuality is much more important than absolute accuracy. The reason for calling for these returns is that the higher authorities may know how many Reinforcements to ask for.

The above reports will in no way affect the normal daily report.

10. MAPS AND ORDERS.

No papers or orders are to be carried by Officers or men taking part in the Attack except the German Trench Map. All Officers will carry a note book, and the skeleton map (map 14) with message form on back.

11. VERY PISTOLS.

Will be taken over on the scale of *at least* 1 per platoon. Ammunition will be issued by Battalion H. Qrs.

12. COMMUNICATION TRENCHES.

IN.

1. ROUTE B. (i.e. PROMENADE) - ROUTE C. (i.e./ over the open past VALLEY COTTAGES) - MAPLE TRENCH - GAP STREET.
2. ROUTE B as above - ZILLEBEKE STREET - DAVIDSON STREET.

3. North side of ZILLEBEKE LAKE - VINCE STREET.

OUT.

DUCK WALK from LIVING TRENCH - ROUTE C - or ZILLEBEKE STREET from West side of MAPLE COPSE to ZILLEBEKE.

All Officers and as many N.C.Os., Runners and stretcher bearers as possible and 8 men per Coy. who may be required as Guides must know the routes East of the YPRES - DICKEBUSCH Road.

All Officers and a proportion of the O.Rs. mentioned above (except stretcher bearers) must, as far as possible, make themselves acquainted with Routes West of above line. O.C. Coys. will be held responsible for the instruction of all ranks of their Coys.

The Transport Officer must know the best routes to Battalion H. Qrs.

13. AMMUNITION.

A daily return made up to 12 Noon and 8 p.m. of the S.A.A. Bombs and Rifle grenades expended since the last return will be forwarded to Battalion H. Qrs. as soon after Noon and 8 p.m. as possible, starting on Z day.

Demands for fresh supplies will be sent to Battalion H. Qrs as they are required.

14. FLARES.

One flare will be carried by each man. O.C. Platoons will be responsible that N^3 are lit in their platoons when called for by Contact Aeroplane by means of a WHITE light. The N^3 flares must be grouped together and about 50 yards away from the next group of $N.^3$

15. BOMBS, etc.,

The following Bombs, etc., will be carried over on Z day Carriers will be detailed as follows :-
'B' Coy.   28 men.
'C' "   14 "
'D' "   42 "

These men will be organised in sections of 7. Each section will carry the following :-
No. 1. Two sandbags with 12 bombs in each, and 1 shovel slung.
No. 2.   do.   do.   do.   do.
No. 3.   do.   do.   do.   do.
No. 4. Contents of 1 box S.A.A. (slung).
No. 5.   do.   do.   do.
No. 6. Two sandbags with 12 Rifle grenades in each.
No. 7.   do.   do.   do.   do.

Rifles grenades will be carried in sandbags with a big black patch on both sides. Bombs not carried in buckets will be carried in sandbags with a big yellow patch on both sides.

250 Lachrymatory bombs will also be distributed.

In addition to the above, the two throwers and the two Bayonet men of Nos. 5, 7, 8, 10, 12, 15 & 16 platoons will each carry 24 bombs in two buckets.

Every man in the Battalion will carry a bomb in each pouch, (except Runners). Men of bombing squads and men of Rifle grenade sections will carry them in the two breast pockets. Men of Rifle grenade sections will carry two sandbags with six rifle grenades in each. They will also carry (slung) one bandolier of blank S.A.A. in clips. To each two sandbags of 12 bombs, i.e. those carried by the carrying parties will be added one bandolier of blank S.A.A. in clips.

The No. 2 of each Lewis Gun team will carry four filled magazines in a bucket. Nos. 3 & 4 will each carry two buckets with four filled magazines in each bucket. A dump of filled magazines in addition to above will be made at Battalion H. Qrs. during the night Y/Z.

Every man in the Battalion (with the following exceptions will carry 10 rounds S.A.A. in each pouch and three bandoliers slung. (a) Carriers as detailed above will only carry 50 rounds S.A.A. (b) Men of Rifle grenade squads, Bombing squads and Runners will only carry 20 rounds S.A.A. (c) Nos. 1 & 2 of Lewis gun teams will only carry 24 rounds of revolver ammunition.

O.C. 'B' & 'D' Coys. must arrange to have their bombs, etc., dumped at I.30.b.20.15. and I.30.a.97.10. respectively O.C. 'C' Coy. will arrange to dump his bombs near the Northern end of IMAGE SUPPORT. The two bombs carried by each man must be collected into these dumps as soon as possible. It must be impressed upon all ranks that bombs must not be thrown indiscriminately. In all probability, the supplies carried over by the assaulting troops will have to last till dusk.

16. MESSAGES.

All officers must be careful to put the time of despatch on all messages whether sent by Signal or Runner. They should also notice how long a message has taken to arrive and they must be prepared to continue the investigation if the message has been unduly long in transit.

Captain & Adjutant.
11th (S) Battalion,
THE SHERWOOD FORESTERS.

Issued to :-

Copy No. 1. O.C. 'A' Coy.
" " 2. O.C. 'B' "
" " 3. O.C. 'C' "
" " 4. O.C. 'D' "
" " 5. Signalling Officer.
" " 6. Quartermaster.
" " 7. Major C.E.HUDSON,M.C.,
" " 8. War Diary.
" " 9. H. Qrs. 70th Inf. Bde.
" " 10. Office.
" " 11. Transport Officer.

SECRET.

9

2nd ARMY OFFENSIVE.

ADDITIONS to OPERATION ORDER No. 1b.

1. **MESSAGES.**

   The following will be the code words used when referring to the points tabulated below. On arriving at these points, the Senior Officer or N.C.O. on the spot will immediately send back to B.H.Q. to that effect. These messages will be prepared beforehand. Failure to send reports may mean that Artillery is turned on them as it will be understood that they are not occupied by our troops.

   Strong point I.30.a.o.5.   STRAW
   Apex of triangle I.30.d.20.65.   SWALE
   Junction of Communication Trench with)
     Objective I.30.d.25.75.   )   HARRISON
   I.30.b.70.10.   VOS
   I.30.a.35.90.   GIBSON

2. **TRENCH GARRISON.**

   1 Officer and 6 Lewis gun teams will be detailed by O.C. 9th K.O.Y.L.I. as garrison for our present front line from 'C' Sap to ST.PETER'S ST. These guns will take up the following positions on Y/Z night and will come under the orders of the O.C. Battn. when the line is taken over on Y/Z night. They will be warned to watch particularly the left flank of the attack. None of these guns will be withdrawn from the front line without orders from G.O.C. Bde.

3. **GAS & SMOKE.**

   (a) One sub-section (4 guns) of No.2 Special Company R.E., in emplacements in WINNIPEG STREET (North of ST. PETER'S STREET about I.35.a.55.35. will fire Lacrymatory and Lethal Shells into CLONMEL COPSE (J.1.a.c.) at the following times :-

   (1) Zero. 100 C.G. and 100 S.K. as rapidly as possible.

   (2) Zero plus 1 hour and 30 minutes. 100 C.G. and 100 S.K.

   (3) Zero plus 3 hours. 100 S.K.

   Firing will take place in any wind between S.W. and N.W. The decision as to the suitability of the wind lies with the Commander of the Special Company R.E.

   (b) Arrangements are being made for a smoke discharge to cover the left flank of the Brigade at Zero hour and subsequently for a projector discharge to prevent the enemy assembling in SHREWSBURY FOREST. Details of this will be forwarded later.

4. BLOCKS.

O.C. "A" Coy. will be responsible for blocking IMAGE
RESERVE & IMAGE CRESCENT at their junction (I.30.a.40.45)
in addition to blocking other trenches.

5. CONSOLIDATION.

As soon as the Objective has been gained, consolidation
will begin on the following lines :-
(a) A Front line in the vicinity of the Objective joining
up with our present Front line through 'G' Sap.
(b) A Support line from junction of IMAGE LANE & IMAGE
SUPPORT, about I.30.a.90.60, to a point in the enemy front
line about I.30.a.95.10. O.Cs. 'A', 'B' & 'D' Coys. will
be responsible for that part of (a) which is covered by the
portion of the objective allotted to them.
O.C. 'C' Coy. will be responsible for (b) and also for
establishing a Strong point at I.30.a.90.60. which should be
able to hold 20 riflemen and 2 Lewis, or Machine guns. 1
Machine gun from the 4 supporting this Battn. will be sent
to this S.P. as soon as it is constructed.
O.C. 'D' Coy. will be responsible for continuing 'F'
Sap across NO MAN'S LAND as early as possible. O.C. 'B' Coy.
will be responsible for continuing 'G' Sap and making it
into a Fire trench.

6. REPORTS.

O.C. Coys. will report by Zero - MINUS 3/4 an hour that
they are in assembly positions in our trenches ready to
advance to the assault. Crawling forward over our parapet
in anticipation of Zero hour must be done on the initiation
of O.C.Coys.

7. REMOVAL OF WIRE.

Starting on W/X night the 9th York. & Lancs. Regt.
will arrange to gradually thin out our wire along the
Brigade Front. This will be continued on X/Y night so that
on Y/Z night the removal of the remaining wire will be a
matter of only a few minutes.

8. ARTILLERY SUPPORT.

One 18 pdr. Battery & 1 4.5 How. Battery will be at
the disposal of G.O.C. Bde. If O.C. Coys. want Artillery
support at any place other than the fixed barrage all
necessary information must be sent to Battn. H.Qrs.

9. STOKES MORTARS.

1. DISTRIBUTION OF GUNS.

    No. II - LIVING TRENCH.
    III - LIVING TRENCH.
    IV - 'F' SAP.
    V - 'G' SAP.
    VI - DAVIDSON STREET.
    VII - DAVIDSON STREET.
    VIII - WINNIPEG STREET.
    IX - WINNIPEG STREET. (Alternative)

Army Form C. 2118.

WAR DIARY
or
INTELLIGENCE SUMMARY.
(Erase heading not required.)

June 1917
11th Batt" Sherwood Foresters

Vol 21

Place	Date	Hour	Summary of Events and Information	Remarks and references to Appendices
TRENCHES	June 1st		The Batt" were heavily shelled during the day. At morning Stand To 2nd Lieut A. Knight and a party of men were heavily fired at by a party of about 25 of the enemy who appeared in the Sap running from the hostile front line about 30 yards distant from our own. As the first discharge all the men except 2nd Lieut KNIGHT and 70560 Pte HARRIS.A became casualties. The Officer however & Pte HARRIS from his position all their bombs were finished, when HARRIS was down the trench to obtain more, or his return after being away a few moments he found 2nd Lieut KNIGHT lying on the bottom of the trench severely wounded; the enemy had however disappeared. The hostile party undoubtedly intended to raid the [?] of the Batt" line & would have accomplished their object but for the bravery of 2nd Lieut KNIGHT & Pte HARRIS. Batt" Relieved by 13th Batt" DURHAM LIGHT INFANTRY During the night the Batt" had the following Casualties 86th BRIGADE Between 28th May & the evening of June 1st the Batt" had the following Casualties. Officers Killed Captain R.W. MILES Wounded Captain T.T. OTTOWELL 2nd Lieut J.H. Lacey. Died A.T. KNIGHT. OR.s Killed 3. Died of Wounds 1. Wounded 31.	

WAR DIARY or INTELLIGENCE SUMMARY

Army Form C. 2118.

Place	Date	Hour	Summary of Events and Information	Remarks and references to Appendices
HALIFAX CAMP.	June 2nd		The BATTⁿ arrived at HALIFAX CAMP about 4 a.m. in the morning of June 2nd but it had been heavily shelled and the men were put under Bivouac Sheets on old TRANSPORT lines at TORONTO CAMP. In the evening the BATTⁿ took over St. LAWRENCE CAMP.	
St LAWRENCE CAMP	June 3		During the morning the Divisional Commander spoke to the Officers of the Battⁿ about the coming offensive. The 16th Battⁿ when in billets near BRANDHOEK had one a football team killed and hurt no by 3 girls L I. To play the Battⁿ and beat no by 3 goals to 1. The Battⁿ left Camp at 8.15 p.m. proceeded to their position in HALF WAY HOUSE and RITZ STREET which they were to occupy prior to taking up their Assembly position. The men who accomplished without a casualty although the enemy shelled the Bridges heavily & several of the pack horses & mules were hit. Lieut (Hon^d) H? WATSON Eng ASC was admitted to hospital. Lieut H. MARCHER admitted on June 8th.	
TRENCHES/June 6th			2nd Lieut A.T. KNIGHT was reported died of wounds on June 3rd. At 10.30 p.m. the Battⁿ left their position and moved up into their Assembly position which they reached at 2.30 a.m. on June 7th.	

WAR DIARY or INTELLIGENCE SUMMARY

Army Form C. 2118.

Place	Date	Hour	Summary of Events and Information	Remarks and references to Appendices
TRENCHES	June 7th		The Battn formed the left attacking Battn of the whole attack, zero hour was at 3.10 a.m. at which hour the mines were exploded. The Battn occupied their objective with few casualties. (Attacked to a depth of 70 metres) The majority of casualties took place from enemy's shell fire after the trenches had been gained. MAJOR A.D. WAYTE who in Command of the Battn owing to the absence of Lieut Colonel WATSON in hospital. Colonel H.F. WATSON rejoined the Battn TRANSPORT LINES but did not go up to the trenches. During the night of the 10th the Battn came out of the trenches 9 men killed and in Cavas in SCOTTISH LINES. The were relieved June 7th and June 10th (incuss) by the Battn. we follows:– Officers killed Lieut AUBRIGHT wounded 2nd Lieuts S.BYARD, A STRAW, W.A BAVLEY. JVOS Lieut A.B.ENNETT & 2nd Lieut A.MOORE. ORs killed 41 wounded 169 missing 15. Of the last mentioned 3 have since been discovered as wounded. Lieut G.H.T.SHIFT and 2nd Lieut E.W.NIGHTINGALE were evacuated sick to England on 31st & 30th respectively, & struck off on strength.	

Army Form C. 2118.

WAR DIARY
or
INTELLIGENCE SUMMARY.
(Erase heading not required.)

Place	Date	Hour	Summary of Events and Information	Remarks and references to Appendices
SCOTTISH LINES	June 11th		18109 L/Cpl Capt DUNN M and 14134 Pte POGSON E. were awarded the MILITARY MEDAL.	
	June 12		The Batt. was inspected at 10.6.m by the DIVISIONAL COMMANDER who visited it marched to REST BILLETS near METEREN. It was a very hot day & the march was very trying — Nr close to REMINGHELST we passed the 1st Batt. who were marching up to the line — MAJOR A.B. WAYTE took over command of 1/5th Batt ROYAL LANCASHIRE REGT.	
METEREN	June 14		Lieut. General Sir T.L.N. MORLAND K.C.B. K.C.M.G. D.S.O. Commanding 10 Corps came to the billets & congratulated the Batt. on its behaviour 2nd Lieut A.T. KNIGHT (died of wounds) was awarded the Military Cross.	
	June 15		The Batt. was moved in lorries to a camp close to the ETANG at DICKEBUSCH to be employed (& mend) the roads in the direction of STELOI and CAFE BELGE	
DICKEBUSCH	June 16		Captain C.B. Fylde who awarded a Military Cross in the London Gazette of 5.6.17.	
	June 17		70560 Pte HARRIS A. died of wounds on 11-6-17 was granted the Military Medal for gallant conduct on June 1st	

Army Form C. 2118.

WAR DIARY
or
INTELLIGENCE SUMMARY.
(Erase heading not required.)

Place	Date	Hour	Summary of Events and Information	Remarks and references to Appendices
	18/9/17		Lt Col H.F. WATSON C.M.G. D.S.O. took over temporary command of the 70th Brigade and Major C.E. HODSON command of the Battalion. A draft of one S/Sgt, one Cpl and 52 O.R's arrived practically all three had served with the B.E.F. before, all with various battalions of the Regiment.	
	21/9/17		The Battalion returned by lorry to its former billets at PROVEN BOOM.	
	22/9/17		The Battalion played the 9 B. YORK & LANCASTER REGT at cricket in the semi-final of the BRIGADE competition and won - the 9th scoring 53 runs we scored 180 for 2 wickets - Capt L.R. HALFORD making 81 runs.	
	23/9/17		The final of the above competition was played against the BRIGADE H.Q. the Battalion winning by [illegible] Bn H.Q. 70 runs the Battalion 140 runs. Attached is a list of MILITARY MEDALS awarded to the Battalion by the G.O.C. in C. A divisional Horseshow was held at BERTHEN and was a great success the Battalion won the 3rd prize in the single Horse turnout.	
	25/9/17		2nd Lieut R.W. CLARK was awarded the MILITARY CROSS for his gallant conduct whilst in charge of a bomb dump at ZILLEBEKE during the Battle of MESSINES.	
	26/9/17		The Battalion marched to MICMAC CAMP near DICKEBUSCH and became reserve Battalion to the BRIGADE the rest of which were in the line at HILL 60.	
	28/9/17		Attached is a list of further honours granted the Battalion for the action on June 7th 1917.	

B. Hudson Major
Commanding 1/5 Sherwood Foresters

SECRET.   Copy No. 6

               2nd ARMY OFFENSIVE.

               MOPPERS - UP.   3rd JUNE, 1917.

1.   Before throwing a M.S.K. or P. Grenade into a dugout, "moppers-up" will be instructed to shout down each entrance to ascertain if the dugout is occupied; If there is no sign of the enemy, a Mills Bomb will be thrown down each entrance. Should there still be no signs of the enemy the dugout will be examined. Should it appear that the dugout is occupied and that the enemy means to fight, an M.S.K. Grenade or P. Bomb. will be thrown into each entrance.

2.   Dugouts which have been cleared and into which no M.S.K. or P. Bombs have been thrown will be marked with a WHITE flag.
        Dugouts into which an M.S.K. or P. Bomb has been thrown will be marked with a RED flag and a sentry will be posted at each entrance.
        Dugouts so marked must only be entered when wearing Gas helmets until it is ascertained that the dugout is clear of gas when the RED flag will be removed.

                                          [signature]
                                          Captain & Adjutant.

Issued to :-
   No. 1.   O.C. 'A' Coy.
   "   2.   'B' "
   "   3.   'C' "
   "   4.) Office
   "   5.)
   "   6.   O.C. 'D' Coy.
   "   7.   War Diary.
   "   8.   Signalling Officer.
   "   9.   Major C.E. HUDSON, M.C.,
   " 10.   Headquarters, 70th Inf. Bde.

SECRET.   Copy No. 9.

2nd ARMY OFFENSIVE.

ADDITIONS and AMENDMENTS.   4th JUNE, 1917.

I.   Ref. MOPPERS-UP.
For WHITE flag in every case read BLUE flag.

II.   Ref. CAPTURED ARMS, etc.,
A report of those captured will be sent to Bn. H. Qrs. as soon as possible.

III.   Ref. para 15 ADMINISTRATIVE DETAILS.
Bombs will now be carried in sandbags with a RED patch on either side and not a YELLOW one.

IV.   Ref. PRISONERS.
These will now be sent from Bn. H. Qrs. to the Bde. Collecting Station in PROMENADE TRENCH, I.22.b.1.3. the route to which all escorts must know in case there is no one to take them over at Bn. H. Qrs.

V.   Bombing sections carry the following number of bombs :-
2 Throwers - 4 bombs each.
2 Bayonet men - 4 bombs each.
2 Carriers - 2 buckets each with 12 bombs in each bucket.
1 spare man with 2 buckets with 12 bombs in each bucket.
    Total for squad - 88 bombs.

VI.   All ranks are to be warned that there is no such word as 'RETIRE' and that anyone using such a word is in all probability a German.

                                     Captain & Adjutant.
                                       11th (S) Battalion,
                                   THE SHERWOOD FORESTERS.

Issued to:-
Copy No. 1.   O.C. 'A' Coy.
"   "   2.   O.C. 'B' "
"   "   3.   O.C. 'C' "
"   "   4.   O.C. 'D' "
"   "   5.   Signalling Officer.
"   "   6.   War Diary.
"   "   7.   Major C.E.HUDSON, M.C.,
"   "   8.   Quartermaster.
"   "   9.   Headquarters, 70th Inf. Bde.
"   " 10.) Office.
"   " 11.)

LIST of AWARDS in connection with Offensive of June 7th.

DISTINGUISHED SERVICE ORDER

Major C.E.HUDSON, M.C.,

MILITARY CROSS

Lieut. A. BENNETT,
2nd Lieut. R.W. CLARK,
2nd Lieut. H. MOORE,

DISTINGUISHED CONDUCT MEDAL

19088 Sgt. W. ELLIS,
73014 " J. WILSON,
17957 " H.E. ANTCLIFFE,
70560 Pte. A. HARRIS.

MILITARY MEDAL.

15739 Sgt. C. ROBINSON,
16843 " T. FLOWERS,
73008 " A.V. COX,
21787 Cpl. A. FRANCE,
22479 " J. DEEKS,
18736 " J. HAYWOOD,
16982 L/C J.J. McCOY,
23919 " M. HEAVEY,
265091 " A. SMITH,
73134 " J.A. MILLS,
15969 Pte. A. MATHER,
18108 " W.E. TALBOT,
36401 " A. BOYCE,
32251 " G.H. WALKER,
4748 " T. TOOP,
17428 " I. BERESFORD,
27332 " G. BATES,
50584 L/C E. WYNNE,
71777 Pte. LYNES J.
73060 " F. GARFIELD,
71854 " I. FREEDMAN,
71863 " F.J. SELWAY,
71870 " A. FALCONBRIDGE,
47814 " W. DEAN,
42805 " C. BROWN,
22550 " G. BRADSHAW,
71787 " C.C. BENNEWORTH,
35438 " S. KEYS,
15465 " E. JONES,
15975 " E. CONSTERDINE,
14286 " W. PLANT,
18246 " J. BIGGS,
19281 " B.S. HULME,
16493 " J. BUSBY,
19540 " T. FINNEY.

WAR DIARY
or
INTELLIGENCE SUMMARY

Army Form C. 2118.

1st Batt (Shewin) Field

Vol 22

Z.22

Place	Date	Hour	Summary of Events and Information	Remarks and references to Appendices
WINDMILL CAMP near CARNOY	1917 July 1st		The anniversary of the first day of the SOMME OFFENSIVE. 2nd Lieut J.A. GREVILLE, T. HODSON, F.H. BAINES, H.A. WATTS, A.S. HIBBS, F. IBBOTSON & J.F. TANNER joined the Battn. The Battn took over the Left Section of the Brigade front from 9th Batt York & Lancaster Regt. R. Two infty kft Head 2/6th HEDGE STREET dug ok. 2nd Lieut H.P. ELLIS also reported to the Battn from the Labour Bn Yorkshire Regt.	
	July 3 July 4 July 5		At Night. H/155 R.O.C men joined the Battn. At Night A/B/C/D & B COY 4 men joined the Battn 9th Batt came out of the trenches in the night of July 5/6 & moved back to MICHAEL Camp	
MICHAEL CAMP	July 6		2nd Lieut R.A. ANDERSON & 2 Lieut T.F. DISON joined the Battn. During the tour in the trenches 18 O.Rs was killed. 5 O.Rs wounded Serjt. shot by J.G. HARRISON reported & employed from 2.4.17 & Temp attached — HODGSON M.E.C., a former Coy Serjt went from the wound rect. 7437 Pte HOHN 452562 Pte Brundyth Welch 45377 Pte Bailey 32616 Pte Walley wounded	

WAR DIARY
or
INTELLIGENCE SUMMARY.

(Erase heading not required.)

Army Form C. 2118.

Place	Date	Hour	Summary of Events and Information	Remarks and references to Appendices
MICMAC CAMP	July 12ᵗ		The Battⁿ. entrained at ONDERDOOM SIDING for GODEWAERSVELDE marching from thence to billets near STEENVOORDE. Extracts from the Gazette. Tempy. Lieut. N.W. COATES M.C. to be Tempy. Captain 2ⁿᵈ June 1917. 2ⁿᵈ Lieuts. B.H. BIRD & R. GROVES to be Tempy. Lieuts. 8ᵗʰ April 1917 & 2ⁿᵈ June 1917.	
STEENVOORDE	13ᵗ		Battⁿ. billets rather scattered.	
PINCHBOOM	18ᵗʰ		The Battⁿ. marched to the billets previously occupied by them at PINCHBOOM near METEREN. Parade grounds were very limited on account of the cultivation but great use was made of the Range, the Bullet and Bayonet & Bombing Course.	
	21ˢᵗ		The Battⁿ. played 8 Battⁿ. Yorks. Lancaster Regᵗ at Cricket but were beaten by 40 runs. Major R.S. HART reported his arrival & took over 2ⁿᵈ in Command of the Battⁿ.	
	22ⁿᵈ			
	23ʳᵈ		The Battⁿ. was inspected by the G.O.C. 23ʳᵈ Division.	
	24ᵗʰ		The Battⁿ. played the 70ᵗʰ Brigade Staff at Cricket & beat them by 32 runs.	

Army Form C. 2118.

WAR DIARY
or
INTELLIGENCE SUMMARY.
(Erase heading not required.)

3

Instructions regarding War Diaries and Intelligence Summaries are contained in F. S. Regs., Part II. and the Staff Manual respectively. Title pages will be prepared in manuscript.

Place	Date	Hour	Summary of Events and Information	Remarks and references to Appendices
PINCHBOOM	23rd		2nd Lieut C. H. TURNEY reported his arrival was taken on the strength of the 24th D Company under the Command of MAJOR L.R. HALFORD, proceeded to 10th Corps School at INGLINHEM for duty and remained there for the remainder of the month.	
	26th		Cadet F.T. HILL who had been attached for Instruction to D Company left for England with a view to being granted a Commission. Major R.S. HART left the Battn to take the Command of the 9th Battn Yorkshire Regt.	
	31st		Captain G.B. FYLDES M.C. left the Battn on being attached for duty to the 23rd Division Staff. An attack was commenced on the enemys lines NORTH of YPRES	

H. Walker Lieut Colonel
1st Battn Shropshire Infantry

WAR DIARY
or
INTELLIGENCE SUMMARY.
(Erase heading not required.)

Army Form C. 2118.

Vol 23

1/1 Batt^n Newton Fletre

Y.23

Place	Date 1915	Hour	Summary of Events and Information	Remarks and references to Appendices
METEREN	Aug 4		The Bn the hrs down latterly & held August 5th my little talk bookworth.	
ARGUES	Aug 6		The Batt^n entrained at CAESTRE at 6 P.M. arriving at ARGUES at 8.30 P.M. and went into billets for the night	
WEST BEDFORD	Aug 7		Marches from ARGUES to WEST BEDFORD the hd. Qrtrs of general of the men Pay 8.	
			2nd Mont-CASSEL & 2nd West H.G. HUNTINGTON joined the Batt^n were taken on the strength August 8th	
	Aug 10		Passed E. HATTEN and started from Rue E. PROVEN going into Camp between PROVEN & POPERINGHE.	
			The Camp was one of the worst that the Batt^n had been in, the ground was very limited	
			The Brigade was them moved from the Setting into a strong ground 15th Corps commanded by Lieut General Sir LUIS/MASSE KCB CVO DSO the 66th & 69th Brigades remained in them transport Area	

WAR DIARY
or
INTELLIGENCE SUMMARY.
(Erase heading not required.)

Army Form C. 2118.

2.

Place	Date	Hour	Summary of Events and Information	Remarks and references to Appendices
ST JULIEN BELGN	Aug 11		The Brigade was held in support to 145 Brigade who were holding the line near ST JULIEN. In the event of that Brigade being unable to retain position the Brigade was to be in readiness to take on the position that they held. The attack was however unsuccessful & the Brigade did not go into the line.	
	Aug 12		A number of Officers & N.C.Os reconnoitred the line to be held.	
	Aug 13		2nd Lieut ROCHESTER reported his arrival & was taken on the strength. The Battn. in the evening played the 7 Bedn. BLACK WATCH who were in billets at BRANDHOEK at water polo & won by 5 goals to 0.	
	Aug		2nd Lieut L.A.S. HIBBS left the Battn on being transferred to the Flying Corps on being transferred to the —	
	Aug		Information was received that the Divison was to be transferred to the II Corps.	
	Aug 23rd		The Battn marched from camp to DEVONSHIRE CAMP near BUSSEBOOM	
DEVONSHIRE CAMP	Aug 24		all Officers & most of the N.C.O.s & men to look at a large scale model of the hostile line in front of POLYGON WOOD. The chief points of interest being INVERNESS COPSE & GLENCORSE WOOD	

WAR DIARY
or
INTELLIGENCE SUMMARY

(Erase heading not required.)

Army Form C. 2118.

Place	Date	Hour	Summary of Events and Information	Remarks and references to Appendices
DEVONSHIRE CAMP	Aug 2nd		The Bn being detailed to the relief of Troops into the lines to fit the support trenches round HALF WAY HOUSE near ZILLEBEKE, three Officers & 2 N.C.O.'s per company sent up to reconnoitre the trenches & the route from Bivouac area – The Brigade was ordered to hold a line approximately the west of INVERNESS COPSE across the YPRES–MENIN ROAD in front of CLAPHAM JUNCTION along the west of GLENCORSE WOOD to the north and thence towards Mt DONNON to support the right flank of the Brigade if the Brigade on the right (25th) of the Brigade line = The Bn was to support the 9th Bn Black Watch sent to North Trenches camp & CHATEAU SEGARD where it bivouaced. The Bn moved off at (?) as told on arrival at (?) (?) the route within 1/2 effort a very unpleasant night – men dog tired specially (?) a mile of the Bivouac. Most of the men relieved by seep towards Bivouac Sheet turn for at the Baths (divine)	
CHATEAU SEGARD	Aug 3rd		Very wet day – Bn did not leave the Camp as no supplies of rations at 2pm to take over the trenches (?) HALFWAY HOUSE in the west of INVERNESS Recce of the Battle (?) in the system of trenches to the north	
HALFWAY HOUSE	Aug 4th		The Battn have been detailed to looking & assisting parties	

Army Form C. 2118.

WAR DIARY
or
INTELLIGENCE SUMMARY.
(Erase heading not required.)

Place	Date	Hour	Summary of Events and Information	Remarks and references to Appendices
HALFWAY HOUSE	Aug 29		Sent the Officers (non-coms) (Imployees up to see the Front line trenches which the Batt would take over.	
			Batt did not take over the front line trenches as anticipated, but the Brigade sent Platoons of the 7 Inf Brigade moved into the ASYLUM at YPRES. Platoons sent now out into Issues & billeted men WIPPENHOEK.	
WIPPENHOEK	30		Brigade M.G. camp at ABEELE. Found the Company comfortable - spent the day cleaning up & fitting the men.	

A H Watson Lieut Colonel
u/c Batt 7th Hunts? Brigade

Army Form C. 2118.

WAR DIARY
or
INTELLIGENCE SUMMARY.
(Erase heading not required.)

1st Batt Sherwood Foresters

Vol 24

Place	Date	Hour	Summary of Events and Information	Remarks and references to Appendices
WINNEZEELE	Sept 1917		2nd Lieut C.H. HARWOOD was transferred to Royal Flying Corps (the other 2nd Lieuts of the Batt'n having been killed)	Nominal Rolls
	Sept 3		The Battⁿ —	
			The Brigade marched from WINNEZEELE to OOST-HOEK.	
			A.M. C. in C. came to the evening	
			St BAINES was transferred to Labour Corps.	
	Sept 4		2nd Lt Bruce Bairnsfather attached to Brigade Scheme	
			The Lecturer had been a Brigade Scheme. He was informed Kitchener	
			The "Battⁿ" taught the Machine Gun Battⁿ on the morning of same	
			The "SUNDAY GAZETTE" MAJOR C.E. HUDSON D.S.O. M.C. to be second in	
			Command (vice 2nd Lieutenant Lighton)	
			Left OOST-HOEK and arrived near NOORDPEENE	
NOORDPEENE	13		Left NOORDPEENE and the next took place EAST of STEENVOORDE	
			up STEENVOORDE and marched to SHERWOOD CAMP DICKEBUSCH	
DICKEBUSCH	15		The Battⁿ moved up to relieve 1st Royal Fusiliers 17th Brigade on the left Sub sector but	
			upon reaching the MENIN ROAD Lt Col Batt H.Q. at CLAPHAM JUNCTION	
			the 47 Division are on the left of the Batt, the 9th Brigade is on the right	
			the 70 Brigade of the Batt N. and there became very strong.	

WAR DIARY
or
INTELLIGENCE SUMMARY.

(Erase heading not required.)

Army Form C. 2118.

Place	Date	Hour	Summary of Events and Information	Remarks and references to Appendices
In the LINE	Sept 16		The 47th Division carried out a hostile straffing opposite the junction of the front lines. 36 prisoners were taken & the left Company of the Battn killed a number of the enemy who retired across their front. From information gained by photos from the Battn & parts to left had sent men to as a strong point in the MENIN ROAD was accurately located & adalts the 9th York Lancaster Regt who relieved us knocked a successful raid.	
	Sept 17		The Battn was relieved in the front line and took out into support with HQ at STIRLING CASTLE	
	Sept 19		The Brigade was relieved in the Line and the Battn went back to MICMAC CAMP	
MICMAC CAMP	Sept 19		The Battn was (now) with the Battle Stores and a fatigue party was left at a strong	
			point it had recently taken on the YPRES CANAL BANK.	
			Rain fell heavily.	
	Sept 20		ATTACK DAY - 70th Brigade formed the Reserve Brigade 68 & 69 Brigades formed the attacking Brigades. The Australians (cops Div) on the left The 41st Division on the right.	
			ZERO hour was 5.40 a.m. AT ZERO HOUR all the Battn moved forward to the rear of ATRENCH position near ZILLEBEKE Hd K two lst officer + 6 men	

WAR DIARY or INTELLIGENCE SUMMARY

Army Form C. 2118.

Place	Date	Hour	Summary of Events and Information	Remarks and references to Appendices
STIRLING CASTLE	Sept 20th		Was that time the Batt. again moved forward and they themselves into Trenches and JAM SUPPORT LINE with H.Q. at STIRLING CASTLE remaining there that night and the whole of Sept 21st. Bryde. Our offensive position being immediate to Westing Batt. before the Enemy Follow line. The 70th Bryde. relieved the 63rd Bryde in the Real front line - the Batt.	
	22nd		formed the left front Batt. of the Bryde. front about 500 yards. The right of the Battn. being NORTH of the MENIN ROAD the left being too yards SOUTH of it. REUTELBEEK STREAM. The AUSTRALIANS were on the left & the 9th YORK and LANCASTER Regt on the right. The 9th Yorks had orders to take TOWER HAMLETS a defensive work. The formed by the Batt. on our right. & the Germans of the 68 Bryde to left in the line. Bother had known that to DUMBARTON LAKES.	
IN H. LINE	23rd		The day was spent consolidating the line taken. The Enemy were shelling constantly from TOWER HAMLETS.	
	24th		The 33rd Division relieved the Bryde taking up ASSEMBLY Position for a further Attack. The Battn was relieved by the 2nd KINGS 2nd Batt. WORCESTER Regt & GLASGOW HIGHLANDERS (H.L.I. 9.AM) The relief was completed in heavy shelling	

Army Form C. 2118.

WAR DIARY
or
INTELLIGENCE SUMMARY.
(Erase heading not required.)

Instructions regarding War Diaries and Intelligence Summaries are contained in F. S. Regs., Part II. and the Staff Manual respectively. Title pages will be prepared in manuscript.

Place	Date	Hour	Summary of Events and Information	Remarks and references to Appendices
IN LINES	Sept 24th		The Battⁿ was taken back in billets in bivouac to MICREM BRIDGE Camp near REMINGHELST	
MICREM BRIDGE	25th		2nd Lieuts H.L. ELLIS and G.E. PEARSON are posted TEMPLIEUTS (July 1st 1917).	
	27th		The Battⁿ marched at 9 a.m. to BEDFORD HOUSE NORTH OF YPRES CANAL, remaining there for the day. After dark the Battⁿ took over the front line from the 33rd Division on left Battalion on the REUTELBECK STREAM & on right NORTH OF THE MENIN ROAD. The Battⁿ took over from the Some Buffs on left has handed over to on the 24th. The Division taken over attacked and has been unable to realise the contemplated attack. The attack was completed on that day being too. The Battⁿ was relieved from the front line by 6 Yorks & Lancs to Rifle and that ret close Support line with HQ at TORR TOP DUG OUTS	
IN LINE 29th	Oct 1st		The Battⁿ Hd Qrs moved to 42 Battⁿ K.O.S.B. J 5 5 Bivouac & came back to SWAN & DEAR CORNER near DICKEBUSCH. The casualties to the Battⁿ since the commencement of operations were as follows	

2353 Wt. W2544/1454 700,000 5/15 L. D. & L. A.D.S.S./Forms/C. 2118.

Army Form C. 2118.

WAR DIARY
or
INTELLIGENCE SUMMARY.
(Erase heading not required.)

5

Place	Date	Hour	Summary of Events and Information	Remarks and references to Appendices

Officers wounded 2nd Lieuts. J F TANNER C A RYDE W MEAKIN
ORs killed 27 died of wounds 10 wounded 131 missing 23
The following have been awarded the Military Medal by the GOC Commanding
In for Gallantry in the field
1/89 L/Cpl JACKSON A. 3065 Pte MALLETT T 10148 Pte OGDEN F.
The following officers were recommended in Batt. orders [?] for their bravery when
wounded
Lieut R FERRIS. 2nd Lieuts H A WATTS. J F TANNER. 1 M RIDE
A further list of N.C.Os + men was sent in by Br. Buckley [?] and the
name of Sickey Thos Perry Pte Barton's team with Pte Saunders [illegible]

A [?] White Lieut Col
Commg 1 Batt. Manch Regt

SECRET.

Second Army G.353.
X Corps G.101/17/32.
23rd Divn. S.G.181/1/11.

X Corps.

The evidence gained from captured documents all tends to show that the enemy intended to launch a heavy attack on the Second Army front on October 3rd and that in order to gain a better footing a preliminary attack was made on 1st October.

This was so heavily dealt with by 23rd Division that it so dislocated the further attack that General von Finckenstein, Commanding 4th Guard Division, who was in charge of the operations, evidently decided to postpone his attack from 3rd to 4th October.

The result of this postponement is well known. The Army Commander wishes the 23rd Division to be informed of the far reaching results of their determined resistance and to congratulate and thank all ranks concerned on behalf of himself and the Second Army.

7th October, 1917.

(sd) C.H. HARINGTON,
M.G.G.S., Second Army.

2.

With reference to the above, while some troops were more immediately engaged than others, I feel confident that whatever troops had been concerned the result would have been the same and that the enemy will, as he always has done, meet with heavy defeat at the hands of the 23rd Division.

9th October, 1917.

Major-General,
Commanding 23rd Division.

SECRET.   Copy No. 5.

11th. (S) Battalion THE SHERWOOD FORESTERS Order No. 50.

Reference Map 1/10000 GHELUVELT.   15th. October 1917.

1. It has been found necessary to send 1 Company into the front line tonight. 'C' Coy. will therefore proceed to HOOGE CRATERS by 4.15 p.m. today. There guides from 9th. YORKS Regt. will meet them and take them to the positions selected for them by O.C. 9th. YORKS Regt. under whose command they will come at 4.15 p.m. today.

2. O.C. 'D' Coy. will hand over to O.C. 'C' Coy. 1 day's preserved rations, also enough pairs of socks to complete the number required by 'C' Coy.

3. The following stores will be issued to 'C' Coy. on their arrival at HOOGE CRATERS by Lieut. SWALE :-

    15 Tins of water,
    12 S O S Grenades (1 box),
    6 Boxes Bombs,
    20 Shovels,
    10 Picks.

4. O.C. 'C' Coy. will draw water for 17th. from Battalion Headquarters as early as possible on the 17th. and rations for the 18th. from the same place as early as possible on that day.

5. 'C' Coy. will again come under the command of the O.C., 11th. SHERWOOD FORESTERS on the completion of the relief of the 9th. YORKS Regt. on the night 16/17th. October. On completion of the relief of 9th. YORKS Regt. on night of 16/17th. 'C' Coy. will become right support as already ordered. The completion of this move on the night of 16/17th. Oct. will be reported to Battalion Headquarters by the two Battn. H.Q. runners at present with 'C' Coy. These runners will then be retained at Battn. H.Q.

6. Completion of taking over positions tonight will be reported to O.C. 9th. YORKS Regt.

Captain & Adjutant.

Issued at 11.45a.m. to
O.C. 'C' Coy. Copy No. 1
  " 'D' "   " " 2
O.C. 9th. YORKS Regt. Copy No. 3
File   Copy No. 4
War Diary   "   " 5

War Diary

SECRET. Copy No. 2

11th. (S) Battalion THE SHERWOOD FORESTERS Order No. 51.

Reference Map 1/10000 GHELUVELT. 15th. October 1917.

1. The Battalion will relieve the 9th. YORKSHIRE Regt. in the right sector during the night 16/17 October.

2. 'C' Coy. has already proceeded into the front line. This Coy. will move to the position of right support Coy. on relief of 9th. YORKS tomorrow night.

3. Dispositions will be as follows :-

    'B' Coy. right front line Coy. taking over from 'A' Coy. 9th.YORKS
    'D' "   left   "   "   "   "   "   'B' "   "   "
    'C' "   right support   "   "   "   "   'C' "   "   "
    'A' "   left   "   "   "   "   'D' "   "   "

    Battalion Headquarters will be at the MOUND J.10.a.7.8.

4. 2 Guides per platoon from 9th. YORKS Regt. will meet the Battn. at HOOGE CRATERS at a time to be notified later, as it depends on the visibility. It will probably be about 4 p.m.

5. Companies will move independently by platoons in order 'B', 'D' 'A' and at quarter of an hour intervals between Coys. on receipt of orders from Battn. H.Q.

6. The following stores will be issued to each Coy. at HOOGE CRATERS by the Quartermaster on their arrival there :-

    12 S.O.S. Grenades (1 Box),
    6 Boxes Bombs,
    20 Shovels,
    10 Picks,
    10 tins of water.
    Some bandoliers of ammunition, Bombs, etc. will be taken over from 9th. YORKS Regt. together with all maps, etc.

7. Two complete days' rations will be carried. Care must be taken that water bottles are full when the BUND is left. Water must be issued as sparingly as possible in the line.

8. Completion of relief will be reported by outgoing Coys. of 9th. YORKS Regt. The 2 Battn. H.Q. runners with each coy. however will be sent to Battn. H.Q. as soon as possible after relief but not before they are thoroughly acquainted with the position of their Coy. H.Q.

9. In order to simplify the relief of the Battalion, guides must continually explore the route between Company and Battalion H.Q. Some must also know their way to and from HOOGE CRATERS. Prospective guides should therefore be used for carrying parties etc. as much as possible and excused routine work as the situation permits.

10. Water for consumption on the 18th. will be brought to Battn.H.Q. by the Quartermaster on the 17th. on the scale of 10 tins per Company and 10 for H.Q. These will be drawn by Companies as early as possible on the 18th. Rations and water for 'A', 'B' & 'D' Coys. and H.Q. for consumption on 19th. will be brought up on the 18th. and drawn from Battn. H.Q. by Coys. as early as possible that day.
    Orders for the delivery of rations to 'C' Coy. for consumption 19th. will be issued when their situation on that day is known.

P.T.O.

11. Casualty Reports)
    Strength Returns)
    Intelligence Reports)
    will be sent to Battn. H.Q. before 12 noon each day. They will all be sent at the same time. It will not be possible of course for Casualty Reports to cover the period noon to noon and care must therefore be taken not to report casualties twice over.

12. The line must be kept in as sanitary a condition as possible and shell holes are not to be used as latrines indiscriminately. Where possible pits are to be dug.

13. Companies will bury all dead in their areas. The RED IDENTITY DISC and personal effects will be forwarded to Battn. H.Q. together with location of the grave, which should be marked on the ground when possible.
    The Regimental Aid Post is at Battn. H.Q.

14. Patrols are to be actively employed during the night and during the foggy weather. Posts will be out at night at the following places :-

    Cross Roads at J.12a.45.55 by 'B' Coy.
    About J.12.a.45.95 by 'D' Coy.

    Patrols will visit these posts continually and will also be pushed forward down the roads and tracks approaching our lines in addition to any other places selected by Os. C. Coys.

15. Every endeavour is to be made to wire both the front and support lines and to make the trenches continuous. There is a large dump of wire on the road about J.10.a.30.95.
    There is no telephonic communication forward from Battn. H.Q. so communication trenches and taped routes must be made.

16. The offensive spirit is to be cultivated in every way. Snipers are to be posted and they must avail themselves of the many opportunities which arise of killing Germans. Low flying aeroplanes must be driven off by Rifle and Lewis Gun fire.

                                          Captain & Adjutant.

Issued at   p.m. to
O.C. 'A' Coy.   Copy No. 1
  " 'B' "   "   " 2
  " 'C' "   "   " 3
  " 'D' "   "   " 4
QrMr.   "   " 5
9th. WORKS)   "   " 6)
70th. Bde.)   "   " 7) for information.
War Diary   "   " 8
File   "   " 9

SECRET.   Copy No. 9

11th. (S) Battalion THE SHERWOOD FORESTERS, Order No.52.

Reference GHELUVELT 1/10.000 Map.   19th. October 1917.

1. The Battalion will be relieved by the 8th. YORK & LANCS REGT. during night 19/20 Oct.

2. On relief Headquarters and 3 Companies will proceed to the Camp near ZILLEBEKE BUND where the accomodation will be taken over from the 8th. K.O.Y.L.I. 'A' Coy. will take from the Company of the 8th. K.O.Y.L.I. now in position about J.5.c.2.3. and will come under the orders of the O.C. Left Battalion.

3. No position will be vacated till it has been occupied by the corresponding troops of the relieving Battalion. Completion of relief will be verbally reported to Battn. H.Q. by an Officer as the Company passes on the way out. O.C. 'A' Coy. will report his arrival in support position to O.C. Left Battn. 'A' Coy. will rejoin the Battalion at H.30.c.9.1. after relief during night 20/21 October.

4. Advance parties of 1 N.C.O. per platoon and 1 man per Coy. H.Q. from 'B', 'C' & 'D' Coys. will leave the line at 5.30 a.m. 19th. and proceed to new camp, and take over from 'B', 'C' & 'D' Coys. 8th. K.O.Y.L.I.

5. 1 N.C.O. per Coy. as guide to Advance Parties will proceed to HOOGE CRATERS tonight. They will report to Bde. Major, 69th. Bde. at 5.15 a.m. 19th. Two guides from each platoon will report at Battn. H.Q. 6 a.m. 19th.; they will then be sent to HOOGE CRATERS where they will await arrival of Battalion at 4 p.m. 19th.

6. All maps, trench stores, bombs and one bandolier per man will be handed over.
These orders must be destroyed when they have been read.

G.B.FYLDES, M.C., Captain & Adjutant.

Issued at 5.30 p.m. by runner to :-

O.C. 'A' Coy. Copy No. 1
 " 'B' "   "   " 2
 " 'C' "   "   " 3
 " 'D' "   "   " 4
Major HOLFORD, D.S.O. Copy No. 5
O.C. 8th. YORK & LANCS "   " 6
File   "   " 7
Transport Officer   "   " 8
War Diary   "   " 9

COPY.

31st. October 1917.

ROUTINE ORDERS by

    Brigadier General H.GORDON, C.M.G., D.S.O.

    Commanding 70th. Infantry Brigade.

Commander -in- Chief's Inspection.

    The G.O.C. the Brigade has much pleasure in publishing for the information of all ranks that the Commander-in-Chief expressed himself as highly satisfied with the appearance and general turn-out of the troops on parade today.

The Commander-in-Chief also congratulated all ranks of the Brigade on their good work during the recent operations and ordered that this be communicated to those concerned.

                                        S.L.KIND, Captain,
                                           a/Staff Captain,
                                    70th. Infantry Brigade.

MESSAGE FORM.

To :—　　　　　　　　　　　　　　　　　　　　　No.

1. I am at.................... (Note :—Either give Map Reference or mark your position by a 'X' on the Map on back.

2. I have reached limits of my Objective.

3. My Platoon / Company is at........................... and is consolidating.

4. My Platoon / Company is at........................... and has consolidated.

5. Am held up by (a) M.G. (b) Wire at.................(Place where you are).

6. Enemy holding strong point...............

7. I am in touch with.....................on Right / Left. at............

8. I am not in touch with...................on Right / Left.

9. Am shelled from......................

10. Am in need of :—

11. Counter Attack forming at................

12. Hostile (a) Battery
    (b) Machine Gun   active at......................
    (c) Trench Mortar

13. Reinforcements wanted at.......................................

14. I estimate my present strength at........... rifles.

15. Add any other useful information here :—

　　　　　　　　　　　　　　　　　　　Name...........................
　　　　　　　　　　　　　　　　　　　Platoon........................
Time............. m.　　　　　　　　　Company......................
Date............. 1917.　　　　　　　Battalion......................

(A). Carry no maps or papers which may be of value to the Enemy.

(B). Give no information if captured, except the following, which you are bound to give :—

　　　Name and Rank.

(C). Collect all captured maps and papers and send them in at once.

ATTACHED 8TH DIVISION
70TH INFY BDE 23 DIV

11TH BN NOTTS & DERBY
OCT 1915 - MAY 1916